TRANSACTIONS

OF THE

AMERICAN PHILOSOPHICAL SOCIETY

HELD AT PHILADELPHIA
FOR PROMOTING USEFUL KNOWLEDGE

NEW SERIES—VOLUME 64, PART 5
1974

BENJAMIN RUSH: PHILOSOPHER OF THE AMERICAN REVOLUTION

DONALD J. D'ELIA

Professor of History, State University of New York, New Paltz

THE AMERICAN PHILOSOPHICAL SOCIETY
INDEPENDENCE SQUARE
PHILADELPHIA

September, 1974

For my brother, Anthony, who having conquered death
sleeps in the peace of Christ

Copyright © 1974 by The American Philosophical Society
Library of Congress Catalog
Card Number 74–77911
International Standard Book Number 0-87169-645-2
US ISSN 0065-9746

PREFACE

I think Benjamin Rush would have agreed with pleasure that the historian's work is a modest and gradual, yet necessarily victorious struggle against death. For every historian, whatever his claim to our attention, mixes the living present of at least one man with the past in the very nature of his enterprise and recovers a part of what had once been lost. In the history of men, as in all things, we must believe with the poet that death shall have no dominion. No conviction was more tenaciously held by Rush than this. And truly death shall have no empire over us so long as we can think in terms of the past as well as in terms of the present and future. The present writer hopes that he has thought in terms of the past not meanly.

This study owes its existence to Professor Ira V. Brown of the Department of History of the Pennsylvania State University and to Professor H. Trevor Colbourn, formerly of the department. I wish also to express my gratitude to Professor Mason W. Gross and the late Professor Mark M. Heald of Rutgers University for their kind personal and scholarly interest in me. And to the late Professor Henry A. Finch of the Department of Philosophy of the Pennsylvania State University, I am likewise proud to hold myself in the relation of student.

Dr. Charles Coleman Sellers, Librarian Emeritus of Dickinson College, and Dr. George W. Corner, Dr. Whitfield J. Bell, Jr., and the late Dr. Richard H. Shryock of the American Philosophical Society encouraged me in many ways and provided valuable scholarly assistance. Dr. Lyman H. Butterfield's edition of Rush's letters and his other essays provided me with many insights which I have tried to develop. Mr. Edwin Wolf 2nd and the staff of the Library Company of Philadelphia were warmly generous in helping me use the Rush manuscripts at that venerable institution, as was Dr. Nicholas B. Wainwright and his staff at the Historical Society of Pennsylvania. I wish also to thank Dr. Stephen G. Kurtz, former Director of the Institute of Early American History and Culture, and the editorial staff of the Institute, the librarians of the Pennsylvania State University Library, the Indiana University Library, the Library of Congress, the Bloomsburg State College Library, and the Library of the State University College at New Paltz. Certainly, all of the libraries in the interlibrary loan system deserve the profound gratitude of every historical researcher.

Parts of Chapter Six appeared in the *Proceedings of the American Philosophical Society* **110** (August, 1966) and **114** (April, 1970). Chapter Seven appeared in slightly different form in *Pennsylvania History* **33** (April, 1966), and Chapter Six derives from the Boyd Lee Spahr Lecture in Early American History at Dickinson College, November 1966. Parts of Chapter Two and Eight appeared in the *Journal of General Education* **19** (July, 1967), the *Journal of Medical Education* **43** (July, 1968), and the *Journal of the History of Ideas* **30** (July–Sept., 1969).

In quoting from Rush, I have left the prose as I found it, although never to the detriment of meaning or style. Punctuation and underscoring here have been to some extent modernized.

Finally, I am thankful beyond words for the help and encouragement of my wife, Margaret, and my children, Keith, Gregory, Nancy, and Anthony.

D.J.D'E.

New Paltz, New York

ABBREVIATED TITLES OF WORKS FREQUENTLY CITED IN THE NOTES

Autobiography: *The Autobiography of Benjamin Rush: His "Travels through Life" Together with His Commonplace Book for 1789–1813*, George W. Corner, ed., Mem. Amer. Philos. Soc. 25 (Philadelphia, 1948).

DAB: *Dictionary of American Biography*, Allen Johnson and Dumas Malone, eds. (20 v., New York, 1928–1936).

Diseases of the Mind: Benjamin Rush, *Medical Inquiries and Observations, upon Diseases of the Mind* (Philadelphia, 1812).

DNB: *Dictionary of National Biography*, Leslie Stephen and Sidney Lee, eds. (63 v. and supplements, London, 1885–1912).

Goodman: Nathan G. Goodman, *Benjamin Rush, Physician and Citizen, 1746–1813* (Philadelphia, 1934).

"Paris Journal": J. Pierpont Morgan Library MS, Benjamin Rush's account of his visit to Paris, 1769.

Rush Essays: Benjamin Rush, *Essays, Literary, Moral and Philosophical* (2nd ed., Philadelphia, 1806).

Rush Letters: *Letters of Benjamin Rush*, Lyman H. Butterfield, ed., Mem. Amer. Philos. Soc. 30 (2 v., Philadelphia, 1951).

Rush MSS: Benjamin Rush's papers in the Library Company of Philadelphia.

"Scottish Journal": University of Indiana Library MS, Benjamin Rush's account of his visit to Edinburgh, 1766–1768.

BENJAMIN RUSH: PHILOSOPHER OF THE AMERICAN REVOLUTION

Donald J. D'Elia

CONTENTS

INTRODUCTION

There is nothing more common, than to confound the terms of *American Revolution* with those of *the late American war*. The American war is over: but this is far from being the case with the American revolution. On the contrary, nothing but the first act of the great drama is closed. It remains yet to establish and perfect our new forms of government; and to prepare the principles, morals, and manners of our citizens, for these forms of government, after they are established and brought to perfection.

So declaimed Dr. Benjamin Rush to a Philadelphia audience gathered together on Independence Day, 1787.[1] He himself, as a revolutionary patriot, signer of the Declaration, and volunteer physician in the War, had played a major role in the "first act of the great drama" of which he spoke. And known to many of his listeners that day was the further role he was performing as a social and cultural revolutionary in trying to complete the great dramatic work of the American Revolution. Indeed, few Americans, if any, were more wary than Benjamin Rush of confounding the "terms of *American Revolution* with those of *the late American War*." And we can do no better in introducing this study than to borrow, as it were, a great man's phrase and say that

it is essentially a discussion of what the term "American Revolution" meant to Benjamin Rush.

Discovering the historical Rush, whose revolutionary thought we would study, is not easy. From that Christmas Eve of his birth in 1745, Old Style, to his death on April 19, 1813, exactly thirty-eight years after Lexington and Concord, Rush acted out a life which remains controversial to this day. Patriot and conspirator against George Washington, disinterested man of science and dogmatic bleeder, educator and philistine, cosmopolitan and chauvinist—so he has been represented in the writings of those who have evaluated his status in American history.

Harry G. Good, in a pioneer treatment of Rush's life and educational works, observed that Rush afforded "material enough for four lives of ordinary men."[2] The diversified activities of Rush's life in medicine, politics, social reform, education, and religion were indeed striking. But there was an even more fascinating universality in Rush's thought and experience which, as the following study argues, may be seen most clearly in the vigorous middle period of his life.

In few instances does the character of a man figure so prominently in his historical reputation as it does with Rush.[3] Opinion about the nature of the man and his work was polar while he was alive, and even at the distance of almost two centuries the problem seems to many as vexing as ever. Early biographers and eulogists of Rush—usually but not always his medical students—were unanimous in exalting his character. He was described as a champion of free inquiry, a man of discrimination, and a great thinker of "brilliant imagination" and "comprehensive understanding."[4] As a physician and scientist, he was represented as a practical man of "unwearied research," grubbing out facts and organizing them with uncommon intelligence in earnest and dedicated service to his fellow man.[5]

---

[1] Rush, "An Address to the People of the United States. . . . On the Defects of the Confederation," *American Museum* 1 (January 1787): pp. 8–11, reprinted in H. Niles, *Principles and Acts of the Revolution in America* (Baltimore, 1822), p. 234; Goodman, p. 75.

[2] *Benjamin Rush and His Services to American Education* (Berne, Ind., 1918), p. 95.

[3] Lyman H. Butterfield, "The Reputation of Benjamin Rush," *Pennsylvania History* 17 (1950): pp. 3–22.

[4] David Ramsay, *An Eulogium upon Benjamin Rush, M.D.* (Philadelphia, 1813), pp. 27–29, 97–98; William Staughton, *Eulogium in Memory of the Late Dr. Benjamin Rush* (Philadelphia, 1813), p. 16; James Thacher, *American Medical Biography: Memoirs of Eminent Physicians Who Have Flourished in America. To Which is Prefixed a Succinct History of Medical Science in the United States, from the First Settlement of the Country* (2 v., Boston, 1828) 2: pp. 34–35, 55, 66.

[5] Ramsay, *Eulogium*, pp. 9–10, 101; Staughton, *Eulogium*, p. 19; Thomas D. Mitchell, *The Character of Rush; An Intro-*

When Rush died in 1813, two fellow revolutionaries of '76 towered above petty controversy to eulogize his memory. Said Thomas Jefferson: "a better man than Rush could not have left us, more benevolent, more learned, of finer genius, or more honest." [6] And John Adams affirmed in reply that he knew "of no Character living or dead, who has done more real good in America." [7] A kind, perceptive, thoughtful, and undogmatic figure was set forth in these accounts; a man with acknowledged limitations as a physician, but not as a man.

Much of the laudatory opinion on Rush in the first half of the nineteenth century was reverential, if not idolatrous. Acclaiming the Philadelphian's devotion to his patients during the yellow fever epidemic of 1793, in which Rush himself risked and almost died from infection, one eulogist wrote that had he lived "in the dark ages of the Christian era, he would have been canonized, and worshipped as a saint." [8] This perhaps overgenerous attitude towards Rush was doubtless explainable in large part by what Lyman H. Butterfield has called the "inspirational force of his personality." [9] But even the impact of a forceful, inspiring personality must have been limited in its effect upon mature individuals and teachers in their own right. The early eulogies, written as they were by men who had known Rush as a teacher and a friend, cannot be entirely dismissed on the ground of a closeness-to-the-man bias. Dr. Thomas D. Mitchell, writing thirty-five years after the death of his teacher, could still praise him as "the *beau ideal* of moral, intellectual, and professional greatness," while he himself scorned "a blind adhesion to any man or to any system." [10]

The system that Mitchell alluded to was Rush's celebrated and, indeed, notorious theory of disease. And it was this system of pathology, with its therapeutics of bloodletting and purging, which was in very large measure to discredit him in the eyes of his fellow Americans and to create the image of the ruthless bleeder. Even today, Rush is still commonly known as a signer of the Declaration of Independence and as a bleeder, the deed of the pen alone saving him from the total disgrace of the lancet. And as if his heavy reliance upon bloodletting were not enough to assure his historical obloquy, Rush dared to commit the unforgivable sin of criticizing George Washington. [11] With the same courage or temerity with which he attacked the common medical practices of the day, he assailed the common hero of the day. Posterity has forgotten neither.

The year 1918 marked the beginning of critical and objective scholarship on Rush, for it was then that Harry G. Good published a careful and well-documented study of Rush. The study made available Rush's educational writings, but it also included a judicious life of the physician-educator. On the so-called Conway Cabal, to which Rush was by now inextricably tied, Good soundly maintained that there was no proof. With regard to the other scandalous aspect of Rush's life, however, his theory and practice of medicine, Good wrote that "little need be said to the non-professional reader . . . the physician already knows that the less said, the better." [12] Rush was wrong in purging and bleeding, he continued, but we know this only from the vantage point of the twentieth century. "We need to introduce no qualification in speaking of Benjamin Rush, no matter what his errors of practice may have been," Good generalized. Rush was an egoist of all-devouring ambition and "impetuous temper," yet in some of his many controversies he was in the right. Posterity, Good concluded, had forgotten his self-acknowledged "frailties and errors." [13]

Good was incorrect on one point, however, obvious to any modern student of Rush: posterity had not forgotten the faults of Benjamin Rush. True, the presence of Rush behind the Conway Cabal was generally to remain the exclusive image of the nineteenth century, but the image of the lancet-wielding doctor was fast becoming the common property of the twentieth. Still, if our century has not nobly forgotten Rush's bleeding, it has, on the positive side, remembered much of incontrovertible value in another phase of his life—social reform.

As evidence of this new orientation in Rush scholar-

---

ductory to the Course on the Theory and Practice of Medicine in the Philadelphia College of Medicine (Philadelphia, 1848), p. 15; Delaplaine, *Repository of the Lives and Portraits of Distinguished Americans* (2 v., Philadelphia, 1816) **1**: pp. 28, 33–36; Thomas G. Morton and Frank Woodbury, *The History of the Pennsylvania Hospital, 1751–1895,* (rev. ed., Philadelphia, 1897), pp. 492–494.

[6] May 27, 1813, Andrew E. Lipscomb and Albert E. Bergh, eds., *The Writings of Thomas Jefferson* (20 v., Washington, 1903) **13**: p. 246.

[7] June 11, 1813, "Microfilms of the Adams Papers," Letter book, Pt. ii, Box 95, Massachusetts Historical Society (Boston, 1955). "Why is not Dr. Rush placed before Dr. Franklin in the Temple of Fame? Because cunning is a more powerful divinity than simplicity. Rush has done infinitely more good to America than Franklin. Both have deserved a high rank, among benefactors to their Country and mankind, but Rush, by far the highest," John Adams to Richard Rush, July 22, 1816, *ibid.,* Box 122.

[8] Ramsay, *Eulogium,* pp. 91–92.

[9] Butterfield, "The Reputation of Benjamin Rush," *Penna. Hist.* **17** (1950): p. 11; Mitchell states that "there was a sort of magic influence about the man; a something in every look and word and thought, that enlivened, warmed and even electrified," *The Character of Rush,* pp. 17–18.

[10] Mitchell, *The Character of Rush,* pp. 22, 6. Cf. Rush, "Introductory Lecture to a Course of Lectures on the Theory & Practice of Physic," Rush MSS, call number Yi2/7400/F1, pp. 16–18.

[11] The nature and extent of Rush's criticism of Washington and his relationship to the so-called Conway Cabal have been discussed by Lyman H. Butterfield, ed., *Rush Letters* **2**: append. i, pp. 1197–1208.

[12] Good, *Benjamin Rush and His Services to American Education,* pp. 85, 53.

[13] *Ibid.,* pp. 85, 97–98.

ship, two historians of the Prohibition era, John Allen Krout and Herbert Asbury, accorded Rush status as a pioneer in the American temperance movement.[14] His work with the mentally ill in the Pennsylvania Hospital, capped by his *Medical Inquiries and Observations upon the Diseases of the Mind,* was hailed by Albert Deutsch in 1937 as the first scientific treatment of mental illness in America.[15] And Rush's humane enterprise in prison reform and abolition was similarly recalled with commendation.[16]

The progressive historical discovery of Benjamin Rush and the mounting interest in his life and work were reflected in 1934 by the publication of the first detailed biography by Nathan G. Goodman. *Benjamin Rush; Physician and Citizen, 1746–1813,* still the best biography of Rush after more than a quarter of a century, was based upon exhaustive research into Rush materials. The tradition of Rush scholarship begun by Good was further developed by Goodman's wide and careful use of all known Rush sources, paving the way for future historical studies. Goodman denied that any evidence existed to show that Rush was connected in any way with the Conway Cabal. His portrait of Rush revealed a man of intense patriotism, one in sympathy with Washington insofar as they were both concerned with the same great end—the independence of America—although they disagreed on the urgency of different means. Washington saw the war as commander-in-chief; Rush saw only the miserable sick and wounded in army hospitals and the need for victory. As a physician, Rush's belief in phlebotomy, Goodman observed, "seems today to be little short of preposterous." But any judgment of his place in the history of medicine must be relative to the medical environment of his times; we must not, cautioned Goodman, evaluate him in the light of present-day medical knowledge.[17] Goodman's biography gave Rush definite status in American history, but it did not treat of his philosophy of the American Revolution. Aside from his obvious medical and social thought, Rush the thinker remained virtually undiscovered.[18]

One of the most distinguished of the new Rush scholars of the nineteen-forties was the medical historian, Richard H. Shryock, who viewed Rush with the historical perspective that Good and Goodman had recommended. In two articles, Shryock undertook an evaluation of Rush's controversial place in American medicine, declaring that in psychology he was "both a theorist and original observer . . . far in advance of other Americans in the field."[19] Rush was caught between two traditions: that of speculative pathology in which he had been trained at Edinburgh; and the tradition of local pathology which became so popular in the nineteenth century. Although to some extent marked by a "credulity" in his work, Shryock continued, Rush made use of a limited amount of clinical evidence. As a physician and scientist, Rush was further ahead of his times than a casual reader of his works might suppose. Shryock's major criticism of Rush seemed to be that of his adhering to "a traditional approach to the problem of disease, in a day when more promising procedures were already being adopted in European centers."[20]

Equally distinguished was the work of George W. Corner in editing Rush's autobiography, then recently acquired by the American Philosophical Society, which had been practically inaccessible to scholars since Rush's death, except for a limited, expurgated version privately published in 1905.[21] In his introduction to the *Autobiography,* Corner described Rush as a great man with "weaknesses of temperament and of thought," a complex personality of "tense spirit" easily misunderstood through over-simplification.[22] Scholarly and insightful, Corner's edition of the autobiography was a landmark in Rush scholarship.

Rush's *Autobiography,* like all works of the kind, must be used with care. For although he drew upon his contemporary student journals, family records, and commonplace books—and did so with an impressive

[14] John A. Krout, *The Origins of Prohibition* (New York, 1925), p. 296; Herbert Asbury, *The Great Illusion; An Informal History of Prohibition* (New York, 1950), p. 27.

[15] Albert Deutsch, *The Mentally Ill in America; A History of Their Care and Treatment from Colonial Times* (Garden City, N.Y., 1937), p. 72; Rush, *Medical Inquiries and Observations upon the Diseases of the Mind* (Philadelphia, 1812); Norman Dain, *Concepts of Insanity in the United States, 1789–1865* (New Brunswick, 1964).

[16] Negley K. Teeters, "Benjamin Rush, Pioneer Prison Reformer," *Prison Journal* 23, 2 (April 1943): p. 306; Negley K. Teeters and John D. Shearer, *The Prison at Philadelphia, Cherry Hill* (New York, 1957), p. 225; George S. Brookes, *Friend Anthony Benezet* (Philadelphia, 1937), p. 93.

[17] 114–115, 250, 351–352. David F. Hawke's skillful biography, *Benjamin Rush, Revolutionary Gadfly* (Indianapolis, Ind., 1971), is the most recent contribution to the literature on Rush.

[18] I. Woodbridge Riley in an article, "Benjamin Rush as Materialist and Realist," wrote that Rush was "a living com-

promise between various divergent schools of thought." Although Riley concluded that Rush, despite his inconsistencies, was "in the main a materialist," his emphasis upon inconsistencies in Rush's thought made it fashionable among later students either to treat Rush as a confused materialist or to dismiss him altogether as a serious thinker; *Bull. Johns Hopkins Hospital* 18 (1907): p. 89, and his subsequent book, *American Thought; from Puritanism to Pragmatism and Beyond* (New York, 1915). Cf. Herbert W. Schneider, *A History of American Philosophy* (New York, 1947), and Joseph L. Blau, *Men and Movements in American Philosophy* (Englewood Cliffs, 1961).

[19] "The Psychiatry of Benjamin Rush," *Amer. Jour. Psychiatry* 101 (January 1945): pp. 429, 430–431; "Benjamin Rush from the Perspective of the Twentieth Century," *Trans. the College of Physicians of Philadelphia,* 4th ser., 14 (1946): p. 117.

[20] *Ibid.,* pp. 119–120.

[21] The earlier and expurgated volume was *A Memorial Containing Travels Through Life or Sundry Incidents in the Life of Dr. Benjamin Rush . . . also Extracts from His Commonplace Books as Well as a Short History of the Rush Family in Philadelphia,* ed. Louis Alexander Biddle (Lanoraie, Penna.).

[22] pp. 10–11.

degree of accuracy—the *Autobiography* was undertaken late in life and written, Rush said, for the "entertainment and instruction" of his family. Thus, the perspective of the year 1800, the year in which the fifty-four-year-old Rush began his "Travels Through Life," is evident throughout the work. Also clear is the need he felt to explain—even justify—to his children and to posterity his life, his thought, and his activities in behalf of truth and country. This testament, though, even if we conceive it narrowly in this way is, along with his correspondence, lectures, and published books and articles, the record of Benjamin Rush. It is a record which provides the materials for a reconstruction of his life and thought and enables Rush to explain himself, as it were, to posterity in the most general and true sense. If Rush's explanation of his life and thought was ideal, as indeed it was, this is because he was an idealist. His favorite literary character, we know, was Don Quixote and like that romantic Rush must have life on his own terms. The central fact—rather the ideal— of Rush's life was the American Revolution, and practically everything he wrote, including the *Autobiography,* was deeply colored by that fact and ideal.

While the autobiography was being edited for publication, Lyman H. Butterfield was engaged in the difficult task of editing Rush's letters. The publication of the *Letters of Benjamin Rush* in 1951, a work as rich in commentary as in original materials, set the precedent for the research that Butterfield himself had suggested in earlier articles on Rush.[23] Now, Rush could be seen through at least half of his known letters—the more important ones—as well as in his *Autobiography.*

Dr. Butterfield described Rush as "pugnacious and domineering" and revealing "symptoms and expressions of mild paranoia"; yet, he went on, Rush exhibited some "amiable traits" in his character.[24] In an appendix to the *Letters,* Butterfield agreed that Rush's unsigned letter to Patrick Henry, long held to be proof of Rush's treachery, suggested the removal of Washington, but, in extenuation of Rush's conduct, Butterfield noted that many other patriots had also criticized the general.[25] However suggestive his editorial commentaries on Rush, Butterfield's really outstanding achievement was that of rescuing a great man from an ill-deserved oblivion.

Although studies of Rush as a major figure and thinker in the Revolutionary and early national periods

should have begun in full earnest as a result of the preparatory work of Corner and Butterfield, this was deplorably not to be the case. Students of the times, apparently following the promising comparative method of historians like Daniel J. Boorstin, have tended to view Rush not as an autonomous historical personality, significant in his own right, but as a representative of a movement or a circle.[26] Thus, the old practice of forcing the historical Rush into a class—as conspirator, bleeder, and even signer and patriot, for example—has not been abandoned but merely transformed. And it seems that, despite the new evidence and penetrating insights of those scholars whose work we have discussed above, Rush as a philosopher of the American Revolution remains unappreciated.

In what follows, we shall attempt to show on the basis of a systematic examination of Rush's thought that he, far from being a secondary historical character, was a leading—perhaps the chief—philosophical exponent of the American Revolution. The claim is large, indeed, but the range of the man's thought was large, and his philosophy of the American Revolution more comprehensive in its objects than that of any other patriot thinker.

Benjamin Rush was a revolutionary in an age of revolution, a man of action in a century of men whose imaginations were astir with great purposes and historic commissions, a visionary among visionaries whose special eighteenth-century place in history commanded the sweep of past centuries and discerned the contours of the future. Yet Rush's revolutionary mission was unique. It was unique in point of time and place to late eighteenth-century America; and it was a Christian revolutionary mission, broadly and peculiarly understood within Rush's own terms, in an era when revolution and Christianity were hardly thought compatible.

Revolution and Christianity were compatible in Rush's thinking, as we shall see, because of his education in Great Awakening "Schools of the Prophets" where Presbyterian evangelists like Gilbert Tennent, Samuel Finley, and Samuel Davies taught him the eschatology of millennialism. His was an age, he was taught to believe, of Christian revolution, when all things were changing radically to make the world ready for Christ's Second Coming. The Great Awakening and the Enlightenment, he was told, were signs of this

---

[23] Notably "Benjamin Rush as a Promoter of Useful Knowledge, (1760–1797)," *Proc. Amer. Philos. Soc.* 92, 1 (1948): pp. 26–36, and "The Reputation of Benjamin Rush," previously cited.

[24] *Rush Letters,* introduction, pp. lxx–lxxi; *ibid.,* index, p. 1275. *Cf.* John H. Powell's study of Rush in the yellow fever epidemic of 1793, *Bring Out Your Dead; The Great Plague of Yellow Fever in Philadelphia in 1793* (Philadelphia, 1949), pp. 115, 124, 122, 202, 127, 199, 128.

[25] pp. 1197, 1202. *Cf.* Bernhard Knollenberg, *Washington and the Revolution, A Reappraisal* (New York, 1940).

[26] For example, see: Daniel J. Boorstin, *The Lost World of Thomas Jefferson* (Boston, 1960); Brooke Hindle, *The Pursuit of Science in Revolutionary America, 1735–1789* (Chapel Hill, 1956); Merle Curti, *The Growth of American Thought* (2d. ed., New York, 1943); Edwin T. Martin, *Thomas Jefferson: Scientist* (New York, 1952); and Constance Rourke, *The Roots of American Culture and Other Essays,* ed., with a preface, by Van Wyck Brooks (New York, 1942). Texts in American history, as one might expect, show this tendency even more emphatically.

Christian revolution, but the clearest sign of all—which he read for himself—was the American Revolution and its creation of the world's first Christian Republic.

As a Christian revolutionary, Rush interpreted the American Revolution as heralding the advent of the New World Christ—not the Christ of oligarchic Puritan New England but the Christ of republican America. For Rush, affixing his signature to the Declaration of Independence in 1776 was no mere political act; it was, instead, a vital preliminary to the laying of a new civilization in which true Christianity would flourish among free men. In what he conceived to be a Christian utopia, whose establishment would climax millennia of human and divine effort, freeborn sons of America would enjoy "private and public temporal happiness" with the happy expectation of universal salvation of all souls in the world to come. There, in a paradise regained, the forces of reason and revelation would ultimately triumph over physical and moral evil.

Benjamin Rush's revolutionary mission was that of disseminating the gospel of divine and human benevolence.

PART ONE

THE MAKING OF THE CHRISTIAN REVOLUTIONARY

I. SCHOOLS OF THE PROPHETS

This, my dear Ebenezer, is our forming time.—to Ebenezer Hazard, May 21, 1765.[1]

It is fitting that what is today part of the City of Brotherly Love was the birthplace of Benjamin Rush, for the American physician's life was a career of benevolence. But this career of benevolence, sufficient as it was to deserve praise in any age, was not all. Rush was the founder of a nation. The Revolutionary generation in which Rush was a leading figure also traced its source to Philadelphia and combined, as Rush did so paradoxically in his own life and thought, philanthropy, religion, and revolution.

Byberry, where Rush drew his "first breath" on January 4, 1746 (December 24, 1745, Old Style), was already in 1746 the ancestral home of the Rushes. There in 1683 John and Susanna Rush, English Quakers, had made a home for their children and grandchildren, free at last to worship God as they pleased. Benjamin Rush, the senior male descendent of the fifth generation of John Rush's line, was too much the republican to busy himself with elaborate English genealogies when he wrote his autobiography over a half-century later; it was enough for him to know, he declared, that John Rush had "fought for liberty, and migrated into a remote wilderness in the evening of his life in order to enjoy the privilege of worshiping God according to the dictates of his own conscience." [2] In a very real sense, Benjamin Rush translated his ancestor's early quest for religious and political freedom into American republican terms. To the author of the Declaration of Independence, Rush later confided that "to the respect and admiration which I was early taught to cherish for his virtues and exploits I owe a large portion of my republican temper and principles." [3]

Rush's father and mother, John and Susanna Hall, were farmers in Byberry. There and later in Philadelphia, John plied the gunsmith's trade like his father before him, until his early death in 1751 widowed Susanna for the second time. Mrs. Rush, a Presbyterian, supervised Benjamin's religious education at home; and, after the death of her husband, a communicant in the Episcopal Church, took young Rush to services at Rev. Gilbert Tennent's Second Presbyterian Church in Philadelphia. Accordingly, Benjamin's religious understanding was carefully shaped to Tennent's "highly calvinistical" principles both at home in Philadelphia and at West Nottingham Academy, Maryland, where his mother arranged for his further education. She was, he recalled in the twilight of his life, an "excellent mother," to whom equally with his wife he owed more than to any other human being.[4]

Gilbert Tennent, whom Mrs. Rush trusted with her son's early religious education, was the first of several Great Awakening evangelists whose personal and theological influence was important in Rush's life. Indeed, Tennent, along with Samuel Finley, Samuel Davies, and Elhanan Winchester—New Light preachers to be discussed later—led Rush by the example of their religious idealism to his matured synthesis of the opposing traditions of evangelical religion and the new science of the Enlightenment.

Tennent was tall and well-proportioned in appearance and of a "Naturally calm" disposition, as young

[1] *Rush Letters* **1**: p. 14.

[2] Rush to James Thornton, September 3, 1792, *Rush Letters* **1**: p. 621; Rush to John Adams, July 13, 1812, *ibid.* **2**: pp. 1150–1152; *Autobiography,* pp. 23–25.

[3] Rush to Thomas Jefferson, October 6, 1800, *Rush Letters* **2**: p. 826.

[4] *Autobiography,* pp. 25–26, 163; Rush to John Adams, June 13, 1811, *Rush Letters* **2**: p. 1083. Susanna Rush bore seven children to John Rush, of whom Benjamin Rush was the fourth, Goodman, p. 3.

Rush noted in his eulogy of 1764.[5] From his pulpit in Philadelphia's new Second Presbyterian Church, to which he had been called in 1743, Tennent preached revivalistic sermons like those of his circuit days, when he had followed George Whitefield to New England in search of souls for Christ. But Tennent, after accepting the charge from the Whitefieldian congregation in Philadelphia, had become steadily more moderate in his views. Never again was he to preach a sermon like *The Danger of an Unconverted Ministry* (1740), which had attacked the majority of Presbyterian clergy as hypocrites and provoked schismatic controversy in the Church. Whitefield's "Son of Thunder" who "doth not fear the Faces of Men" grew more conciliatory with the Old Lights after 1743, calling for a reunited Presbyterian Church in his *Irenicum Ecclesiasticum* (1749).[6]

When Tennent died in 1764, Rush was living in Philadelphia as a medical apprentice to Dr. John Redman. Rush's uncle and preceptor at West Nottingham Academy, Rev. Samuel Finley, was at the time of Tennent's death, president of the College of New Jersey. Finley was a close friend of Tennent. He had studied at Gilbert's father's "Log College," and had joined with Whitefield and Gilbert Tennent in converting souls in New Jersey. Finley eulogized his friend in *The Successful Minister of Christ, Distinguished in Glory* (1764), and in recognition of the special bond between Rush and Tennent seems to have asked the young man to write a eulogy of his own.

Rush's "Funeral Eulogy," the earliest of his published writings, reveals more than the great respect in which Rush held his first religious teacher. It shows, as do Rush's letters of the time, an increasing awareness of what another teacher of Rush—Rev. Samuel Davies—had called "public spirit" and urged upon his students in his valedictory address, *Religion and Public Spirit*, to Rush's graduating class at the College of New Jersey in 1760.[7] "The Rich, and the Poor, Black and White had equally free Access to his Person," Rush made a point of observing about Tennent. Tennent loved all who loved Christ, "whatever Mode of Worship they professed."[8] And Rush seemed to delight in his pastor's rejection of Quaker pacifism and political submissiveness. "The Liberties and Constitution of his Country," Rush wrote of Tennent, "he ever held in the highest Veneration; and always endeavoured to

promote a vigorous Defence of them, when the Invasions of the Enemies of BRITAIN made it necessary."[9] The example of Tennent's patriotism, like that of Finley and Davies, helped Rush later to overcome any religious scruple about his part in the War for Independence. Although it is true that in the disillusionment of his final years he came to accept a kind of pacifism.

When young Rush gathered together his thoughts and feelings about Tennent, he reflected the inner struggle between religion and public spirit which was developing within his own nature. Like Tennent in his early years, Rush in 1764 was studying medicine because he felt a spiritual "incapacity" for the ministry.[10] "To be sure," he had written a fellow graduate of the College of New Jersey,

to have officiated in the Sacred Desk would be my most delightful employment; to spend and be spent for the Good of Mankind is what I chiefly aim at. Though now I pursue the study of Physic, I am far from giving it any preeminence to Divinity.[11]

Unlike Tennent, however, Rush never experienced the necessary conversion to satisfy himself that he was fit for the ministry. Yet, in his years of medical apprenticeship in Philadelphia, when he wrote the eulogy on Tennent, Rush's thoughts were full of death, the grave, and his personal need for justification.[12] At the same time that he sought to prepare his soul for that necessary infusion of grace, in keeping with the Calvinistic teaching of Tennent, Rush was being drawn more deeply into the world of men, of epidemic disease and politics. It was the tension of religion and public spirit, to use Samuel Davies's phrase.[13]

Gilbert Tennent's influence on Rush in his earliest years was profoundly Calvinistic, as Rush's writings show. "Wherever he went," Rush powerfully characterized his teacher, "the Kingdom of Satan trembled."[14] He, too, was to exhibit in the Revolution and in life a fiery, uncompromising spirit—like that which had inspired Tennent's attacks upon the unconverted Presbyterian ministry in the Great Awakening. And Rush, too, was to have his "Scribes and Pharisees" in the Tories and false patriots of the Revolution.

Young Rush next came under the influence of his maternal uncle, Rev. Samuel Finley, whose Academy at West Nottingham was well known. Finley had been called to Nottingham in 1744 after laboring with George Whitefield and Gilbert Tennent to spread the

[5] *A Funeral Eulogy, Sacred to the Memory of the Late Reverend Gilbert Tennent,* appended to Samuel Finley, *The Successful Minister of Christ Distinguished in Glory. A Sermon Occasioned by the Death of the Late Reverend Mr. Gilbert Tennent* . . . (Philadelphia, 1764), p. xii; *Rush Letters* 1: p. 23, n. 3.

[6] See Harris E. Starr in *DAB, s.v.* "Tennent, Gilbert."

[7] *Religion and Public Spirit, A Valedictory Address to the Senior Class, Delivered in Nassau Hall, September 21, 1760* . . . ([New York,] 1761).

[8] Rush, *A Funeral Eulogy,* pp. x, xii.

[9] *Ibid.,* pp. xi–xii. See Tennent's *The Late Association for Defence Encourag'd, or, the Lawfulness of a Defensive War* (1748).

[10] Rush to Enoch Green, 1761, *Rush Letters* 1: p. 3; Starr, "Tennent, Gilbert."

[11] Rush to Enoch Green, 1761, *Rush Letters* 1: p. 3.

[12] Rush to Ebenezer Hazard, March 19, 1765, *ibid.,* pp. 10–11.

[13] Rush to Ebenezer Hazard, September 27, 1762, and to Enoch Green, 1761, *ibid.,* pp. 5–6, 3–4.

[14] Rush, *A Funeral Eulogy,* p. ix.

word of God throughout the Middle Colonies and New England. Like his friend Gilbert Tennent, with whom he had preached at the Second Presbyterian Church of Philadelphia, Finley had no patience with unconverted ministers. His sermon *Christ Triumphing, and Satan Raging* (1741) and Tennent's *The Danger of an Unconverted Ministry* (1740), both on this subject, were in fact given in Nottingham and only several months apart.

At Nottingham, then, a center of the Great Awakening made famous by Finley's and Tennent's schismatic preaching, Rush in 1754 continued his religious and secular education. Here he memorized the Shorter Catechism of the Church of Scotland and repeated it dutifully to his uncle at the end of each week. Mornings and evenings before prayers he listened to the preacher's exegesis of the Scriptures, noting at least the sincerity, if not the meaning, of the learned commentaries. Not that Finley's presence was as commanding as that of Tennent. He was short of stature, ruddy-complexioned, and without any of the grave expressions of his honored colleague. But Finley was just as animated when he preached to Rush and the other students that "the Kingdom of God is come" in their very day and that the "Spirit of God" was casting out "Devils" everywhere.[15] And he poured scorn on the enemies of George Whitefield and those other converted ministers who, like himself, were proclaiming the long-awaited Millennium. "For many will hate and contradict," he asserted, "what they are unable to confute."[16] It was all very much like what Rush had heard from his mother and Gilbert Tennent.

There was one lesson in particular which made a deep impression on young Benjamin Rush, a kind of late Sunday evening affirmation of the week's work. In this instruction, Rush remembered in his autobiography, Finley would adduce "in a plain way some of the most striking and intelligible evidences of the truth of the Christian Religion."[17] He would, moreover demonstrate the truth of his Christian belief by using many of the best arguments, which he characteristically tried to express with, he said, "plainness, not nicety, a familiar, not an ornate Stile."[18] These proofs of the

Christian religion were deeply convincing to Rush. Almost a half-century later, after he had abandoned much of Finley's Calvinistic theology, he could attribute to Finley's arguments his never having a doubt as to "the divine origin of the Bible."[19]

Finley liked to emphasize that he spoke and wrote not for "the learn'd but the Common People" and "that it is better to be understood by all, than admired by any."[20] *The Approved Ministers of God* (1749) was an ideal self-description as well as the title of one of Finley's sermons. The perfect minister, he wrote, "should study rather to speak instructively than learn'dly, and suppress a Thousand flowery Expressions for the sake of one that is pertinent, and level to the capacity of his Hearers."[21] This was not to despise learning, though, for Finley's ideal minister should

> be stor'd with *Knowledge*. . . . He should be able to apprehend Things clearly, Methodize his Conceptions regularly, and Reason solidly. It is not enough that he has good natural Parts, but these must be cultivated by Learning. Acquaintance with the learned Languages, Rhetoric, and Philosophy, secures him from Contempt, and at the same Time is greatly subservient to Divinity, his main Study.[22]

Rush learned that the approved minister of God must be an excellent teacher and must be judged by his results. He learned that "The Minister of God should be a Man of Universal Benevolence: A Lover of Mankind, especially of those who are Good."[23] But the approved minister of God must work for sinners, too, and, in Finley's words—which Rush would use later himself—"he will gladly spend and be spent, for them."[24]

That Rush tried to model his life after that of Finley's ideal man of God is clear. He failed, of course, in the obvious sense that he never felt secure in possessing that gift of grace he thought necessary for the ministry. Like Gilbert Tennent, and, significantly, on the recommendation of Finley—who himself seemed to favor medicine next to divinity—Rush felt compelled to save bodies rather than souls.[25] As we shall see, he did

---

[15] Finley, *Christ Triumphing, and Satan Raging. A Sermon on Matthew XII, 28. Wherein is Proved, That the Kingdom of God is Come unto Us at This Day . . . . January 20, 1740* (Philadelphia, 1741), pp. 40, 33; see Harris E. Starr in *DAB*, s.v. "Finley, Samuel"; William B. Sprague, *Annals of the American Pulpit; or Commemorative Notices of Distinguished American Clergymen of Various Denominations, from the Early Settlement of the Country to the Close of the Year Eighteen Hundred and Fifty-Five* (9 v., New York, 1857–1869) 3: pp. 96–101; *Autobiography*, pp. 28–31. Finley married Sarah Hall, Mrs. Rush's sister, *ibid.*, pp. 25–26.

[16] Finley, *Christ Triumphing*, preface, p. iv.

[17] *Autobiography*, p. 31.

[18] Finley, *A Charitable Plea for the Speechless: or, the Right of Believers' Infants to Baptism Vindicated* (Philadelphia, 1746), preface, p. vi.

[19] *Autobiography*, p. 31.

[20] Finley, *A Charitable Plea*, Preface, p. vi; Finley, *Christ Triumphing*, preface, p. iv.

[21] *The Approved Ministers of God* (Philadelphia, 1749), p. 7.

[22] *Ibid.*, pp. 5–6.

[23] *Ibid.*, pp. 9–10.

[24] *Ibid.*; "to spend and be spent for the Good of Mankind is what I chiefly aim at," Rush to Enoch Green, 1761, *Rush Letters* 1: p. 3.

[25] E.g., Rush to John Adams, July 21, 1789, *ibid.*, p. 524; Rush to Mrs. Rush, August 26, 1787, and August 15, 1791, *ibid.*, pp. 438, 603. In his medical lectures, Rush liked to pay tribute to the influence of his great teacher. He often quoted Finley as teaching his students to "esteem truth the only knowledge, and that labouring to defend an error, is only striving to be more ignorant," Rush, "On the Necessary Connexion Between Observation, and Reasoning in Medicine," *Sixteen Introductory Lectures, to Courses of Lectures upon the Institutes and Practice of Medicine. . . . To Which are Added, Two*

experience "conversions" in politics, medicine, and even theology, but he never discovered within his soul the certainty of that grace that fitted men like Tennent, Finley, and Davies for the ministry and made them approved ministers of God. In another and perhaps more important sense, Rush came very close to achieving Finley's ideal. He was no less theological than Finley's approved minister in his conception of the world; and he did not fail by much in acting on Finley's precept that the man of God's "Life and Doctrine should be of a Piece." [26] And there is absolutely no denying, however controversial his life was in some other ways, that it was, in Finley's expression, "a Pattern of good Works." [27]

Finley's arguments for the Christian religion, presented with love, vigor, and his characteristic simplicity of explanation, convinced Rush of the logical nature of the process by which one arrived at truth: how "indelible" arguments "fixed in the understanding" worked upon the judgment in a mental process known "to yield as necessarily to the impression of truth as vision in a sound eye succeeds the impression from the rays of light." [28] Thus Rush discovered philosophy and that "The truths of philosophy and Christianity dwell alike in the mind of the Deity, and reason and religion are equally the offspring of his goodness." [29] Never afterwards did Rush genuinely doubt the correspondence of philosophy and Christianity. For him the truth was one, however arrived at: "Like its divine author, it is an eternal unchangeable UNIT." [30]

Although religion was the directing principle of Rush's education at the country school, it was by no means Finley's exclusive concern. In his strict, disciplinarian way, the schoolmaster taught Latin, Greek, English, and certain of the arts and sciences. When he looked back over the years, Rush found his master's teaching of English praiseworthy but his lectures in the arts and sciences hopelessly confined to the primitive

knowledge of the times. The arts and especially the sciences of 1800, Rush believed, were so far advanced beyond those of 1755 as to constitute a revolution in learning. As for the years spent in tedious drilling in Greek and Latin, Rush deemed them practically valueless, an opinion one might have expected from the defiant republican anti-classicist. Much more enduring in importance for Rush was Finley's tabletalk with Mrs. Finley and occasional visitors to Nottingham. Forced to listen with what he later described as "a reluctant and impatient ear," the twelve-year-old scholar nevertheless acquired many "seeds of useful knowledge." [31] Moreover, Rush, by listening to good, instructive conversation (and some of the finest sermons of the Great Awakening) developed an appreciation for oral expression, which inclined him to the study of rhetoric after his matriculation at the College of New Jersey. Indeed, the mature Rush attached so much value to conversation that he kept elaborate records of information he collected in this way, and interspersed such facts and opinions throughout his published and unpublished writings. [32]

The day's lessons for young Rush were not all sedentary. At harvest time he and the other students learned "practical agriculture" by working in Finley's fields. Barely in his teens, Rush discovered the pleasures of the countryside and afterwards treasured every idyllic memory of Nottingham's meadows, orchard, and fields. In 1800 he liked to think, too, that his pastoral labors gathering up the harvest and making hay "begat health, and helped to implant more deeply . . . the native passion for rural life." [33] It was easy to idealize Nottingham some fifty years later when Rush, after many disillusionments with the modern world, wrote his autobiography for his children. Yet the real and lasting influence of Finley's Nottingham is not hard to see.

Lectures upon the Pleasures of the Senses and of the Mind, with an Inquiry into Their Proximate Cause (Philadelphia, 1811), p. 13. On Finley's recommending medicine as second only to divinity, and his favorite use of medical analogies in his sermons, see, e.g., *The Approved Ministers of God,* p. 18 *et passim,* and *The Madness of Mankind, Represented in A Sermon Preached in the New Presbyterian Church in Philadelphia on the 9th of June 1754* (Philadelphia, [1754]), pp. 15–16, 21, 28; *Autobiography,* p. 37. Tennent at first chose medicine as a profession only because he felt spiritually unqualified for the ministry, Starr, "Tennent, Gilbert."

[26] *The Approved Ministers of God,* p. 14.

[27] *Ibid.*

[28] *Autobiography,* p. 32.

[29] Rush, "An Inquiry into the Influence of Physical Causes upon the Moral Faculty," *Medical Inquiries and Observations* (5th ed., 2 v., Philadelphia, 1818) 1: p. 123.

[30] Rush, "An Enquiry into the Consistency of Oaths with Reason and Christianity," *Rush Essays,* p. 126. Also, see Rush, "Introductory Lecture to a Course of Lectures on the Theory & Practice of Physic," Rush MSS, call number Yi2/7400/F1, pp. 37–38.

[31] Rush to John Adams, July 21, 1789, *Rush Letters* 1: p. 524; *Autobiography,* pp. 30, 32; Rush, "On the Application of Metaphysicks to Medicine," Rush MSS, call number Yi2/7400/ F2, pp. 22–35. In June, 1789, Rush had published in the *American Museum* 5: pp. 525–535, an attack upon the Latin and Greek languages as unrepublican. Adams strongly disagreed with his views, and Rush was trying in this letter to make his argument more emphatic by referring to his own real or idealized education. The fact that young Rush had had sufficient interest in Greek to translate Hippocrates' aphorisms into English shows that he was now overstating his own case against the classical languages. But this is the very point of Rush's life and thought. In his personal idealism and revolutionary republican ideology life must be fitted to thought, fact to ideal. His *Autobiography* and other writings illustrate this well. And this was essentially what he was doing in the present instance.

[32] E.g., *Autobiography, passim;* Rush, "An Inquiry into the Cause of Animal Life in Three Lectures," *Medical Inquiries and Observations* (5th ed.) 1: p. 38. The latter, originally published in 1799 as *Three Lectures upon Animal Life,* remains an important explanation of the fundamental nature of animal life.

[33] *Autobiography,* p. 32.

Nottingham, like the College of New Jersey where Rush was soon to continue his education, was what Gilbert Tennent called a "School of the Prophets." [34] It was for young Rush and ever remained a virgin seminary of divine learning, protected by the rural innocence of the countryside against the evils of Philadelphia and the outside world. For, as Dr. Rush would later pronounce, "The country life is happy, chiefly because its laborious employments are favourable to virtue, and unfriendly to vice.[35] Cities were the legacy of Adam's sin. "I consider them in the same light that I do abscesses on the human body," Rush wrote Jefferson in 1800, "viz., as reservoirs of all the impurities of a community." [36] Nottingham Academy and the College of New Jersey were places of health as well as virtue, Rush theorized, because of the salutary effects of rural odors on the human system. When Rush helped found Dickinson College in 1783, and projected it as a kind of "School of the Prophets" like those he had attended at Nottingham and Princeton, he calculated the advantages to the health of the students to be derived from the country location of the new college.[37] He characteristically employed his new science of animal life in the cause of religious education, hoping to make his "School of the Prophets" at Carlisle as modern and effective as possible.

But, of course, Nottingham was a "School of the Prophets" neither because of its bucolic setting nor because of the formal subjects that Samuel Finley taught there. It was a seminary for preparing a "faithful Ministry" for the New Side Presbyterian church, inspired by William Tennent's Log College, which Finley and Gilbert Tennent had attended. In his *The Danger of an Unconverted Ministry,* preached in Nottingham, Gilbert Tennent had called for establishing "Private Schools of the Prophets" where "poor Youths" of "good natural Capacity, and great Desires after the Ministerial Work" should be educated.[38] Mrs. Rush's sons, Benjamin and Jacob, qualified in the ways Rev. Tennent prescribed, and she sent both of them to Nottingham school and then to the College of New Jersey. And although it seems they never received that converting grace essential to change them, in Tennent's phrase, from natural men to "God's Ministers," they

were men of deep piety in their life's work of medicine and law.[39]

Finley hoped to educate his students to form with other true Christians what he called a "Party for Jesus Christ." [40] Those belonging to this party of Christ, according to Finley and other revivalists, were those of the laity and clergy who followed Christ even when to do so meant crossing local and denominational lines. The true followers of Christ, as Gilbert Tennent had said, were not "great Bigots to small Matters in Religion," not little men of "Party-Zeal." [41] Prudence, Finley declared, was no real Christian virtue (Rush would later say in another, if analogous, context that it was no republican virtue either).[42] "I look upon all Neuters, as Enemies, in Affairs of Religion," Finley thundered. "Away with your carnal Prudence! And either follow God or Baal. *He that is not with us, is against us; and he that gathereth not with us, scattereth abroad. . . ."* [43] In the "School of the Prophets," whether conducted by Tennent or Finley, there was no compromising with evil. Either one followed God or Baal. Rush possessed the same kind of either-or, for-or-against mentality, and the same censorious disposition.

To Rush, Finley was himself a prophet—one of those divinely appointed men, like the Tennents and Blairs, sent to awaken and revive the people to God. In his own life Rush was to feel the same kind of evangelistic purpose. While it is true that he was never called to the "faithful Ministry," he was to be a preacher of the Gospel nevertheless. His systems of politics, medicine, and education—to be discussed later—rested on the Gospel. As we shall see, Enlightenment ideas shaped Rush's life and thought too, especially in the 1770's and 80's when he articulated his vision of a post-Revolutionary American utopia. But in the end, disillusioned with America and the world, and realizing what Finley many years before had called the "Madness of Mankind," Rush was to fall back on the Gospel truths of his Nottingham days.[44]

Like the prophets of the Old Testament, Finley and Tennent were judges and censors of public policy. "They and we," said Finley proudly, "are Turners of the World upside down, Subverters of Peace and Church-Government, and the like." [45] Their prophetic mission was that of opposing the sins and wrongs of the day, while preparing for the coming Kingdom of

[34] *Danger of an Unconverted Ministry* in Alan Heimert and Perry Miller, eds., *The Great Awakening, Documents Illustrating the Crisis and Its Consequences* (Indianapolis, 1967), p. 85.
[35] Rush, "Influence of Physical Causes upon the Moral Faculty," *Med. Inq. & Obs.,* (5th ed.) 1: p. 109.
[36] October 6, 1800, *Rush Letters* 2: p. 824. "Towns and cities are the jails and graves of the human species," Rush, "Lectures on Pathology," Rush MSS, call number Yi2/7396/F19, p. 120.
[37] Rush, "Three Lectures upon Animal Life," *Med. Inq. & Obs.* (5th ed.) 1: p. 13; Rush, "Lectures on Pathology. On the Influence of Different Religions on the Health of the Body," Rush MSS, call number Yi2/7396/F23, pp. 320–321.
[38] Heimert and Miller, eds., *The Great Awakening,* p. 85.

[39] On Jacob Rush (1747–1820), see Butterfield's note, *Rush Letters* 1: p. 44.
[40] *Christ Triumphing,* p. 27.
[41] *Danger of an Unconverted Ministry* in Heimert and Miller, eds., *The Great Awakening,* p. 75.
[42] *Christ Triumphing,* p. 38; Rush to John Adams, July 9, 1807, *Rush Letters* 2: pp. 949–951.
[43] *Christ Triumphing,* p. 38.
[44] Finley, *Madness of Mankind;* Rush to John Adams, August 8, 1812, *Rush Letters* 2: p. 1159.
[45] *Christ Triumphing,* p. 30.

God on earth. Finley believed, and in this he was a typical Great Awakening evangelist, that the times presented Christians with a crisis as well as a promise: Christ was triumphing (to paraphrase the title of his famous sermon) but Satan was raging. "Woe to the Inhabitants of the Earth, for the Devil is come down with great Wrath, because he knows his Time is short." [46] It was imperative that men of the Gospel try to put the world right for Christ's Second Coming.

The idea of the Christian revolution, of the new creation, of God's erecting in this world a Kingdom of Christ, was the common possession of the American evangelists. Jonathan Edwards, of course, was the leading spokesman of millennialism in the Great Awakening, as he was the leading theologian of the movement. In his *Christ Triumphing, and Satan Raging* (1741), Finley preached chiliastic ideas like those of Edwards's *History of Redemption* (1739). It was manifest that Christ was coming, declared Finley, for "Devils" were being "cast out" by the "Spirit of God." The conversion of deists and papists was another sign of His coming. And, in an allusion to the Enlightenment, which he hailed as another evidence of the redeeming of the world, Finley observed that "even the Graceless are increased in knowledge" and "Pious and Soul-searching Books, that formerly lay neglected, are now in great Request." [47] These and other Great Awakening ideas on the nature of the millennium—which we associate more with Edwards and Samuel Hopkins than lesser evangelical thinkers like Finley and Gilbert Tennent—were basic in Rush's thinking about the meaning of his times. He was to conceive the greatest event of his life, the American Revolution, as fulfilling in his dream of the Christian Republic the millennial expectation of the new Zion.

Samuel Finley died in Philadelphia in July of 1766, seven years after Rush's departure from Nottingham and about a month before he left Philadelphia for the University of Edinburgh. By now a College of New Jersey bachelor of arts and an experienced medical apprentice, Rush attended his dying master "every other night for several weeks, and finally performed the distressing office of closing his eyes." [48] While the young apprentice sat by the bedside of his uncle, he may have revolved in his mind the curious fact of his having been advised to study medicine by the very patient he was attending. Six years earlier, on taking his degree at the College of New Jersey, Rush had intended to study law. A chance meeting with Finley at Nottingham, however, had caused Rush to change his plans. The preacher had counseled his nephew to avoid the "temptations" of law and to study medicine; but in any case, Finley had insisted, "set apart a day for fasting and prayer, and ask God to direct you in

your choice of a profession." [49] Admittedly, Rush did not follow this last piece of advice, but he did abide by his revered preceptor's injunction to study physic and later saw "the hand of heaven clearly in it." [50]

The intervening years between 1759, when Rush left Nottingham, and July of 1766, when his twelve-year relationship with Finley was ended by the preacher's death, were years spent at the College of New Jersey and in Philadelphia. The College of New Jersey, which later became Princeton University, was about as old as Rush when he matriculated there in the spring of 1759. After taking examinations, he was granted junior class status in the Presbyterian college. In August, the eminent New Side minister, Samuel Davies, became the fourth president of the school, which since the death of the great Jonathan Edwards had been without a permanent head.[51] Trained in evangelism at William Tennent's Log College, Davies had carried the Calvinistic revival to Hanover County, Virginia, in 1755, and had established the first southern Presbytery.[52] The new president soon developed a special interest in young Rush's aptitude for verse, composition, and public speaking. In his own poetry, for which he was admired by his friend and co-worker, Samuel Finley, Davies reflected the influence and style of the British poets, Edward Young and James Thomson, both of whom became Rush's favorites.[53] No doubt, as a pulpit orator of great distinction—an orator of "thoughts sublime," as Finley was to say—Davies was quick to discern his student's rhetorical promise. Rush, moreover, impressed Davies academically by the ease with which he memorized the day's lessons. Very probably unknown to young Rush at the time was the fact of Davies's earlier and likewise favorable impression of another young American, George Washington, whom he foresaw to have a unique destiny in his country's history.[54]

[46] *Ibid.*, preface, p. v.

[47] *Ibid.*, p. 33.

[48] *Autobiography*, p. 33.

[49] *Ibid.*, pp. 36–37.

[50] *Ibid.*, p. 37.

[51] *Ibid.*, p. 35; on Samuel Davies (1721–1761), see Sprague, *Annals of the American Pulpit* 3: pp. 140–146.

[52] William W. Sweet, *Religion on the American Frontier* (4 v.) 2: *The Presbyterians, 1783–1840, A Collection of Source Material* (New York, 1936), p. 6.

[53] *Autobiography*, p. 36; Finley's eulogy on Davies, *The Disinterested and Devoted Christian: A Sermon Preached at Nassau-Hall, Princeton, May 28, 1761 Occasioned by the Death of Rev. Samuel Davies, A.M.*, in Samuel Davies, *Sermons on Important Subjects, To Which Are Now Added, Three Occasional Sermons . . . Memoirs and Character of the Author, and Two Sermons on Occasion of His Death, By the Rev. Drs. Gibbons and Finley* (3 v., 5th ed., New York, 1792) 1: p. xxii; Davies, "The General Resurrection," *Sermons on Important Subjects* 1: p. 463; Alan Heimert, *Religion and the American Mind: From the Great Awakening to the Revolution* (Cambridge, Mass., 1966), p. 173; "Scottish Journal," p. 77; Rush to David Petrikin, April 21, 1812, *Rush Letters* 2: p. 1130; *Rush to John Adams*, October 2, 1810, *ibid.*, p. 1067.

[54] For Finley's praise of Davies's "thoughts sublime," *Disinterested and Devoted Christian* 1: p. xxii; *Autobiography*, p. 36; Samuel Davies, *Religion and Patriotism the Constituents*

Rush did know of the fierce patriotism that Davies shared with Finley and Gilbert Tennent. Like Finley's French-and-Indian-War sermon, *The Curse of Meroz, or, The Danger of Neutrality in the Cause of God, and Our Country* (1757), Davies's *Religion and Patriotism the Constituents of a Good Soldier* (1755) exhibited what Gilbert Tennent praised in Finley as "a disinterested and undaunted Zeal for God, his King, and Country." [55] This patriotism, Rush would later understand, was only one expression of what Samuel Davies called "public spirit" in his valedictory address to Rush's graduating class in September, 1760. This sermon, which Rush cherished through the years, not only capped his education in the "School of the Prophets" but dramatically helped him to resolve the problem of religion and public spirit, of how he could try to be in but not of the world, of how he could serve God and man at the same time. In short, Davies's *Religion and Public Spirit* was to be for Rush a handbook of Christian revolution. It was to provide him with the theological means by which to synthesize the apparently contradictory otherworldly and secular ideals of the Great Awakening and the Enlightenment.

Be like the Biblical David, President Davies had said to Rush's senior class, David *"the Servant of God and his Generation."* "He suffered, he fought, he reigned, he prophecied, he sung, he performed every Thing, to serve his Generation, according to the Will of God." [56] Religion and public spirit together formed "the truly good and useful Man; a proper Member of human Society; and even of the grand Community of Angels and Saints." Davies continued:

Public Spirit and Benevolence without Religion, is but a warm Affection for the Subjects, to the Neglect of their Sovereign; or a Partiality for the Children, in Contempt of their Father, who is infinitely more worthy of Love. And Religion without Public Spirit and Benevolence, is but a sullen, selfish, sour and malignant Humour for Devotion, unworthy that sacred Name. "For if a Man love not his Brother, whom he hath seen, how can he love God whom he hath not seen?" [57]

In Davies's ideal of "the truly good and useful Man" —which he shared with Gilbert Tennent, Samuel Finley, and other evangelists of the Great Awakening —public spirit and benevolence formed "a beautiful Symmetry; they adorn, cherish and perfect each other;

they contain the Substance of all Obedience to the divine Law, which is summed up in the Love of God, and the Love of Man." [58]

President Davies on that September day in 1760, Rush remembered, had called upon him and every other graduating senior to emulate David and become "the good, the useful, and public-spirited Man." [59] Whether the graduates planned to

appear in the sacred Desk ... to make Men wise, good and happy; or whether you appear at the Bar, as Advocates for Justice, and the Patrons of the Opprest; or whether you practise the healing Art in the Chambers of Affliction ... whatever, I say, be your Place, permit me, my dear Youth, to inculcate upon you this important Instruction, imbibe and cherish a publick spirit. Serve your Generation. Live not for yourselves, but the Publick. Be the Servants of the Church; the Servants of your Country; the Servants of all. [60]

And neither Rush nor anyone else in Nassau Hall was surprised when Davies—who was as famous for his secular learning as for his piety—emphasized his point by quoting from Alexander Pope's *Essay on Man* in order to show how reason, too, dictated "one close System of Benevolence." [61] Then, after charging each of his students with "an indispensable Obligation" to do good as "proper Agents" of God, the evangelist had stressed the need for "Regeneration . . . that divine Change of the Principles of Action . . . the great Foundation of true Religion and social Virtue; without which, you can never arrive at the finished Character of good and great Men." [62]

Human nature, Davies as Calvinist believed, was too depraved to allow for the union of true religion and true public spirit "till there be 'a new Creation; till old Things pass away, and all Things be made new.' " [63] Rush and the other College of New Jersey graduates, Davies said, must go into "publick Life with a new heart and a new spirit. . . . Therefore let this saying sink deep into your Hearts, the new birth is the beginning of all genuine religion and virtue." [64]

Alan Heimert has remarked that this graduating class was to produce many outstanding leaders of the Revolution.[65] The effect of his valedictory address and Davies's personal example on all these young Revolutionaries to be, would be a study in itself. This much,

of a Good Soldier (Philadelphia, 1755), p. 9n. Later, Rush not only learned of Davies's prediction but caused it to be published, Rush to John Adams, February 12, 1812, *Rush Letters* **2**: p. 1125, Butterfield's note.

[55] Tennent's preface to Samuel Finley, *The Curse of Meroz, or, The Danger of Neutrality in the Cause of God, and Our Country* (Philadelphia, 1757), p. iii; "It is known," Finley wrote of Davies, "what an active instrument he was in stirring up a patriot spirit, a spirit of courage and resolution in *Virginia*, where he resided during the late barbarous *French* and *Indian* ravages," *Disinterested and Devoted Christian* **1**: p. xxiii.

[56] *Religion and Public Spirit*, p. 4.

[57] *Ibid.*, pp. 4–5.

[58] *Ibid.*, p. 5.

[59] *Ibid.*, p. 3.

[60] *Ibid.*, pp. 6–7. The spelling of "public" varies throughout the printed sermon.

[61] *Ibid.*, p. 7n; on Davies's learning, see the biographical memoir by Dr. Thomas Gibbons in Davies, *Sermons on Important Subjects* **1**: pp. xil–xlii.

[62] *Religion and Public Spirit*, pp. 8–9, 12.

[63] *Ibid.*, p. 13.

[64] *Ibid.*

[65] *Religion and the American Mind*, pp. 328–330. *Religion and Public Spirit* "would be republished several times in the next ten years and would provide many Calvinists with their definition of patriotism through the early years of the Revolution," *ibid.*, p. 328.

however, is clear with regard to one of them. Davies's sermon for Rush was a call for personal conversion, regeneration, and reform—in the tradition of the Great Awakening—but it was more. It was a call for social conversion, regeneration, and reform—in the tradition of the Enlightenment as well. In Rush's view, the American Revolution was to be the historic opportunity for regenerated men, men like himself of "new heart" and "new spirit," to found the New Jerusalem of the millennium, whose beginnings in America Davies had proclaimed in his sermons. These new men, in whom true, awakened religion and true, enlightened public spirit were to be joined for the first time in relatively large numbers, Rush was to call republicans or Christian republicans, and their new, ideal society, the Christian Republic.[66]

Samuel Davies, like the other prophets Gilbert Tennent and Samuel Finley, was in background a man of humble beginnings and unpretentious education, as Rush happily realized decades later when, as educator and social reformer, he argued for the establishment of "Schools of the Prophets" to be modeled after William Tennent's Log College and Samuel Blair's Fagg's Manor, where Davies had studied.[67] Rush's Great Awakening teachers, as Finley himself had said in his funeral sermon on Davies, had no time for "merely curious and amusing researches."[68] The approved ministers of God, to use Finley's phrase—preachers like Tennent, Finley, and Davies—were ever wary of "abstruse and unedifying Speculations, or doubtful Disputations; or at best, such as are but superficially Practical."[69] True religion and true public spirit, the essential qualities of the approved minister of God, could not exist one without the other, as Davies had said; and Rush agreed with Davies and his other teachers that pedantic, esoteric, or useless learning was just as deadly a threat to real public spirit as (in Finley's words) "unministerially pragmatical" activism was to real religion.[70]

Davies was largely self-educated, but as Rush later noted in his autobiography Davies had "surmounted the disadvantages of scanty circumstances and a confined education by the strength and activity of a great and original genius."[71] Rush was not alone in attributing genius to Davies. The revivalist's learning was so far above suspicion of narrow pedantry as to be celebrated in Britain as well as America. His scholarly reputation in ancient literature, rhetoric, and philosophy had been acknowledged by the trustees of the College of New Jersey in 1753 when they had asked him to accompany Gilbert Tennent on a fund-raising mission to England and Scotland. Perhaps it was while he was abroad that Davies became so interested in "Mathematics and the Newtonian Philosophy" as to make the new science a key academic program when he became president of the College of New Jersey in 1759.[72] In any case, there was no doubt in Rush's mind, when he looked back on his student days at Princeton, that Davies had come to his new post after having learned much from his association in Britain with "the most eminent Scholars and Divines among the dissenters."[73] Rush was himself to meet many of these same men—including Davies's intimate friend and biographer, Dr. Thomas Gibbons—while continuing his medical studies in London.[74]

By his own confession in his autobiography, Rush, like many other students then and now, did not learn as much as he could from his teacher. He was at the College of New Jersey less than two years, but even so Rush studied closely enough with Davies in that time to observe that his teacher was consumed with "a love of knowledge."[75] Davies was, in fact, to die shortly after Rush graduated, as the result of a weakened condition brought on, it was said, from excessive study.[76] In his memoirs, Rush regretted his lost opportunities at Princeton to take from Davies all the hard-won knowledge that he was so willing to share. Rush did, however, learn from his gentle teacher to love knowledge and how to seek it out. To this end, Davies taught Rush the advantages of keeping a "Liber Selectorum" or commonplace book in which he should record highly interesting passages from his reading in the classics. As a scholar, Davies was careful to take notes on what he read and thought and young Rush was sufficiently impressed by the value of this practice as to keep abundant journals and commonplace books throughout his own life.[77]

Davies, then, inspired Rush in many ways. He inspired him, as had Finley and Tennent, with religious awe. Davies, especially, was no compromiser of Calvinistic doctrine; and his eulogist writes that he agonized constantly over the fate of himself and his children and all men, knowing as he did the depraved

---

[66] E.g., Rush to Charles Nisbet, May 15, 1784, *Rush Letters* 1: pp. 334–335. See below, ch. VIII.

[67] Rush to Ashbel Green?, May 22, 1807, *Rush Letters* 2: pp. 946–947, and Butterfield's note, pp. 947–948.

[68] *Disinterested and Devoted Christian* 1: p. xii.

[69] *The Approved Ministers of God*, p. 17.

[70] *Successful Minister of Christ*, p. 19. See below, ch. VI.

[71] *Autobiography*, p. 35; Rush must have been greatly impressed by President Davies's "Synoptical Compend Metaphysicks," a formidable outline indeed, which he copied in his senior year at Princeton and which can be found in Rush MSS, call number Yi2/7402/F1.

[72] Francis L. Broderick, "Pulpit, Physics, and Politics: The Curriculum of the College of New Jersey, 1746–1794," *Wm. and Mary Quart.*, 3d Ser., **6**, 1 (1949): pp. 52, 57.

[73] *Autobiography*, p. 35.

[74] *Ibid.*, p. 57.

[75] *Ibid.*, p. 36.

[76] Davies, *Sermons on Important Subjects* 1: append., p. xxxiv.

[77] *Autobiography*, p. 36. Later, as a teacher, Rush emphasized the value of keeping commonplace books and diaries by citing the precedent of their use by John Locke, Voltaire, Benjamin Franklin, and others, "On the Means of Acquiring Knowledge," *Sixteen Introductory Lectures*, pp. 346, 351–352, 355–356.

nature of man.[78] After graduating from the College of New Jersey, and while a medical apprentice in Philadelphia surrounded by sickness and death, Rush exhibited in his letters and other writings an awed reverence for God and a foreboding which derived from Davies's influence on his sensitive nature as much as, if not more than, it did from the influence of Finley and Tennent. Davies inspired Rush with "public spirit," as we have seen. And, in his final tribute to his Princeton mentor in his autobiography, Rush wrote that Davies's "mode of teaching inspired me with a love of knowledge, and that if I derived but little from his instructions, I was taught by him how to acquire it in the subsequent periods of my life." [79] By his example, Davies taught Rush the art of inquiry, in its most basic form, which another of Rush's teachers, Dr. William Cullen of the University of Edinburgh, would later help to develop more systematically in Rush's thinking.

In September 1760, considerably less than two years after he had entered the College of New Jersey, Rush was awarded the Bachelor of Arts degree. It was at this juncture, as we have already seen, that young Benjamin, after a false start in the direction of law, chose a medical apprenticeship. By doing so, he followed the advice of Finley and not of Davies, who "believed I should make a better figure at the bar," said Rush, "than in the walks of a hospital." [80] Acquiescing in Rush's decision, Davies wrote a letter of recommendation to Dr. John Redman, a "Log College" alumnus and Philadelphia's leading physician, requesting an apprenticeship for the fourteen-year-old graduate of the College of New Jersey.[81] The request granted, Benjamin Rush took leave of Davies, whose months of life were already numbered, and embarked upon a new career in Philadelphia.

When Rush entered Dr. Redman's "shop" in February, 1761, he began what was to be a career against sickness and death. As if symbolically, in that very month, he learned of the premature death of Davies at thirty-eight, an event which shook him by its strange, unexpected character:

Oh, it is a wound too fatal—the stroke is almost too severe. When the silver locks of old age and unusefulness are taken away, then indeed it's vain to grieve. But when the charms of beauty, vigor, health, and youth, and all the united splendors of utility are snatched away, the blow is heavy and portends something important. Oh, my friend, you and I have lost a father, a friend. He was the bright

source of advice and consolation, the focus of every earthly virtue, and alas he bore too much of the Divine Image—he had too much of the spirit of the inhabitants of Heaven to be a long sojourner here on Earth. He labored fast—and soon finished his worldly task. Oh, it is an example worthy of imitation—for to use his own words, he has served his generations and fallen asleep.[82]

Rush here remembered Davies's valedictory sermon on *Religion and Public Spirit* in which he had urged Rush and the other students to emulate David, "who served his own Generation according to the Will of God, and then, as a weary Labourer, gently fell on Sleep, and sweetly rested from his generous and pious Toils." [83] The fatherly Davies had fallen asleep and soon Finley, too, would sleep in the grave. In the years that followed, Rush's experience of premature death, especially in the Philadelphia epidemics of his times, became wider and deeper. The phenomenon of early death gradually took on disturbing religious significance for Rush. And in the decade of the 1780's, when four of his own children died in infancy, Rush came to know deeply the enormity of premature death.[84] His theodicy, "An Inquiry into the Causes of Premature Deaths," published in 1806, was an attempt to reconcile divine benevolence and early death.[85]

As medical apprentice to Dr. Redman, young Rush served his master well for "six long years," pounding his mortar and posting his books. He lived in the physician's house, from which, he proudly recalled, he had absented himself for only three evenings during his entire stay; equally impressive and gratifying for Rush, as a man of unremitting industry, was his record of only eleven days lost from Dr. Redman's business over the five-year period.[86] The doctor's "shop" was a busy one; in fact, the busiest in Philadelphia at the time. Young Rush, at first having "an uncommon aversion" to the scenes of medical practice, was soon hardened to the extent of calmly assisting Dr. Redman with the severest surgical operations. Still, as he learned to minister to the sick and dying, and to wield the crude instruments of eighteenth-century surgery, his awareness of the fundamental material condition of man obtruded:

This earthly frame, a minute fabric, a center of wonders, is forever subject to Diseases and Death. The very air we breathe too often proves noxious, our food often is armed with poison, the very elements conspire the ruin of our

---

[78] Dr. Thomas Gibbons in Davies, *Sermons on Important Subjects,* 1: pp. xliv–xlv.

[79] *Autobiography,* p. 36.

[80] *Ibid.*

[81] *Ibid.,* p. 37; Whitfield J. Bell, Jr., "John Redman, Medical Preceptor, 1722–1808," *Penna. Mag. History and Biography* 81, 2 (April, 1957): p. 157; Dr. Redman to Benjamin Rush, April 4, 1767, Rush MSS, XXII, p. 10. A Leyden medical graduate, Dr. Redman (1722–1808) was the great man of Philadelphia medicine at this time, Richard H. Shryock, *Medicine and Society in America: 1660–1860* (Ithaca, N.Y., 1962), p. 66.

[82] Rush to Enoch Green, 1761, *Rush Letters* 1: p. 4.

[83] P. 3. As a graduate of the College of New Jersey, class of 1760, Enoch Green had been present with Rush when Davies gave this sermon. "It deserves," Rush wrote his classmate, "to be printed in letters of gold in every young candidate's heart," 1761, *Rush Letters* 1: p. 4.

[84] Susanna Rush, Elizabeth Graeme Rush, William Rush, and Benjamin Rush all died within the first five months of life, *Autobiography,* append iii, pp. 371–372.

[85] *Rush Essays,* pp. 310–316.

[86] Rush to John Morgan, July 27, 1768, *Rush Letters* 1: p. 62; *Autobiography,* p. 38.

constitutions, and Death forever lies lurking to deceive us.[87]

It was a thought that Dr. Redman, as a profoundly religious man, could appreciate too.

Rush had added reason to lament the precariousness of human life in the fall of 1762 when yellow fever swept the city. True to his notebook habit, he recorded that the epidemic "began in August and prevailed in September, October, November, and December, carrying off for some time twenty persons in a day."[88] It was one of the worst plagues in the history of Philadelphia. Rush, in his round of apprentice duties, beheld "pale Death spreading fear throughout the world."[89] Desperately, young Rush and his master purged the countless victims in the accepted Boerhaavian manner. The epidemic, however, subsided only when temperatures dropped at the approach of winter.[90] For Rush, the yellow fever plague of 1762 was an object lesson, the first of many, in the killing power of epidemic disease. "Enter the World with a deep Sense of your Mortality," Samuel Davies had urged his students.[91] Sixteen-year-old Rush, who was destined to risk death again and again fighting yellow fever over the next half-century, was now coming to understand Davies's meaning.

At Dr. Redman's house, Rush read the standard medical works of Hermann Boerhaave, the great Leyden teacher, and Thomas Sydenham, the "English Hippocrates."[92] In fact, Dr. Redman had taken his medical degree at Leyden, which under Boerhaave's influence had become a center of study for many prominent eighteenth-century physicians. Naturally enough, Rush's master had him study Boerhaave's works on physiology and pathology "with the closest

attention."[93] Similarly, Rush pored over Gerard van Swieten's famous multivolume commentary on Boerhaave's aphorisms, acquiring as he did a general understanding of the state of medical knowledge in the early eighteenth century. Sydenham's works figured importantly in Rush's early study of medicine, and continued to do so over the years. Dr. Redman had presumably labored over the great Englishman's medical writings at Leyden, where Boerhaave had earlier proclaimed himself a disciple of Sydenham in his teaching and practice; hence, Dr. Redman's apprentice pondered Sydenham's texts, especially those dealing with his epidemiological theories. Some of these theories Rush was later to adopt himself. His edition of Sydenham's works in 1809 was a tribute to the great man's influence in Rush's medical thinking.[94] Likewise, Rush attended to Hippocrates' aphorisms and translated them into English.[95] These and other authors were read by Rush and their learned and wise observations were duly recorded in the apprentice's prized notebook.[96]

Rush's first exposure to Hippocratic medical literature under Dr. Redman was most important in his future development as a physician and, more broadly, as a philosopher. This was so, not from any strict adherence to the leading theoreticians of that literature —Hippocrates, Sydenham, and Boerhaave—but because of his turning away from the first principle of the Hippocratic tradition: the healing power of nature.[97] Both Sydenham and Boerhaave in their emulation of the fifth-century Greek philosopher accepted the doctrine of the curative power of nature in disease. As a student with Dr. Redman, Rush did too. But in his post-Edinburgh years, after studying another and different medical curriculum, Rush was of the opposite conviction:

The natural, moral, and political world exhibit every where marks of disorder, and the instruments of this disorder, are the operations of nature. Her influence is most obvious in

---

[87] *Ibid.,* Rush to Enoch Green, 1761, *Rush Letters* 1: p. 3.

[88] Rush copied this extract from his apprentice notebook of 1762 in a letter to Mrs. Rush, September 1, 1793, *ibid.,* 2: p. 646. Delaplaine claims that Rush's account of the yellow fever epidemic of 1762, from which Rush took the above extract, was "the only record then extant of the malignant fever which had prevailed in Philadelphia in the year 1762," *Repository of the Lives and Portraits of Distinguished Americans* (Philadelphia, 1816) 1: p. 31; Prof. Butterfield cites Dr. Charles Caldwell, a former student of Rush, as the author of the anonymous essay in Delaplaine herein quoted, "The Reputation of Benjamin Rush," *Penna. Hist.* 17 (1950): p. 9.

[89] Rush to Ebenezer Hazard, July 23, 1765, trans. from the Latin by Lyman H. Butterfield, ed., "Further Letters of Benjamin Rush," *Penna. Mag. Hist. Biog.* 78 (January, 1954): p. 5.

[90] Rush to John R. B. Rodgers, October 3, 1793, *Rush Letters* 2: pp. 695, 698. The eclectic medical system of Hermann Boerhaave (1668–1738) prevailed among Philadelphia physicians at this time, especially his therapeutics of purgation, Wyndham B. Blanton, *Medicine in Virginia in the Eighteenth Century* (Richmond, Va., 1931), p. 4. Rush to Mrs. Rush, October 20, 1793, *Rush Letters* 2: pp. 720–721; see Henry R. Viets in *DAB,* s.v. "Redman, John."

[91] *Religion and Public Spirit,* p. 15.

[92] *Autobiography,* p. 38, and Dr. Corner's note; Lester S. King, *The Medical World of the Eighteenth Century* (Chicago, 1958), ch. iii and p. 34.

[93] *Autobiography,* p. 38.

[94] *Ibid.;* King, *Medical World of the Eighteenth Century,* p. 64; *The Works of Thomas Sydenham, M.D., on Acute and Chronic Diseases. . . . With Notes, Intended to Accommodate Them to the Present State of Medicine, and to the Climate and Diseases of the United States,* by Benjamin Rush (Philadelphia, 1809).

[95] Rush, "An Inquiry into the Natural History of Medicine among the Indians of North America, and a Comparative View of Their Diseases and Remedies with Those of Civilized Nations," *Med. Inq. & Obs.* (5th ed.) 1: p. 78; Rush to Ebenezer Hazard, June 27, 1765, *Rush Letters* 1: p. 17. Both Sydenham and Boerhaave esteemed Hippocrates greatly, Joseph F. Payne, "History of Medicine," *Encyclopaedia Britannica* (11th ed., 29 v., 1910–1911), 18: pp. 50–51.

[96] *Autobiography,* p. 38.

[97] George Sarton, *A History of Science; Ancient Science through the Golden Age of Greece* (Cambridge, Mass., 1960), p. 343; Rush, ed., *Works of Thomas Sydenham,* 1815 ed., p. iv. Boerhaave's inaugural lecture on the institutes of medicine at Leyden recommended Hippocrates as a model for his students, "Boerhaave, Hermann," *Encyclopaedia Britannica,* (11th ed.), 4: pp. 115–116.

the production of diseases, and in her hurtful or ineffectual efforts to remove them.[98]

The physician, Rush believed, should be the master, not the servant of nature.[99] By identifying his name with nature Hippocrates had done incalculable "mischief" to humanity, resulting in the death of millions. As for his humoral physiology and pathology, the former was "fanciful" and the latter "erroneous" in many places.[100] Suffice it to say at this point that Rush's opposition to the "nature" and humoral schools of medicine, which crossed in the teaching of Boerhaave and Sydenham, was based on religious as well as medical scruples if, indeed, the two can be disentangled in his thought.

Busy as he was assisting Dr. Redman, Rush still found time to observe the practice of other physicians who, with Dr. Redman, formed the staff of the Pennsylvania Hospital. He was also fortunate in receiving instruction in anatomy and materia medica from two recent Edinburgh graduates, Dr. William Shippen, Jr., and Dr. John Morgan, both of whom represented the ascending influence of Edinburgh in colonial medicine. Dr. Shippen's lectures on anatomy, the prototype of their kind in America, were illustrated by dissection, and it is quite possible that Rush at this time dissected his first cadaver.[101] With Dr. Morgan, who had preceded Rush as a student at Nottingham and Dr. Redman's "shop," the young apprentice inaugurated a lasting friendship. Dr. Morgan spoke devoutly to Rush of his medical preceptor at Edinburgh, Dr. William Cullen, calling him the Boerhaave of his times.[102] Morgan in this way fired Rush's enthusiasm for study under the great Scottish medical teacher.

Notwithstanding his tight medical schedule, which sometimes included substituting for Dr. Redman days at a time, Rush closely followed religious and political events. In 1764, when Gilbert Tennent died, Rush eulogized his beloved religious teacher anonymously in his earliest published writing.[103]

Privately, in correspondence with Ebenezer Hazard, he revealed his active participation in congregational affairs at the Second Presbyterian Church, which was bereft of its pastor.[104] One day in May of 1765 Rush was present when George Whitefield, the great English evangelist, revisited Philadelphia on his seventh American tour. He wrote ecstatically:

Nothing could equal the solemnity of the day. Mr. Whitefield when he came down from the pulpit and began to speak to the communicants seemed as if he had come fresh from Heaven and glowed with all the seraphic love of a Gabriel. When he spoke of the dying love of a Mediator in instituting the Feast of his Supper the night in which he was betrayed, when he traced the Son of God through all his sufferings and beheld him wounded for our sins and bruised for our iniquities, his soul catched fire at the thoughts, and earth seemed scarce able to contain him. 'Twas a Heaven upon Earth I believe to many souls. . . .[105]

At this time, or earlier during Whitefield's visit in 1754, Rush was introduced to the evangelist.[106] The young Philadelphian was certainly no stranger to Whitefield's theology, which was essentially what he had been taught by Tennent, Finley, and Davies. It was perfectly natural, then, that he should respond feelingly to the master preacher. Moreover, these for Rush were years of intense, personal religious experience, as we have seen. In true revivalistic fashion, he condemned the apostasies of his generation and prayed that the Son of God might make him and his dear friend and Princeton classmate, Ebenezer Hazard, "feel our vileness and undone situation, and earnestly cry aloud to Jesus till he opens our eyes to behold his all-sufficiency and fitness to be our Redeemer." [107] Hazard, who had also been educated by Finley and Davies in the "Schools of the Prophets," at Nottingham and the College of New Jersey, understood and appreciated Rush's anxieties. Rush had begun the drama of his salvation. It started conservatively enough in Calvinism; it would end in revolutionary universalism.

Rush's last year in Philadelphia, before leaving for Edinburgh, was marked by political as well as religious

[98] Rush, "Outlines of the Phenomena of Fever," *Med. Inq. & Obs.* (3rd ed. rev. and enlarged, 1809) **3**: pp. 31–32. Also, for the "confused and irregular operations of nature" in mental disease, see *Diseases of the Mind*, pp. 28–29. See William Cullen's lecture, "Introductory to the Practice of Physic," quoted by John Thomson, *An Account of the Life, Lectures, and Writings of William Cullen, M.D.* (2 v., Edinburgh, 1859) **1**: pp. 118–119.

[99] Rush, "Natural History of Medicine among the Indians," *Med. Inq. & Obs.* (5th ed.) **1**: p. 76. In this his first oration before the American Philosophical Society, given in 1774, Rush advanced this idea which was to become the cardinal principle of his system of revolutionary medicine.

[100] Rush, "On the Opinions and Modes of Practice of Hippocrates," *Sixteen Introductory Lectures*, pp. 285–286.

[101] *Autobiography*, p. 39; Rush to Ebenezer Hazard, November 18, 1765, *Rush Letters* **1**: p. 20. Shippen (1736–1808) and Morgan (1735–1789) received medical degrees from Edinburgh in 1761 and 1763, respectively, Francis R. Packard in *DAB*, s.v. "Shippen, William," Whitfield J. Bell, Jr., *John Morgan* (Philadelphia, 1965); Goodman, p. 12, George W. Corner, *Two Centuries of Medicine; A History of the School of Medicine, University of Pennsylvania* (Philadelphia, 1965), p. 12.

[102] Rush, "Introductory Lecture to a Course of Lectures on the History & Practice of Physic," Rush MSS, call number Yi2/7400/F1, pp. 1–16; Rush to John Morgan, November 16, 1766, *Rush Letters* **1**: p. 29. On the influence of Edinburgh M.D.'s at America's first medical school, the College of Philadelphia, see James T. Flexner, *Doctors on Horseback; Pioneers of American Medicine* (New York, 1939), p. 22.

[103] Rush to Ebenezer Hazard, July 2, 1766, *Rush Letters* **1**: pp. 24–25; Ramsay, *Eulogium*, p. 136.

[104] August 2, 1764, November 7, 1764, April 10, 1765, May 21, 1765, June 27, 1765, November 8, 1765, November 18, 1765, December 23, 1765, March 29, 1766, *Rush Letters* **1**: pp. 7–9, 11–24.

[105] May 21, 1765, *ibid.*, p. 14.

[106] *Autobiography*, p. 55; Finley knew Whitefield closely enough to be acknowledged publicly by the great evangelist as "a worthy friend of mine abroad," Starr, "Finley, Samuel." Presumably, then, it was Finley who introduced Rush.

[107] Rush to Ebenezer Hazard, August 2, 1764, *Rush Letters* **1**: p. 7.

commitment. Like David, Rush must attain the "Character of the good, the useful, and public-spirited Man," as Samuel Davies had charged him to do.[108] In November of 1765, the month in which the Stamp Act was scheduled to go into effect, Rush espoused the patriot cause in letters to his New York friend, Ebenezer Hazard. Assailing Franklin and the Quakers for backing the Parliamentary measure, he approved the hanging of stamp officers in effigy and praised the recently adopted nonimportation agreements. "My next letter I hope will contain a full history of something more spirited," he further confided to Hazard after speculating upon the disgruntled mood of Philadelphia mechanics.[109] When news of the repeal of the Stamp Act reached America in the spring of 1766, the twenty-year-old patriot was overjoyed. Like so many of his fellow colonists who were appealing to Greek and Roman history for analogies by which to understand their own times, he thrilled with the vision of Pitt's "declaiming with more than Roman eloquence in favor of his distant oppressed countrymen!"[110] Rush was not yet prepared, however, for a basic change in political ideology. He might dissent from an Act of Parliament, as he did in the crisis over Grenville's stamps; but from royal authority there was for him no conceivable dissent—politically, he was too intellectually naïve and unskeptical to question ancient pieties.[111] Indeed, in the "Schools of the Prophets" he had been educated in such ancient pieties as God, king, and country. And he was not yet prepared in thought or action to find in the millennial teachings of Gilbert Tennent, Finley, and Davies a call to—and a rationale for—political revolution. In short, Rush in Philadelphia was a rebel and not a revolutionary. The political skepticisms of Edinburgh, which nurtured the Pennsylvania revolutionary, were still in the future.

Rush had originally planned to leave for England in the summer of 1765. Changing his mind, he decided to spend one more year in Philadelphia in order to prepare himself better for medical study abroad.[112] This proved to be a critical decision for Rush as it afforded him the opportunity of becoming the favorite student of Dr. Morgan, who not only later recommended him to Dr. Cullen at Edinburgh but promised weighty support for Rush in obtaining the professorship of chemistry at the College of Philadelphia upon his return.[113] Consequently, when Rush departed Phil-

adelphia for Edinburgh in August of 1766, he did so with the brightest of prospects for a medical career. Only the poet within him demurred on that "mournfull Sunday" when the sky darkened and he "fancied all nature around me corresponded with: the gloomy Situation of my Mind."[114]

Beyond the Atlantic in Scotland lay a different school of thought for Benjamin Rush, a school of reason and science, whose teachers were not Great Awakening prophets like Tennent, Finley, and Davies but progressivists, skeptics, and liberals of the Enlightenment. Their party was not Finley's "Party for Jesus Christ" but Voltaire's "Party of Humanity," and their utopianism was not millennial but secular and scientific. Rush was now to come under the influence of the *philosophes,* of their rationalism, political and religious liberalism, and experimental Newtonian science.

II. EDINBURGH AND THE SCOTTISH ENLIGHTENMENT

I now suspected error in every thing I had been taught, or believed, and as far as I was able began to try the foundations of my opinions upon many other subjects.[1]

Rush's transatlantic passage aboard *Friendship* was hardly routine. Twice, unknown to the youthful passenger at the time, the ship risked destruction off Ireland and Wales. Most harrowing of all, during a perilous crossing, was the "violent Gale of Wind" which buffeted the ship eighteen days out of Philadelphia. Again, as he had in the yellow fever epidemic of 1762, Rush faced the "King of Terrors," and again he did so helplessly save for his faith:

What feint inadequate Ideas do we form of a Storm at Sea while we live secure on Land! All my Courage and Firmness was now vanquished, and I waited every moment with trembling Anxiety for the fatal wave that should engulph us for ever in the Sea. . . . Riches and power could have afforded no Comfort in this important Hour. 'twas Religion alone that could support the Soul, and bear her up amidst the awfull prospects of approaching Death. happy the Man to whom Heaven bestows this most precious Gift of divine Bounty! The Sea may rage and roar. Winds may blow wth: all their Fury and Destruction may appear on all sides ready to devour him: still will his Soul be calm and serene, nay he will welcome Death tho' clad in these his horrid Forms wth: all the Triumph of a Conqueror. Would to Heaven this had been my happy Case![2]

Providence and good Captain Pearse, however, determined otherwise, and *Friendship* docked safely at Liverpool on the 21 of October.

108 *Religion and Public Spirit,* p. 3.
109 November 8, 1765, *Rush Letters* 1: p. 18.
110 Rush to Ebenezer Hazard, October 22, 1768, *ibid.,* p. 68; Howard Mumford Jones, *O Strange New World, American Culture: The Formative Years* (New York, Viking Press ed., 1968), p. 251 *et passim.*
111 *Autobiography,* p. 46.
112 Rush to Ebenezer Hazard, May 21, 1765, *Rush Letters* 1: p. 14.
113 Rush to John Morgan, November 16, 1766, *ibid.,* p. 28; *Autobiography,* p. 81.

114 Rush to Thomas Bradford, October 25, 1766, Butterfield, ed., "Further Letters of Benjamin Rush," *Penna. Mag. Hist. Biog.* 78 (January, 1954): p. 7.
1 *Autobiography,* p. 46.
2 Rush to Thomas Bradford, October 25, 1766, Butterfield, ed., "Further Letters of Benjamin Rush," *Penna. Mag. Hist. Biog.* 78 (January, 1954): p. 8; *Autobiography,* p. 40.

In a letter to Thomas Bradford, his Philadelphia friend and co-worker in resisting the Stamp Act, young Rush described the English port city and complained that "Custom House Officers here exercise a kind of Vigilance and Authority over the Ships which almost approaches to Tyranny." His and other passengers' trunks, he wrote indignantly, were "carried to the Custom House, and there searched narrowly and for this peice of unmannerly Ceremony we were Obliged to pay half a Crown. Pray how do you think the free born sons of America bore this unacustomed Treatment?"[3] There was little difference in principle, Rush in fact was beginning to conclude, between this violation of the political rights of men and that of their bodies, as witnessed also in Liverpool harbor where ships of the African slave trade were teeming with black cargoes. "Inhuman practice!" he noted on October 28, "that men Oh? grow rich by the Calamities of their fellow-creatures!"[4]

Cabined with Rush aboard ship had been Jonathan Potts and James Cummins, the former a prospective Edinburgh student and the latter a Scottish merchant bound for home after sojourning in the West Indies. The three men during the long, dangerous voyage learned to know one another well. Cummins, broken in health and fortune after an unsuccessful business venture in the West Indies, spoke often and nostalgically of his aged parents in northern Scotland to whom he was returning. One night Cummins dreamt that he and Rush were to die shortly after landing at Liverpool. Three days after disembarking from *Friendship*, Cummins died in the "utmost Agony," while Rush, Potts, and an English physician looked on in despair. In his journal, Rush penned this sorrowful epitaph: "By foreign hands his Eyes were closed.—Strangers followed him to his Grave."[5] Death and young Rush, it seemed, were inseparable fellow travelers.

Ironically, the death of James Cummins was the occasion of Rush's making his first and most important student friendship at the University of Edinburgh. By way of arranging for the interment of Cummins in Liverpool, Rush met the aunt of a certain John Bostock, who was already studying medicine at Edinburgh. Bostock, who will be discussed later, introduced Rush to the writings of Algernon Sidney and other classical republican thinkers of the seventeenth century. But for Cummins's death, the two might never have met. As it was, Rush carried a letter to Bostock when he left Liverpool.[6]

From the port city, the day after he arrived, Rush posted a letter to Benjamin Franklin in London, requesting the doctor's recommendation for himself and Mr. Potts. Dr. Franklin, as Pennsylvania's agent and, in fact, spokesman for all the colonies, enjoyed as high a reputation in Edinburgh as he did in London. Dr. Franklin had visited Edinburgh in 1759 and had been given the freedom of the city. Rush knew that Franklin was a friend of William Cullen and other Edinburgh philosophers. Franklin complied by writing to Dr. Cullen in behalf of the two Americans and similarly announced their visit to Sir Alexander Dick, the celebrated Edinburgh host. This assured their entry into the social life of the city. Accordingly, when the Pennsylvanians left for Edinburgh in late October, they did so with the confidence born of having recommendations to the medical faculty there not only from Dr. Morgan in Philadelphia but from the cosmopolitan and prestigious Dr. Franklin. So impressive were these recommendations, that by the middle of November Rush and Potts had already spent an evening with Cullen's family.[7]

Dr. Morgan had counseled Rush to attend the lectures of Drs. Alexander Monro, secundus, Joseph Black, James Russell, and the great William Cullen. These men, notably Cullen and Black, were the pride of the University of Edinburgh and the Scottish Enlightenment. As friends of David Hume and Adam Smith, as members of a philosophical circle whose fame was known throughout the Western world, Cullen and Black had much more to offer Rush than the practical training he at first sought. He would later understand this. But in November of 1766, when Rush began classes at the university, his plan was simply to learn medicine and chemistry from two of the world's outstanding teachers. In this way, as Dr. Morgan had said, Rush could qualify himself for a teaching position in chemistry at the College of Philadelphia.[8]

William Cullen and Joseph Black were names familiar to anyone interested in the new science of chemistry. Black, especially, was already famous in 1766 as the discoverer of carbon dioxide. He had been Cullen's student and close associate at the University of Glasgow, where in 1754 he had succeeded his master as lecturer in chemistry. Refusing to compete with his teacher and friend for the chair of chemistry at the University of Edinburgh, which Cullen accepted in 1755, Black later succeeded him in that position too.

[3] Rush to Thomas Bradford, October 25, 1766, Butterfield, ed., "Further Letters of Benjamin Rush," *Penna. Mag. Hist. Biog.* **78** (January, 1954): pp. 9–10.

[4] "Scottish Journal," p. 13.

[5] *Ibid.*, p. 17; *Autobiography*, pp. 40–41.

[6] *Ibid.*, p. 41.

[7] Rush to Benjamin Franklin, October 22, 1766, *Rush Letters* **1**: p. 27; Charles R. Fay, *Adam Smith and the Scotland of His Day* (Cambridge, 1956), p. 125; Franklin had earlier in 1761 recommended Dr. Morgan to Edinburgh, James T. Flexner, *Doctors on Horseback; Pioneers of American Medicine* (New York, 1939), p. 13; Mrs. Thomas Potts James, *Memorial of Thomas Potts, Junior, Who Settled in Pennsylvania* (Cambridge, Mass., 1874), pp. 172–174; for Cullen's superlative estimate of Franklin, see Dr. William Cullen to Dr. Benjamin Rush, August 16, 1785, Rush MSS, XXIV: p. 58; "Scottish Journal," November 29, 1766, p. 23; Rush to John Morgan, November 16, 1766, *Rush Letters* **1**: p. 28.

[8] *Ibid.*, p. 29. These illustrous men will be identified and discussed below.

So Rush, not only in his course with Black on chemistry but in Cullen's classes on the Institutes of Medicine, studied "chemical philosophy." [9]

Cullen, the teacher of Black, of the great anatomist and obstetrician William Hunter, and of scores of other eminent men of science was very popular in the classroom. Tall, thin, and striking in appearance, Cullen had that quality of intelligence and alertness that Rush later possessed as a doctor and teacher. When, young Rush wrote in his student journal, Cullen lectured on the "most abstruse Causes of Diseases," he spoke with characteristic ease and clarity.[10] His lectures were in simple English, not Latin, a fact which by itself does much to explain why Rush and other students lauded him for his powers of observation and expression. Throughout his lectures, and in private conversation with his students, Cullen insisted on the necessity of medical systems: facts without organization, he warned, could never lead to true science. "A system," Dr. Cullen often told his students,

> as well as we can make it, is to be attempted, for these reasons; 1st, as the best means for collecting and remembering the facts already known; 2dly, as the best means of rendering them in the mean time as useful as possible; and, lastly, as the best means of discovering where facts are wanting, and therefore of leading us to that diligence and attention in observation and experiment that are the only means of supplying our deficiencies. I admit, therefore, and I plead, therefore, for the utility of system, but still it is with a constant distrust of it as such, and that distrust, too, is always the greater in proportion as the system is more general.[11]

Always looking beyond particular facts to general explanations, Cullen was the medical systematizer *par excellènce*. Medical systems should be devised to fit the advancing knowledge of each generation, he urged. Later, Rush would take this instruction to heart in the development of his own revolutionary theory of the unity of disease.

In 1777 Dr. Cullen was to be elected a Fellow of the Royal Society of London, presumably as much for his essay "On the Construction and Operation of the Plough"—a study of its mathematical principles—as for his writings on medicine. Young Rush marveled at his teacher's ingenuity in handling the most difficult

questions, as his "Scottish Journal" reveals.[12] In this he was only one of a great number of admirers, including Cullen's hundreds of students and celebrated philosophers and scientists like David Hume, Lord Kames, Dr. William Hunter, and Dr. Joseph Black. But Hume, Kames, Hunter, Black, and other leaders of the Scottish Enlightenment, with whom Cullen was intimate, admired the doctor less for his "great Turn for System"—to use Rush's words of praise—than they did for his powers of close observation, judgment, precise definition, and inductive and deductive reasoning.[13]

Cullen was, in fact, David Hume's physician in theory as well as practice. He attended to the philosopher's health and that of his Edinburgh circle, and sought to improve the teaching and practice of medicine by using Hume's empirical methods of inquiry. "All our knowledge of nature," Cullen agreed with his friend, "consists in experience." [14] The doctor even went so far as to accept Hume's radical views on causation, that from experience one can know only the order of events. "My business is not," Cullen made clear his inductive philosophy, "so much to explain how this and that happens, as to examine what is truly matter of fact. . . . My anxiety is not so much to find out how it happens, as to find out what happens." [15]

If Rush never fully understood his master's cautious empiricism, his challenging of *a priori* ideas like causation, which indeed was the case, he was not alone. It seems that many of Cullen's students and rivals in the teaching of medicine failed to appreciate the philosopher's use of hypothesis or what he called "system." For Cullen, as he said repeatedly in his lectures over the years, his and other medical systems were only provisional organizations of facts useful in leading to the acquisition of more facts of an increasingly general nature. Systems were means, not ends. They had heuristic value, and no value in themselves. Ultimately, it was true, Cullen believed that the perfect system of medicine would be achieved through a kind of dialectical clash of systems, but this was to be a remote development, according to the great teacher:

> The system, "quem animo metimur," to use Lord Bacon's phrase, is indeed of immense extent, and is not to be reached in the course of one man's life; and measuring matters in this way, I have indeed done very little; but comparing with what had been done before, I flatter myself that I have done a great deal.[16]

---

[9] Douglas Guthrie, *A History of Medicine* (Philadelphia, 1946), p. 223; Sir William C. Dampier, *A Shorter History of Science* (Cambridge, 1945), p. 83; William P. D. Wightman, "William Cullen and the Teaching of Chemistry," *Annals of Science, A Quarterly Review of the History of Science Since the Renaissance* 11, 2 (June, 1955): pp. 154–165; Andrew Kent, ed., *An 18th Century Lectureship in Chemistry* (Glasgow, 1950); Henry, Lord Brougham, "Joseph Black," in Eduard Farber, ed., *Great Chemists* (New York, 1961), pp. 211–225.

[10] "Scottish Journal," September 1767, p. 59; John Thomson, *An Account of the Life, Lectures, and Writings of William Cullen, M.D.* (Edinburgh, 1859) 1: pp. 59, 156; see G. T. Bettany in *DNB, s.v.* "Cullen, William."

[11] Thomson, *William Cullen* 2: p. 96; Richard H. Shryock, *The Development of Modern Medicine* (Philadelphia, 1936), pp. 24–25.

[12] September 1767, p. 59; Thomson, *William Cullen* 1: p. 65; 2: p. 218.

[13] "Scottish Journal," September, 1767, p. 60; Dr. Thomas D. Mitchell, who was certainly no enemy of Rush, observed that with Rush "love of *order*" practically amounted to a passion, *The Character of Rush*, p. 19; Thomson, *William Cullen* 2: pp. 679, 675.

[14] Quoted in Thomson, *ibid.* 1: p. 112.

[15] *Ibid.* 2: pp. 132, 131.

[16] *Ibid.*, pp. 97–98.

Cullen's inductive philosophy of medicine, it seems, was, like Hume's positivism, too advanced for the times.

Rush was typical of Cullen's students in that he was so eager to become a disciple that he oversimplified his idol's teaching about systems. "My general doctrines," Cullen characteristically declared, "are to be only so many general facts." [17] His theory, he warned over and over again, was not to be understood merely as "a deduction of reasoning." Nor, he said, was his differing with the Boerhaavians in their system to be construed as a violent innovation, for he esteemed Dr. Boerhaave as "the author of a system more perfect than any thing that had gone before, and as perfect as the state of science in his time would permit of." [18] Boerhaave's system had now to be abandoned in the progress of medicine. Young Rush, in his adulation of Cullen, missed the fine points of what his master was teaching about the aims and methods of science, points which eluded Rush even later in his career after many years of professional experience. In Edinburgh he was looking for a master like Finley and Davies and a system of medicine that would enable him to attract patients in Philadelphia. He found these in William Cullen and "Cullenism"; and, while he could not understand his teacher's advanced doctrine of positivism then, and apparently never could, Rush did appreciate enough of Cullen's skepticism and freedom of inquiry to reexamine many of his traditional beliefs.

Cullen, then, like Dr. Joseph Black—who also insisted vigorously on the danger of premature generalization—exerted no deep philosophical influence upon Rush. They could have, had Rush been receptive, for they were both progressive scientific thinkers like their greater contemporary and friend, David Hume. Their empiricism was really unintelligible to Rush, at Edinburgh and later. Aside from the chemistry and practical medicine that Rush learned from Cullen and Black, he somehow derived from their instruction and attributed to Cullen, if not to Black, a doctrine of strict rationalism.

The system of Cullen in medicine answered all of Rush's questions as did the system of religion which the young evangelist has acquired from his other masters, Tennent, Finley, and Davies. It was characteristic of Rush to think in terms of systems in religion, medicine, politics, etc.—and, of course, this was typical of many other eighteenth-century thinkers. The Enlightenment which, next to the more important event of the Great Awakening, explains Rush's philosophical development, offered Newtonianism and Cartesianism as systems of thought. And while it is true that Rush declaimed later from his professor's chair "On the Necessary Connexion between Observation and Reasoning in Medicine," and properly revered the names of Locke and Francis Bacon, his way of reasoning was ontological and deductive, more in the Continental tradition of Descartes than in the tradition of British empiricism. The mature Rush was observant, it has been said, but not a good observer.[19] He was an *a priori* thinker, unlike Cullen and Black, who were striving to free themselves from the narrow rationalistic systems of the past. Rush could not be a good observer, he could not be a real empiricist, because his attitude towards the world of experience was deeply theological, like that of William Paley, Bishop Butler, David Hartley, and his great American contemporary, Jonathan Edwards.

In 1767 Rush noted in his "Scottish Journal" that, even when his demonstrations in class failed him, Cullen was equal to the occasion with conjecture so ingenious that "it was impossible not to assent to it." [20] The doctor was, above all, suggestive in his teaching, allowing his fertile imagination wide scope in an age when the chaos of recently discovered facts in biological science was making speculative pathology again necessary.[21] Here was a man, perhaps Rush thought, whose mastery of fact did not blind him to the essential values of synthesis and interpretation. No mere Philadelphia empiric, indeed, Dr. Cullen was a philosopher of medicine.

Order and ingenuity were marks of Cullen's genius which particularly struck Rush as he sat in the doctor's lecture hall or followed him in his circuit of the infirmary. In his student journal, a little masterpiece of Boswellian portraiture, Rush chronicled his dilemma of which to admire more: Cullen's order or his ingenuity. The dilemma, however, was overnice; Rush's religious, middle-class background, then and afterwards, valued order above all else. There was room in his universe for the absence of ingenuity, but never for the presence of disorder. He was too much the Newtonian, too much the Christian universalist, to see arbitrariness at the center of things. Such a perception was alien to his age and his character. In the meantime, as we have seen, Cullen dazzled the youth endlessly with his "great Turn for System."

Sometimes, in the midst of his lecture, the tall, stooping professor would stop his exposition of doctrine and indicate weaknesses in his own arguments. When necessary, he would admit his mistakes to the class, taking obvious pleasure in doing so. "It is not improperly said," Dr. Cullen told his class after a dissection, "that the earth hides the faults of the physician. If every patient that

dies were opened, as ours has been, it would but too often discover the frivolity of our conjectures and practice. In these lectures, however, I hazard my credit for your instruction, my first views, my conjectures, my projects, my trials, in short, my thoughts, which I may correct, and

---

[17] *Ibid.* **1**: p. 260.
[18] *Ibid.*, pp. 118–119.

[19] E.g., Richard H. Shryock in *DAB, s.v.* "Rush, Benjamin."
[20] September, 1767, p. 59.
[21] Shryock, "Benjamin Rush from the Perspective of the Twentieth Century," *Trans. College of Physicians of Phila.,* 4th ser., **14** (1946): pp. 115–116.

if necessary change; and whenever you yourselves shall be above mistakes, or can find any body else who is, I shall allow you to rate me as a very inferior person.[22]

It was as though the doctor were in dialogue with himself and concerned only with discovering the truth. All doctrines, he said, including his, must be rigorously and thoroughly examined; and if any of his doctrines were accepted by the students, they should only accept them with—in Cullen's words—"a slow-consenting academic doubt."[23] Rush found Cullen's skeptical method remarkable and unprecedented in his academic experience, and the doctor's example made Rush appreciate, as fully as his rigid evangelical character would allow, the tentativeness of scientific conclusions. That is to say, the impact of Cullen's skepticism was great but limited by Rush's absolutistic, Great Awakening mentality.

Cullen's skepticism in medical philosophy, however, was one thing for Rush; his religious skepticism, after David Hume, was quite another. "There is one thing however wanting in Dr. Cullen to constitute his Character a complete One," he inscribed in his journal, "viz: a Regard to Religion."[24] It was not that Cullen was blasphemous or even mildly disrespectful of religious matters. On the contrary, Rush knew that he was a man of "innate Dignity and Superiority of Soul," whose religious skepticism was always inoffensive. Indeed, he openly and frequently acknowledged his belief in the existence of the soul and its immaterial and immortal nature. But concerning revealed religion—and this precisely was his grievous shortcoming in Rush's eyes— he was publicly and frankly skeptical. His religious orthodoxy notwithstanding, Rush forgave and revered Cullen like an admiring son.[25]

Once, Rush confessed, he was late in keeping an appointment with Cullen, for which the master "warmly reproved" him. However, the young man's chagrin was all for the good, since he learned the value of punctuality. Always quick to moralize, he wrote: "Men who break Appointments are generally to be suspected of greater Breaches of Honour and Faith."[26] In the light of this belief, it is easy to accept the plausibility of the report that in his thirty years of attendance at the Pennsylvania Hospital, Rush was never observed to be more than two minutes late for his appointments.[27] Punctuality occupied an eminent place in his hierarchy of values as the habit of men who used their time wisely. In the "Schools of the Prophets" and at worldly Edinburgh, Rush's teachers were agreed on this, whatever their philosophical differences. Every minute must be used to advantage, never wasted. Cullen himself

was always in a hurry, as his letters show. Rush was the same way, and he was fond of justifying his busy life by saying with his Nottingham mentor, Samuel Finley, that he "was ashamed to take rest here. Eternity will be long enough to rest in."[28] Rush held, in good utilitarian fashion, that the salutary effects of punctuality constituted it a virtue—certainly an easy belief for a physician.[29]

In class, Rush was an industrious, almost compulsive, notetaker. Twice he took Dr. Cullen's course, and each time he was unfailingly rewarded by some fresh display of the doctor's genius and erudition. Probably most surprising for Rush of all Cullen's theses was that which attacked Boerhaave and the humoralists and deployed arguments recommending Friedrich Hoffmann's system. Following Hoffmann, Cullen drew attention to the nervous system in disease, which evoked Rush's keenest interest. The doctor, employing to some degree the works of Hoffmann and Albrecht von Haller, the great Swiss experimental physiologist, advanced a theory of pathology which sought to explain disease in terms of tension and laxity of the nervous system. This theory of disease was fundamental to Cullen's iatrophysical system. Hence, the physician, according to Cullen, could restore health to the patient by reducing tension or increasing nervous activity. As to the nature of the nervous system itself, the very crux of the doctor's physiology, Cullen made clear that he did not accept David Hartley's theory of nervous action, but rather argued—perhaps with von Haller— for the existence of a nerve fluid to communicate motion. Even so, despite this treatment of Hartley, Rush became acquainted with the work of the English philosopher, who subsequently exerted a shaping influence upon his thinking.[30]

[22] Thomson, *William Cullen* 1: pp. 108–109.
[23] *Ibid.*, p. 637n.
[24] "Scottish Journal," September, 1767, p. 66.
[25] *Ibid.*, pp. 66, 69. Cullen's *First Lines of the Practice of Physic, For the Use of Students in the University of Edinburgh* (Edinburgh, 1776–), which Rush edited in 1781, is wholly secular in character.
[26] "Scottish Journal," pp. 75, 63.
[27] Cited by Mitchell, *The Character of Rush*, pp. 19–20.

[28] Rush to Mrs. Rush, November 11, 1793, *Rush Letters* 2: p. 744.
[29] Mitchell, *The Character of Rush*, p. 19; Rush, "On the Means of Acquiring Business and the Causes which Prevent the Acquisition, and Occasion the Loss of It, in the Profession of Medicine," *Sixteen Introductory Lectures*, p. 233; for the primacy of "actions" or effects in Rush's ethics, see "Influence of Physical Causes upon the Moral Faculty," *Med. Inq. & Obs.* (5th ed.) 1: pp. 96–97.
[30] Rush to John Morgan, January 20, 1768, *Rush Letters* 1: p. 51; G. T. Bettany in *DNB, s.v.* "Cullen, William"; Friedrich Hoffmann (1660–1742), first professor of medicine at the University of Halle, explained health and disease in terms of the equilibrium or disequilibrium of "tonus," Guthrie, *A History of Medicine*, p. 217; Shryock, "Benjamin Rush from the Perspective of the Twentieth Century," *Trans. College of Physicians of Phila.*, 4th ser., **14** (1946): p. 115; a distinguished student of Boerhaave, von Haller (1708–1777) is regarded as the first modern physiologist, Guthrie, *A History of Medicine*, pp. 223–224. See Dr. Corner's discussion of von Haller's influence upon Cullen, *Autobiography*, append. i, pp. 362–363. David Hartley (1705–1757) explained his doctrine of vibrations in *Observations on Man, his Frame, his Duty, and his Expectations* (2 v., London, 1749); G. S. Brett, *History of Psychology*, ed. and abridged by R. S. Peters (London, 1953), pp. 587–590; Rush, "On the Application of Metaphysicks to Medicine," Rush MSS, call number Yi2/7400/F2, pp. 22–35.

The impact of Cullen on Rush was total and lasting, so much so that almost a quarter century later he candidly admitted his excessive veneration of the master. Medically, where Rush's confession was most relevant, the truth of his observation is easily seen. From July, 1769, when he returned to Philadelphia, until October, 1789, when he was named to succeed the late Dr. Morgan as professor of the theory and practice of medicine in the College of Philadelphia, Rush was the disciple—if not the partisan—of Cullen. Only with his election to the duties of the chair of the theory and practice of medicine did he feel constrained to formulate his own "System of principles in medicine," which had been evolving from his experience and thought as a physician.[31] Rush may have remembered on that occasion Dr. Cullen's advice to his classes:

When a student has learned one system, if he cannot think for himself, he should keep to the system of his master as religiously as he can, and allow no other views to disturb him; but if a student can think for himself, and every one believes that he can, he will no sooner have learned a particular system than he will be disposed to differ from it; he will immediately find that others also do so, and that the conflict of opinions is unavoidable. He will, therefore, wish to view matters in different lights, and, though he prefers no one Professor, yet, by comparing them, he becomes stronger in reasoning, and firmer in his own conclusions.[32]

However, even with the formulation of his own iatrophysical system, Rush's rebellion was more apparent than real, since the framework of his thought remained Cullenian. When the luminary of the Edinburgh school died in 1790, Rush delivered the eulogy to the College of Physicians of Philadelphia, freely declaring Cullen's genius and placing him in the company of the giants: "While Astronomy claims a Newton, and Electricity a Franklin, Medicine has been equally honoured by having employed the genius of a Cullen."[33]

Cullen's philosophic temper, his experimental habit of mind, was in the Baconian tradition of the Enlightenment; and young Rush's "Scottish Journal" reveals his efforts, as a student of the Great Awakening prophets, to understand and assimilate what to him was a radically different way of thinking. Unlike Rush's American teachers, including Dr. Redman who was theological rather than scientific in outlook, Cullen was exploratory, skeptical, and tentative in methodology, while undogmatic in his thinking. Like his friend, David Hume, and his seventeenth-century predecessors in science, Francis Bacon, Thomas Sydenham, and John Locke,

Cullen represented an empirical challenge to the received knowledge of the times. He planned, in fact, to edit Sydenham's works—a project which Rush later carried out—and to write a biography of the great medical empiricist with whom he was congenial in thought. Just as Sydenham had applied to medicine the empiricism of his friend, the philosopher John Locke, so Cullen accepted David Hume's radically empirical views on causation and sought to introduce them into medical theory and practice. Rush himself, though more as a social philosopher than as a physician, would later follow this precedent, as we shall see, by using the psychological ideas of the physico-theologian David Hartley in his new, moral science for reconstructing post-Revolutionary America.

Cullen's adoption of Hume's positivism and, especially, his rejection of Boerhaave's doctrines caused a public outcry against his teaching. He was called a "whimsical innovator" as a result of his discarding the Boerhaavian humoral pathology and boldly articulating an original solidistic pathology centered upon the nervous system. Cullen was supremely alive to the possibilities of medical speculation—too much so according to his contemporary and nineteenth-century critics who, like Rush and other worshiping students, failed wholly to appreciate his advanced experimental methodology. "There must be a tub to amuse the whale," Cullen used to say about all theories, including his own.[34] Systems, he taught, were essential to medicine, but were all expendable in the progressive development of medicine towards perfection. Rush, as we have observed, never fully understood this experimental philosophy, but he liked to think that he did; and in his classes at the University of Pennsylvania he tried to emulate Cullen by encouraging freedom of inquiry and discussion among his students. David Ramsay wrote that Rush welcomed criticism of his own theory of disease and urged his students "to think and judge for themselves, and would freely, and in a friendly manner, explain his principles, resolve their doubts, listen to their objections, and either yield to their force, or show their fallacy."[35] It should also be pointed out, however, that Dr. Charles Caldwell, another student of Rush, was firmly of the opinion that Rush was intoler-

[31] *Autobiography*, pp. 87–88; Goodman, p. 129; John T. Rees, *Remarks on the Medical Theories of Brown, Cullen, Darwin and Rush* (Philadelphia, 1805). See below, ch. vi.
[32] Quoted in Thomson, *William Cullen* 1: pp. 620–621.
[33] Rush, "An Eulogium in Honor of the Late Dr. William Cullen," *Rush Essays*, p. 331. "I consider Dr. Cullen as the Columbus of Medicine," Rush, "Introductory Lecture to a Course of Lectures On the History & Practice of Physic," Rush MSS, call number Yi2/7400/F1, p. 33.
[34] Quoted in Ralph H. Major, *A History of Medicine* (2 v., Springfield, Ill., 1954) 2: p. 591. The originality of Cullen's system is attested by Henry T. Buckle, *History of Civilization in England* (2 v., 2nd ed., New York, 1873) 2: p. 426, an insightful treatment of Rush's master teacher and his work. Dr. Cullen's letters to Rush are revealing of the former's tentative and undogmatic temperament, e.g., June 28, 1783, and October 16, 1784, Rush MSS, XXIV: pp. 55–57. See Dr. Redman's letters to Rush, e.g., April 4, 1767 and May 12, 1768, *ibid.* XXII: pp. 10–11. Cullen never completed his work on Sydenham's life and writings, Thomson, *William Cullen* 1: pp. 79–80.
[35] Ramsay, *Eulogium*, pp. 29–30; Rush to John Adams, March 15, 1806, *Rush Letters* 2: p. 916.

ant of disagreement with his views.[36] It is true that Rush, like his great Edinburgh teacher, believed in the perfectibility of medicine—the inevitability of perfection—but, essentially, his reasons were theological not scientific, more having to do with the redemptive powers of Christ than with Cullen's natural causes. The Great Awakening, not the Enlightenment, was the primary influence in his character and thought.

Rush's ultimate tribute to Cullen, which bespeaks at the same time his all-consuming belief in divine providence, discloses as much of the ambitions of the eulogist as it does of the eulogized: "Who can think of the talents, virtues, and services of Dr. Cullen, without believing that the Creator of the world delights in the happiness of his creatures, and that his tender mercies are over all his works!"[37] That anyone could do so was inconceivable to Rush, for whom God's benevolent design was omnipresent and nowhere so incontrovertibly present as in medicine and in the persons of the great physicians.[38] It was his lifelong ambition to be one of them.

If at Edinburgh Rush's attention to Dr. Joseph Black was overshadowed by his homage to Cullen, there was good reason for it. In his late thirties, despite his accomplishments in chemistry, Black had not yet established himself as a famous lecturer. He was, moreover, only the brilliant student of Cullen, in Rush's view, and still not a towering figure in his own right. Rush was perceptive enough, however, with not a little encouragement from Dr. Morgan, to realize the value of Black's lectures in chemistry, which he attended twice and

scrupulously recorded.[39] These, he knew, would fortify his application for the chemistry position at the College of Philadelphia, for which Morgan was promoting him. So persevering was Rush in his studies with Black, that by the time of his graduation in 1768 he had become an expert in Black's system of chemistry, probably the best available at that time. "As to the experiments you speak of," he wrote Morgan, who counseled him to master Black's lecture demonstrations for use in Philadelphia, "there is scarcely one of them but what I have seen twice performed either publicly or privately by Dr. Black."[40] Thus, in chemistry, at least, Rush easily assimilated the elements of scientific method which he later applied in his own investigations. For the techniques of chemistry, as he understood them, posed no philosophical difficulty to him as an *a priori*, theological thinker. When he assumed the professorship of chemistry at the College of Philadelphia in 1769, Rush based his lectures upon his notes from Black's course at Edinburgh, although not to the point of slavish imitation. The first American-written text in chemistry, Rush's *Syllabus of a Course of Lectures on Chemistry* (1770), essentially followed Black's system.[41]

Rush's interest in chemistry at this time and later was more than narrowly careeristic. Indeed, the converse was hardly possible in the speculative world of mid-eighteenth-century Edinburgh. Cullen, as has been remarked, was far from being dryly factual and ingenuous in his thinking; and Black, very much his master's disciple at least in this respect, was equally imaginative. The latter's theory of latent heat, which he verified by experiment, was not only revolutionary but highly speculative in its implications. Among other things, it raised a challenge to our sense knowledge about heat in particular and by doing so questioned the reliability of the senses in general.[42] Black's skepticism here was no doubt worthy of the example of his friend, David Hume, whose heterodoxies were less discreet.

Whether Rush was aware at the time of Black's epistemology is problematical; he did, however, over and against his immediate practical purpose, discover

[36] Harriot W. Warner, ed., *Autobiography of Charles Caldwell, M.D.*, with a new introduction by Lloyd G. Stevenson, M.D. (New York, 1968), pp. 296, 421–422, *et passim*. Lyman H. Butterfield suggests parallels between the careers of Cullen and Rush, of which Rush was mindful: their common beginnings as teachers of chemistry; their learning, brilliance, and popularity as lecturers; their worship-inspiring generosity to students; their medical system-making; and the obscure fate of their doctrines in the nineteenth century, *Rush Letters* 1: p. 30n. Joseph Carson, too, pointed out similarities between Rush and Cullen, *History of the Medical Department of the University of Pennsylvania* (Philadelphia, 1869), pp. 83–84. For Rush on the importance of freedom of inquiry see, e.g., "On the Causes Which Have Retarded the Progress of Medicine, and On the Means of Promoting Its Certainty, and Greater Usefulness," *Sixteen Introductory Lectures*, pp. 150, 165; "Observations upon the Duties of a Physician, and the Methods of Improving Medicine, Accommodated to the Present State of Manners and Society in the United States," *Med. Inq. & Obs.* (5th ed.) 1: pp. 261–262.

[37] "An Eulogium in Honor of Cullen," *Rush Essays*, pp. 327, 333–334; on the dialectical mechanism by which the perfect system will be evolved, see Rush, "Observations upon the Cause and Cure of Dropsies," *Med. Inq. & Obs.* (5th ed.) 1: pp. 120–121. For Cullen's ideas on this, see, e.g., Thomson, *William Cullen* 2: pp. 24–25, and Cullen, "Announcement . . . of the short Course of Lectures on the Practice of Physic," (1768), *ibid.* 1: append., pp. 619–621.

[38] Rush, "An Eulogium in Honor of Cullen," *Rush Essays*, p. 327; Rush, "On the Vices and Virtues of Physicians," *Sixteen Introductory Lectures*, pp. 128–129, 132–134.

[39] Josiah C. Trent, "Benjamin Rush in Edinburgh, 1766–1768," *Science, Medicine and History, Essays on the Evolution of Scientific Thought and Medical Practice, Written in Honour of Charles Singer*, ed. E. Ashworth Underwood (2 v., London, 1953) 2: p. 183; Rush to John Morgan, January 20, 1768, *Rush, Letters* 1: p. 51.

[40] *Ibid.*, July 27, 1768, 1: p. 61; Brougham, "Joseph Black," in Farber, ed., *Great Chemists*, pp. 211–225; Wyndham D. Miles, "Benjamin Rush," *ibid.*, p. 306.

[41] *Ibid.* One can easily imagine how gratifying it was for Rush to receive the tribute his master lavished on him for his classic work on yellow fever, Dr. Joseph Black to Dr. Benjamin Rush, August 18, 1795, Rush MSS, XXIV: p. 20.

[42] For the revolutionary character of Black's work on heat and his use of experiment, see Charles Singer, *A Short History of Scientific Ideas to 1900* (New York, 1959), p. 350; Buckle, *History of Civilization in England* 2: p. 389.

that, as he put it, chemistry "is not only a science of importance in itself, but serves as a key to a thousand other sources of knowledge." [43] This discovery led Rush eventually to apply the methods of chemistry, as he understood them, to many and diverse phenomena from cookery to morals. And nowhere was this more evident than in his adoption of David Hartley's principle of the association of ideas, which very probably attracted him by its chemical analogy of simple ideas combining into complex ideas. It is, accordingly, routine to find in his writings the chemical analogy of mixing, combining, and proportioning.[44] Chemistry, or chemical analysis, was for Rush, as for Black, a new organon. But in Rush's case, unlike Black's, a prevailing habit of analogical reasoning—more theological than scientific—marked his thinking upon all subjects. He was, by Great Awakening training and native character, really incapable of understanding chemistry, medicine, or any other science on its own terms. In his thinking about science, and about life in general, Rush was more like his seventeenth-century favorite, the physician Sir Thomas Browne, than like Black or even Cullen. Rush and the author of *Religio Medici* were congenial, if unequal, minds in their purpose of analogizing from what happened in the world to a higher kind of knowledge rather than simply trying to explain natural phenomena. Like Browne and other seventeenth-century thinkers, Rush was always looking for analogies and metaphors by which to understand ultimate reality. Black's perspective on science was different; as an experimentalist he was concerned only with phenomena themselves. His major contribution to modern chemistry was quantitative analysis, which Rush understood well enough to conduct himself on returning to Philadelphia.[45] But what Rush derived

from Black's—and to a lesser extent Cullen's—chemical philosophy and retained in his own scientific mentality was the analogy of mixing, combining, and proportioning simple and complex ideas. This general principle of thought, which in his lectures Black credited to Francis Bacon and Sir Isaac Newton, Rush (after studying David Hartley's *Observations on Man*) came to regard as a universal and unifying conception in all fields. We shall see that it led him into psychology, where his theological bias did not prevent him from making a significant contribution. And we shall see, too, that he urged the study of chemistry for its general educational value in teaching boys and girls how to think correctly.

Black explained to Rush and his other students at the University of Edinburgh that the science of chemistry "had arisen from the reflections of ingenious men on the general facts which occur in the practice of the various arts of common life." [46] This scientific interest in "the various arts of common life" was the hallmark of the philosophical society to which Black and Cullen belonged, an intimate society whose members included many of the founders of modern science and philosophy. Black and Cullen (chemistry), James Hutton (geology), David Hume (philosophy), Adam Smith (economic science), and Adam Ferguson (sociology) were all ingenious men and close observers of the common arts of the new industrial culture that was forming around them in Scotland. The inventive genius of this circle was James Watt, who had employed Black's discovery of the latent heat of steam in devising his famous steam engine. Watt's use and application of his friend's research on heat to industrial processes, the first instance of advanced technology, laid the foundation for modern industrial civilization. The ideas and inventions of Black and Watt, of scientist and engineer, led to the new science of thermodynamics, of the mechanical action of heat, the basic science of the new industrial society of the nineteenth and twentieth centuries.[47] Rush, as a student of Black, heard his teacher often describe the chemist as one who "studies the effects produced by heat and by mixture, in all bodies, or mixtures of bodies, natural or artificial, and studies

---

[43] Rush to Jonathan Bayard Smith, April 30, 1767, *Rush Letters* 1: p. 41.

[44] There are countless examples of this analogy in Rush's works. A sample might include: "An Enquiry into the Effects of Public Punishments upon Criminals, and upon Society," *Rush Essays*, pp. 151, 154; "Three Lectures upon Animal Life," *Med. Inq. & Obs.* (5th ed.) 1: p. 39 "A Defence of the Use of the Bible as a School Book," *Rush Essays*, p. 94; "Thoughts upon Female Education, Accommodated to the Present State of Society, Manners, and Government, in the United States of America," *ibid.*, pp. 75, 83; "On the Origin of Evil of Every Kind," Rush MSS, call number Yi2/7399/F36, pp. 4–19.

[45] For examples of Rush's use of quantitative analysis and scientific method in general, see: "Observations upon Worms, and upon Anthelmintic Medicines," *Med. Inq. & Obs,* (5th ed.) 1: pp. 203–214, in which he gave "an account of some experiments which I made in the year 1771, upon the common earthworm, in order to ascertain the anthelmintic virtues of a variety of substances" (p. 209): *Diseases of the Mind*, p. 26, where he demonstrated skillful use of inductive reasoning; and "An Account of the Late Dr. Hugh Martin's Cancer Powder, with Brief Observations on Cancers," *Trans. Amer. Philos. Soc.* 2 (1786): pp. 212–217, in which Rush presented the results of his analysis of Martin's cancer powder, showing arsenic to be its only active ingredient, Brooke Hindle, *The Pursuit of Science in Revolutionary America, 1735–1789* (Chapel Hill,

1956), pp. 297–298. Referring to this analysis, L. H. Butterfield applauds Rush's "impeccably scientific methods," "Benjamin Rush as a Promoter of Useful Knowledge, 1760–1797," *Proc. Amer. Philos. Soc.* 92, 1 (1948): p. 33. On the "learned and pious" Sir Thomas Browne, whose *Religio Medici* (1642) Rush treasured, see his letters to John Adams, June 4, 1812, April 5, 1808, and November 4, 1812, *Rush Letters* 2: pp. 1139, 963, 1165; *Autobiography*, pp. 345–346n. There is an excellent discussion of Joseph Black's scientific ideas and development in J. G. Crowther, *Scientists of the Industrial Revolution* (London, 1962), pp. 9–92, esp. pp. 54–55.

[46] Quoted in *ibid.*, p. 49.

[47] *Ibid.*, introduction, p. 3, *et passim*; Robert E. Schofield, *The Lunar Society of Birmingham; A Social History of Provincial Science and Industry in Eighteenth-Century England* (Oxford, 1963).

them with a view to the improvement of arts, and the knowledge of nature." [48] It is clear that Rush understood the practical applications of chemistry to medicine; his doctoral thesis on digestion, in which he analyzed the contents of his own stomach, amply demonstrates this. And it is improbable that such a momentous event as Watt's improvement of the steam engine was totally unknown to the practical-minded American. In any case, by the spring of 1768 Rush was already thinking in terms of introducing applied chemistry into the colonies by establishing a china factory in Philadelphia, which would have the desired effect of stimulating colonial manufactures in the face of Parliamentary displeasure. He wrote from Edinburgh to his friend, Thomas Bradford, in Pennsylvania, about the need for "encouraging American manufactures. I have many schemes in view with regard to these things. I have made those mechanical arts which are connected with chemistry the particular objects of my study. . . . Yes, we will be revenged of the mother country." [49] Rush was already a member of the American Society Held at Philadelphia for Promoting Useful Knowledge when he wrote these lines. In word and deed, he was to strive to win economic as well as political independence for the colonies by carrying the Industrial Revolution to America.

Of two other teachers at the University of Edinburgh, Dr. Alexander Monro, secundus, the anatomist, and Dr. James Russell, the natural philosopher, Rush took little notice. Perhaps, in respect of natural philosophy, he felt himself unequal to handling Dr. Russell's mathematical interpretations of nature, much in vogue in the Newtonian world of the eighteenth century, for he spent the following summer of 1767 privately studying mathematics. As we have noted, Rush's schooling with the Great Awakening prophets was theological and practical and—except for a general encouragement of science by Samuel Davies—included no serious work in mathematics. At Princeton there had been few books on mathematics and Newtonian natural philosophy, and this helps explain young Rush's weakness in the subject. Remembrance of this deficiency must have been vivid in his mind when, years later as a natural philosopher himself, he advocated that all candidates for medical degrees at the University of Pennsylvania receive extensive instruction in natural philosophy. [50]

Even then, however, mathematics was still only peripheral to Rush's own understanding of nature, which was physico-theological rather than scientific in any modern sense.

While it is true that Rush ultimately derived his understanding of nature from his Great Awakening teachers and personal religious experiences, and never really comprehended the secular meaning of Enlightenment science as it was being taught at Edinburgh by Cullen, Black, and Russell, he did acquire from his new studies the idea of secondary causes to explain natural events. At Nottingham and Princeton, Finley and Davies had trained their young scholar essentially to account for all things by invoking God, the first cause. Their explanations of the physical world were supernatural, not natural. After studying medicine and natural philosophy at the University of Edinburgh, Rush came to understand the distinction between primary and secondary causation, and how he could synthesize his Great Awakening view of God as the primary cause of the physical world with the Enlightenment doctrine of secondary, natural causes. His mature philosophy of animal life, published in 1799, shows this. [51] In this and other works, Rush adapted the ideas of the Enlightenment to his theological mentality.

His second year at Edinburgh, Rush attended a course in the practice of medicine given by Dr. John Gregory, who alternated with Dr. Cullen in lecturing on the subject. New to the university, having come from King's College, Aberdeen, and having recently been appointed to his post, the forty-three year old professor could boast a distinguished intellectual background. While at Aberdeen as a student, Gregory had been influenced by his cousin, Thomas Reid, the philosopher, who later founded at King's College the Scottish school of philosophy. After having received a medical degree from Aberdeen, he had lectured in philosophy at King's College, resigning the position in 1749 in order to attend to his practice of medicine. As a member of the Aberdeen Philosophical Society, organized by Reid in 1758 largely for the criticism of Hume's philosophy, Gregory was associated with some of the best analytic thinkers of Scotland: Thomas Reid, George Campbell; James Beattie; and Alexander Gerard. Further, enjoying as he did the intimate friendship of David Hume and some of his chief antagonists, Gregory was a close student of the outstanding philosophical dialogue of the times. In 1765, a year after his removal

[48] Quoted in Crowther, *Scientists of the Industrial Revolution,* p. 50. Black, like Cullen, experimented with the bleaching of cloth, Henry Hamilton, *An Economic History of Scotland in the Eighteenth Century* (Oxford, 1963), p. 140.

[49] April 15, 1768, *Rush Letters* 1: p. 54. The Lunar Society, of which Watt and Black were members or associates, was an organization very friendly to the American cause, Nicholas Hans, "Franklin, Jefferson, and the English Radicals at the End of the Eighteenth Century," *Proc. Amer. Philos. Soc.* 98, 6 (December, 1954): p. 426.

[50] On Monro, Secundus, (1733–1817), see Guthrie, *A History of Medicine,* p. 229; little seems to be known about Dr. Russell, except for what Rush tells us in his letter to John Morgan,

November 16, 1766, *Rush Letters* 1: p. 29, as given above. Benjamin Franklin referred to a "Dr. Russel" as professor of natural philosophy in a letter to Lord Kames of Edinburgh, January 1, 1769, John Bigelow, ed., *The Life of Benjamin Franklin, Written by Himself* (3 v., 3rd ed. rev., Philadelphia, 1893) 2: p. 31; *Autobiography,* p. 42; Rush to George Clymer, November 25, 1809, *Rush Letters* 2: p. 1023.

[51] "Three Lectures upon Animal Life," *Med. Inq. & Obs.* (5th ed.), pp. 1–54.

to Edinburgh, Gregory published his principal contribution to the Scottish philosophy, *A Comparative View of the State and Faculties of Man with Those of the Animal World,* while he encouraged his very intimate Aberdeen friend, James Beattie, to war on Hume and his Edinburgh circle of skeptics.[52]

Rush found Dr. Cullen's rival in the professorship of medicine to be a man of considerably lesser brilliance. In fact, he may have joined with the other students in petitioning Cullen to give the lectures in place of Gregory, which the doctor agreed to do. Except for this, Rush noted secretly, "I shd. have returned but little wiser in the practical parts of Medicine." [53] Rush, however, was discriminating enough to separate the philosopher from the medical teacher in Gregory. He wrote in his journal: "He professes a full Belief in Christianity, and used occasionally to introduce into his Lectures such Refutations upon Infidelity as had a good Tendency to convince young minds that true Honour could only consist in a Regard to Religion." [54] Rush, then, in the same passage, noticed Gregory's *A Comparative View,* describing it as "a very ingenious little Essay" of "many original Tho'ts." If Rush had read the work, which is very likely from the context here and from his owning a copy of the book in 1790, then he knew of the philosopher's common sense appeal to what he had called the "few and simple" religious truths knowable to all men. This view of self-evident religious truth, direct and unselfconscious, was the doctrine of the Aberdeen group, before whom Gregory had read his treatise. His denunciation of "monstrous systems of metaphysical subtlety" in religion was likewise typical of the Scottish school. Later, in his famous *Medical Inquiries and Observations Upon the Diseases of the Mind* (1812), Rush was to go one better than Gregory and the other Scottish realists in classifying such "monstrous systems of metaphysical subtlety"— Bishop Berkeley's extreme idealism, for example—as pure and simple disorders of the mind.[55] In the meantime, the young evangelist liked what he read in Greg-

ory's philosophical essay. The question of the extent to which Rush was influenced by Gregory personally in his thinking is, of course, moot. But there can be no doubt that Gregory served prominently in introducing Rush to the Scottish Philosophy of Common Sense in its classical age.

Dr. Gregory also introduced Rush to Dr. William Robertson, principal of the University of Edinburgh and the celebrated author of *History of Scotland.* Rush's characterization of Robertson in his contemporary journal was narrow and political. It was not in Robertson's capacity as historian that the American took the measure of the Scot. Rush, at the time, knew and respected Robertson's *History of Scotland.* And the Scottish historian's later books on Charles V and on America were to be standard works in Rush's library, as his catalogue of 1790 and his letters show. Robertson as the leader of the moderate party of the General Assembly, as the friend of Hume and other unbelievers, as the opponent of George Whitefield and the Great Awakening—this was the Robertson that concerned the diarist. Rush, as was his wont, sharply characterized the liberal divine. With an enmity otherwise foreign to his nature, he portrayed Robertson as a veritable antichrist, who was the "Patron and open advocate of all irreligious Clergymen, but the professed Enemy and Persecutor of such as are truly pious. This Haughty Prelate," he averred,

if it lay in his power would be but little inferior to Arch-Bishop Laud himself . . . his intimate Connection with the Earl of Bute has given him many advantages in carrying his Schemes into Execution wherever they are any ways connected with the civil power.[56]

Robertson, then, was anathema to Rush on more than one account: he was not only religiously moderate but politically Tory, a shameless conspirator against the "good old cause" who had thrown in with the notorious Bute. The former prime minister's speech against repeal of the Stamp Act was, of course, offensive to Rush as it was to other colonists who had declared themselves for repeal. In November, 1767, two months after Rush had written this entry in his journal, he was to join Edinburgh's Revolution Club, where enemies of the "good old cause" like Robertson and Bute were held in contempt.[57] His comparing Dr. Robertson to Archbishop Laud demonstrates that Rush, finding parallels between eighteenth- and seventeenth-century

[52] *Autobiography,* p. 43; S. A. Grave, *The Scottish Philosophy of Common Sense* (Oxford, 1960), p. 1; James McCosh, *The Scottish Philosophy, Biography, Expository, Critical from Hutcheson to Hamilton* (New York, 1875), pp. 231, 263, *et passim;* Sir William Forbes, *An Account of the Life and Writings of James Beattie, LL.D.* (new ed., London, 1824) 2: p. 35; James Beattie to Mrs. Montagu, May 3, 1773 and John Gregory to James Beattie, June 16, 1767, *ibid.* 1: pp. 242, 95–96.

[53] "Scottish Journal," September, 1767, p. 72; he was a bit more generous of Gregory in a letter to Dr. Morgan, January 20, 1768, *Rush Letters* 1: p. 51.

[54] "Scottish Journal," September, 1767, pp. 72–73.

[55] Gregory is quoted in McCosh, *The Scottish Philosophy,* p. 263. For an analysis of the place of metaphysics in the Scottish Philosophy, see Grave, *The Scottish Philosophy of Common Sense,* pp. 146–147. Rush's "Catalogue of Books," Rush MSS, lists the titles in his library for the year 1790. See ch. xi, "Of Derangement in the Principle of Faith, or the Believing Faculty," in Rush's *Diseases of the Mind,* esp. pp. 273–274.

[56] "Scottish Journal," September, 1767, pp. 112–114; *Autobiography,* p. 50. Robertson (1721–1793) was the living symbol of Scotland in her Augustan age, George S. Pryde, *A New History of Scotland* 2 v., 2: *Scotland from 1603 to the Present Day* (London, 1962), p. 177.

[57] See Thomas Seccombe in *DNB, s.v.* "Robertson, William." Rush's certificate of membership in Edinburgh's Revolution Club is in Rush MSS, call number Yi2/7402/F2.

figures, was already beginning to think as a True Whig or Commonwealthman.[58]

Entirely different were Rush's impressions of Dr. John Erskine, colleague of Robertson in Old Grey-friars' Church, Edinburgh, and leader of the evangelical party. Erskine's faction in the Church of Scotland was pro-American, as opposed to the moderates, and no evangelical minister was more sympathetic to the colonists than he. His pamphlet, *Shall I Go to War with My American Brethren?*, published two years later and again in 1776, made that clear enough. With Erskine, friend of George Whitefield and America, Rush struck up an enduring friendship. The Edinburgh theologian immediately commanded the young American's religious allegiance as the ecclesiastical opponent of Robertson and the moderate clergy. More-over, Erskine had corresponded at length with his close friend, Jonathan Edwards the elder, and with other American clergymen on religious subjects, notably the Great Awakening. Erskine had already edited the works of Edwards in cooperation with the younger Jonathan Edwards, who at this time was a tutor at the College of New Jersey and known to Rush, although not intimately. Possessing such credentials, Erskine was naturally attractive to Rush, steeped as he was in New Side Presbyterianism.[59]

More than acceptable, too, was Robert Walker, asso-ciate minister of the High Church, Edinburgh, Rush's church while at the university. Walker, unlike his colleague at High Church, the moderate Hugh Blair, was no friend of Robertson, Hume, and company. Instead, he was solidly in Erskine's evangelical party, regularly drawing to his afternoon service the faithfully evangelical, among whom was the stalwart Rush. Walker, whom Rush judged the finest of preachers he had heard abroad, emphasized the Deity's primary interest in man and repudiated the "false notion" that He attends first to the angels. Another of Walker's "Original Sentiments," which appealed to the young

evangelist, was that of Christ's place at the right hand of God, making known each man to Him. For Rush, listening to these and other sermons by Walker on "practical subjects" in High Church was like being transported back to the "Schools of the Prophets." Just as Gilbert Tennent, Finley, and Davies had done before him, Walker emphasized the difference between the true man of God and the pharisee, and urged sinners "to flee for refuge to that Almighty Saviour, who alone can deliver them from the wrath to come." [60] Words like these had a special meaning for Rush who, at the time, was painfully aware of his own sinfulness and prayed that he might be blessed with the regenerate nature of his beloved teachers of the Great Awakening.[61]

Most important of all the clergymen Rush met in Scotland was John Witherspoon, pastor at Paisley. Like Erskine and Walker, Witherspoon attacked the moderate clergy, whom he called "paganized Christian divines" in the Church of Scotland.[62] This sentiment, which Witherspoon had expressed in several acid pam-phlets on the controversy between moderates and con-servatives in the Scottish ministry, was faultless in young Rush's view, as we know from his diary. As a leader of the Popular Party of the Church of Scotland, Witherspoon attacked Robertson and other moderates whom he, Walker, and other orthodox clergymen held to be more humanistic than religious, substituting En-lightenment science and moral philosophy for traditional Christian piety. In his brilliant satire *Ecclesiastical Characteristics* (1753), Witherspoon mocked—to use the language of Gilbert Tennent—the "unconverted ministry" of the Church of Scotland, those clergymen like Robertson who based their understanding of Christianity upon the arguments of Leibnitz, Shaftes-bury, and Hutcheson rather than upon the truths of revelation.[63] Rush and Witherspoon first came to know each other on business relating to the College of New Jersey. With Samuel Finley dead and the college sorely in need of a president, the trustees had elected Witherspoon. Rush had been asked to help persuade the reluctant president-elect to accept the call.

[58] The best discussion of this tradition is Caroline Robbins, *The Eighteenth-Century Commonwealthman: Studies in the Transmission, Development, and Circumstances of English Liberal Thought from the Restoration of Charles II until the War with the Thirteen Colonies* (New York, 1968), intro-duction, pp. 3–21, *et passim*.

[59] See Rev. Prof. Blaikie in *DNB, s.v.* "Erskine, John"; Dal-phy I. Fagerstrom, "Scottish Opinion and the American Revo-lution," *Wm. and Mary Quart.*, 3d ser., 11, 2 (1954): p. 265. That Rush carefully followed events of the General Assembly may be inferred from the evangelical John Witherspoon's letter to him, October 8, 1768, Lyman H. Butterfield, ed., *John Witherspoon Comes to America; A Documentary Account Based Largely on New Materials* (Princeton, 1953), p. 79; Rush to John Montgomery, September 11, 1785, *Rush Letters* 1: pp. 369–370 and n. 3; Ola E. Winslow, *Jonathan Edwards, 1703–1758; A Biography* (New York, 1940), pp. 331, 365–366; see Benjamin Wisner Bacon in *DAB, s.v.* "Edwards, Jonathan" (1745–1801); John T. McNeill, *The History and Character of Calvinism* (2nd ed., New York, 1957), pp. 358–359; *Auto-biography*, p. 267; "Scottish Journal," September, 1767, p. 104.

[60] *Sermons on Practical Subjects* (3rd ed., Philadelphia, 1772), pp. 70–71, 64–69; "Scottish Journal," September, 1767, p. 107; *Autobiography*, p. 47, and n. 21.

[61] Later, Rush was to write in his *Autobiography:* "The early part of my life was spent in dissipation, folly, and in the practice of some of the vices to which young men are prone. The weight of that folly and those vices has been felt in my mind ever since. They have often been deplored in tears and sighs before God. It was from deep and affecting sense of one of them that I was first led to seek the favor of God in his Son in the 21st year of my age. It was thus the woman of Samaria was brought to a repentance of all her sins by the Son of God reminding her of but one of them, viz. her living criminally with a man who was not her husband" (p. 164).

[62] See John E. Pomfret in *DAB, s.v.* "Witherspoon, John."

[63] *Ecclesiastical Characteristics: or, the Arcana of Church Policy. Being An Humble Attempt to Open the Mystery of Moderation . . .* (7th ed., Philadelphia, 1767), pp. 28–30.

His eventual decision to come to America in 1768 as the sixth president of the College of New Jersey was largely the work of young Rush who simply would not take no for an answer from Witherspoon whom he regarded as the only fitting successor to his beloved teacher, Samuel Finley.

The influence of John Witherspoon in America was perhaps the greatest of any Scot. Not only as president of the College of New Jersey for over a quarter of a century—which office he used to carry religiously acceptable ideas of the Scottish Enlightenment, especially those of the "common sense philosophy," to generations of Princeton students—but as organizer of the American Presbyterian Church, signer of the Declaration of Independence, and leading revolutionary patriot, Witherspoon acted out a career unique by any standard. As it turned out, Rush's convincing Witherspoon to heed the call to Princeton provided revolutionary America with one of her most articulate Whig spokesman. For in his teaching and writings at the College of New Jersey Witherspoon combined Scottish Enlightenment philosophy with republican ideas of government.[64]

The very month Rush arrived in Edinburgh, November, 1766, he met David Hume at a dinner given by Sir Alexander Dick, to whom Benjamin Franklin had recommended him. Hume, Rush reported in his journal, was

well known in the Literary World from his History of England, and ingenious Moral Essays. Mr. Hume's Appearance was no ways engaging.—his Person was rather ungenteel [?] and clumsy. he spoke but little, but what he said was always pertinent and sensible. he acknowledges himself a Deist and has wrote much in Defence of his Principles. his political books are much esteemed.[65]

Less than a year later, in his biting characterization of Dr. Robertson, he elaborated his impressions of Hume. Hume and the moderate Scottish clergyman and dramatist, John Home, were Robertson's "bosom Friends," he observed sourly. Yet, for all his Deism, Hume, Rush continued, was "a Gentleman of the most amiable private Character, and much beloved by every Body that knows him." A generous benefactor of the poor, Hume was always inoffensive in speech and never reproachable in conduct.[66]

Rush's commendation of Hume as a man was shared by many of his Christian contemporaries. It was, therefore, to young Rush's credit that, while finding Hume's religious views disagreeable, he magnanimously admitted those personal traits of the great man which all men of good will have since conceded. However repugnant Hume's philosophic writings were to him as a partisan of the evangelical party, which had attempted to censure the philosopher before the General Assembly, Rush could not forbear reading Hume's *History of England* while abroad. Its Tory character notwithstanding, the American revolutionary later employed the *History's* arguments and information while a delegate to the Second Continental Congress. And he even found a place for Hume the historian in his classic work on mental disease published in 1812. The Scot's principles in religion and politics might have been objectionable, but his style of writing was magnificent and Rush frankly confessed his emulation.[67]

The last recorded meeting between Rush and Hume mentioned in the *Autobiography* occurred in London in the spring of 1769, when Rush returned from his visit to Paris. Apparently insensible of the historic occasion, Rush carried a letter from Denis Diderot to Hume, recollecting many years later only that Hume had displayed a picture of Rousseau which the philosopher had observed to bear the likeness of the Genevan's "peevish countenance."[68] No doubt Hume had at the time painfully recalled the embarrassing events of 1766–1767, when he had tried abortively to settle Rousseau in England. At any rate, Rush in no way showed a real appreciation then or later of two of the most significant men of the eighteenth century. But this was understandable in a young man of intense evangelical feeling: Diderot, after all, was known to be scarcely a theist and Hume was, in Rush's view, the notorious and still unpunished infidel. "David," to use Rush's figure, had not yet appeared on the field of battle to slay the "giant of infidelity."[69] He did appear a year later, according to Rush, in the person of James Beattie, whose *Essay on the Nature and Immutability of Truth in Opposition*

[64] Francis L. Broderick, "Pulpit, Physics, and Politics: The Curriculum of the College of New Jersey, 1746–1794," *Wm. and Mary Quart.*, 3d ser., 6, 1 (1949): pp. 59, 67.

[65] "Scottish Journal," November 29, 1766, p. 23; *Autobiography*, p. 49; Sir Alexander Dick (1703–1785), was the friend, host, and correspondent of Dr. Franklin. The famous American, as well as many other celebrities of the times, visited Dick's mansion at Prestonfield outside Edinburgh, Carl Van Doren, *Benjamin Franklin* (New York, 1938), p. 282, and Robert Harrison in *DNB, s.v.* "Dick, Alexander."

[66] "Scottish Journal," September, 1767, pp. 114–115; Hume at this time was under-secretary of state and lived in Edinburgh, where his literary following included such eminent figures as Robertson, Adam Smith, and Lord Kames, McCosh, *The Scottish Philosophy*, p. 129; John Home (1722–1808), the intimate friend of David Hume, enjoyed the patronage of Bute and tutored the Prince of Wales, who later became George III, Ernest C. Mossner, *The Life of David Hume* (Austin, Texas, 1954), pp. 274–278.

[67] Rush to John Adams, July 21, 1789, *Rush Letters* 1: p. 524; Mossner, *The Life of Hume*, ch. xxv, pp. 336–355; *Autobiography*, pp. 116–117; *Diseases of the Mind*, p. 339; Rush, "Lectures on Pathology," Rush MSS, call number Yi2/7396/F22, pp. 283–284; Rush to David Ramsay, November 5, 1778, *Rush Letters* 1: p, 219.

[68] *Autobiography*, p. 69.

[69] Rush to James Kidd, May 13, 1794, *Rush Letters* 2: p. 748.

to *Sophistry and Scepticism* (1770) Rush and other believers considered to be a decisive refutation of Hume's arguments. "I cannot think of him," Rush said of Dr. Beattie, "without fancying that I see Mr. Hume prostrate at his feet."[70] Rush so treasured Beattie's *Essay* in his personal library that Charles Willson Peale, when he executed his famous portrait of Rush, painted the spine title of the book in the background. Ironically, Rush himself subsequently embraced religious principles which laid him open to charges of infidelity.[71]

While unyielding in his religious orthodoxy at Edinburgh, i.e., never doubting the basic ideas and doctrines of Great Awakening evangelism, Rush was aroused to a compelling skepticism of his other accepted opinions. This was certainly true in the classroom, where Dr. Cullen made Rush aware of the importance of skeptically examined principles in medicine; it was even more true outside the classroom, where a fellow student, John Bostock, plied him with anti-monarchical arguments from Algernon Sidney's *Discourses Concerning Government* (1698), thus creating serious doubts in Rush's mind about the legitimacy of kingly power. In this way, Bostock introduced the colonial patriot to the literature of seventeenth-century English republicanism; and Rush now found, as many other Americans were finding too, a political hero in Sidney, who had been martyred for his Whig opposition to arbitrary government. As he read Sidney's famous refutation of Robert Filmer's argument in *Patriarcha or the Natural Power of Kings* (1680) that one should not "meddle with mysteries of state," Rush noted the Whig martyr's call to his countrymen "to examine the original principles of government in general, and of our own in particular. We cannot distinguish," Rush further noted in Sidney's *Discourses,* "truth from falsehood, right from wrong, or know what obedience we owe to the magistrate, or what we may justly expect from him, unless we know what he is, why he is, and by whom he is made to be what he is."[72] Then the republican

Sidney argued, and Rush approvingly read, that the original principles of government which honest men sought were natural, rational, and Scriptural, the principles of universal liberty and equality, and that "the constitution of every government is referred to those who are concerned in it, and no other has any thing to do with it."[73] The object of the English government, wrote Sidney—as of all legitimate governments derived from the free consent of the people—was the good of the people. This was, of course, the kind of argument being heard increasingly in the colonies, and it made sense to the young American who had recently defied the Stamp Act. That Act had been arbitrary, Rush believed, and Sidney asserted that arbitrary power must be limited even if it took a revolution to do so. The evangelist was also pleased to read in the *Discourses* that the contrary absolutist doctrines of men like Filmer, Thomas Hobbes, and Archbishop Laud could "have no title to Christianity."[74]

John Bostock, to whom Rush had carried a letter from Liverpool, proudly claimed to be descended from an officer in Cromwell's army, whereupon Rush informed his new friend that his ancestor, Captain John Rush, had served in Cromwell's cavalry. As a "free born son of America," Benjamin cherished the stories of Captain Rush's heroism in the great English war against tyranny, stories which formed a major part of Rush family tradition. Bostock confessed his attachment to the compact theory of government as advanced by Sidney and John Locke and invoked the memory of his and Rush's heroic ancestors to win the colonial patriot to the "good old cause." The effect of this personal appeal, combined with Rush's new liberal studies and colonial political experience, was dramatic:

Never before had I heard the authority of Kings called in question. I had been taught to consider them nearly as essential to political order as the Sun is to the order of our Solar System. For the first moment in my life I now exercised my reason upon the subject of government.[75]

This new skepticism about government prepared Rush for what can only be described as his conversion to republicanism, for he reasoned now that the doctrine of hereditary kingly power was patently false and absurd, as Sidney and Bostock argued, and that there could be only one true, rational, and constitutional species of government; namely, "that which is derived from the Suffrages of the people who are the subjects of it."[76] This truth of reason was illustrated by the experience

[70] *Ibid.;* Grave, *The Scottish Philosophy of Common Sense,* p. 1; James Beattie to Thomas Blacklock, January 9, 1769, Forbes, ed., *An Account of the Life and Writings of James Beattie* 1: pp. 120–127.

[71] I am indebted to Charles Coleman Sellers, the biographer of Charles Willson Peale, for this reference; Mitchell, *The Character of Rush,* p. 16.

[72] *The Works of Algernon Sydney, A New Edition* (London, 1772), iii, ch. i, pp. 6–7; John Bostock (1740–1774), too, was an admiring student of Cullen, Thomson, *William Cullen* 1: p. 461; John Bostock, Jr. to Benjamin Rush, June 4, 1805, Rush MSS, XXV: p. 71; *Autobiography,* p. 46. Algernon Sidney (1622–1683), the English politician, paid dearly for his extreme republicanism with his life. On Sidney's general influence in America, see Caroline Robbins, "Algernon Sidney's *Discourses Concerning Government:* Textbook of Revolution," *Wm. and Mary Quart.,* 3d ser., 4, 3 (1947): pp. 267–269. Rush, like John Adams and other Revolutionary leaders, read Sidney's *Discourses* in his youth, Rush to John Adams, March 13, 1809, *Rush Letters* 2: pp. 997–998; John Adams to Thomas Jefferson,

September 18, 1823, Lester J. Cappon, ed., *The Adams–Jefferson Letters; The Complete Correspondence Between Thomas Jefferson and Abigail and John Adams* (2 v., Chapel Hill, 1959) 2: p. 598.

[73] *The Works of Algernon Sydney,* 16: ch. i., p. 36; *ibid.* 2: ch. i, pp. 3–5; *ibid.,* 10, ch. i, pp. 21–22; *ibid.* 41, ch. iii, pp. 481–485.

[74] *Ibid.* 5: ch. ii, pp. 82–83; *ibid.* 2: ch. i, p. 3.

[75] *Autobiography,* p. 46.

[76] *Ibid.*

of England and of all nations, as Sidney had shown in the *Discourses*.[77] That it was still held as a truth in Rush's own day, the American believed, was demonstrated by resistance to the Stamp Act and other unconstitutional measures. Republicanism was true for Rush not because of the lessons of experience, nor because of the bookish authority of Sidney, nor by virtue of the persuasive arguments of Bostock, but because of its rationality—a rationality that withstood every test of doubt.

Once admitted into Rush's thought, doubt cut deeply and generally. "I now suspected error in every thing I had been taught, or believed," Rush confided to his memoirs some thirty years later, "and as far as I was able began to try the foundations of my opinions upon many other subjects."[78] This intellectual discovery, reminiscent of Descartes and basic to the philosophy of the Enlightenment, of employing doubt in the service of truth, marked the beginning of Rush the revolutionary. His beliefs in many areas, now exposed to new and searching criticism, proved untenable. Kings, Cullenism (as well as rival systems of pathology), oath-taking, severe and capital punishments, the priority of classical languages, traditional penal and medical institutions—all of these and more were sincerely questioned by Rush at various times in his life and found wanting in rationality.[79]

But his skepticism did not end in mere negation. As we have noted, the subtleties of David Hume were too much for him. Rather, doubt for Rush as for Descartes and the *philosophes* was always preliminary to certainty or near certainty; it was inconceivable to him that doubt might be an end-in-itself and not a means. Hence, one might doubt the rationality of one form of government, say monarchy, but this only meant that another form of government, i.e., the republic, must be rational. It was unthinkable to him that all forms of government might be irrational. Both "schools" of the Enlightenment and the Great Awakening rejected this possibility. Thus, for Rush, republicanism was the only rational plan of government. He began his revolutionary career as a political republican, while finishing it as a religious, social, and medical republican.

In typical Enlightenment fashion, Rush believed in the amenability of human problems, whatever their contexts, to human reason. While this is not to deny that revealed Christianity, with its doctrine of the Fall of Man and his redemption in Christ, was to remain the organizing principle of Rush's life and thought, and not Enlightenment rationalism, it is to say that, at Edinburgh, Rush discovered reason and science as valuable means by which to understand the natural, if not the supernatural, world. Like Sir Thomas Browne, David

Hartley, and many other seventeenth- and eighteenth-century thinkers, Rush was more medieval than modern in his understanding, extolling reason but treating it as ultimately subordinate to religious faith. His own religious faith, Rush tells us in his *Autobiography,* became more liberal and tolerant while he was abroad, although it was never in danger of slipping into Unitarianism or any other rational creed. The severity of his Great Awakening belief in man's depravity as a result of the Fall was moderated by the Enlightenment optimism and progressivism of teachers like William Cullen and Joseph Black and fellow-students like John Bostock. Cullen and Black as *philosophes* belonged to Voltaire's and Franklin's "Party of Humanity," and in their teaching and scientific work held out the promise of a scientific utopia where reason would triumph forever over superstition and prejudice. The Enlightenment's scientific utopia and the millennium of the Great Awakening were analogous ideas that Rush could easily accept as the program of the future. Samuel Finley's "Party for Jesus Christ" was, after all, dedicated to the same reconstruction and improvement of human society as were the *philosophes*. To be sure, they disagreed about the nature of the ideal society—whether it would be one of the reign of Christ or reason—but the means of social reform that the new prophets and *philosophes* employed were basically the same. Both "parties" of Christ and humanity put their faith, as it were, in reason; although the prophets, unlike the secular rationalists, could ultimately appeal to the God above reason.[80]

Thanks to the scientific teaching of Cullen and Black and, especially, the political rationalism of Bostock and Sidney—which helped the young American make sense of his colonial experience as a rebel against British authority—Rush came under the influence of Enlightenment liberalism with its Baconian empiricism and absolute trust in reason. As one of the "Party for Jesus Christ," he rejected the extreme rationalism of the Enlightenment, but accepted in his philosophy of reform certain ideas of the secular philosophers, like the ideas of social and physical science, progress, and benevolence. These he could accept because they were ideas of secondary causes and, hence, theologically consistent with his Great Awakening belief in God as the primary cause of all things. After leaving Edinburgh in 1768, Rush was to continue his education in the school of Enlightenment liberalism among the Whigs and *philosophes* of London and Paris.

It would be misleading, however, to think that the excitements of this intelligent American in his early twenties were purely intellectual. Indeed, he tells us that his behavior as a student in Edinburgh was quite

[77] *The Works of Algernon Sydney* **18**: ch. i, pp. 45–46, *et passim*.

[78] *Autobiography*, p. 46.

[79] *Ibid.*, p. 89; Rush, "On Imposture in Medicine," Rush MSS, call number Yi2/7400/F5, p. 2.

[80] *Autobiography*, pp. 164–165, p. 79; Donald J. D'Elia, "Benjamin Rush, David Hartley, and the Revolutionary Uses of Psychology," *Proc. Amer. Philos. Soc.* **114**, 2 (April, 1970): pp. 109–118.

ordinary despite his new theoretical radicalism. Rush fell deeply and helplessly in love—or so he thought—with two women, an American and a Scotswoman, during his residence in Edinburgh. Both romances, with Mary "Polly" Fisher at home in Philadelphia and Lady Janes Leslie of Edinburgh, ended in defeat and separation.

Polly Fisher, who so infatuated Rush that he paced his floor through the night, was finally abandoned, as it were, in favor of his family obligation to provide for his widowed sisters and their children, but not without heartbreak. At Rush's ostensible urging, his friend, Thomas Bradford, married Polly in 1768. Rush wrote Bradford:

Her merit and virtue I shall ever esteem, and shall think too that my knowledge in physic was too dearly purchased when I sacrificed an opportunity of making myself happy by coming abroad: for had I obeyed the dictates of my own will, I should have married and settled in some obscure place in the country immediately after I was free—but Heaven hath ordered it otherwise.[81]

Providence, he went on to say in the same place, had directed him to care for his relatives. Still, he owned with characteristic eighteenth-century sentimentalism, that Polly was his first and last true love. It was a confession worthy of the melancholy romanticism of his favorite poet and author of *Night Thoughts*, Edward Young.[82]

Even while Rush was successfully persuading Bradford to marry their mutually beloved Polly, he was admiring—if not worshiping—Lady Jane Leslie. At fifteen, an age when Rush suggested feminine charms of youth, beauty, and virtue are at their fullest expression, Lady Jane was not only irresistibly charming but accomplished in music, French, and the social graces. She was, moreover, the daughter of David Leslie, Earl of Leven and Melville, and consequently of a wealthy and high-ranking family.

Despite his Pennsylvania resolve "to avoid forming connections with persons of great distinction" (which one suspects to have been more a youthful patriotic affectation than a conviction), Rush soon became an intimate of the Leslies.[83] He was almost beside himself with loving praise of Lady Jane:

The Law of Kindness is written in her Heart. words like Honey drop from her Tongue. In a word Heaven is in her Eye—Grace is in her Look—in every Step there is Dignity and Love. Methinks She possesses Charms eno' to revive the Garden of Eden and restore the joys of Paradise itself.[84]

Rush, who was first introduced to the Leslies by a mutual friend, Thomas Hogg, a local banker, visited the family at their Edinburgh and Melville residences. At Melville, the county seat of Lord Leven, he experienced the absolute joy of living intimately with the family for several weeks, always close to his youthful inamorata, in a primitive, if contrived, state of nature which he romantically declared superior to the insipidities of academic life. The Rousseauian scene at Melville was made complete by the perfect happiness of a peasant couple to whom Lord Leven introduced Rush, a peasant couple uncorrupted by the sense and use of money, yet self-sufficient on their modest farm, cognizant of the outside world but wanting none of it. "One visit methinks to this happy Cottage," Rush mused, "if rightly inspired would cure all the ambition in the world." [85]

But, actually, his ambition was too vast to be so romantically dismissed, and Melville, Lady Jane, and artlessly happy peasants were all really tangential to the serious business of getting ahead in the bourgeois world of eighteenth-century Philadelphia. Rush's work at the university might have been dull and lifeless contrasted to the bucolic wonders of Melville, but only at the former place might his career be furthered. It was unmistakably clear that he dearly loved Lady Jane and that his affection for the Leslies was genuine. But clear, too, was his determination "to make a figure in Europe," and for this perservering, unromantic study was indispensable.[86] For in the background of his life in Edinburgh was the intrusive reality of family obligations at home, which enhanced his natural sobriety and made a serious relationship with Lady Jane impracticable.

Rush's express purpose in studying at the University of Edinburgh was that of qualifying himself for a successful medical and academic career in America.

[81] Rush to Thomas Bradford, April 15, 1768, and June 3, 1768, *Rush Letters* 1: pp. 52–54, 60; *Autobiography*, p. 46; "Scottish Journal," September, 1767, pp. 89–93; Lyman H. Butterfield, "Love and Valor," or Benjamin Rush and the Leslies of Edinburgh," *Princeton Univ. Library Chronicle* 9, 1 (November, 1947): pp. 1–12.

[82] References and allusions to Young (1683–1765) are dispersed throughout Rush's writings, e.g., "Scottish Journal," September, 1767, pp. 77–78; Rush to Ebenezer Hazard, November 7, 1764, *Rush Letters* 1: p. 8; Rush to John Witherspoon, April 30, 1768, *ibid.*, p. 59. Witherspoon, like Rush and his Great Awakening teachers, thought highly of Young's religious poetry, *Ecclesiastical Characteristics*, p. 20.

[83] Butterfield, "Love and Valor," *Princeton Univ. Library Chronicle* 9, 1 (November, 1947): pp. 1–12; Rush to Jonathan Bayard Smith, April 30, 1767, *Rush Letters* 1: p. 40, n. 3 to p. 43.

[84] "Scottish Journal," September, 1767, pp. 90–92.

[85] *Ibid.*, pp. 88, 86–87; *Autobiography*, pp. 47, 51; Rush to Colina Campbell Hogg (Mrs. Thomas Hogg), July 5, 1768, Butterfield, ed., "Further Letters of Benjamin Rush," *Penna. Mag. Hist. Biog.* 78 (January, 1954): p. 11.

[86] Rush to Ebenezer Hazard, May 21, 1765, *Rush Letters* 1: p. 14. Lyman H. Butterfield, who has sketched Rush's relationship with the Leslies, says Rush was under Lady Jane's spell at least until 1773, about five years after he left Edinburgh, "Love and Valor," pp. 4–5. In 1773 Rush met Sarah Eve of Philadelphia, whom he planned to marry in December of the following year. But it was not to be. The young woman died three weeks before the date set for their wedding, Eva Eve Jones, ed., "Extracts from the Journal of Miss Sarah Eve. Written while Living Near the City of Philadelphia in 1772–73," *Penna. Mag. Hist. Biog.* 5, 1 (1881): pp. 19–20.

From this middle-class purpose he would not be deflected, however tempting the blandishments. The fatherless son of a Philadelphia grocerwoman, Rush's driving ambition for professional respectability overshadowed every other consideration. He was even willing to submit to what he regarded as the perfunctory teachings of the London physicians in order to increase his reputation.[87] It is not uncharitable to observe that he knew the value of connections—and well-dropped names—in his rise to the top, but this was as much an expression of laudable aspiration to greatness as it was of expediency. Professional and social acceptability at home, he knew, were prerequisite to his calling as a defender of life against the forces of death. Thus, he studied long and hard at the university to prepare himself for his great work.

In this purpose at Edinburgh, he was unswerving. But something happened in the course of his experience as a student to transform his program of routine medical studies into an adventure of intellectual discovery: he awakened, as it were, to the reality of doubt. Even when we allow for the long passage of time between Rush's stay in Edinburgh, when he penned youthful impressions in the "Scottish Journal," and his recollections in the *Autobiography* written as an old man, the shaping influence of Edinburgh—of Enlightenment thinkers like Cullen, Black, Gregory, and Bostock—upon Rush's life and thought is clear. "The two years I spent in Edinburgh," he summarized, "I consider as the most important in their influence upon my character and conduct of any period of my life." [88] Edinburgh, the Edinburgh which will be known as the city of Hume so long as men cherish honest and courageous dissent, emancipated Rush from the unexamined life.

III. THE LONDON SCHOOL OF POLITICS: ENGLISH LIBERTIES AND THE RIGHTS OF MAN

I am but a young scholar in the school of politics, although I have made great progress in the love of liberty; for this, let me assure you, madam, was among the first passions that warmed my breast.—to Catharine Macaulay, January 18, 1769.[1]

On June 19, 1768, Rush received his medical degree, versed and examined to be sure in Dr. Cullen's arguments for rational principles in medicine and against bloodletting; in his polar concepts of tension and relaxation; and in the all-importance of the "nerve principle." Rush's thesis on the digestion of food in the stomach was based upon personal experimentation and the principal dedication was to Rush's patron, Dr. Franklin, "worthy delegate to the Britannic Court, known far and wide." [2] Rush's dedication was as much a tribute to Franklin's influence among the great men of London as it was to his science, for Rush wrote to an American friend there that he was confident of the same advantages from Franklin's patronage in London as he had enjoyed in Edinburgh.[3] In this expectation, as we shall see, Rush was not to be disappointed.

Although dubious about the value of study under the London empirics, Rush followed precedent by deciding to "walk" the great hospitals of Middlesex and St. Thomas. Here his sense of expediency overrode his conviction that medical philosophy languished outside Cullen's Scotland. Rush's certainty on this point, that the medical system he had learned at Edinburgh was the one true rational system, was, ironically, philosophically inconsistent with the teachings of both Cullen and Black, as we have seen. Later, when he saw fit to abandon Cullen's system for one of his own, he came to appreciate to some degree his Scottish master's ideas on the progress of medical systems. For now, however, young Rush considered himself as a man of true systems: Cullen's in medicine and—even more important for his future—Sidney's in politics.

In London in the fall of 1768, he studied anatomy and dissection under the celebrated William Hunter and William Hewson. Hunter, too, had been a favorite student of William Cullen, and was now the leading teacher of anatomy in Britain. Rush recalled later that he had been dissecting a body when Hewson, next to him, succeeded experimentally in proving that fish possess lymphatic vessels, a demonstration of capital importance.[4] At Middlesex, a center of practical medicine, Rush was very graciously received by Dr. Richard Huck, a friend of Dr. John Morgan. Now, after following Huck and other Middlesex physicians in their rounds, the Edinburgh graduate relented somewhat in his harsh characterization of the London doctors, granting at least their "useful" information if not their "philosophical principles." When Huck left Middlesex Hospital for St. Thomas' in December, 1768,

---

[87] Rush to John Morgan, July 27, 1768, *Rush Letters* 1: p. 61.
[88] *Autobiography*, p. 43.
[1] *Rush Letters* 1: p. 71.

[2] Rush's thesis has been translated and edited by David F. Musto, "Benjamin Rush's Medical Thesis, 'On the Digestion of Food in the Stomach,'" *Transactions and Studies of the College of Physicians of Philadelphia*, 4th ser., 33, 2 (October, 1965): pp. 121–138; Ramsay, *Eulogium*, p. 16; Rush to John Morgan, January 20, 1768; *Rush Letters* 1: p. 50.
[3] Rush to Samuel Fisher, July 28, 1768, *ibid.*, p. 63.
[4] *Autobiography*, pp. 52–53, and Dr. Corner's n. 35 to p. 53; William L. Sachse, *The Colonial American in Britain* (Madison, 1956), p. 60; William Hunter (1718–1783), the famous anatomist, owed his medical career to his teacher and friend, Dr. William Cullen, see G. T. Bettany in *DNB, s.v.* "Hunter, William." William Hewson (1739–1774), anatomist, was the distinguished student and partner of William Hunter, whose premature death resulted from a self-inflicted dissection wound, see J. F. Payne in *DNB, s.v.* "Hewson, William."

Rush accompanied him with obvious and full appreciation of the doctor's social and medical connections.[5]

Rush learned to know Huck well enough to sample his political beliefs as well as his more accessible medical opinions. "In his politicks," he wrote, the doctor "was a high toned Royalist, and never discovered any irritability of temper, except when he spoke against the claims of America, or the conduct of the opposition to the British Court."[6] One is tempted to speculate whether the ardent colonial Whig ever divulged his own political opinions about Bute and George III to this former army physician. In any case, Rush must have been piqued at Huck's often made observation that his traveling experience confirmed the least free of people to be the most happy.[7] The wise course for Rush was probably the one he followed of not mixing politics and medicine, especially when his own politics and medicine were vulnerably radical.

Through Huck, whose reputation was considerable, Rush met Sir John Pringle and secured an invitation to attend weekly medical discussions at the eminent physician's home. Pringle at sixty-one was indeed famous at home and abroad. Among his intimate friends, he numbered von Haller and van Swieten, names enchantingly distant and great to Rush, fresh out of Edinburgh. Sir John, a native Scot, was no ordinary London physician after the manner of Rush's definition. Rather, he was a physician of philosophical background, Fellow of the Royal Society, and a leading member of the Royal Society Club, where his intimate friend and Rush's patron, Dr. Franklin, often dined. After taking his degree at Leyden, Pringle had removed to Edinburgh where in 1734 he had been called to the relatively new joint professorship of metaphysics and moral philosophy at the university. There, if we may trust to the accuracy of Rush's later commentary, Pringle was neither strictly a Christian nor a republican, finding conviction in these matters only very late in life. In Edinburgh, Sir John had been a member of the Rankenian Club, a distinguished company of liberal religious and political thinkers. His religious heterodoxy, though, had not been as extreme as that of his friend, David Hume, whose skepticism prevented his succeeding Pringle in the chair of philosophy at Edinburgh in 1744. By the time Rush was introduced to Sir John, the celebrated physician was a Christian and very likely of the Unitarian persuasion. His Christianity was heavily rationalistic, suggesting closeness to the views of Thomas Reid and the other Scottish philosophers.

If Rush and Pringle ever discussed religion, as evangelist vis-à-vis rationalist, there is no extant record of it.[8]

Rush next enjoyed the warm hospitality of Dr. John Fothergill, Quaker and—like Pringle—a close friend of Franklin, who had earlier recommended Drs. Shippen and Morgan to the Pennsylvania Hospital. Fothergill, whose interest in the colonies and kindness to traveling Americans was already well established, possessed his medical degree from Edinburgh, which made him all the more partial to Rush. The older man invited Rush to his home, where he talked spiritedly and characteristically about his philanthropic enterprises, for which he was already widely known. Rush remembered years later, after he himself had embraced pacifism, that Fothergill had repeatedly denounced war in his presence. It is not unlikely that the two men discussed relations between the colonies and the mother country, since the Quaker physician had some three years earlier written a pamphlet arguing for repeal of the Stamp Act and was at this time working closely with Franklin in an effort to bring about reconciliation. Moreover, Fothergill was a member of the Honest Whigs, a London club of whiggish politics, which included such notables as Franklin, Dr. Joseph Priestley, Peter Collinson, Dr. Richard Price, and John Pringle. He was, therefore, politically as well as medically congenial to the young American.[9]

---

[5] Rush to John Morgan, October 21, 1768, *Rush Letters* 1: p. 66; Richard Huck Saunders (1720–1785), took his M.D. at Aberdeen and studied at Edinburgh, served a tour of duty in America as army physician during the Seven Years War, and at this time was on the staff of the Middlesex Hospital, see W. W. Webb in *DNB*, s.v. "Saunders, Richard Huck"; *Autobiography*, pp. 53–54.

[6] *Ibid.*

[7] *Ibid.*

[8] *Ibid.*, p. 53; Sir John Pringle (1707–1782), a medical graduate of Leyden, established modern military medicine in his classic and widely acclaimed work, *Observations on the Diseases of the Army* (1752), see J. F. Payne in *DNB*, s.v. "Pringle, Sir John"; Verner W. Crane, "The Club of Honest Whigs: Friends of Science and Liberty," *Wm. and Mary Quart.*, 3d ser., **23**, 2 (1966): pp. 212–213; Pryde, *A New History of Scotland*, **2**: *Scotland from 1603 to the Present Day*, p. 106; Rush to Thomas Jefferson, August 22, 1800, *Rush Letters* **2**: p. 821. According to the *DNB*, Pringle became a Unitarian near the end of his life. On Pringle and the Rankenians, see Robbins, *The Eighteenth Century Commonwealthman*, pp. 218, 163, 202. Sir John attacked the Stamp Act, as noted by James Boswell, Frank Brady and Frederick A. Pottle, eds., *Boswell on the Grand Tour: Italy, Corsica, and France, 1765–1766* (New York, 1956), p. 291. On Pringle and David Hume, see A. H. Basson, *David Hume* (London, 1958), p. 11, and *DNB*. Possibly Rush kept a London journal or extended his Scottish journal to include his experiences in England, Lyman H. Butterfield, *Benjamin Rush's Reminiscences of Boswell & Johnson* (Somerville, N. J., 1946), p. 2n.

[9] *Autobiography*, pp. 54–63; see J. F. Payne in *DNB*, s.v. "Fothergill, John." Fothergill (1712–1780) was the first Edinburgh graduate to be admitted to the licentiate of the London College of Physicians. Whitfield J. Bell, Jr., has discussed Fothergill's patronage of American students, "Philadelphia Medical Students in Europe, 1750–1800," *Penna. Mag. Hist. Biog.* **67**, 1 (January, 1943): p. 5. That Fothergill was interested, with Dr. Cullen and others, in extending the influence of Edinburgh in America may be seen in his promotion of a Philadelphia medical school and his recommendation of Morgan, Shippen, and Rush, all Edinburgh graduates, Flexner, *Doctors on Horseback*, p. 18; Crane, "The Club of Honest Whigs," *Wm. and Mary Quart.*, 3d ser., **23**, 2 (1966): pp. 211, 218; Betsy Copping Corner, "Dr. Fothergill's Friendship with

The Club of the Honest Whigs was one of the many informal philosophical societies which Dr. Franklin enjoyed while in London. It was not as large or as prestigious as the Royal Society Club, a more formal body whose membership consisted mostly of Fellows of the Royal Society. But it was, like the larger organization, more scientific than literary, drawing its members from Britain's men of science and technology, some of whom belonged to both clubs. Franklin's Honest Whigs, however, was singular among the great clubs of London for its membership of political and religious dissenters and other pro-American Commonwealthmen. Joseph Priestley and Richard Price, close friends of Franklin—and later of Rush—were members. Dr. Thomas Gibbons, M.A. of the College of New Jersey, another dissenting minister and friend and eulogist of Samuel Davies, whom Rush knew in London, may have been a member, too. In any case, before long Franklin's social patronage and Rush's own Commonwealth ideals, more the former than the latter, had enabled the twenty-two-year-old doctor to find his way into the company of Honest Whigs.[10]

His letters of introduction and new friendships in London allowed Rush intimate contact with other leading members of English society. He visited George Whitefield, now in London, and reaffirmed the greatness of the man and his evangelical purpose as he had done earlier in Philadelphia and in Edinburgh, where the English revivalist had stopped over during Rush's stay at the university. "Were I to record all the original, pious and eloquent sayings of this great man during my visits to him," Rush wrote at the beginning

of the nineteenth century, "a volume would not contain them."[11] What a pity that he did not do so!

It was by now customary for Americans visiting in the capital city to avail themselves of the widely known hospitality of Pennsylvania-born Benjamin West, and so Rush enjoyed the painter's company on frequent occasions. West, in turn, introduced his compatriot to Sir Joshua Reynolds, the portrait painter, who with Dr. Samuel Johnson had some years before founded the Literary Club. At Reynolds's table, Rush heard the conversation of Drs. Johnson and Oliver Goldsmith, writing later that the former "spoke a good deal, and always in a manner that commanded respect."[12] Dr. Johnson's "conversation was highly respectful to religion," Rush further noted, "and though he was now and then offensive in his manners, I left his company under an impression that I had passed a day which deserved always to be remembered with pleasure." The subject of John Wilkes was raised among the guests when Heaton Wilkes, the brother of the extreme Whig, denounced the use of weapons in putting down the St. George's Fields riot, by which several Wilkites had been killed. Dr. Johnson was seemingly unimpressed, but Rush, for whom as an American Wilkes bulked large, arranged to have an interview with the English radical.[13]

For Rush as for many other colonists in the winter of 1768–1769 John Wilkes was the staunchest defender of the balanced English Constitution which alone seemed to guarantee the rights of America against George III's arbitrary government. Wilkes's *North Briton, No. 45* and other attacks upon Lord Bute, the king's Scottish prime minister, of course endeared him to Rush who believed, as we have already seen, that Bute was leading a royal conspiracy to destroy the constitutional liberties of Englishmen. Although he had been legally elected

---

Benjamin Franklin," *Proc. Amer. Philos. Soc.* **102**, 5 (October, 1958): p. 416; R. Hingston Fox, *Dr. John Fothergill and His Friends; Chapters in Eighteenth Century Life* (London, 1919), pp. 319, 370. Fothergill had, in fact, written a denial of Franklin's alleged partisanship to the Stamp Act, *ibid.*, pp. 319–320; Carl Van Doren, *Benjamin Franklin* (New York, 1938), p. 421. Joseph Priestley (1733–1804), chemist, philosopher, and theologian, doubtless referred to this club in his memoirs, Ira V. Brown, ed., *Joseph Priestley; Selections from His Writings* (University Park, Pa., 1962), p. 52. Peter Collinson (1694–1768), an English Quaker of broad scientific interests, had in 1751 arranged the London publication of Franklin's *Experiments and Observations on Electricity*, to which Fothergill wrote the preface, I. Bernard Cohen, *Franklin and Newton: An Inquiry into Speculative Newtonian Experimental Science and Franklin's Work in Electricity as an Example Thereof* Mem. Amer. Philos. Soc. **43** (Philadelphia, 1956): p. 432. Richard Price (1723–1791), the Welsh philosopher, whose reputation largely derived from his *Review of the Principal Questions in Morals* (1757), was outstandingly Whig in his politics, as was his intimate friend, Priestley, Carl B. Cone, *Torchbearer of Freedom; The Influence of Richard Price on Eighteenth Century Thought* (Lexington, Ky., 1952), pp. 53–55, 199.
[10] Crane, "The Club of Honest Whigs," *Wm. and Mary Quart.*, 3d ser., **23**, 2 (1966): pp. 210–212, 223.

[11] *Autobiography*, pp. 55–56; "Never did the Beauty of Religion appear more evident than in this great Man," "Scottish Journal," June 21, 1768, p. 35. Presumably, Rush gave serious thought to the conception of such a memoir, *Autobiography*, p. 355.
[12] Sachse, *The Colonial American in Britain*, p. 173; *Autobiography*, pp. 58–59; see Mantle Fielding in *DAB*, *s.v.* "West, Benjamin." James Boswell dedicated his *Life of Johnson* to Sir Joshua Reynolds, see Cosmo Monkhouse in *DNB*, *s.v.* "Reynolds, Sir Joshua"; Rush to James Abercrombie, April 22, 1793, *Rush Letters* 2: p. 632; Sir John Hawkins, *The Life of Samuel Johnson*, ed., abridged, and with an introduction by Bertram H. Davis (New York, 1961), pp. 178–179. For a treatment of Rush, Johnson, and Boswell, see Butterfield, *Benjamin Rush's Reminiscences of Boswell & Johnson*, and Charles G. Osgood, "An American Boswell," *The Princeton Univ. Library Chronicle* **5**, 3 (April, 1944): pp. 85–91.
[13] *Autobiography*, pp. 59–60. See J. M. Rigg in *DNB*, *s.v.* "Wilkes, John"; George F. Rudé, *Wilkes and Liberty; A Social Study of 1763 to 1774* (Oxford, 1962). The intense political antagonism between Johnson and Wilkes is attested in James Boswell, *Life of Johnson* ed. R. W. Chapman (3d ed., London, 1953), p. 1147. Dr. Johnson's politics is valuably discussed in Donald J. Greene, *The Politics of Samuel Johnson* (New Haven, 1960), esp. pp. 20, 253–254.

and re-elected to Parliament, Wilkes's position was never secure because of the persecution of the ministry, which had him expelled several times and even arrested on a controversial general search warrant. Wilkes was serving a term in King's Bench prison when Rush met him in January of 1769; and as heir to Hampden, Sidney, and other seventeenth-century Whig victims of Stuart despotism, he personified to Rush and other Whigs the English Constitution which was being violated so flagrantly at home and in the colonies. "Wilkes and Liberty" was the toast of America, and groups as varied as the radical Boston Sons of Liberty and members of the South Carolina Assembly contributed money to Wilkes's cause which was identified with the cause of British liberty itself. At issue, Rush, Wilkes, and other patriots argued, was whether the government of George III could succeed in imposing upon the British people again the unjust and arbitrary measures of the Stuart monarchy, measures like the Stamp Act, the Quartering Act, writs of assistance, and illegal seizures and trials, all of which had been condemned by the Revolution of 1688. The historic background to what was happening in their own day, these Whigs knew, was the seventeenth century, whose problems seemed to be reappearing with alarming frequency.[14]

The intermediary for Rush's meeting with Wilkes was the Virginian, Arthur Lee, Edinburgh M.D. and good friend of the notorious agitator, who suggested that Rush join him and others for dinner with Wilkes. Comfortable in his apartments, in which he received friends of both sexes, Wilkes continued to press for a representative Parliament. Rush found Wilkes to be witty, interesting, and chaste in his conversation—a far sight from the "monster of immorality" which he had preconceived him to be. The exchange between the republican hero and his guests turned inevitably upon politics, with Rush extremely impressed by Wilkes's political genius. "I heard a number of sentiments from him," Rush wrote, "that would have done honor to a Sidney or a Hamden. He is an enthusiast for American Liberty, and says if you can but preserve an equality among one another, you will always be free in spite of everything."[15]   The name of Sidney, even when

mouthed, as it were, by the devil himself, was all sweetness to the new republican.

Wilkes mentioned John Dickinson and plied Rush with questions about the author of the *Farmer's Letters,* a work which Wilkes claimed to be the greatest of its kind. The English radical, if a second-hand account of the conversation be credited, broached the subject of John Locke's *Essay Concerning Human Understanding,* whose denial of innate ideas he said he now accepted.[16] What response Rush made to this is not known, although he must have then had at least a rudimentary knowledge of Lockean empiricism on which to judge the remark.

As a student of William Cullen, Joseph Black, and other Edinburgh philosophers, Rush could be expected to have some opinions on Locke's *Essay,* which was of course the key text for the Enlightenment's theory of the mind and its operations. Locke's denial of innate ideas, apart from its deep significance for the theory of knowledge, was also a major contribution to that liberal Whig tradition whose social and political philosophy Locke himself had brilliantly articulated in his *Treatises on Government.* By showing that the mind of man was *tabula rasa* upon which experience imprinted simple ideas which were combined into complex ideas, Locke provided Commonwealthmen and other Enlightenment liberals and reformers with a scientific doctrine of environmentalism. The ways in which D'Alembert, Condillac, and the French *philosophes* tried to apply Locke's sensationalism are clear and well known, but the attempts of English liberals like John Gay (1699–1745), Edmund Law, David Hartley, and Joseph Priestley to increase the virtue and happiness of mankind by developing a theory of the association of ideas from Locke's *Essay* are not. Nevertheless, Locke's ideas, particularly the theory of the association of ideas as it came to be developed, was conceived within the tradition of Whig ideology as providing the moral and scientific means for achieving the ideal society. As we

[14] Pauline Maier, "John Wilkes and American Disillusionment with Britain," *Wm. and Mary Quart.,* 3d ser., **20,** 3 (1963): pp. 375–395. Essential, along with Robbins, *The Eighteenth Century Commonwealthman,* is Bernard Bailyn, *The Ideological Origins of the American Revolution* (Cambridge, Mass., 1967).

[15] Rush to ?, January 19, 1769, *Rush Letters* 1: p. 72. Butterfield maintains that this letter and the letter of January 26, 1769 (*ibid.,* pp. 73–74), both of which were published in the *Pennsylvania Journal,* were written to Jacob Rush, the physician's brother, *ibid.,* p. 72n. John Hampden (1594–1643), famous leader of the Long Parliament, was the chief opponent of King Charles I's "ship money" tax, see C. H. Firth in *DNB, s.v.* "Hampden, John." Thus, many Americans hailed the English statesman as the implacable enemy of despotism, John C. Miller, *Origins of the American Revolution* (Boston, 1943),

p. 426. Rush later used the pseudonym "Hamden" to oppose the Tea Act, *Rush Letters* 1: pp. 83–84; *Autobiography,* pp. 61–62. On the close relationship of Arthur Lee (1740–1792) and Wilkes, see Burton J. Hendrick, *The Lees of Virginia: Biography of a Family* (New York, 1935), p. 166. Lee, no doubt by virtue of his friendship with Wilkes, qualified for inclusion in Boswell's *Life of Johnson,* pp. 774, 767. And even Dr. Johnson granted Wilkes to be a companionable fellow, *ibid.,* p. 776. Wilkes' *Essay on Woman* (1763) was generally condemned as obscene, *DNB;* Peter Quennell, *The Profane Virtues* (New York, 1945), pp. 213–214.

[16] John Macpherson, Jr., to William Paterson, April 9, 1769, in Thomas A. Glenn, *Some Colonial Mansions and Those Who Lived in Them,* 2d ser. (Philadelphia, 1900), pp. 456–457, cited by Butterfield, *Rush Letters* 1: pp. 72–73, n. 1. On Locke, see Maurice Cranston, *John Locke; A Biography* (New York, 1957), esp. ch. xx. *Letters from a Farmer in Pennsylvania,* twelve letters in all, were first published in the *Pennsylvania Chronicle and Universal Advertiser,* starting with the December 2, 1767, issue, Paul Leicester Ford, ed., *Life and Writings of John Dickinson* (Philadelphia, 1895) 1: pp. 279–406.

shall see, the mature Rush—who could now only glimpse this in his conversation with Wilkes—was later to take this conception of a new moral science from the Lockean David Hartley and apply it in a utopian enterprise to reconstruct post-Revolutionary America along new lines.[17]

Another friend of Lee was Catharine Macaulay, the Whig historian. Rush met her at a time when she was eagerly sought out by visiting American libertarians. He attended Mrs. Macaulay's literary and political circle, where he met and listened to the republican conversation of such men as James Burgh and John Sawbridge—friends of Wilkes and America—and the Scottish conservative Whig historian, Adam Ferguson. Dame Thucydides, as her many admirers liked to call Catharine Macaulay, was writing her multivolume *History of England* when young Rush came under her spell. Her first volume had appeared in 1763 and by challenging Hume's Tory history served to rally around her all the Whig elements of British society who, following Wilkes, opposed Lord Bute's patronage of Hume, William Robertson, and other Scots. Rush, as we noted earlier, was furious about what he considered Bute's design to subvert the English Constitution by restoring the odious practices of the Stuarts. The historical perspective of Mrs. Macaulay and her friends, which was essentially the same view of the past as that which Rush had learned from Bostock and Sidney, helped provide Rush with a more fully integrated conception of how American problems fitted into the grand scheme of British liberty. He became more of a Commonwealthman as he heard Mrs. Macaulay, her brother John Sawbridge, and James Burgh draw striking parallels between the unconstitutional taxing, standing armies, and illegal search warrants of the Stuart kings and George III.[18]

Mrs. Macaulay read and knew well the political literature of the Civil War and Interregnum, and her own program of reform included some of the leading ideas of the age of Harrington, Sidney, and Locke. An agrarian, rotation in office, annual and representative parliaments, and manhood suffrage were all high on her list of reforms, a list with which Burgh agreed. Government must be representative of the people, she insisted with her good friend, Burgh. She was lionized by Burgh, Arthur Lee, and all men of the times who believed that she—"our incomparable female historian," as Burgh called her—was demonstrating from the English past that the Stamp Act and other arbitrary "innovations" were parts of "that barbarous system of despotism imposed by the Norman tyrant, on the inhabitants of this island."[19] True patriots learned their history from Mrs. Macaulay. This Rush now discovered, along with Arthur Lee, Thomas Jefferson, John Adams, and other colonial spokesmen for English liberties.[20] And this Whig history taught real patriots that they owed it to their ancestors to oppose tyranny however disguised.

James Burgh, like Mrs. Macaulay, was destined to have great influence upon the leadership of the American Revolution. When Rush met him in 1769, the Scottish teacher and philosopher was reading Sidney, Locke, and Harrington, and becoming increasingly pessimistic about England's future as he noted the failure of Parliament to represent the people. "All lawful authority, legislative, and executive," Burgh was to write in his influential *Political Disquisitions* (1774), "originates from the people. Power in the people is like light in the sun, native, original, inherent, and

---

[17] Robbins, *The Eighteenth Century Commonwealthman*, pp. 305–308, *et passim;* Leslie Stephen, *History of English Thought in the Eighteenth Century* (2 v., New York, Harcourt, Brace & World Edition 1962) 2: pp. 53–59.

[18] Sachse, *The Colonial American in Britain*, pp. 182, 163; *Autobiography*, pp. 60–61; Mrs. Catharine Macaulay (1731–1791) wrote an eight-volume *History of England from the Accession of James I to That of the Brunswick Line* (1763–1783), which was acclaimed by the Whigs as an answer to Hume's Tory *History of England*, see W. P. Courtney in *DNB*, *s.v.* "Macaulay, Catharine," George O. Trevelyan, *The American Revolution* (4 v., New York, 1899–1907) 1, pt. i, p. 41n. Also see Lucy M. Donnelly, "The Celebrated Mrs. Macaulay," *Wm. and Mary Quart.*, 3d ser., 6 (1949): pp. 173–207. For Thomas Jefferson's high opinion of Macaulay's *History of England*, which he subsequently had placed in the University of Virginia library, see H. Trevor Colbourn, "Thomas Jefferson's Use of the Past," *ibid.* 15, 1 (1958): p. 64n. James Burgh (1714–1775) was at this time schoolmaster at his Stoke Newington academy, see Leslie Stephen in *DNB*, *s.v.* "Burgh, James;" Randolph G. Adams, *Political Ideas of the American Revolution; Britannic-American Contributions to the Problem of Imperial Organization, 1765 to 1775* (3d ed., New York, 1958), p. 184. John Sawbridge (1732?–1795), brother of Mrs. Catharine Macaulay and fellow-republican, championed Wilkes

as a member of Parliament. His portrait in Roman attire was done by Benjamin West, see Charles Welch in *DNB*, *s.v.* "Sawbridge, John," Donnelly, "The Celebrated Mrs. Macaulay," *Wm. and Mary Quart.*, 3d ser., 6 (1949): p. 178. There is a letter from Sawbridge to Rush, dated September 19, 1774, evidencing the high esteem in which Rush and other Americans held Sawbridge, Rush MSS, XLIII, p. 18. On Adam Ferguson (1723–1816), see Francis Espinasse in *DNB*, *s.v.* "Ferguson, Adam;" Robbins, *The Eighteenth Century Commonwealthman*, pp. 199–202; Crane, "The Club of Honest Whigs," *Wm. and Mary Quart.*, 3d ser., 23, 2 (1966): pp. 228, 231–233.

[19] Catharine Macaulay, *An Address to the People of England, Ireland, and Scotland, on the Present Important Crisis of Affairs* (3d ed., New York, 1775), p. 8, *et passim;* James Burgh, *Political Disquisitions; or An Enquiry into Public Errors* (Philadelphia, 1775) 1: preface, vi–vii, Bk. i, pp. 1–7; Robbins, *The Eighteenth Century Commonwealthman*, p. 360.

[20] *Ibid.*, pp. 360–361; Donnelly, "The Celebrated Mrs. Macaulay," *Wm. and Mary Quart.*, 3d ser., 6 (1949): pp. 174–175. "A story is told of young Rush, that he was present, some years before the war, at a debating society in London, when some one derided the Americans as having guns but no cannon-balls to put into them. This brought Rush to his feet, declaring that if they had not balls, they would load their guns with the skulls of their ancestors, who had crossed the ocean to vindicate their independence," Fox, *Dr. John Fothergill and His Friends*, p. 371.

unlimited by any thing human." [21] Burgh agreed with
Sidney, Mrs. Macaulay, and all Commonwealthmen that
"history is the inexhaustible mine, out of which political
knowledge is to be brought up." [22] All Whigs maintained that the history of nations in general showed
constitutional government derived from the consent of
the people to be the only true government; the history
of England in the seventeenth and eighteenth centuries
showed how true government had been weakened by
"public errors" and conspiracies to the point where, in
Burgh's day, a small group of men ruled millions in an
outrage against the wisdom of history and nature.
Burgh, however, was not fatalistic about Britain's
decline. As a typical Enlightenment figure, he believed
that men of reason might still prevail in reforming a
corrupt British society. This view he shared with Mrs.
Macaulay, John Sawbridge, and other Commonwealthmen—even with the more conservative Adam Ferguson,
whose acquaintance Rush made at Mrs. Macaulay's. [23]

Adam Ferguson, professor of moral philosophy at
the University of Edinburgh and author of the *Essay
on the History of Civil Society* (1767), was probably
the least radical of Mrs. Macaulay's friends. He was a
close friend of David Hume and William Robertson and
had served as tutor to the family of Lord Bute, credentials that made his presence among the Whigs appear
strange indeed. Moreover, Ferguson was no partisan
of the American colonists and no utopian in his social
and political theory. Yet Burgh saluted him as "my
worthy friend" and used his *Essay on the History of
Civil Society* as an authoritative text to prove that
luxury, vice, and corruption were fatal to a nation and
were causing the decline of Britain as they had caused
the fall of Rome. The London Whigs enlisted Ferguson's historical ideas in their cause, as they did the
historical ideas of his greater French counterpart,
Montesquieu, to whose *Esprit des lois* the Scot's work
was often compared. They also liked Ferguson's
liberalism in opposing slavery and advocating more
equality among men. As a major thinker of that
Scottish Enlightenment culture, whose influence Rush
had felt at Edinburgh, Ferguson represented in the
literary circles of London the new science of man and
society whose principles Burgh, Mrs. Macaulay, and
other Commonwealthmen were adopting and using in
their program of reform. [24] These principles were to

provide Rush as a mature social reformer with a
stronger and more elaborate case for Locke's Whig
doctrine of scientific environmentalism.

"Mrs. Macaulay," Rush remembered, "was sensible
and eloquent, but visionary in some of her ideas of
government." [25] In her doctrinaire way, she insisted
to the evening's company that laws should reward
virtue while punishing vice, an assertion contrary to
Algernon Sidney's teaching which, in Rush's opinion,
was properly challenged by one of the guests who urged
that the world sufficiently rewards virtue by approba-
tion. The point was the kind Commonwealthmen liked
to discuss, for it was essential to the problem of how to
go about reforming Britain and all of mankind. Cato's
republican virtues, it was agreed, must be the foundation
of the ideal state; and every Whig was familiar with
Addison's popular tragedy *Cato* (1713) which drama-
tized the Roman stoic's martyrdom rather than submit
to the tyranny of Caesar. [26] But how to promote these
virtues among the people in order to establish the ideal
state was another and more difficult matter. Even so,
there was agreement in the literary and scientific circles
of Enlightenment Europe—of which Rush's Revolution
Society of Edinburgh and Mrs. Macaulay's London
group were representative—that moral science, like
physical science, was possible, and that people could be
mechanically educated in the virtues of Cato, Sidney,
and other recognized heroes of freedom. John Locke
was the greatest Whig philosopher on this subject, and
it is true that Adam Ferguson's environmentalism was
more derivative than original. But the Scot's observations and ideas on vice, virtue, and national character,
and on the problem of how to increase public morality
by careful environmental changes, were timely and relevant to Burgh's and Mrs. Macaulay's desperate project
of "restoring the Constitution, and Saving the State." [27]

In Mrs. Macaulay's pamphlet rejecting Thomas Hobbes's absolutist political philosophy in favor of republicanism, Rush found many of the same telling arguments
which he had recently discovered in Sidney's *Discourses
Concerning Government*. Here, too, was that same
invocation of the glorious perfections of the ancient
Roman Republic characteristic of the Whig tradition
to which Mrs. Macauley, Sidney, and Burgh belonged.
Her political heroes—Hampden, Sidney, Milton, and

[21] 1, Bk. i, pp. 3–4; Gordon S. Wood, *The Creation of the American Republic, 1776–1787* (Chapel Hill, 1969), pp. 323, 371.

[22] *Political Disquisitions* 1, preface, p. vi; H. Trevor Colbourn, *The Lamp of Experience: Whig History and the Intellectual Origins of the American Revolution* (Chapel Hill, 1965),
pp. 5, 8–9.

[23] Robbins, *The Eighteenth Century Commonwealthman*, pp.
364–368, introduction, pp. 3–21.

[24] Burgh, *Political Disquisitions* 3, Bk. i, p. 85; Robbins,
The Eighteenth Century Commonwealthman, pp. 199–202;
Stephen, *History of English Thought in the Eighteenth Cen-
tury* 2: pp. 181–183.

[25] *Autobiography*, p. 61.

[26] *Ibid.*; Sidney, *Discourses Concerning Government* 21, ch.
ii, p. 169; Colbourn, *The Lamp of Experience*, p. 24. Like all
true Whigs, Rush agreed with Oliver Goldsmith's judgment in
his *Roman History* (London, 1769) 2: p. 16, that Cato Uticensis
was "one of the most faultless characters we find in the Roman
history." Rush owned a copy of Goldsmith's work, "Catalogue
of Books," Rush MSS. For him as for many other leaders of
the American Revolution—most notable being Nathan Hale
who paraphrased Addison's *Cato* on the gallows—the martyred
Roman hero was the paragon of republican virtue, Rush to Mrs.
Rush, June 1, 1776, July 23, 1776, and to John Adams, July 13,
1780, *Rush Letters* 1: pp. 101, 105, 253.

[27] Burgh, *Political Disquisitions* 1: title page.

Locke—were names now dear to Rush. First and foremost on her list was Hampden, whose opposition to arbitrary taxation, although of a different age, entitled him to a high place in the estimation of every republican, including Rush. Small wonder that the Philadelphian, when he later adopted a pseudonym in his epistolary war against the Tea Act, chose the stirring name of "Hamden." By 1773 ship money and East India tea were to be, in Rush's Whig mentality, indistinguishable as outrages upon the English Constitution. "Remember, my countrymen," this American Hampden was to write in the tradition of Mrs. Macaulay and the Commonwealthmen, "the present era—perhaps the present struggle—will fix the constitution of America forever. Think of your ancestors and of your posterity." [28]

From the Pennsylvania Coffee House, a favorite gathering place for Americans where Dr. Franklin was often to be seen, Rush in January, 1769, penned an admiring letter to Mrs. Macaulay which included criticisms of her plan of government for Corsica. The island of Corsica, as Rousseau had noted in his *Social Contract* (1762), was a "country still capable of legislation"; and he, Mrs. Macaulay, and other liberal political thinkers idolized the Corsican patriot, General Pasquale Paoli, while they sought to devise perfect governments for his people. Rush's letter shows that he, too, was caught up in the excitement of writing constitutions for places like Corsica that often existed more in the imagination of political utopians than in reality. Citing Mrs. Macaulay's distinction as the only woman to earn the plaudits of mankind for her defense of liberty, he took modest issue with two of the propositions in her plan of democratic government for Corsica. Rush protested deferentially but firmly Mrs. Macaulay's inclusion of military officers in the legislature and her division of the taxing authority between the representative assembly and the senate. Only the representative assembly, Rush argued in true American fashion, should tax the people, as it represented a larger and more universal segment of the people. Mrs. Macaulay's republicanism was not radical enough for this colonial student of Sidney who knew the menace of a standing army and its influence first-hand, not just from seventeenth-century accounts, and for whom opposition to the Stamp Act was more than the academic exercise that it sometimes appeared to be among the London Whigs. "Perhaps I am wrong in both these observations," he selfconsciously ended his letter,

If I am, I expect to be rectified by you, madam, who are so well skilled in the science of government. I am but a young scholar in the school of politics, although I have made great progress in the love of liberty; for this, let me assure you, madam, was among the first passions that warmed by breast.[29]

Mrs. Macaulay was impressed, for she published young Rush's letter along with her plan of Corsican government in a second edition.

Mrs. Macaulay was neither a rational Christian nor a Deist. Like Sidney she was an ardent defender of English Protestantism against papists, Deists, and all enemies of her conventional religious beliefs. Archbishop Laud, Bolingbroke, Hume, and others who, in her view, attacked the traditional pieties suffered Mrs. Macaulay's censure, yet among her personal friends were dissenting clergymen and freethinkers whom she respected. Coming from the tradition of dissent himself, Rush was all the more pleased with Mrs. Macaulay's liberal religious character, which was tolerant of nonconformity without being condescending. "Political freedom includes in it every other blessing," he wrote Mrs. Macaulay. "All the pleasures of riches, science, virtue, and even religion itself derive their value from liberty alone." [30] Rush had been schooled in this conviction of free inquiry by his Great Awakening teachers and the philosophers of Edinburgh, and in Sidney's and Mrs. Macaulay's Whig history and "science of govern-

<hr>

[28] "To His Fellow Countrymen: On Patriotism," *Rush Letters* 1: p. 84; Catharine Macaulay, *Loose Remarks on Certain Positions to be Found in Mr. Hobbes's Philosophical Rudiments of Government and Society. With a Short Sketch of A Democratical Form of Government; In a Letter to Signior Paoli* (London, 1767), pp. 33–35; *idem., The History of England from the Accession of James I to the Elevation of the House of Hanover* (3d ed., London, 1769) 3: pp. 425–432. This is Rush's copy of the *History.*

[29] Rush to Catharine Macaulay, January 18, 1769, *Rush Letters* 1: p. 71. Butterfield proves Rush's authorship of this anonymous letter, which was originally printed in Mrs. Macaulay's *Loose Remarks on Certain Positions to be Found in Mr. Hobbes' Philosophical Rudiments of Government and Society* . . . (2d ed., London, 1769), pp. 29–32. It was to the first edition of this work that Rush was replying, Rush to Catharine Macaulay, *ibid.,* pp. 71–72, nn. 1, 4. On Rousseau, Paoli, and the English liberals, see Chauncey B. Tinker, *Nature's Simple Plan; A Phase of Radical Thought in the Mid-Eighteenth Century* (Princeton, 1922), p. 33 and ch. ii. *Cf.* Rush, *Observations upon the Present Government of Pennsylvania. In Four Letters to the People of Pennsylvania* (Philadelphia, 1777), pp. 5–13. Addison in *The Spectator* had aptly described the coffee-houses of London, which Rush now frequented, as "these our *British* Schools of Politics," No. 305, Tuesday, February 19, 1712, ed. with an introduction and notes by Donald F. Bond (Oxford, 1965) 3: p. 100.

[30] Rush to Catharine Macaulay, January 18, 1769, *Rush Letters* 1: p. 70; Donnelly, "The Celebrated Mrs. Macaulay," *Wm. and Mary Quart.,* 3d ser., **6** (1949): pp. 179, 191; Henry St. John, first Viscount Bolingbroke (1678–1751), the English statesman and Deist, wrote *Essays Philosophical and Theological,* a collection of essays published posthumously (1752–1754) which attacked organized Christianity while praising the simplicities of Jesus's gospel, Herbert M. Morais, *Deism in Eighteenth Century America* (New York, 1960), p. 43; also see Walter M. Merrill, *From Statesman to Philosopher; A Study in Bolingbroke's Deism* (New York, 1949). Rush owned a copy of Bolingbroke's *Letters on the Spirit of Patriotism* and admired his style of writing and "versatility of mind," Rush MSS, "Catalogue of Books," and Rush to David Ramsay, November 5, 1778, *Rush Letters* 1: p. 219, Rush to John Adams, January 8, 1813, *ibid.* 2: p. 1175.

ment" he found his views on freedom of thought confirmed.

The nonconforming clergymen of London, especially Samuel Davies's intimate friend, Dr. Thomas Gibbons —with whom Rush discussed Philip Doddridge, Isaac Watts, and the other great men of dissent—helped Rush appreciate how closely nonconformity and the Whig libertarian tradition were related in English history. Rush's favorite evangelist preacher in London, George Whitefield, teacher and friend of Rush's Great Awakening masters, was pro-American as were so many of these dissenting clergymen. Among them Joseph Priestley and Richard Price, as rational nonconformists, were the most influential in supporting the American cause at the time while they labored within the Whig tradition to secure for all men civil and religious liberty. In Rush's later friendship with these two men, who represented in their lives and thought the highest achievements of nonconformity in the period, one finds the common interests of Whigs and dissenters in political and religious liberty, tolerance, social, legal, and educational reform, representative government, and general plans for the improvement or redemption of society.[31]   In fact, Rush's dream of the Christian Republic, his utopian scheme to reform post-Revolutionary America and make it ready for the Second Coming of Christ, was inspired by this historical outlook.

Quite naturally, Rush during his stay in London visited Parliament and wrote home about it. His reaction to the experience, although mixed with convention and even affectation, shows the colonial patriot and proud defender of the English Constitution. Entering the House of Lords, he informed his comrade, Ebenezer Hazard, "I felt as if I walked on sacred ground. I gazed for some time at the Throne with emotions that I cannot describe." Despite the remonstrances of the guide, Rush mounted the throne and in so doing "was seized with a kind of horror which for some time interrupted my ordinary train of thinking." Sufficiently awed by this experience, in which he revealed himself

to be a not untypical tourist, Rush descended to the House of Commons where, he charged, "the infernal scheme for enslaving America was first broached." Here it was that the "usurping Commons" tried to steal the colonies from the king. Here it was, too, that Pitt —"alas! now Lord Chatham"—had urged repeal of the Stamp Act in eloquent phrases that Rush, on the very spot, once again declaimed to an imaginary house. The "Great Commoner's speech, like Hampden's speech on ship money of an earlier century, was precious to all true Whigs. "I was ready to kiss the very walls that had re-echoed to his voice upon that glorious occasion," Rush waxed romantic, "and to ask them to repeat again the enchanting sounds." [32]

Pitt, Macaulay, and Wilkes, as well as a host of lesser champions of America, were all heroic figures to Rush precisely because they defended opposition to tyranny, whether of king or Parliament. In denouncing unconstitutional taxes, as in the notorious Stamp Act, they were to Rush's vivid historical imagination the Hampdens and Sidneys of the eighteenth century. This was, of course, true for many of Rush's contemporaries who regarded the Stamp Act and ship money as undisguised violations of fundamental law. But what added a special dimension to Rush's historical imagination was his evangelical intensity, his Great Awakening fervor, which converted into a religious crusade what was for Mrs. Macaulay and other Commonwealthmen, including Americans like Jefferson and John Adams, a narrower, legalistic struggle for constitutional justice.

In the "Schools of the Prophets" young Rush had been taught to hate deceit and corruption as the work of the devil and to love simple truth and piety. The new imperial policy of Britain, with all the various evils that he thought accompanied it, was, in Rush's total perspective, not only reactionary but corrupt and sinful. The design was to enslave the American colonists who preserved the Whig and dissenting heritage of freedom and who alone among Englishmen offered the hope of restoring public and private virtue to a decadent civilization. The Great Awakening, Rush knew, was a providentially directed movement by guardians of Christian virtue and piety to stop the spiritual decline of British and Western civilization—a decline which even secular thinkers like Adam Ferguson agreed was taking place. The same diabolical forces that snared men into questioning ancient religious truths, revealed in Scripture, were deceiving men into accepting political

---

[31] *Autobiography*, pp. 55–57. Dr. Gibbons, M.A. College of New Jersey (1760), was the biographer of both Davies and Isaac Watts. When Rush met him, Gibbons was no doubt collecting materials for his *Memoirs of the Rev. Isaac Watts, D.D.*, which was to appear in 1780, see Edwin Cannan in *DNB*, s.v. "Gibbons, Thomas." Rush remembered that the dissenting minister had shown him Dr. Watts's annotated "Greek testament" and letters from Samuel Davies and Philip Doddridge, *Autobiography*, p. 57. Whig and pietistic himself, formed in American "Schools of the Prophets" that came out of the same evangelical tradition as the dissenting academies of England, Rush admired in Watts, Doddridge, and other nonconformists their combination of Sidney's and Locke's political ideas with the simple religious truths of the Great Awakening, Robbins, *The Eighteenth Century Commonwealthman*, pp. 246–251, 254–257, and ch. vii; Rush to Mrs. Rush, October 6, 1793, *Rush Letters 2*: p. 705, *Autobiography*, pp. 186, 348, 254. On Samuel Davies's and Gilbert Tennent's friendship with Whitefield, see Stuart C. Henry, *George Whitefield, Wayfaring Witness* (New York, 1957), pp. 89–90.

[32] October 22, 1768, *Rush Letters 1*: pp. 68–69. William Pitt, first earl of Chatham (1708–1778), had emphatically argued for the American distinction between internal and external taxation, denying that Parliament had the authority to raise revenue by levying internal taxes and commending the Americans for their resistance to the Stamp Act, Adams, *Political Ideas of the American Revolution*, p. 15. Such visits to Parliament as this of Rush, fraught with dramatic meaning, were quite common among Americans abroad, Sachse, *The Colonial American in Britain*, p. 26.

slavery, as imposed by Bute and Grenville, and human slavery, as imposed by the Africa Company's parliamentary monopoly of the Negro slave trade.[33] With God's help, Rush believed, men must defeat these forces of sin or suffer the tragic consequences, for as Gilbert Tennent, Samuel Finley, and Samuel Davies had taught him, the times were making ready the Kingdom of God in this world and, in the words of the Great Awakening millennialists, presented Christians with a crisis as well as an opportunity. By 1774 religious, historical, and social ideas like these were to combine and evolve in Rush's understanding to the point where he could write of growing evils like Negro slavery and Parliamentary tyranny as presenting the British empire and the world with a crisis in freedom almost beyond hope. In his mind, as we shall see, this crisis in freedom was to be desperate but not hopeless, for it was to be surmounted by a revolution in world history designed by God and infinitely greater than the Revolution of 1688. The American Revolution, in Rush's ideal conception, was to be the fulfillment of the millennial promise and would climax and perfect the Great Awakening, the Enlightenment, and all the movements and traditions of history that revealed fallen man's struggle to regain the friendship of God.

To Rush in 1769 King George's ministers and their collaborators in Parliament were acting the role of anticonstitutionalists in an historical drama whose scenes and characters were those described in Mrs. Macaulay's Whig history of the seventeenth century. Rush believed that relations between America and Britain had taken a turn for the worst, although like most colonists he was not yet ready to follow the logic of historical precedent and Sidney's arguments to the extreme conclusion of civil war, and instead patriotically sought ways of rescuing his "sinking country" from total collapse. He had from the start of his British tour evinced a high degree of interest in the factories which now seemed to mark the land. At the University of Edinburgh, William Cullen and Joseph Black, pioneering scientists of the Industrial Revolution, had advanced Rush's interest in manufacturing by demonstrating, among other things, the practical uses of chemistry, especially in the bleaching of cloth. As relations between the colonies and the mother country worsened in the late 1760's, with passage of the Townshend Acts and revival of nonimportation, Rush came to believe that American economic development was an absolute necessity in the contest with Parliament. In London he inspected "the large and curious manufactures," and described what he saw in his notebooks for use at home. With increased conviction, he now wrote that only by expanding and otherwise developing American manufactures might the colonies endure. Wine, sheep, silk, chinaware—in fact, every necessity and luxury might be produced, even perfected, in certain of the colonies. In this way, the economic patriot continued, more colonial workers would be employed at higher wages, since more products would be consumed by Americans.[34] The general effect on the colonies would be prosperity and economic independence. This was economic republicanism at its best. Rush was extrapolating the republican insight into economics, as he would do later into medicine and other departments of thought.

In February, 1769, Rush, as was the custom of visiting Philadelphia medical students, left London for Paris and what was to be an uncommonly brief grand tour of the continent. Again, he was well prepared with letters of introduction, notably from Dr. Franklin to his "philosophical friends" among the French *literati*. This time the venerable doctor generously provided a letter of credit as well, guaranteeing a happy visit abroad to one whose financial resources must have been modest.[35] The prospect of visiting a truly foreign country, where men spoke neither English nor its dialects, was exciting for Rush, who was by now a practiced and discerning traveler in a century of great travelers. So, when he arrived in Paris in mid-February, after an uneventful journey, he endeavored to lay aside his Anglo-Saxon prejudices and see French civilization on its own terms. In this, understandably, he failed; but he failed through no lack of conscious sincerity.

The chief person to whom Dr. Franklin recommended Rush was Dr. Jacques Barbeu Dubourg, physician, thinker, and friend of Franklin and America. A

[33] Rush to Granville Sharp, July 9, 1774, John A. Woods, ed., "The Correspondence of Benjamin Rush and Granville Sharp 1773–1809," *Jour. Amer. Studies* 1, 1 (April, 1967) : pp. 8–9; Bailyn, *The Ideological Origins of the American Revolution*, chs. iii and iv, pp. 55–143, 144–159; Oscar and Mary F. Handlin, "James Burgh and American Revolutionary Theory," *Mass. Hist. Soc. Proc.* 73 (1961): pp. 38–57; Heimert, *Religion and the American Mind*, pp. 387–389, 460–463, *et passim.* "If domestic Slavery is agreeable to the Will and Laws of God, political Slavery is much more so. Then it follows, that our British Constitution was obtained unjustly. King Charles the First did no wrong. Passive Obedience was due to Oliver Cromwell. King James the Second was the Lord's Anointed. The Revolution was a Rebellion. King William was a Tyrant. The illustrious House of Hanover are Usurpers and the Right of the British Parliament to tax the American Colonies, is unlimited and indisputable," Rush, *A Vindication of the Address, To the Inhabitants of the British Settlements, on the Slavery of the Negroes in America, in Answer to A Pamphlet Entitled, "Slavery Not Forbidden by Scripture; Or A Defense of the West-India Planters . . ."* (Philadelphia, 1773), p. 49.

[34] Rush to ?, January 26, 1769, *Rush Letters* 1: pp. 74–75; *Autobiography,* p. 65. Rush seems to have taken part in the meetings of the "Society for the Encouragement of Arts—Manufactures and Commerce" while in London, for in 1772 he was elected a corresponding member, Rush MSS, call number Yi2/7402/F3.

[35] *Autobiography,* p. 66; Bell, "Philadelphia Medical Students in Europe, 1750–1800," *Penna. Mag. Hist. Biog.* 67, 1 (January, 1943) : pp. 23–24; Goodman, p. 19. Rush drew upon Dr. Franklin's letter of credit while in Paris and repaid the debt soon after. It was, he appreciatively recalled, "a delicate act of paternal friendship in Dr. Franklin," *Autobiography,* p. 74.

member of a circle of Physiocrats, Dr. Barbeu Dubourg was busily translating John Dickinson's *Farmer's Letters* into French and presumably already laboring on his celebrated French translation of Franklin's works. A "real republican," as Rush later described him to John Adams, Barbeu Dubourg was a close and sympathetic observer of American affairs, and he excitedly introduced the young Philadelphian to other liberals, including the elder Mirabeau. At the latter's home, Rush was quizzed on the character of John Dickinson. The mixed company of men and women sipped coffee and talked economics, liberty, and government, preparing the way, as Rush observed in his memoirs a quarter-century later, for the epoch-making French Revolution.[36]

In 1769 Barbeu Dubourg was the most influential Frenchman supporting the American cause, which as a *philosophe* he characteristically identified with the cause of liberty throughout the world. Franklin and Dickinson, whose works he was translating to prove the moral and intellectual superiority of the Americans, were to Barbeu Dubourg names that conjured up visions of an idyllic Pennsylvania where Quakers and Indians lived at peace with nature and themselves. This primitivism and utopianism Barbeu Dubourg shared with his good friend, Jean Jacques Rousseau, and with certain of his fellow Physiocrats who, like himself, found in distant America the realization of every dream of reason. When Rush met these *philosophes,* their greatest American idol—next to Franklin himself—was John Dickinson's "Pennsylvania Farmer," whose common-sense views on men and government were admired as a perfect expression of Enlightenment reason. The French liberals were as eager to talk with Rush about John Dickinson and the "rights of man" as the London Whigs had been to talk about Dickinson and the inherited rights of Englishmen. Barbeu Dubourg himself, as a friend of Viscount Bolingbroke and translator of his *Letters on the Study and Use of History,* was exceptional among the *philosophes* in knowing enough about the English past to appreciate in an historical sense the constitutional problem uppermost in the minds of Dickinson, Rush, and the Commonwealthmen. This

ability to incorporate thinking about English rights into the more general Enlightenment philosophy of the "rights of man" suggests Barbeu Dubourg's contribution to Rush's philosophical development over the ten years that they exchanged their ideas in letters and published writings.[37]

So great was this *philosophe's* impression upon the young American that Rush while abroad described his new friendship with Barbeu Dubourg as the highlight of his French trip. Why Rush reacted this way is not difficult to infer from entries in his contemporary "Paris Journal" and from his later correspondence with Barbeu Dubourg. The French liberal's obvious recommendations in 1769 were his philosophical friendship with Franklin and his well-known command of the English language. The latter, indeed, made possible the former, as it did Barbeu Dubourg's important cultural and political role as the earliest French spokesman for American rights—"le Don Quichote de l'Amérique Angloise," he was to describe himself in a letter to Rush.[38] The rights of Americans, he argued in the pages of the Physiocratic journal *Ephémérides du Citoyen* and elsewhere, were no less than the "rights of man" that the God of Nature bestowed upon all thinking creatures. In their pre-eminence as men of reason, untrammeled by Old World errors and restraints, Franklin and Dickinson, Barbeu Dubourg believed, were heralding the new rational order of things that he himself as a *philosophe* was writing about in this and other journals and in his major contribution to Enlightenment thought, *Petit code de la raison humaine* (1768), which was dedicated to Franklin. The *Petit code* described a natural universal order of reason, liberty, and benevolence which, Barbeu Dubourg idealistically maintained, already prevailed in Quaker Philadelphia, from which it was destined to reform the world. This, of course, was flattering to Rush as a native of Philadelphia. And one can see from his journal and correspondence that he was proudly conscious of the honor and advantage of having his name associated in Barbeu Dubourg's mind with Franklin, Dickinson, and William Penn's ideal City of Brotherly Love.[39]

Barbeu Dubourg asked his new friend to read his *Petit code* and Rush did so. He read and generally approved this book of Enlightenment principles, a work admired by Catherine the Great and Diderot, favorably compared to Rousseau's *Social Contract,* and later in 1789 authorized as necessary reading for French revolutionaries. Barbeu Dubourg's Deistical religious principles in the *Petit code* were clearly unacceptable to

---

[36] *Ibid.,* pp. 66–68; Alfred O. Aldridge, "Jacques Barbeu Dubourg, A French Disciple of Benjamin Franklin," *Proc. Amer. Philos. Soc.* **95** (1951) : pp. 331–392; idem, *Franklin and His French Contemporaries* (New York, 1957), p. 240, n. 16; "Paris Journal." Barbeu Dubourg's translation of Franklin's works appeared in two volumes in 1773 with a highly flattering preface, Van Doren, *Benjamin Franklin,* p. 432. In the "Paris Journal" Rush said that, at the time he first met Barbeu Dubourg, the Frenchman was at work translating Dickinson's *Farmer's Letters;* in the *Autobiography,* written over thirty years after Rush's visit to Paris, he referred to the French translation as an accomplished fact at the time of his Paris sojourn, p. 68. The above text follows the journal-keeper rather than the autobiographer. See Barbeu Dubourg's letters to Rush, Rush MSS, XLIII, Library Company of Philadelphia; Rush to John Adams, January 22, 1778, *Rush Letters* **1** : p. 192. Barbeu Dubourg, Rush noted in his "Paris Journal," said Dickinson's farmer was more eloquent than Cicero.

[37] Rush to Barbeu Dubourg, April 29, 1773, *Rush Letters* **1** : p. 77, n. 1; Aldridge, "Jacques Barbeu Dubourg," *Proc. Amer. Philos. Soc.* **95** (1951) : pp. 345–349 *et passim;* Stephen, *History of English Thought in the Eighteenth Century* **2** : pp. 142–152.
[38] Cited in Aldridge, "Jacques Barbeau Dubourg," *Proc. Amer. Philos. Soc.* **95** (1951) : p. 348.
[39] *Ibid.,* pp. 346, 362, 365–375; "Paris Journal."

Rush; and in his journal he excused them as the erroneous belief of good men like Barbeu Dubourg who were prevented by a tyrannical state church from exercising "Freedom of Enquiry in Religious matters." [40] As a Great Awakening evangelist, jealous of his own dissenting background and that of his country, he resented the power of the established Roman Catholic Church over the minds of philosophers like Barbeu Dubourg and called for its overthrow. Rush could tolerate Barbeu Dubourg's rationalistic Christianity which, after all, was not essentially different from what Rush believed to be the sincere but narrow unevangelical religious beliefs of English dissenters like Joseph Priestley and Richard Price. And he must have known that there was an even closer similarity in religious ideas between Barbeu Dubourg and Rush's senior friend and patron, Dr. Franklin, whom the French liberal acknowledged as inspiring his writing of the *Petit code*. But apart from Barbeu Dubourg's mild Deism, which to the evangelist was more a grievous failure of understanding than anything else, the radical Enlightenment ideas of this genial friend of America were a positive influence in Rush's thinking. This can be seen in the most general way by comparing the freer, more worldly and liberal entries of his "Paris Journal" with the record he kept while a student in Edinburgh. Barbeu Dubourg, Mirabeau, and the other *philosophes* were more humanistic and cosmopolitan than any other society that Rush had attended at home or in Scotland and London. They were truly a "Party of Humanity," as Voltaire, the greatest of them, liked to say; and even the Scottish philosophers and London Whigs seemed provincial in comparison.

Rush's "Paris Journal" reveals throughout an elaborate interest in agriculture. In it he mirrors the Physiocratic doctrine of Barbeu Dubourg and his circle that "Agriculture is [the] only solid Basis of [the] Riches of any country." This was why the American colonies were prospering, Rush further noted in agreement with Barbeu Dubourg's ideas: "where Agriculture is encouraged, there will be Riches, where there are Riches, there will be Power, and where there is Power, there will be Freedom and Independence." [41] These were ideas that Barbeu Dubourg was contributing in 1769 to the Physiocratic *Ephémérides du Citoyen;* and we know from his letters to Rush that he made a gift of these papers and other works of the French Enlightenment to his junior friend. Barbeu Dubourg's philosophical influence, in essence that of the continental Enlightenment, was deeply important in Rush's mature thinking and can be seen in any examination of the American's publications over the next five years. Rush sent Barbeu Dubourg a copy of his *Sermons to Gentlemen upon Temperance and Exercise* (1772), a topic

of great interest to Barbeu Dubourg and his good friend, Rousseau, and one on which both primitivistic thinkers had written. Rush published the *Sermons* anonymously, conscious of the "fate of reformers in religion—politics and science"—a favorite subject in Barbeu Dubourg's letters—but knowing, too, of the "sacred power of truth." [42] "Civil society and agriculture began together," Rush asserted in this pamphlet which, except for its theological ideas, either Barbeu Dubourg or Rousseau could have authored. Agriculture, Rush went on,

has always been looked upon among the first employments of mankind. It calls forth every individual of the human race into action. It employs the body in a manner the most conducive to its health. It preserves and increases the species most; and lastly, it is most friendly to the practice of virtue. [43]

And in his first oration before the American Philosophical Society, *An Inquiry into the Natural History of Medicine Among the Indians of North America and a Comparative View of Their Diseases and Remedies, with Those of Civilized Nations* (1774), which Rush dedicated to Barbeu Dubourg because of his friend's great interest in the subject, the influence of Barbeu Dubourg and the French Enlightenment is even more apparent.

The *Inquiry*, like the journal he kept while enjoying Barbeu Dubourg's company in Paris, showed the *philosophes'* concern with comparisons between savage and civilized European nations; but only in the journal did Rush reveal the full, naïve primitivism of Rousseau and Barbeu Dubourg. Nothing in the *Inquiry* equalled his declaration of 1769 that "there is no life so agreeable as that of [the] savage. It is free and independant, and in this consists [the] highest happiness of man. When he is removed from it he is perpetually striving to get back to it again." [44] The author of the *Inquiry* did not hold civilization responsible for the "vices of mankind"; he did maintain with Barbeu Dubourg, however, that "their number and malignity increase with the refinements of polished life." [45] Rush further exhibited the influence of Barbeu Dubourg and the *philosophes* by using one of their favorite allusions to the enlightened people of China to demonstrate that civilization and natural health were not necessarily incompatible. Because European civilization was effete and corrupt, Rush argued, it was diseased. "America," on the contrary, had "advanced but a few paces in luxury and effeminacy. There is yet strength enough in her vitals to give life to those parts which are decayed.

[40] *Ibid.;* Aldridge, "Jacques Barbeu Dubourg," *Proc. Amer. Philos. Soc.* **95** (1951): pp. 346, 331, 384–385.
[41] "Paris Journal."

[42] Philadelphia, pp. 11–12; Aldridge, "Jacques Barbeu Dubourg," *Proc. Amer. Philos. Soc.* **95** (1951): pp. 347, 333–334, 338.
[43] P. 28.
[44] "Paris Journal."
[45] *Med. Inq. & Obs.* (5th ed.) **1**: p. 73.

She may tread back her steps." [46] Rush's program for guarding America against the corrupting influence of Europe was one that Barbeu Dubourg himself could have written. It included reforming the education of children along natural lines, preventing the use of spirituous liquors, and being "cautious what kind of manufactures we admit among us." [47] Barbeu Dubourg had championed all of these reforms in France, as Rush knew from the Frenchman's conversation and writings. Rush's *laissez-faire* attitude toward government's role in this program—which attitude, incidentally, he was to change later—was also, of course, agreeable to Barbeu Dubourg's Physiocratic beliefs.

Rush concluded his *Inquiry* with a tribute to "Agriculture . . . the true basis of national health, riches, and populousness." [48] Barbeu Dubourg and all other French reformers and enthusiasts for America were thrilled to read in this work of the Philadelphian's vision of his country's future greatness, a vision which took on new meaning for them in 1774 as a consequence of Rush's apparent success the year before in helping bring about a prohibitive tax on the importation of Negro slaves into Pennsylvania. [49] "It is impossible to tell, from history," Rush in reality addressed the philosophical idealists of France as well as the members of the American Philosophical Society,

what will be the effects of agriculture, industry, temperance, and commerce, urged on by the competition of colonies united in the same general pursuits, in a country, which for extent, variety of soil, climate, and number of navigable rivers, has never been equalled in any quarter of the globe. America is the theatre, where human nature will probably receive her last and principal literary, moral and political honours. [50]

---

[46] *Ibid.*, 88, 86; Aldridge, "Jacques Barbeu Dubourg," *Proc. Amer. Philos. Soc.* **95** (1951): p. 391.

[47] "An Inquiry into the Natural History of Medicine Among the Indians of North America," *Med. Inq. & Obs.* (5th ed.) **1**: pp. 88–89.

[48] *Ibid.*; Aldridge, "Jacques Barbeu Dubourg," *Proc. Amer. Philos. Soc.* **95** (1951): pp. 389, 375, 362, 348.

[49] *Ibid.*, pp. 347, 377; Rush to Barbeu Dubourg, April 29, 1773, *Rush Letters* **1**: pp. 76–77. After acknowledging his authorship of *An Address to the Inhabitants of the British Settlements in America, upon Slave-Keeping* (1773), a copy of which he was sending to Barbeu Dubourg by way of Dr. Franklin, Rush happily reported that the pamphlet "has been reprinted in New York and in Boston, where it has aroused the zeal of a number of ardent and eloquent defenders of justice, liberty, and humanity, all of which are violated by this iniquitous practice of slave-holding." Then, knowing full well Barbeu Dubourg's idealization of Quaker Pennsylvania, Rush gratified it by adding that he had "refused a thousand guineas a year lately offered to me in Charleston, South Carolina. I am too attached to my own country, this dear province where one owes one's ease only to free and honest toil, to be tempted to exchange it for a country where wealth has been accumulated only by the sweat and blood of Negro slaves." (p. 77)

[50] "An Inquiry into the Natural History of Medicine Among the Indians of North America," *Med. Inq. & Obs.* (5th ed.) **1**: 89; *cf.* Barbeu Dubourg's preface to his translation of the *Farmer's Letters* in Ford, ed., *Life and Writings of John Dickinson* **1**: pp. 297–304, esp. p. 299.

We shall see that Rush's own idealism, so evident here, was to be made bolder with the coming of the American Revolution and to culminate in his vision of a Christian utopia founded upon physico-theological principles.

Barbeu Dubourg was Rush's philosophical friend and correspondent. As a romantic idealist, much like Rush in the '70's and '80's, whose dreams of man's progress and perfection were more congenial in spirit with Rousseau and Condorcet than with Franklin and Jefferson, Barbeu Dubourg did more than contribute to Rush's knowledge and understanding of the French Enlightenment. Barbeu Dubourg was a revolutionary, a world-changer; his vision of what must be done was not bounded by history, as was too often the case with Mrs. Macaulay and the Whigs. Like Rush's teachers in the Great Awakening "Schools of the Prophets," Barbeu Dubourg (and other continental reformers whose ideas he helped make availabe to Rush) worked for a general redemption of man and society which was conceived by both parties of Christ and humanity as new and historically unique. The means of accomplishing this were the "rights of God" and the duties of man. The enthusiasm of the Great Awakeners and the *philosophes* was the same, as were many of the reforms that the parties of Christ and humanity believed necessary in order to realize the "millennium" which they understood in different ways. In the '70's and '80's Rush was to find no great difficulty in belonging, so to speak, to both parties, and could justify his work as a reformer by appealing to the rights of God and man together. It was in this period of his development, too, when the American Revolution appeared to be the final crisis of history before the Second Coming of Christ, that Rush attempted to synthesize the universal ideas of the Great Awakening and the Enlightenment with the more particular ideas of the Whig tradition. This was, in essence, his vision of a worldly Christian Republic, a vision which began to fade only as he became more and more disillusioned with man's nature which in post-Revolutionary America and in a war-torn world seemed, despite his own youthful idealism and the teaching of Enlightenment optimists, to be more corrupt than ever. In the end, as we shall see, Rush was to declare the world literally "mad" and find the only hope for man in the forgiving love and absolute power of Christ.

While in France in 1769 Rush met Jean Baptiste Le Roy, another very close friend of Franklin, who had defended the American's experiments in electricity before the Académie Royale des Sciences. Other new scientific acquaintances opened to him by his letters of introduction were the French chemists Antoine Baumé and Pierre Joseph Macquer, who were to distinguish themselves subsequently as pioneers in the study of combustion. In 1790 when Rush cataloged his personal library, Macquer's *Dictionnaire de Chymie* was among his honored titles. Most famous of all those whom

Rush met in Paris was Denis Diderot, friend of Barbeu Dubourg, *philosophe* and co-editor of the *Encyclopédie.* Aside from carrying Diderot's letter to David Hume, as previously noted, Rush presumably enjoyed no special relationship with the great man. Physiocrats and *philosophes,* chemists and purely literary figures—such were the men to whom the genial and intelligent American was introduced. The times were astir with ideas, daring ideas of liberty, equality, fraternity, and the "rights of man," ideas that would soon explode upon the world in two of the greatest Revolutions of history. Rush, student of Sidney and Macaulay and enthusiast for liberty, was introduced to these revolutionary ideas of the French Enlightenment by Barbeu Dubourg. So powerful was the influence of the Enlightenment in shaping his thinking, along with seventeenth-century Whig ideas, that only later with the coming of Napoleon did Rush conclude that, like all vanities of reason, the *philosophes'* "rights of man" were doomed to fail. Rush was to rationalize and justify the American Revolution and the early stages of the French Revolution by invoking the ideas of the Enlightenment and the Whig tradition; but, as his disappointments with both Revolutions multiplied, he came to reject these ideas and retained only his theological justification of the two Revolutions as pre-millennial.[51]

There was a more commonplace side to Rush's visit to Paris, and that was his sight-seeing. On his medical agenda were tours of the public hospitals, to which he did not seek admission as a student, probably on account of his belief that French medicine had little to teach a graduate of Cullen's Edinburgh and one who had walked the London hospitals. His expenses were mounting, contrary to all expectation, and it was necessary for him to return to the British capital as soon as possible. This did not, however, preclude visits to the churches and galleries of the city, where Rush delighted in the paintings and statuary. In the Church of the Carmelites, the young M.D. was greatly impressed by a painting of a weeping Mary Magdalen; and in Notre Dame, his sensibilities were deeply touched by a canvas of a priest administering the last sacrament to a plague-stricken woman near death. "Pain, sickness, sallowness, and despair," he wrote later, "appeared in every feature and expression of her face. The sight of this picture . . . seemed for a moment to disorder the stomach."[52] Rush's impression of this scene became even more poignant after his attendance upon a dying victim of yellow fever in 1802.[53]

The Pennsylvania republican was soon driven by curiosity to Versailles, where he examined the garden, the palace, and the conduct of King Louis XV during a mass in the royal chapel. Rush found the garden and palace "magnificent and beautiful" and the king's behavior in church unimpeachable. "He had a good eye, and an intelligent countenance," remembered Rush in a charming vignette, "and hence he was said to be 'the most sensible looking fool in Europe.'"[54] On another occasion, Rush witnessed the king and, presumably, Madame Du Barry together and wrote angrily in his journal:

Let such as maintain [the] Divine Right of kings come and behold this monarch, sitting at a toilet with a common Prostitute, picked up a few years ago from the Streets of Paris . . . and then let them declare if they can, that they believe him to be [the] Lord's annointed. It is Blasphemy itself to suppose, that God ever gave an absolute command over 18 million of his creatures.

There were parliaments in France, Rush went on to note, but they were "mere Courts of Justice, and have no Power of any Kind as a legislative Body." At one time these parliaments had been "as free and independant as our own," the American Commonwealthsman observed historically, but now they existed only at the "King's Pleasure."[55] The same fate, it was clear, awaited the legislatures of British America unless true Whigs resolved to follow John Wilkes and emulate Hampden, Sidney, and the other heroes of the seventeenth century in opposing arbitrary government.

[51] *Autobiography,* pp. 67–69; Aldridge, *Franklin and His French Contemporaries,* p. 23; Van Doren, *Benjamin Franklin,* p. 657; J. R. Partington, *A Short History of Chemistry* (3d ed., rev. and enlarged, New York, 1960), p. 88; Rush, "Catalogue of Books"; "Paris Journal"; R. R. Palmer, *A History of the Modern World* (New York, 1953), p. 302. "The members of this Society," Rush wrote at the turn of the century, referring to these Physiocrats, *Encyclopedistes,* and *philosophes,* "consisted of some men who bore an active part in the events of the first years of the French Revolution. The seeds of the Revolution, it has been said by one of its enemies, were sowed by the meetings and publications of this Society," *Autobiography,* p. 68, and Dr. Corner's note 82.

[52] Rush to William Smith, August 10, 1802, *Rush Letters* 2: p. 852; "Paris Journal"; *Autobiography,* pp. 69, 74. For Rush as esthetician, discoursing on the principles of beauty, see his "Paris Journal." On visual beauty, e.g., he observed that "architecture is carried to much greater perfection here than in Engld."
[53] Rush to William Smith, August 10, 1802, *Rush Letters* 2: p. 852.
[54] *Autobiography,* p. 70.
[55] "Paris Journal." Barbeu Dubourg's "Abraham Mansword, Citoyen de Philadelphie," and his "Samuel Jones, Trembleur de Philadelphie" (pseudonyms which he used to write about Anglo-American problems, etc., in French journals) are spokesmen for the liberal social and political ideas that Barbeu Dubourg associated with Rush and his other ideal Americans, Franklin and Dickinson, Aldridge, "Jacques Barbeu Dubourg," *Proc. Amer. Philos. Soc.* 95 (1951): pp. 380, 368, 369. In their views of the English Parliament as corrupt and unrepresentative of the people, of the republic as the best form of government for Britain and America (possibly for France, too, but Barbeu Dubourg was cautious here because of his fear of censorship), of social evils as caused by the environment, and of the need for separation of church and state and religious and intellectual freedom, Rush and Barbeu Dubourg were perfectly agreed, *ibid.,* pp. 368–375, 380, *et passim.* The French reformer developed these and other ideas later in his *Calendrier de Philadelphie, ou Constitutions de Sancho-Panca et du Bon-Homme Richard, en Pensylvanie* (1777 or 1778), *ibid.,* p. 380n.

About Louis XV and the royal family, Rush had little to say that was good. The Dauphin, whom he saw dine in public, was characterized in Johnsonian fashion as seeming "dull in his intellects and vulgar in his manners." As for the daughters of the king, they were unremarkable save for their generous rouge.[56] All in all, Rush discovered the French people—except for Barbeu Dubourg and a few other good men—to be as corrupt as John Wilkes had told him they were.[57] And church and state were the causes of this corruption.

The Philadelphia medical students who toured England and the Continent at that period were not keen philosophical judges of national character, except Rush. Undeterred by the brevity of his stay among the French—little over a month and that almost exclusively in Paris—he generalized later about the French character and its antithesis to the English. Whereas the English appeared a highly various people in manners, Rush proudly observed, the French seemed alike in manners, dress, and the forms and topics of conversation.

Oddly enough, he found more similarities between the French and the Indians of North America than he did between the French and the English. "The highest degrees of civilization border upon the savage life," Rush philosophized.[58] This is so, he continued, because the civilized, barbarian, and savage classes of mankind were parts of a circle, with extremes necessarily impinging upon each other; hence, the superlatively civilized French nation was adjacent to the savage North American Indians on the circle. A few of the similarities between the French and the Indians that Rush instanced were their sex mores, their use of facial cosmetics, their fondness of hunting and fishing, and their aversion to labor and commerce.[59]

Such comparisons and national characterizations—of the English, French, North American Indians, and even of the remote Turks and Chinese—were as irresistible to Rush as they were to Barbeu Dubourg, Montesquieu, and other Enlightenment writers. In his lectures upon animal life of 1799, he went so far as to endow national characters with medical and philosophical importance. Ultimately, and consistent with his belief in utopian republican society, Rush found the American character the most salutary.[60]

Rush departed Paris on March 21 for Calais and, thence, London. Traveling by carriage to the British capital, he made an emergency delivery of a baby boy to a poor, distressed English woman along the roadside. "She was speechless for some time afterwards," Rush recalled in his memoirs after more than a quarter century of service to the poor of Philadelphia, "but in this state she took my hand and pressed it to her lips in the most affecting manner." [61] The doctor always liked to think that he understood the indigent. The circumstances of his own early life had indeed been far from affluent; and now, as a young, unestablished physician, Rush must look to Philadelphia and heed the example of Drs. Cullen and Fothergill in catering to the destitute as his first patients. There was simply no alternative, practically speaking. Besides, it was the duty of a physician to care for the poor.[62]

Rush's last two months in London must not have been thought noteworthy, since he recorded little in the *Autobiography*. He did list his presentation of Diderot's letter to Hume and his expression of thanks to Dr. Franklin for the financial aid received during his sojourn in Paris. When Captain Salmon's ship *Edward* left Gravesend for New York on or about May 26, Rush was aboard. He described the scene retrospectively :

We lost sight of land in a few days. The last view I took of the white cliffs of Britain from the stern of our ship was an affecting one. All the ancient and modern glory of that celebrated and highly favoured island rushed upon my mind. I enjoyed in silence this pensive retrospect of the first country in the world, 'till distance snatched it for ever from my sight.[63]

Thus, Rush severed his physical ties with Britain; in seven years, as a Signer of the Declaration of Independence, he would also cut himself and his posterity away from all political connection with the "first country in the world."

On board the *Edward* with Rush were fellow travelers of highly diverse character. They were all British and, as if to give point to Rush's earlier characterization of the British, all very interestingly different from one another. The Boswellian American, freshly come from meetings with extraordinary personalities like David Hume and Dr. Johnson, Barbeu Dubourg and Diderot, found relief from the long voyage in studying each of his fellow passengers with as penetrating a scrutiny as he directed to his borrowed law books and German grammar. As usual, Rush's judgments on character were lapidary and credible. That John Fricke lived, however obscurely, appears certain after reading Rush's

[56] *Autobiography*, p. 70. Rush, interestingly enough, defended the moderate and artful use of rouge, analogizing it to gardening in the enhancement of beauty, "Paris Journal."

[57] *Autobiography*, p. 71.

[58] *Ibid.*, pp. 70–73; Bell, "Philadelphia Medical Students in Europe, 1750–1800," *Penn. Mag. Hist. Biog.* 67, 1 (January, 1943) : p. 27.

[59] *Autobiography*, pp. 71–73. Cf. Rush, "An Inquiry into the Natural History of Medicine Among the Indians of North America," *Med. Inq. & Obs.* (5th ed.) 1: pp. 55–92.

[60] E.g.: *Diseases of the Mind*, pp. 68–69; "Inquiry into the Cause and Cure of Pulmonary Consumption," *Med. Inq. & Obs.* (5th ed.) 1: pp. 94–95; "Three Lectures upon Animal Life," *ibid.*, pp. 38–40.

[61] *Autobiography*, p. 73.

[62] Rush, "Observations upon the Duties of a Physician, and the Methods of Improving Medicine, Accommodated to the Present State of Manners and Society in the United States," *Med. Inq. & Obs.* (5th ed.) 1: p. 260; Staughton, *Eulogium*, p. 30; *Autobiography*, p. 79.

[63] *Ibid.*, pp. 74–75, 69.

entry on his transatlantic companion. The Philadelphia traveler bestowed historic credibility on anyone who was fortunate enough to win a place in his journal.[64]

The passage from Gravesend to New York consumed almost two months, an extended period in any case, but especially long and monotonous for the garrulous and expansive Dr. Rush. It was sheer torture for him to be cabined for so long and, to make matters worse, he soon exhausted the personality resources of his company. For during these years Rush, while a discerning observer in some ways, was not a profound one, as John Adams was secretly to note a few years later when he described Rush as "too much of a Talker to be a deep Thinker. Elegant not great." [65] Adams, it is true, would feel compelled to revise this estimate of Rush after many years of friendship with the American philosopher—and justly so, we might add—but Adams's characterization of Rush in this stage of his development is a perceptive one. The homeward-bound radical, smug in his feeling that there was no more to learn from the conversation of the ship's company, turned to books for the ideas and information that he could find nowhere else—not his books, but other people's, since he had sent his library ahead to Philadelphia.[66]

Two books were particularly interesting to him: Blackstone's *Commentaries on the Laws of England* and Foster's work on crown law.[67] Blackstone was unmistakably "Tory," arguing the paramountcy of Parliament. It was no accident that the tomes were lent to Rush by Daniel Coxe, a lawyer and, subsequently, a distinguished loyalist. "To the reading of these books," Rush explained later, "I ascribe in part the relish for political science which I felt in the beginning of the American Revolution." [68] Probably, what Rush meant was that these books had for the first time made fully known to him arguments for the supremacy of Parliament, a principle which he condemned as asserted in the Declaratory Act of 1766 and which he would later reject in his attack upon the Pennsylvania Constitution of 1776 and in his criticism of the Articles of Confederation.

Rush was now, as he crossed the Atlantic, becoming familiar with the practical questions of government or what he called political science. Blackstone's *Commentaries,* as a popularization of English law, served his purpose admirably, after Rush made allowances for its defense of the *status quo.* True, he was already a republican in principle, but he had not yet addressed himself to the problem of the organization of government, except, perhaps, in his coffee-house to Mrs. Macaulay. Constitution-making was a proper activity of all Commonwealthmen, Rush knew from his study of seventeenth-century English history; and Blackstone's *Commentaries* provided him with more material for the ideal "balance-of-power" constitution that Commonwealthmen liked to design. Equally important, Blackstone's exposition of the laws of England, which Rush "read with uncommon attention and pleasure," helped give a more practical direction to the Enlightenment "natural rights" philosophy and Whig ideology of the returning American colonist. Rush now began to see and condemn British colonial policy in the wider perspective of English law, English history, and the "rights of man." In a sense, then, as the *Edward* drew nearer to the colonies, Rush's political thought became less speculative and more concrete. His republicanism, conceived in skepticism and accordingly tentative and incomplete, was now taking on the flesh of American political reality.[69]

On the morning of July 14, while Rush was absorbed in the study of German, a language which he regarded as highly useful to a beginning Philadelphia physician, the ship made its American landfall. Not untypically, the homesick American was thrilled by the prospect of his native country and the sweet anticipation of home. That afternoon Rush took leave of the good ship *Edward* in New York harbor and enjoyed the company of his friend, Ebenezer Hazard, who met him at the wharf.

Rush's powers of minute and comparative observation did not fail him this side of the Atlantic. New Yorkers, he remembered, were paler, more slouched in gait, and walked more slowly than Londoners as they went about their daily business. In addition to these social observations, Rush made observations of his own physical and mental reactions to life ashore. His first food and drink after leaving the ship, he noted, possessed a uniquely satisfying taste; and for about a day the young doctor who was later to be recognized as America's first psychiatrist "felt an uncommon depression of spirits, the usual effect of a high tide of joy upon the system." [70] Rush medically used this personal experience of a relationship between great joy and extreme depression to satisfy himself that such a relationship existed. Moreover, he "now believed the many accounts which have been published, of melancholy and even suicide following

---

[64] *Ibid.,* pp. 75–77.

[65] Lyman H. Butterfield, ed., *Diary and Autobiography of John Adams* (4 v., Cambridge, Mass., 1961), 2: p. 182; *Autobiography,* pp. 74–77.

[66] *Ibid.*

[67] *Ibid.,* p. 77.

[68] *Ibid.;* Bailyn, *The Intellectual Origins of the American Revolution,* pp. 31, 174, 229, 201–202; Adams, *Political Ideas of the American Revolution,* p. 140; Colbourn, *The Lamp of Experience,* pp. 188–189.

[69] *Autobiography,* p. 77; Wood, *The Creation of the American Republic,* pp. 7, 14, 299n, 10, 264–265, 350, *et passim.*

[70] *Autobiography,* pp. 77–78. Rush maintained his interest in the relationship between food and taste, see his "An Inquiry into the Relation of Tastes and Aliments to Each Other, and into the Influence of This Relation upon Health and Pleasure," *Med. Inq. & Obs.* (5th ed.) 1: pp. 135–143.

similar emotions of the mind." [71] Self-observation of this kind was not alien to Rush as a discoverer. He had employed it as a medical student at Edinburgh in proving his doctoral thesis on fermentation in digestion, and he would use it afterwards in various profitable ways.[72]

Rush left New York for Bristol and Philadelphia, meeting his brother at Bristol and returning home to a joyful family on the evening of July 18. He had been away from Philadelphia for three years. While overseas he had met some of the great men of Britain and France; at home, he was unknown. Clearly, then, Rush must build a practice among the rich and the influential; and, as already suggested, he determined to attain rank among the prominent families of the city by first treating the poor. Success would not come easily, he knew, but although his family was not socially important, he enjoyed the advantage of having studied at Edinburgh and under the celebrated Hunters. Moreover, Rush—true to Dr. Morgan's promise and with the strong recommendation of Dr. Cullen—was soon appointed professor of chemistry at the College of Philadelphia, a position which not only afforded him some income but which enabled him to acquire public reputation.

Success finally did come to Dr. Rush after six years of ceaseless work and study. Professional success, when it came, might have been reward enough for another gunsmith's son, but for Benjamin Rush it was not enough. He did not bend to the opportunity for easy middle-class respectability and abandon the revolutionary principles of Edinburgh, London, and Paris. Abroad something had happened to Benjamin Rush. It had happened first in Edinburgh—that damp, skeptical city where, he said, his "character and conduct" had been most significantly fashioned. It had also happened in London, that capital of learning and "epitome of the whole world." [73] And in Paris it had happened too. Rush had in all these places been initiated into the changing universe of ideas. Through John Bostock, as we have noted, Rush had been introduced to Sidney's radical *Discourses* and other Whig classics of the seventeenth century. In Scotland, too, where scientific ideas about man and society formed a major part of Enlightenment culture, he had become aware for the first time of liberal social and political philosophy. The Scottish science of man and society, identified with famous thinkers like David Hume, Adam Smith, and Francis Hutcheson offered philosophical support for the political and social ideas which Rush, Bostock, and other Whigs

found in seventeenth-century republicanism. Hutcheson, a founder of the Scottish Philosophy of Common Sense, and John Witherspoon, who as president of the College of New Jersey was to be its chief spokesman in America, were representative thinkers of the new social and political science which emphasized—as did seventeenth-century republicanism—government by social compact and the right to resist tyranny. Rush's friends and teachers in Scotland were like these men careful students of Harrington's *Oceana,* Sidney's *Discourses,* and Locke's *Treatises of Government.* Troubled by many problems within her own society, it was "the interest of Scotland," as Caroline Robbins has shown, to preserve, cherish, and advance this revolutionary tradition.[74]

William Cullen, Joseph Black, and John Gregory were Scottish Commonwealthmen in their acceptance of the revolutionary tradition of social, political, economic, and intellectual freedom. In their liberal public spirit and concern for the general welfare, these men had much in common with Rush's Great Awakening teachers. Theirs, though, was the "Party of Humanity" —as we have seen—not Finley's "Party for Jesus Christ." And their faith was in reason and Newtonian science as promising, especially in the social and psychological doctrines of John Locke, a certain means for reforming and perfecting society.

In the London school of man and politics, Rush had found Whig thinkers who echoed the liberal ideas of the Scottish Enlightenment. James Burgh and Adam Ferguson were Scots themselves, and with Burgh the American kept up a correspondence after returning to the colonies. Burgh was a member of the "Honest Whigs," which attracted to its meetings the leading Commonwealthmen of the day. At gatherings like these, where conversation turned on John Wilkes, parliamentary corruption, and the abuse of the American colonies, Rush had heard Commonwealthmen like Burgh, John Sawbridge, and Mrs. Macaulay confirm his colonial views on the Constitution and seventeenth-century English history. The only hope for England's salvation, Burgh and the other Commonwealthmen had insisted along with Sidney—whom Burgh placed first on his list of political authorities—was reformation of parliamentary government. And in his *Political Disquisitions,* which Rush, Jefferson, and others caused to be published in an American edition of 1775, Burgh was to go so far as to allow the people's "vindicating their liberties by force." [75]

Beyond the encouragement and support that these Commonwealthmen had lent to Rush's colonial position on the unconstitutionality of the Stamp Act, standing armies in peacetime, placemen and pensioners, unrepresentative government, and ministerial tyranny in

---

[71] *Autobiography,* pp. 77–78. In his renowned work, *Diseases of the Mind,* Rush dealt elaborately with this theme, e.g., pp. 65–66.

[72] Ramsay, *Eulogium,* p. 16; Rush to Mrs. Rush, October 29, 1793, *Rush Letters* 2: pp. 732–733; Rush to Vine Utley, June 25, 1812, *ibid.,* pp. 1142–1143.

[73] Rush to James Rush, May 1, 1810, *ibid.,* p. 1043; *Autobiography,* pp. 43, 83–85, 78–79, 70–81.

[74] *The Eighteenth Century Commonwealthman,* p. 177, and ch. vi, pp. 177–220.

[75] 1: pp. 6–7; 3: p. i.

general—all of which perversions of the Constitution Burgh, Mrs. Macaulay, and others vigorously attacked —the London Whigs in their conversations and writings helped Rush to realize more clearly than ever that the conflict between true English liberty and tyranny was historical. Rush, by degrees, especially after reading Mrs. Macaulay's *History of England,* came to see himself, too, as a faithful Whig of the "good old cause," trying to preserve that Constitution which Sidney and other heroes of the seventeenth century had dedicated their lives to upholding. His role as a revolutionary, however, was not to be only that of a conservative in this sense. Like the Scottish and English Commonwealthmen, and like the *philosophe* Barbeu Dubourg, whom Rush met in Paris and who in a lasting correspondence shared with him many ideas on social reform, the mature Rush believed in revolutionary progress by means of free inquiry and Enlightenment social and psychological science.

On his return to Philadelphia in 1769, Rush was supremely alive to the possibilities of reforming his city, his province, and his world. Abroad he had been educated in the Enlightenment school of reason and science, with its fundamental beliefs in the natural order of the universe, the unity of knowledge, and the existence of a body of truths on all subjects including nature, man, and society. His own adventure in the Enlightenment had begun with the realization that government, like physical nature and all things, had natural principles that could be discovered by observation and reasoning. This revelation led Rush to study Enlightenment social, political, and psychological science which, he came to understand, derived mainly from Locke's *Two Treaties of Government* and his *Essay Concerning Human Understanding.* Locke's sensationalism and liberalism confirmed Rush in his Great Awakening belief that Christ had provided natural as well as supernatural means for the reformation of man and society prior to His Second Coming. The dissenting tradition —especially as seen in Price's and Priestley's championing of the "rights of man" also confirmed Rush in this belief. The parties of Christ and humanity must now in the eighteenth century work together for the betterment of mankind, so Finley and Davies had suggested in the "Schools of the Prophets," and so Rush, after studying progressive ideas about improving man and society, believed. Imbued with the scientific optimism of the Enlightenment, while tempered and sanctified by his Great Awakening piety, Rush was a Christian revolutionary. He conceived and articulated his radical doctrine in bold republican philosophies of history, education, science, and religion over the years from his return to Philadelphia in 1769 to his death in 1813. Together, these parts of Rush's revolutionary thought describe his vision of a Christian utopia in America. And he devised this heroic conception of an ideal Christian America out of the materials of his education

and his revolutionary experience as a leading patriot in the 70's and 80's.

IV. OLD WORLD THEORIES AND AMERICAN REALITIES: THE VISION TAKES FORM

I was actuated by the double motives of the safety of my country, and a predilection to a Republican form of government which I now saw within her grasp. It was a blessing I had never expected to possess, at the time I adopted republican principles in the city of Edinburgh.[1]

Upon returning home to Philadelphia in 1769, Benjamin Rush was not so absorbed in the Cullenian medical heresies he was about to propagate as to neglect social and political realities. Some three years earlier, as an apprentice in Dr. Redman's shop, he had taken time to write another young College of New Jersey graduate, Ebenezer Hazard of New York, of the injustice of the recently enacted Stamp Act: "Our merchants have followed your example and entered into an association to import no more goods from London— a resolution of great importance to *America!* and which in my opinion promises more for us than anything hitherto attempted."[2] Rush, at nineteen, had been very much involved in the political controversies of the day. And, as we have seen, his political interests had not withered during his travels abroad.

In Scotland and England, Rush had enjoyed the hearty republican fare of Britishers and fellow colonists; in France he had taken coffee with *philosophes,* discussing the *Farmer's Letters,* the "rights of man," and enjoying their arguments against French and British mercantilism. Now, back in his native city, he began attacking medical and social evils like Boerhaavism, Negro slavery, and spirituous liquor, while championing American liberty against parliamentary taxation.[3] Not surprisingly, the pen name Rush chose for his newspaper assaults upon the Tea Act was "Hampden," a name sacred to all republicans and to none more so than Mrs. Macaulay's disciple. In October of 1773, Rush, with Col. William Bradford, Thomas Mifflin, and a few others, organized to prevent the landing of East India tea in Philadelphia. The American "Hampden" appealed to his readers in the *Pennsylvania Journal:*

Let us with one heart and hand oppose the landing of it. The baneful chests contain in them a slow poison in a political as well as a physical sense. They contain something worse than death—the seeds of slavery. Remember, my countrymen, the present era—perhaps the present struggle—will fix the constitution of America forever. Think of your ancestors and of your posterity.[4]

The plea was effective, for when the ship *Polly* arrived

[1] *Autobiograpy,* p. 115.
[2] November 8, 1765, *Rush Letters* 1: p. 18.
[3] *Autobiography,* pp. 81–83.
[4] Rush to "His Fellow Countrymen: On Patriotism," October 20, 1773, *Rush Letters* 1: p. 84; Rush to John Adams, August 14, 1809, *ibid.,* 2: pp. 1013–1014.

in December, laden with East India tea, her captain was refused permission to unload his cargo.

Many years later Rush credited these newspaper articles as winning for him recognition by John Dickinson and other political leaders. When the First Continental Congress met in Philadelphia he enjoyed the social patronage of the delegates, especially of John and Samuel Adams who stayed in his home, but Rush was less decisive in his political sentiments than John Adams, who urged war and independence in his presence. Only later in April of '75, after he had received news of the battle of Lexington, did he decide on the necessity of independence:

The battle of Lexington gave a new tone to my feelings, and I now resolved to bear my share of the duties and burdens of the approaching Revolution. I considered the seperation of the colonies from Great Britain as inevitable. The first gun that was fired at an American cut the cord that had tied the two countries together. It was the signal for the commencement of our independance and from this time all my publications were calculated to prepare the public mind to adopt that important and necessary measure.[5]

Now Rush was committed. In the newspapers and among the delegates to the Second Congress, assembled in May, he promoted American independence in every way. "I was actuated by the double motives of the safety of my country, and a predilection to a Republican form of government which I now saw within her grasp," he recalled at the turn of the century. "It was a blessing I had never expected to possess, at the time I adopted republican principles in the city of Edinburgh." [6]

In his new enthusiasm for independence, Rush conceived the idea of a pamphlet addressed to the American people on the necessity of separation from Great Britain. Such a publication, he thought, would do far more good in carrying independence than the articles he was writing for the local newspapers. Rush's nerve, though, seemed to fail him when he considered the effect an ill-timed pamphlet might have on his medical practice. Mr. Thomas Paine, Rush's new friend from England, had no such inhibitions about the enterprise when Rush urged it upon him in the fall of 1775. Paine set to work at once, reading the pamphlet to Rush chapter by chapter as it came from his skillful hand. The ideas were Paine's, Rush insisted many years later, not his. But the title *Common Sense* was Rush's, and it was he who arranged for the publication of the pamphlet on January 10, 1776, when it "burst from the press," as Rush dramatically noted, "with an effect which has rarely been produced by types and paper in any age or country." [7]

On May 10, 1776, the Second Continental Congress urged that British charters in all colonies be replaced by independent state governments, a resolution which Rush heartily approved. Although already a member of the local Committee of Inspection, established to implement the resolutions of Congress, which duties he performed along with superintending the manufacture of gunpowder and acting as fleet surgeon to the new Pennsylvania navy, Rush eagerly accepted appointment to the conference formed to give Pennsylvania a state constitution. The officially elected legislative body, the conservative Pennsylvania Assembly, had been declared unacceptable by revolutionaries led by Thomas McKean, who scheduled a meeting of the radical conference for June 18. Rush was very active in this and other meetings of the conference, and on June 23 he moved that Pennsylvania proclaim independence. Elected chairman of the drafting committee, Rush presented the committee's report the following day, a report that anticipated many of the ideas and phrases of the Declaration of Independence itself. With the adoption of the report by the conference, the delegates agreed to submit their independence committee's work to Congress, which was done on June 25.[8]

Rush's reward for his outstanding part in declaring Pennsylvania free was nothing less than election to Congress, by his state's new constitutional convention, and the privilege of signing the Declaration of Independence on August 2. Others might fail to appreciate the epoch-making significance of American independence, but not this son of the Great Awakening. The very hand of God was in it. The "language" of American independence, Rush wrote joyfully to his English friend, Granville Sharp, in 1783, "has for many years appeared to me to be the same as that of the heavenly host that announced the birth of the Saviour of mankind. It proclaims 'glory to God in the highest—on earth peace —good will to man.'" [9] How foolish to think, as many

many patients "by giving rise to an opinion that I had meddled with a controversy that was foreign to my business. I now found that a physician's studies and duties were to be limited by the public, and that he was destined to walk in a path as contracted as the most humble and dependent mechanic." (p. 83).

[8] Goodman, pp. 48–54; Rush to Mrs. Rush, May 27 [i.e., 26], 1776, **1**: p. 96; *Autobiography*, pp. 116–117; J. Paul Selsam, *The Pennsylvania Constitution of 1776: A Study in Revolutionary Democracy* (Philadelphia, 1936), chs. iii and iv; Theodore Thayer, *Pennsylvania Politics and the Growth of Democracy 1740–1776* (Harrisburg, Penna., 1953), ch. xiii.

[9] April 7, 1783, Woods, ed., "The Correspondence of Benjamin Rush and Granville Sharp 1773–1809," *Jour. Amer. Stud.* **1**, 1 (April, 1967): p. 17; Rush to Jeremy Belknap, June 21, 1792, *Rush Letters* **1**: p. 620; *Autobiography*, p. 119; Rush to Barbeu Dubourg, September 16, 1776, *Rush Letters* **1**: p. 111. As early as 1771, Barbeu Dubourg was writing in favor of American independence, Aldridge, "Jacques Barbeu Dubourg," *Proc. Amer. Philos. Soc.* **95** (1951): pp. 366–375. In his letter of September 16 Rush went on to tell his friend of the new republican governments that were being established by American revolutionaries who—Rush seemed to imply—like the ideal Quakers of Barbeu Dubourg's imagination, rejected Old World

[5] *Autobiography*, pp. 112, 109–110.

[6] *Ibid.*, p. 115.

[7] *Ibid.*, pp. 113–115; Rush to James Cheetham, July 17, 1809, *Rush Letters* **2**: p. 1008. Rush claimed in his *Autobiography* that his earlier *Address to the Inhabitants of the British Settlements in America, upon Slave-Keeping* (1773) had cost him

did, that men alone had wrought this great event in the history of the world.

In the congressional debates on the plan of confederation, which arrayed the large states against the small, Rush saw a critical test of that political philosophy which he and other republicans had just proclaimed to the world. "I would not have it understood that I am pleading the cause of Pennsylvania," he addressed the Congress with obvious sincerity, "when I entered that door, I considered myself a citizen of America." [10] Freedom itself was at stake. Voting by states, he argued, "will promote factions in Congress and in the States; it will prevent the growth of freedom in America; we shall be loth to admit new Colonies into the confederation. If we vote by numbers," the true republican concluded, "liberty will be always safe." [11] It was a necessary position to take for one who, following Sidney, Locke, and Burgh, believed in the absolute suffrages of the people.

Rush was adamantly opposed to conciliation with Great Britain, declaring with bold eloquence that the war for independence should be a fight to the death if need be. He was vigorously on guard, too, against weakening the powers of Congress in any way. Rising to speak against a motion to authorize General Washington's appointing general officers of the Continental Army, Rush used arguments from Roman history to make his case for exclusive Congressional authority. On this occasion, one is tempted to speculate, his thoughts may have gone back to his youthful letter to Mrs. Catharine Macaulay on the evils of military officers interfering in civil affairs. Here, too, Rush could have turned to Burgh's *Political Disquisitions* for similar arguments, especially in that he and other patriots had just helped bring out an American edition of the Whig classic. In his many and diverse activities as a delegate to Congress, Rush strove, above all, for unity of decision and action. [12]

On December 12, 1776, Congress, in the face of Howe's impending capture of Philadelphia, adjourned to meet twelve days later in Baltimore. Rush, who had previously made plans to serve with General John Cadwalader's Philadelphia militia, set his private affairs in order and moved quickly to join the general's forces. "Mr. Howe," Rush had earlier in the month confided to John Dickinson, "cannot mean to winter in Philadelphia, unless he is invited here by the slender opposition General Washington now makes against him. A body of 10,000 militia will certainly terrify him into winter quarters. The safety of the continent depends upon the

part Pennsylvania will take upon this occasion." [13] In Rush's view, there was no doubt that a competently led "army of six-months men" would be "an army of heroes," a militia of Cincinnati drawn from the farms of republican America. [14] They were the only hope of the new nation.

The heroic conduct of General Cadwalader's Pennsylvania militia, which thrust into New Jersey after Washington's surprise crossing of the Delaware, strengthened Rush's faith in the effectiveness of citizen-soldiers. And he lost no time in writing from Bordentown of the Pennsylvanians' valor to his confidant and fellow member of Congress, Richard Henry Lee. [15]

With the Philadelphia militia near Trenton, in the midst of a cannonade, Rush saw General Washington ride by in "all the terrible aspect of war." [16] The British fire was accurate enough that bleak afternoon to cause many American casualties. Rush's humanity was shocked and outraged by the violence of war. Trembling, he helped the wounded as best he could and then, with the other surgeons, "lay down on some straw in the same room with our wounded patients. It was now for the first time war appeared to me in its awful plentitude of horrors," Rush remembered in his *Autobiography*. "I want words to describe the anguish of my soul, excited by the cries and groans and convulsions of the men who lay by my side." [17] There were more horrors to come; several days later he was to witness at Princeton "the field of battle still red in many places with human blood." [18] These and other scenes of misery were to give Rush a new cause to champion, for beginning in April, 1777, as surgeon and physician general of the Middle Department (Continental Army) he was to spare neither time nor reputation in trying to improve the inefficient medical service. [19]

Rush was not reelected to Congress by the Pennsylvania Assembly. This, Rush believed, was due to his hostility to the Pennsylvania Constitution of 1776, which he attacked, notably, in his *Observations upon the Present Government of Pennsylvania*. The Constitution provided for a unicameral legislature, whose power was so great as to destroy the independence of the executive and judicial functions of government. [20] This, Rush argued in the true manner of a Commonwealthman, was a gross violation of the simple and historically tested principles of republican government.

---

tyranny and corruption and recognized no authority but that of nature and the will of the people.

[10] Worthington C. Ford, ed., *Journals of the Continental Congress, 1774–1789* (Washington, D.C., 1904–) **6**: p. 1081.

[11] *Ibid.*

[12] Goodman, pp. 60–61; Burgh, *Political Disquisitions* **3**: Bk. i, p. 17; **2**: Bk. iii, pp. 361–389.

[13] December 1, 1776, *Rush Letters* **1**: p. 119; *Autobiography*, pp. 123–125.

[14] Rush to John Adams, October 1, 1777, *Rush Letters* **1**: p. 157.

[15] January 6, 1776 [i.e., 1777], *ibid.*, p. 124.

[16] *Autobiography*, p. 127.

[17] *Ibid.*, p. 128.

[18] *Ibid.*

[19] Rush to Mrs. Rush, April 14, 1777, *Rush Letters* **1**: p. 139.

[20] *Observations upon the Present Government of Pennsylvania. In Four Letters to the People of Pennsylvania* (Philadelphia, 1777), p. 5; Rush to David Ramsay, [March or April 1788], *Rush Letters* **1**: p. 455.

Anyone who read Harrington, Locke, Sidney, Montesquieu, and the other great political writers should know "the extreme folly and danger of a people's being governed by a single legislature," [21] as was the case in Pennsylvania.

Americans, in fact, did not have to rely upon Old World authorities for this political knowledge. Their own fellow citizen, John Adams of Massachusetts, "who is second to no man in America, in an inflexible attachment to the liberties of this country, and to republican forms of government," had made this observation with great force in his excellent *Thoughts on Government* (1776).[22] That Rush himself had learned from Adams was made clear years later. When the odious Pennsylvania Constitution was finally altered and improved in 1790, largely through Rush's efforts, the elated political reformer generously acknowledged Adams's influence in his work. He wrote the vice-president of the United States:

From you I learned to discover the danger of the Constitution of Pennsylvania, and if I have had any merit or guilt in keeping the public mind awake to its folly or danger for 13 years, you alone should have the credit of the former and be made responsible for the latter.[23]

It was an honest testimony from one friend to another.

Rush's brief career as surgeon and physician general was marked by a similar outspokenness, this time against the way the military hospitals were being mismanaged. Dedicated physicians like himself were doing all they could to help the wounded and the sick, but the inefficient and corrupt medical system was killing off more men than they could save. It was a veritable slaughter, and Rush tried desperately to stop it in plea after plea to Congress. On January 30, 1778, frustrated at every turn, he resigned in protest.[24]

The matter, however, was not closed as far as Rush was concerned. In a letter to General Washington, he openly accused Director-General William Shippen, Jr., his former superior in the Continental Army hospitals, of corruption. "What satisfaction," he asked, "can be made to the United States? What consolation can be offered to the friends of those unfortunate men who have perished—or rather who have been murdered in our hospitals—for the injustice and injuries that have been done to them? One half the soldiers who have been thus sacrificed might have proved hereafter the price of a victory that might have established the liberties of America. While our brave countrymen were languishing and dying from the total want or scanty allowance of hospital stores, I am sorry to add that the Director General was employed in a manner wholly unbecoming the dignity of his office and the liberality of his profession in selling large quantities of madeira wine, brown and loaf sugar, &c., &c., which had been transported through the country in hospital wagons and secured as hospital stores under the name of private property.[25]

By this time the Continental medical service itself had been reformed to some extent, at least on paper, by a special committee of Congress. Rush was so pleased with the expected improvements in the hospitals that he deplored his having had to resign from the army. He did not give up his efforts to see Director-General Shippen punished for corruption, efforts which ultimately failed when Shippen was acquitted by a military court in 1780.[26]

Eighteen days before Rush resigned his commission he had posted an unsigned letter to Patrick Henry, then governor of Virginia. In it he urged the absolute necessity of competent generalship to recast the demoralized Continentals into an effective army; and firmly, but tactfully, passed unfavorable judgment on Washington's generalship. As one of Governor Henry's "Philadelphia friends," Rush asserted:

The northern army has shown us what Americans are capable of doing with a general at their head. The spirit of the southern army is no ways inferior to the spirit of the northern. A Gates, a Lee, or a Conway would in a few weeks render them an irresistible body of men.[27]

Men who fought for their republican liberties, he held with Hampden, Burgh, and all true Whigs, needed only competent leaders to make them victorious. And Rush was making the point again to a trusted friend and champion of American liberty.

It is significant that Horatio Gates, the hero of Saratoga, is given priority in the three names Rush lists in the above quotation. Rush, whose own high standards demanded at least competence in others, was much impressed by Gates's military ability. In an earlier letter to John Adams, four days after the American

[21] Rush, *Observations upon the Present Government of Pennsylvania,* pp. 5–6. "Montesquieu (whose writings are oracular in all free countries)," Rush, *Considerations Upon the Present Test-Law of Pennsylvania: Addressed to the Legislature and Freemen of the State* (Philadelphia, 1784), p. 7. See Rush's "Catalogue of Books," Rush MSS, under political titles.

[22] Rush, *Observations upon the Present Government of Pennsylvania,* p. 5. Rush and Adams were later to become very close friends. On meeting Rush in 1775 Adams had noted in his diary: "Dr. Rush came in. He is an elegant, ingenious Body. Sprightly, pretty fellow. He is a Republican. He has been much in London. Acquainted with Sawbridge, McCaulay, Burgh, and others of that Stamp. Dilly [Edward or Charles, London publishers] sends him Books and Pamphletts, and Sawbridge and McCaulay correspond with him." Adams's early judgment of Rush as "too much of a Talker to be a deep Thinker. Elegant not great," was one that he would later revise, Butterfield, ed., *Diary and Autobiography of John Adams* 2: p. 182.

[23] February 12, 1790, *Rush Letters* 1: p. 530; *Autobiography,* pp. 141–142; Robert L. Brunhouse, *The Counter-Revolution in Pennsylvania, 1776–1790* (Harrisburg, Penna., 1942), pp. 225–227.

[24] *Autobiography,* pp. 131–138. See, e.g., Rush to William Duer, December 13, 1777, and to Patrick Henry, January 12, 1778, *Rush Letters* 1: pp. 175–176, 182–183.

[25] February 25, 1778, *ibid.* 1: pp. 202–203.

[26] Goodman, pp. 103–104; Rush to Daniel Roberdeau, March 9, 1778, *Rush Letters* 1: p. 207.

[27] Rush to Patrick Henry, January 12, 1778, *ibid.,* p. 183.

triumph at Saratoga, he had written of Gates's generalship and compared him with Washington:

I have heard several officers who have served under General Gates compare his army to a well-regulated family. The same gentlemen have compared General Washington's imitation of an army to an unformed mob. Look at the characters of both! The one on the pinnacle of military glory, exulting in the success of schemes planned with wisdom and executed with vigor and bravery, and above all see a country saved by their exertions. See the other outgeneraled and twice beated, obliged to witness the march of a body of men only half their number through 140 miles of a thick-settled country, forced to give up a city the capital of a state, and after all outwitted by the same army in a retreat.[28]

Clearly, Rush went on, there should be an investigation. "If our Congress can witness these things with composure and suffer them to pass without an inquiry, I shall think we have not shook off monarchical prejudices and that like the Israelites of old we worship the work of our hands." [29]

General Charles Lee, like Gates a sincere republican in Rush's judgment, appears as a second choice probably because of Rush's opinion of Lee as a competent general but having a fondness for "negotiations and conferences" with the enemy.[30] However, despite his unfavorable opinion of Lee's character, Rush recommended him for his military talents. General Thomas Conway, whom it is doubtful Rush ever met, was praised by Rush in 1777 as having "Lee's knowledge and experience without any of his oddities or vices . . . . the idol of the whole army." [31] In Rush's highly critical view, all three men could lead a desperate America to victory, but only Horatio Gates was a true Whig and "Old Englishman" and possessed Rush's unqualified respect as a man and as a military commander.[32]

That Gates had indeed saved his country by defeating Burgoyne at Saratoga seemed gloriously confirmed to Rush when he learned that France, anxious to prevent Anglo-American reconciliation, had agreed to enter into an alliance with the United States. "Yes," Rush wrote Gates on September 5, 1781, the very day De Grasse's fleet was engaging the British off Yorktown, "while the French alliance is dear to Americans, and a French fleet upon our coast is formidable to Englishmen, your name cannot be forgotten." [33] The words were strikingly appropriate, for the success of the French naval operation begun that day was to lead to

Cornwallis's and Britain's final defeat. Later, as "Leonidas," writing in *The Pennsylvania Journal*, Rush would use the lesson of Yorktown to argue for a powerful American navy.[34]

As the War neared its end, Rush philosophically observed that an even deeper crisis was facing republican America, a crisis of national character. American arms, with French help, were triumphant; but victories in war did not make a nation. Nor did patriotic resentments against the British enemy create a new people, although they did serve, Rush believed, to prevent a counter-revolutionary restoration of English habits and manners. Rush confessed these anxieties in April, 1782, to General Nathanael Greene, his friend and commander of American forces in the south:

. . . I wish Britain for 50 years to come may continue in all her acts of government to call us "rebels" and "deluded subjects." We stand in need of all the follies and vices of our enemies to give us a national character. It is a melancholy truth that most of our virtues have sprung from those impure sources. The patriotism of too many is founded only in resentment. A true republican cherishes no passion but a love for liberty. He draws his sword without malice, and binds up the wounds he inflicts with it. The very blood he sheds is an acceptable offering in the temple of benevolence.[35]

Union of the American states would not by itself produce true republicanism and a distinct national character. But, certain it was, without "perpetual Union" there could be no "future peace, safety, and freedom." [36] America must have permanent and strong governments, Rush was convinced, and so he worked over the next eight years to reform and perfect—in a word, to republicanize—national and state constitutions. But, as he did this, Rush was not distracted from his larger revolutionary purpose of preparing "the principles, morals, and manners of our citizens, for these forms of government, after they are established and brought to perfection." [37]

Rush objected to the single legislature of the Confederation government for the same reason that he found the Pennsylvania government unacceptable. The supreme power of a legislature by whatever name, Congress or Assembly, was in principle as tyrannical to Rush as monarchy itself. Moreover, as he also argued under various pseudonyms in *The Pennsylvania Journal*, the Confederation was intolerably weak. It possessed neither the exclusive power to emit money

[28] October 21, 1777, *ibid.*, pp. 159–160.

[29] *Ibid.*, p. 160.

[30] Goodman, pp. 61–62.

[31] Rush to John Adams, October 13, 1777, *Rush Letters* 1: p. 158.

[32] Rush to Anthony Wayne, June 18, 1777, *ibid.*, p. 150. "General Gates' success has rescued this country in a degree from its idolatry to *one* man. I told him a few days ago that if I thought he *alone* was able to save this country, I should vote for his being banished. 'Yes,' said he with a spirit truly republican, 'you would do better to vote to have my throat cut,'" Rush to John Adams, January 22, 1778, *ibid.*, p. 191.

[33] *Ibid.*, p. 264.

[34] July 4, 1782, *ibid.*, pp. 273–277. *Cf.* Burgh, *Political Disquisitions* 2: Bk. iii, 389–425.

[35] April 15, 1782, *Rush Letters* 1: pp. 268–269. "I hope the war will last until it introduces among us the same temperance in pleasure, the same modesty in dress, the same justice in business, and the same veneration for the name of the Deity which distinguished our ancestors," Rush to John Adams, August 8, 1777, *ibid.*, p. 152.

[36] Rush to Nathanael Greene, April 15, 1782, *ibid.*, p. 268.

[37] Rush, "An Address to the People of the United States. . . . On the Defects of the Confederation," *American Museum* 1, 1 (January, 1787): p. 8.

nor to regulate commerce, both indispensable functions of a soverign government. Like the Pennsylvania Constitution of 1776 and other state constitutions, the Articles of Confederation were conceived more in early Revolutionary anti-monarchism than in mature republicanism. Rush put it this way in his "Address to the People of the United States," a stirring appeal to his countrymen for a more perfect republican government:

We had just emerged from a corrupted monarchy. Although we understood perfectly the principles of liberty, yet most of us were ignorant of the forms and combinations of power in republics. Add to this, the British army was in the heart of our country, spreading desolation wherever it went: our resentments, of course, were awakened. We detested the British name, and unfortunately refused to copy some things in the administration of justice and power, in the British government, which have made it the admiration and envy of the world. In our opposition to monarchy, we forgot that the temple of tyranny has two doors. We bolted one of them by proper restraints; but we left the other open, by neglecting to guard against the effects of our own ignorance and licentiousness.[38]

The second door to tyranny, that of legislative omnipotence, must be closed forever by new federal and state constitutions requiring the separation and balance of powers.

Once again, Rush found many of his Whig political views confirmed in his friend John Adams's writings. The *Defence of the Constitutions of Government of the United States,* which Adams began publishing in London in 1787, was read with such enthusiasm by Rush that spring that he promptly arranged for the first American edition to be printed in Philadelphia. The Federal Convention was about to meet in his city, Rush knew, and what better spokesman was there for the republican doctrines of the separation and balance of powers than John Adams, who was writing his classic *Defence,* ironically, at the Court of St. James itself. By June, Rush was well pleased with his having reprinted the first volume of Adams's study. "Mr. Adams' book," Rush wrote Dr. Richard Price, his English nonconformist friend and intimate of Adams at the time, "has diffused such excellent principles among us that there is little doubt of our adopting a vigorous and compounded federal legislature. Our illustrious minister in this gift to his country has done us more service than if he had obtained alliances for us with all the nations in Europe."[39] There was as much truth as hope in this report, for as Rush penned these lines Edmund Randolph's "Virginia Plan," calling for a bicameral federal legislature, was being debated at the Convention. And Adams's *Defence* was a political text for many of the speakers.[40]

Rush was happy with the prospect of the new national government whose Constitution was finally adopted by the Convention on September 17, 1787; and, at the request of John Dickinson, he published articles and delivered speeches in favor of ratification. The men who opposed the new Federal Constitution in Pennsylvania, Rush observed, were the very ones who defended the state government which he was trying to reform. The two issues were bound up together. Here, then, was a perfect opportunity to serve both his state and nation by helping to found a republican national government as a model for Pennsylvania. Indeed, here was the critical and supreme test of the American Revolution, for the new freedom that had been won for man in America could last only if permanent republican political institutions safeguarded it. "I had resolved and repeatedly declared that I would close my political labors with the establishment of a safe and efficient general government," Rush remembered. "I considered this as an act of consistency, for to assist in making a people free, without furnishing them the means of preserving their freedom, would have been doing them more harm than good, and would have justly exposed me to their reproaches."[41] In the final weeks of September and in October, Rush campaigned hard for the Constitution, confident that his efforts and the efforts of other partisans would lead to ratification by all the states within a year or, at most, eighteen months. This must be the case, he implied to the same English friend and correspondent of long-standing, because the Constitution possessed "all the theoretical and practical advantages of the British Constitution without any of its defects or corruptions."[42] It was the model government that all true Whigs had been seeking over the centuries of English political experience. By November, 1787, Rush, now a member of the Philadelphia delegation to the state ratifying convention, was in an excellent position to convince others of the need to accept the new republican government. He spoke often and eloquently and with effect. His last speech on ratification, delivered on December 12, the same day the vote was taken, represented the proposed Constitution as nothing less than divine in character, and argued—in the words of a reporter—"that he as much believed the hand of God was employed in this work, as that God had divided the Red Sea to give a passage to the children of Israel."[43] When the votes were counted that day, Rush's beloved Pennsylvania became the second state to ratify the Constitution.

The new government, Rush conceded, was not perfect in every way. Yet it fulfilled his every wish of happi-

[38] *Ibid.; Rush Letters* 1: p. 277, n. 1; *Autobiography,* p. 160.

[39] June 2, 1787, *Rush Letters* 1: p. 418; Rush to John Adams, May 19, 1812; 2: p. 1135. See Rush's "Caralogue of Books," Rush MSS, where Adams's *Defence* is listed first among Rush's political books.

[40] Gilbert Chinard, *Honest John Adams* (Boston, 1964), p. 212.

[41] *Autobiography,* p. 161.

[42] Rush to John Coakley Lettsom, September 28, 1787, *Rush Letters* 1: p. 444. Lettsom (1744–1815), the Quaker physician, was a friend of both Rush and Dubourg, Aldridge, "Jacques Barbeu Dubourg," *Proc. Amer. Philos. Soc.* 95 (1951): pp. 340–341.

[43] Quoted in Goodman, p. 80.

ness for his country. Wisely, the framers had not tried in the Constitution to regulate the natural rights of the people, rights which were, after all, theirs alone. In the new Republic of the United States, moreover, the systems of representation and checks and balances would protect the rights of citizens in the very operations of government. This should be clear to every Common-wealthman, Rush maintained. By demanding a bill of rights the antifederalists were, in reality, showing that they continued to think in old, pre-revolutionary political terms—not in the terms of the world's first true republic. "Men who call for a bill of rights," Rush sadly noted, "have not recovered from the habits they acquired under the monarchical government of Great Britain." [44] Somehow they had missed the grand significance of the American political Revolution. As we shall see later, Rush's philosophy of republican education was designed to make sure that future Americans would not revert to old political habits of mind.

Even as he was succeeding in republicanizing American national and state governments, Rush was articulating a revolutionary vision of a new civilization of "good Christians and true whigs," which would be history's counterpart of the new political order. [45] This was to be the Christian republic, a unique organization of humanity, divinely prepared over the centuries especially for the New World and its new people. "All truths are related," Rush explained to Jeremy Belknap,

or rather there is but one truth. Republicanism is a part of the truth of Christianity. It derives power from its true source. It teaches us to view our rulers in their true light. It abolishes the false glare which surrounds kingly government, and tends to promote the true happiness of all its members as well as of the whole world, for peace with everybody is the true interest of all republics. [46]

The deepest, unitary truth revealed to mankind by America's revolutionary experience, then, was the truth of Christian love and peace. "True whigs like true Christians always love one another," Rush insisted. [47] God himself had foreordained that at this particular time in history man would discover the unifying truth of His benevolence, of His universal love, and this profoundest truth would lead to all other truths on all subjects. What Rush and other historical and religious thinkers were witnessing was nothing less than the advent of the world's first Christian Republic with its own world view and culture. So Rush believed, as we shall now try to show.

PART TWO

THE ADVENT OF THE CHRISTIAN REPUBLIC

V. CHRIST, HISTORY, AND THE AMERICAN REVOLUTION

Republican forms of government are the best repositories of the Gospel: I therefore suppose they are intended as preludes to a glorious manifestation of its power and influence upon the hearts of men.—to Elhanan Winchester, November 12, 1791 [1]

Like many other Americans not far removed from their native forebears, Benjamin Rush searched his ancestral past for historic origins and continuities. At first his inquiry was mainly genealogical, arising, he said, from "a natural solicitude in man to be acquainted with the history of his ancestors." [2] The quest for antecedents, natural enough in itself, was more personally intense in the case of Rush because of the early loss of his father and the remarriage of his mother.

Rush's special part in the founding of the Republic also enhanced both his and, potentially, the new nation's interest in the Rush family. In this way, then, Rush first applied himself to the study of history. [3]

What began for Rush as a genealogical project, almost a diversion, expanded with time and thought into a philosophy of history. This was so because the Philadelphian was no ordinary middle-class doctor, interested only in tracing his descent back a few generations. He was, instead, a republican philosopher who had employed Whig and universal history, not antiquarian facts, in a great act of historical courage and belief in affixing his signature to the Declaration of Independence. History thus became for Rush what it was for Jefferson and other eighteenth-century American and European philosophic historians—"philosophy teaching by examples." [4] It would be positively wrong,

[44] Rush to David Ramsay, [March or April 1788], *Rush Letters* 1: pp. 453, 455.

[45] Rush to John Adams, October 21, 1777, *ibid.*, p. 161.

[46] June 6, 1791, *ibid.*, p. 584.

[47] Rush to James Searle, January 21, 1778, *ibid.*, p. 189.

[1] November 12, 1791, *Rush Letters* 1: p. 611.

[2] *Autobiography*, pp. 23, 167.

[3] Rush to Thomas Jefferson, October 6, 1800, *Rush Letters* 2: pp. 825–826; *Autobiography*, pp. 23–28. The eminent psychiatrist, Carl Binger, viewed Rush's early loss of his father as the determining event in his psychology and life, *Revolutionary Doctor: Benjamin Rush (1746–1813)* (New York, 1966), p. 20, *et passim*.

[4] Colbourn, *The Lamp of Experience*, p. 5; R. N. Stromberg, "History in the Eighteenth Century," *Jour. History of Ideas* 12, 2 (April 1951): pp. 302–303; Daniel J. Boorstin, *The Lost World of Thomas Jefferson* (Boston, 1960), p. 218; James W.

however, to ascribe to Rush any collateral *philosophe* rejection of divine agency in history. Ultimately, the nontheological conception of history was as inscrutable to him as to his Great Awakening teachers, Gilbert Tennent, Samuel Finley, and Samuel Davies, as inscrutable as atheism itself or cosmic evil.[5]

Rush's first hero of history was undoubtedly Oliver Cromwell, whose name was especially dear to the posterity of John and Susanna Rush. John Rush, the founder of the line in America, had fought under Cromwell during the English Civil War and was reportedly known well enough by the great soldier to merit his praise. Benjamin Rush, his fifth generation descendant, was proudly aware of his illustrious ancestor's service in the Roundhead cause and treasured with great family piety every souvenir of his forefather's life. In his early twenties, Rush listened to the military exploits of his forebear as described by an aged grandson who had lived with the soldier; and even the militant pacifism of Rush's later years failed to discredit the boyish values he had attached to Captain Rush's English sword. The reason for this abiding heroic celebration of the military virtue of the first American Rush by his scion was clear enough: Captain Rush had wielded his English sword in defense of liberty. More, he had fought alongside the great Oliver Cromwell, whose reputation as a just and good colonial administrator was hailed by patriot spokesmen everywhere in the colonies.[6]

While an apprentice in Philadelphia during the Stamp Act crisis, Rush invoked "good old *Oliver's* spirit" in resisting tyranny.[7] At Edinburgh, as we have already seen, he was drawn in friendship to John Bostock mainly because of the latter's kinship with a Roundhead officer. But then Rush discovered in Bostock's knowledge of the English past—a knowledge

which struck Rush with such force that he emphasized it years later in his memoirs—that Cromwell was perhaps not exclusively important after all; that more consequential than the Ironsides soldier was the republican thinker, Algernon Sidney.[8] Family tradition, as it were, gave way to the study of Whig history and ideology as his approach to the past, and Rush joined the Revolution Club of Edinburgh. The noble political sentiments of Hampden and Sidney, faultless martyrs to the Whig cause, better suited the now intellectually stirring young American. It was a time for new heroes, figures to speak directly to the times. Rush found them in history, in what James Burgh called "that inexhaustible mine."[9] He found his heroes in the Whig tradition from Sidney to Catharine Macaulay.

Rush, at this time, first recognized the nature of history to be more than religious apologetic or simple chronicle. He had read the classics at Nottingham and Princeton to be sure, but it is doubtful that he had studied the ancient historians in any systematic way. History and chronology had been added to the curriculum at Princeton only after Rush's graduation. Moreover, his education and reading before going overseas had been severely restricted by religious and professional circumstances, depriving him of an opportunity for liberal reading. Even if he had had the chance to read widely in secular and lay fields, there is some doubt whether he would have done so. Finley, Davies, Tennent, and Redman were all deeply religious men of the Great Awakening with whom eternal Scripture and Christian truth had come before temporal history and political ideology, and young Rush had been their disciple in the "Schools of the Prophets."[10]

Thompson, *A History of Historical Writing* (2 v., New York, 1942) 2: pp. 94–95; Joseph Priestley, "An Essay on a Course of Liberal Education for Civil and Active Life," Brown, ed., *Joseph Priestley; Selections from His Writings*, p. 84; Rush to John Adams, March 2, 1809, *Rush Letters* 2: p. 996; Rush, "A Plan for Establishing Public Schools in Pennsylvania, and for Conducting Education Agreeably to a Republican Form of Government," *Rush Essays*, p. 4. The phrase "philosophy teaching by examples" is from Bolingbroke's *Letters on the Study and Use of History* (1752), which, as we have seen, Barbeu Dubourg translated into French. For Puritanism as a source of this didactic understanding of history, see Perry Miller and Thomas H. Johnson, eds., *The Puritans; A Sourcebook of Their Writings* (2v., rev. ed., New York, 1963) 1: ch. i, pp. 81–179, esp. p. 84.

[5] Rush, "An Inquiry into the Causes of Premature Deaths," *Rush Essays*, pp. 310–316; Heimert, *Religion and the American Mind*, p. 74. Cf. Sidney, *Discourses Concerning Government*, 11, ch. ii, p. 120, *et passim*.

[6] Rush to John Adams, July 13, 1812, *Rush Letters* 2: p. 1151; *Autobiography*, pp. 23–24; Rush, "A Plan of a Peace Office for the United States," *Rush Essays*, pp. 183–184; John C. Miller, *Origins of the American Revolution* (Boston, 1943), p. 30.

[7] Rush to Ebenezer Hazard, November 8, 1765, *Rush Letters* 1: p. 18.

[8] *Autobiography*, p. 46. Eventually, Rush came to adopt Sidney's harsh judgment on Cromwell as an enemy of "the good old cause," e.g., Rush to "John Dunlap, with a Speech Which Ought to Be Spoken *to* Congress on the Subject of Inflation," July 3, 1779, and to Thomas Jefferson, October 6, 1800, *Rush Letters* 1: p. 235; 2: p. 825. Mrs. Macaulay and James Burgh also condemned Cromwell as—in the words of Burgh—"the mock-patron of Liberty," Colbourn, *The Lamp of Experience*, pp. 44–45.

[9] *Political Disquisitions*, preface, 1: p. vi. See Caroline Robbins, "Algernon Sidney's *Discourses Concerning Government*: Textbook of Revolution," *Wm. and Mary Quart.* 3d ser., 4, 3 (1947): p. 280, and her discussion of Sidney's influence upon Burgh in *The Eighteenth Century Commonwealthman*, p. 367.

[10] Like Finley and Davies, Redman was a graduate of William Tennent's "Log College," Whitfield J. Bell, Jr., "John Redman, Medical Preceptor, 1722–1808," *Penna. Mag. Hist. Biog.* 81, 2 (April, 1957): p. 157. On Redman's piety, see his letters to Rush, April 4, 1767, and May 12, 1768, Rush MSS, XXII: pp. 10–11, in which he warns his former apprentice to be on guard against the temptations of worldliness. On the addition of history and chronology to the program at the College of New Jersey, see Francis L. Broderick, "Pulpit, Physics, and Politics: The Curriculum of the College of New Jersey, 1746–1794," *Wm. and Mary Quart.*, 3d ser., 6, 1 (1949): p. 54. In his attack upon the merely "natural" knowledge of the Pharisees, Gilbert Tennent was one with Jonathan Edwards and other evangelists, *The Danger of an Unconverted Ministry*, Heimert and Miller, eds., *The Great Awakening*, pp. 73–74.

Although the Library Company of Philadelphia had boasted a copy of Sidney's *Discourses Concerning Government* among its earliest volumes, as well as other books on secular history and politics, Rush first learned of Sidney's antimonarchical views from a native Englishman, John Bostock. Reading Sidney, that master of the political uses of history, Rush discovered that the facts of the past established the political truths of the present and future, and that historians like Tacitus demonstrated the origin of government in liberty. The great lesson of history, Rush learned, was that—in Sidney's words—

We know no laws but our own statutes, and those immemorial customs established by the consent of the nation; which may be, and often are changed by us. The legislative power therefore, that is exercised by the parliament, cannot be conferred by the writ of summons, but must be essentially and radically in the people, from whom their delegates and representatives have all that they have.[11]

This experience not only introduced Rush to classical Whig historiography but helped him become aware of the Enlightenment's concern with interpreting the past in secular terms. Bostock and Sidney thus furthered Rush's discovery of the new, nontheological historical science of the seventeenth and eighteenth centuries, which Scottish thinkers like Adam Ferguson were popularizing in their writings. It was to be relatively easy for Rush to proceed, as it were, from a Whig conception of the English past to an Enlightenment conception of universal history as "philosophy teaching by examples" without, however, accepting the full implications of this rationalism.

At the same time that Rush discovered Sidney and the Whig tradition, he met, ironically, the nemesis of the Whig historians, David Hume. "The Tacitus of Scotland," as Edward Gibbon saluted him, had in 1761 completed his monumental six-volume *History of England from the Invasion of Julius Caesar to the Revolution of 1688* (1754–1761), which attacked Whig ver-

sions of the British past.[12] Hume was a friend and admirer of Dr. Benjamin Franklin, as was Sir Alexander Dick, who afforded Rush the chance to meet the literary scourge of the Whigs. The philosophic historian whom Rush dined with at Sir Alexander's that November evening in 1766 was Scotland's leading Enlightenment figure. Like his European counterparts—especially Voltaire—Hume was iconoclastic and anticlerical. In his historiography, he had shattered the Whig idol, Paul de Rapin, whose *Histoire d' Angleterre* (1724) was the official text of English Whiggism.[13] Similarly in philosophy, he had detracted from the power of the orthodox clergy by denying their arguments for the historicity of Biblical miracles. As if all this were not enough to disqualify him in the judgment of the evangelical and Whiggish American youth, Hume admitted himself to be a Deist, or so Rush thought he did.[14]

Hume at fifty-five was the most famous historian in the English-speaking world, and from his birthplace, Edinburgh, his fame radiated to all parts of enlightened Europe. In his native Scotland, where Calvinism held sway, he represented a powerful force on the side of religious moderation and tolerance. Because the clerical opponents of the Scottish Enlightenment were largely Whigs, it has been argued, Hume chose his special kind of "Toryism."[15] In his choice of friends, Hume favored moderates like William Robertson, Hugh Blair, and John Home, all of whom enjoyed like himself some measure of Lord Bute's patronage.[16] Young Rush, an

---

[11] *Discourses Concerning Government,* **44**: ch. iii, p. 496. Sidney emphasized the origin of liberty among the Germans, as described in Tacitus's *Germania,* and treated England and other "Gothic" countries as political descendants of those free people, *ibid.,* **5**: ch. ii, pp. 80–85; **28**: iii, pp. 420–433; **26**: ch. ii, p. 409. There are many references to Tacitus, especially to his *Germania,* in Rush's writings (e.g., Rush, "An Inquiry into the Natural History of Medicine Among the Indians of North America," *Med. Inq. & Obs.* (5th ed.) **1**, pp. 61–62, 89; Rush, *An Address to the Inhabitants of the British Settlements in America, upon Slave-Keeping,* pp. 11–12n). The Roman historian was Rush's favorite among the ancients, as he was Jefferson's, Staughton, *Eulogium,* p. 14; Rush, "Catalogue of Books"; Colbourn, *The Lamp of Experience,* p. 26. Young Rush, as a student at the College of New Jersey, did not read the library's copy of the *Discourses,* listed in its catalogue of January 29, 1760, *ibid.,* pp. 202–203. On the Library Company's copy, see *ibid.,* p. 206, and Louis B. Wright, *The Cultural Life of the American Colonies, 1607–1763* (New York, 1962), p. 148.

[12] Hugh Trevor-Roper, "David Hume as a Historian," *The Listener* **66**, 1709 (December 28, 1961): pp. 1103–1104, 1119; Thompson, *A History of Historical Writing* **2**: pp. 69–72; Colbourn, *The Lamp of Experience,* pp. 28–29, 41–43, 177–180; Robbins, *The Eighteenth Century Commonwealthman,* pp. 217–218.

[13] Trevor-Roper, "David Hume as a Historian," *The Listener* **66**, 1709 (December 28, 1961): p. 1103; Colbourn, *The Lamp of Experience,* pp. 36, 177–180. Rush possessed the English translation of Rapin's history, as his "Catalogue of Books" for 1790 shows. For a discussion of the place of history in Augustan thought, see Herbert Davis, "The Augustan Conception of History" in J. A. Mazzeo, ed., *Reason and the Imagination; Studies in the History of Ideas, 1600–1800* (New York, 1962), pp. 213–229. On Hume's friendship with Dr. Franklin, see Van Doren, *Benjamin Franklin,* pp. 290, 391.

[14] "Scottish Journal," November 29, 1766, p. 23; Hume, "Of Miracles," *An Enquiry Concerning Human Understanding* (1748) in Edwin A. Burtt, ed., *The English Philosophers from Bacon to Mill* (New York, 1939), pp. 652–667. McCosh argued that Hume was neither a Deist nor an atheist; however, his intense prejudices against Hume must be kept firmly in mind, James McCosh, *The Scottish Philosophy, Biography, Expository, Critical from Hutcheson to Hamilton* (New York, 1875), pp. 155–156.

[15] Trevor-Roper, "David Hume as a Historian," *The Listener* **66**, 1709 (December 28, 1961): p. 1104; John T. McNeill, *The History and Character of Calvinism* (2d ed., New York, 1957), pp. 396, 358.

[16] Thomas H. Huxley, *David Hume,* Vol. **5** of John Morley, ed., *English Men of Letters* (New York, n.d.), p. 34; Mossner, *The Life of David Hume,* pp. 274–278.

evangelical Whig, found Hume unsavory on all of these counts.

William Robertson, who with Hume and Edward Gibbon personified Enlightenment historiography in Britain, also incurred Rush's intense disfavor for much the same reason as his more famous colleague and friend. His faults, however, were more grievous—even sacrilegious from a Great Awakening point of view—by dint of his wearing the cloth of the Church of Scotland. It was true that Robertson was more friendly to religion than was Hume, but fundamentally both men were impious to Rush. Also inexcusable in the two Scottish historians, the American radical was bound to conclude, was the conservative nature of their treatments of the past. Hume, as Caroline Robbins has pointed out, accepted the Revolution of 1688 without defending it, a position which Rush as a Whig could not tolerate.[17] Rush in Edinburgh, and afterwards in London and Paris, was looking for liberal political thinkers and historical writings favorable to republicanism and colonial rights. He did not find what he was looking for in the historical sophistications of Hume, nor in the apparent indifference of Robertson. His developing Whig ideology required more positive historical thinkers and studies. Yet he did succumb to Hume's style, while resisting his substance; for as John Adams observed many years later, Hume's pernicious history triumphed over all rivals by virtue of its style rather than its truth.[18] And Rush eventually admitted the books of both Hume and Robertson into his library, where he used them subject, of course, to his own historical ideas.[19]

William Cullen, Rush's mentor at Edinburgh, did not write history, although, as we have seen, he planned to write a biography of Sydenham. Cullen did, however, share with the philosophic historians a didactic purpose in examining the past in terms of its deficiencies. Thus, Hippocrates, Galen, and other ancient medical authorities were reduced by him to what he considered their proper status, which of course from the pinnacle of eighteenth-century achievement was not very high.[20] Towards, say Hippocrates, Cullen felt much the same way as did Robertson towards Ignatius Loyola: his-

torically superior.[21] In religion Cullen was skeptical of revealed authority; and in the candor of his position, he not only acknowledged himself a free-thinker of the Scottish Enlightenment, but indicated the wide degree of academic freedom within the University of Edinburgh. The most striking index of his Enlightenment thought was his utopian belief in historical medical and general scientific progress and perfection. Hume and Robertson offered no clear programs for the future, no certainties of progress calculated to appeal to the buoyant optimism of an American youth of twenty. Cullen did. In his understanding of history, at least with respect to the perfectibility of medicine, Cullen helped significantly to introduce Rush to the eighteenth-century theory of progress, thereby serving as liaison between the British and the French Enlightenments. Rush's republicanism and Cullen's progressivism made for a revolutionary combination.

While in London, Rush mixed with Whigs and libertarians who decried the government's violations of the Constitution. He met and lauded John Wilkes for his vindication of the peoples' rights against a tyrannical ministry. "All Mr. Wilkes' friends are friends to America;" Rush wrote of the London Commonwealthmen; "some of them talk of seeking a shelter from arbitrary power in the peaceful deserts of America." [22] This Wilkes was a man who was so dominated by history—the Whig kind—as to fall to his knees transfixed at the spot where William of Orange had first landed in England.[23] Rush, likewise, felt compelled by the same history to search out the place in the House of Commons where Pitt had called for repeal of the Stamp Act. Rush compared Wilkes to Hampden and Sidney in the highest kind of Whig tribute, for Wilkes like the earlier Whig heroes was a symbol of defiance to arbitrary government.

Whig historical thinking was best represented, however, not in the political activism of the reprobate Wilkes but in the writings of the churchwoman Catharine Macaulay. This remarkable woman, like Rapin and Oldmixon before her, labored to preserve the Whig interpretation of English history from Tory criticism.[24] This Whig interpretation, which Rush enthusiastically accepted, held that the Glorious Revolution had climaxed the victory of good over evil, and that even before the overthrow of James II, the Whigs alone had defended the ancient English Constitution against its Tory enemies. Indeed, Rush as an elected member of Edinburgh's Revolution Club was deeply committed to

[17] The Eighteenth Century Commonwealthman, p. 8; Wallace K. Ferguson, The Renaissance in Historical Thought; Five Centuries of Interpretation (Cambridge, Mass., 1948), pp. 98–99; J. B. Bury, The Idea of Progress; An Inquiry into Its Origin and Growth (New York, 1955), ch. xii, esp. pp. 217–218; Colbourn, The Lamp of Experience, p. 78.

[18] John Adams to Thomas Jefferson, December 16, 1816, Lester J. Cappon, ed., The Adams-Jefferson Letters; The Complete Correspondence Between Thomas Jefferson and Abigail and John Adams (2v., Chapel Hill, 1959) 2: pp. 502–503.

[19] Rush, "Catalogue of Books."

[20] Rush, "An Eulogium in Honor of Cullen," Rush Essays, p. 323. Young Rush observed in his "Scottish Journal" that Cullen was "well acquainted with History-Politics-Belles-Lettres-& Languages," September 1767, p. 58.

[21] William Cullen, "Introductory to the Practice of Physic," in Thomson, William Cullen 2: pp. 72–74. On the place of Loyola in Robertson's thought, see Thompson, A History of Historical Writing 2: p. 73.

[22] Rush to ?, January 26, 1769, Rush Letters 1: p. 74.

[23] John Carswell, The Old Cause; Three Biographical Studies in Whiggism (London, 1954), pp. 5–6.

[24] John Oldmixon (1673–1742) wrote a continuous Whig history of England, Carswell, The Old Cause, p. 202.

this view of the English past.[25] Hume, as we have seen, had attacked such a rigidly dualistic version of English history; and two years after his last volume appeared, Catharine Macaulay published the first of eight volumes designed to refute him. Mrs. Macaulay was really trying to do what another and greater Macaulay, Thomas Babington, would ultimately accomplish, and what lesser Whig historians, like Charles James Fox and Sir James Mackintosh, would soon essay.[26]

As good Whigs should, Mrs. Macaulay and her friends and admirers talked of government, virtue, and constitutions. James Burgh, John Sawbridge, and Adam Ferguson all possessed a decided Whig interpretation of the past; and when Rush met them Ferguson was already at work on his *History of the Progress and Termination of the Roman Republic* (1783) which he was writing to exemplify his republican doctrine and ethical system.[27] Burgh, who believed in the perfection of man and society, as did Ferguson, had earlier written a political utopia reminiscent of Sir Thomas More's and a theodicy equally characteristic of the optimism of the century. Intensely republican in his thinking, Burgh was an outspoken friend of the Americans as was John Sawbridge, Catharine Macaulay's brother. Burgh's *Political Disquisitions,* when it was published in an American edition in 1775, had a quick success among delegates to the Continental Congress; while Sawbridge and his sister were sculptured in wax and painted by admiring Americans.[28] Later, Rush and Sawbridge corresponded about developments in the colonies, with the latter insisting—as all members of the Macaulay circle did—that "Great Britain and her Colonies are entitled alike to a free constitution and that an inability to enjoy property is the characteristic of Slavery." [29]

"There are no means so effectual for communicating the most useful instructions to the minds of men, as making observations upon the facts recorded in history," James Burgh was to write in his *Political Disquisitions,* which—like Sidney's *Discourses*—may be called a "textbook" of the American Revolution.[30] It was for Rush, as for others, a textbook of facts and revolutionary Commonwealth principles. Rush agreed with Burgh that in England "men of power have pursued one uniform track of taxing and corrupting the people, and increasing court-influence in parliament . . . while the constitution was drawing nearer to its ruin, and our country lay bleeding." [31] And he reasoned with Burgh as he did with Sidney that all true patriots must unite in "restoring the Constitution, and Saving the State," even if it meant another bloody civil war.[32] This was what Burgh had concluded from his elaborate study of classical, Whig, and other historical and political writers, including ancients like Tacitus, Plato, and Aristotle, and moderns as various as the Duke of Sully, Harrington, Locke, Sidney, Montesquieu, St. Pierre, Blackstone, and Beccaria. Burgh's three-volume work, when it appeared in 1775, was more than a political treatise. It expressed the general philosophy of Commonwealthmen on history, politics, education, and social reform; and it was this ideology, so ably presented in Burgh's work, that formed—along with other philosophical and theological ideas—Rush's understanding of the American Revolution.[33]

In the 1760's, when Rush made the acquaintance of the London Whigs, Catharine Macaulay and not James Burgh was their leading historical writer. It was she whose *History of England* was praised by Chatham and Horace Walpole before the House of Commons, and who exchanged letters with James Otis, John Adams, and George Washington.[34] And it was she whom Dr. Franklin compared, hyperbolically, to Livy. The comparison was doubtless flattering to her, since she loved the Greek and Roman republics dearly. "From my early youth," Mrs. Macaulay had written in her Introduction to the *History of England,* "I have read with delight those histories which exhibit Liberty in

---

[25] On the Whig interpretation and its historical development, see Herbert Butterfield, *The Englishman and His History* (Cambridge, Eng., 1944); Colbourn, *The Lamp of Experience,* pp. 6–9; Robbins, *The Eighteenth Century Commonwealthman,* pp. 3–21; Bailyn, *The Ideological Origins of the American Revolution,* pp. 33–54.

[26] Trevor-Roper, "David Hume as a Historian," *The Listener* **66**, 1709 (December 28, 1961): p. 1119.

[27] Stephen, *History of English Thought in the Eighteenth Century* **2**: pp. 182–183; Oscar and Mary F. Handlin, "James Burgh and American Revolutionary Theory," *Proc. Mass. Hist. Soc.* **73** (1961): pp. 38–57. Ferguson's earlier work *Essay on the History of Civil Society* (1767) had set forth his belief in social progress, Arthur A. Ekirch, *The Idea of Progress in America, 1815–1860* (New York, 1951), pp. 16–17; Robbins, *The Eighteenth Century Commonwealthman,* pp. 199–202.

[28] *Ibid.,* pp. 363–368; Arthur O. Lovejoy, *The Great Chain of Being; A Study of the History of An Idea* (New York, 1960), ch. vii, esp. p. 208; see Leslie Stephen in *DNB, s.v.* "Burgh, James," and Charles Welch in *ibid., s.v.* "Sawbridge, John"; Donnelly, "The Celebrated Mrs. Macaulay," *Wm. and Mary Quart.,* 3d ser., **6** (1949): pp. 176, 178; Colbourn, "John Dickinson, Historical Revolutionary," *Penna. Mag. Hist. Biog.* **83**, 3 (July, 1959): p. 285, n. 52.

[29] John Sawbridge to Rush, September 19, 1774, Rush MSS, XLIII: p. 18; Lyman H. Butterfield, ed., *Diary and Autobiography of John Adams* **2**: p. 182.

[30] Preface, p. vi.

[31] *Ibid.,* p. v.

[32] *Ibid.,* title page.

[33] Robbins, *The Eighteenth Century Commonwealthman,* pp. 367–368, 9–10.

[34] Donnelly, "The Celebrated Mrs. Macaulay," *Wm. and Mary Quart.,* 3d ser., **6** (1949): pp. 174–175. Mrs. Macaulay's *History of England* has been described as "an imaginative work in praise of republican principles under the title of a History of England," Ian R. Christie, *Wilkes, Wyvill and Reform* (London, 1962), p. 17, cited by Bailyn, *The Ideological Origins of the American Revolution,* pp. 41–42, n. 25.

its most exalted state, the annals of the Roman and the Greek republics." [35] But the great men of her *History* were the English Whigs of the seventeenth century, men like Sidney, Milton, Locke, and, above all, Hampden.[36] In view of this, it is not difficult to understand the reverence young Rush had for Hampden, and why he believed to the end of his life, as he wrote Jefferson in 1800, that "The Republics of America are the fruits of the precious truths that were disseminated in the speeches and publications of the republican patriots in the British Parliament one hundred and sixty years ago." [37] Nor is Rush's antipathy to Thomas Hobbes and Sir Robert Filmer—the political opponents of Locke, Sidney, and Mrs. Macaulay—hard to understand. Most assuredly, too, the life-long enthusiasm Rush felt for the ancient republics had at least one very important source in the Macaulay circle, with its classical sympathies.

On his visit to France, Rush had occasion to attack a foreign king and divine right theory as well with all the vehemence that a dedicated republican could muster. Sidney's *Discourses Concerning Government,* from which Rush and other American Whigs got their anti-monarchical arguments, was highly valued in France; and the martyred Whig's bust was found in literary coteries in a place of honor next to those of Brutus, Voltaire, and Franklin.[38] Dr. Jacques Barbeu Dubourg, the elder Mirabeau, and the other French liberals whom Rush met abroad were all libertarians of the "natural rights" school and close to the Whig position. They all shared, to some extent, the great Montesquieu's admiration for the free Constitution of England. Barbeu Dubourg even planned to edit Montesquieu's *De l'esprit des lois,* and he kept Rush informed about the progress of his work.[39] And certainly these Physiocrats with their *laissez-faire* attack upon mercantilism discovered an eager and approving listener in the young American, who was still faithfully angry about parliamentary interference with colonial trade.

From about 1773 to 1789, the period in which Rush acted out his role as a political revolutionary, his Whig philosophy of history and government, drawn from seventeenth-century classical republicanism and eighteenth-century Commonwealth philosophy sustained

him as it did other patriots like Adams and Jefferson.[40] This is amply proved by the signatures of all three on the Declaration of Independence. Another proximate source of Rush's historical ideas, although less consciously so than the Whig tradition, was his understanding of French Enlightenment philosophy which he seems to have acquired largely from his friendship and correspondence with Jacques Barbeu Dubourg, who as a *philosophe* saw in Rush the fulfillment of the Enlightenment's hopes for man. Even though Rush visited France only long enough to sense the revolution in ideas which preceded the collapse of the *ancien régime,* certain French themes which bulked large in Barbeu Dubourg's *Petit code de la raison humaine* and other Enlightenment writings afterwards pervaded his thinking.[41] These themes did not include Deism or anti-Christian secularism, which fact must absolutely disqualify Rush from the company of *philosophes* like Barbeu Dubourg, Voltaire, Diderot, Rousseau, and even Jefferson.[42] Ultimately, we must remember, Rush's philosophy of life and history was Christocentric, as was all of his thought.

The theory of progress was a major Enlightenment contribution to Rush's thought, although, again, its more general origins were theological. His belief in progress, which he knew to come historically from Bacon and Locke and which justified his every effort at forming and reforming American society, was associated more with French thinkers like Helvétius, Turgot, Condorcet, and Barbeu Dubourg than with English thinkers in the eighteenth century. The *philosophes* urged social progress by governmental action, claiming that society was indefinitely changeable into more perfect forms by enlightened legislative programs. Their British counterparts, educated in a more "negative" understanding of government following Locke and, to a lesser extent, Sidney and emphasizing the protection of order, life, and property—political liberties won in the seventeenth century—were commonly disposed to

[35] 1: p. v.

[36] Donnelly, "The Celebrated Mrs. Macaulay, *Wm. and Mary Quart.* 3d ser., 6 (1949): unnumbered insert and p. 203; Macaulay, *History of England* 3: pp. 425–432.

[37] October 6, 1800, *Rush Letters* 2: p. 825.

[38] See Crane Brinton's article on Sidney in Edwin A. Seligman and Alvin Johnson, eds., *Encyclopaedia of the Social Sciences* (15 v., New York, 1930) 14: p. 49.

[39] Aldridge, "Jacques Barbeu Dubourg, A French Disciple of Benjamin Franklin," *Proc. Amer. Philos. Soc.* 95 (1951): p. 347.

[40] Thomas Jefferson to John Adams, November 25, 1816, Cappon, ed., *The Adams-Jefferson Letters* 2: p. 498; John Adams to Thomas Jefferson, December 16, 1816, *ibid.,* pp. 502–503; Colbourn, *The Lamp of Experience, passim;* Robbins, *The Eighteenth Century Commonwealthman,* pp. 18–19, 84.

[41] For a discussion of Barbeu Dubourg's leading ideas, see Aldridge, "Jacques Barbeu Dubourg," *Proc. Amer. Philos. Soc.* 95 (1951): pp. 361–392. It should be emphasized, however, that, while Rush and Barbeu Dubourg shared a great many ideas about reforming society, the American evangelist rejected the underlying *philosophe* assumption that nature or the physical order determines the moral order.

[42] On this point, see R. C. Collingwood, *The Idea of History* (New York, 1956), p. 76. Ultimately, Rush's philosophy of history was closer to that of Joseph Priestley, Richard Price, and—above all—David Hartley, whose Christian progressivism was, paradoxically, both teleological and reformist. But, intriguing as they are, these are connections which must be developed elsewhere. See R. V. Sampson, *Progress in the Age of Reason, The Seventeenth Century to the Present Day* (Cambridge, Mass., 1956), p. 41, *et passim,* for this seeming paradox in the thought of Hartley and Priestley.

preserve the institutions that already existed.[43] This was well marked in Locke's reservations on the use of revolution, while Sidney was less typical because of his radical acceptance of revolution.[44] Most conservative was David Hume, whose zest for radical reform was nil; and whose skepticism made belief in historical causal relation doubtful, let alone belief in historical progress.[45] Jeremy Bentham's major work on morals and legislation was to come later (1789) and significantly alter the course of English social thought.

It was, moreover, a Frenchman who bequeathed to the eighteenth century, and especially to his native country, a theory of progress. Fontenelle's belief in the progress of knowledge, although foreshadowed by Bacon, Descartes, and Bodin, was uniquely his by virtue of his conception of such progress as not only past and present but future as well; and more, such progress in the future was conceived by him as certain.[46] Rush found this idea of great use in his historical thinking and attributed it, along with other liberal ideas, to Fontenelle.[47] This theory of the progress of knowledge, which Fontenelle justified on the basis of the new Cartesian science, was later expanded into a general doctrine of progress by Barbeu Dubourg and other enlightened thinkers of the Age of Reason, attaining in 1795 its classic expression in Condorcet's *L'Esquisse d'un tableau historique des progrès de l'esprit humain.* Hence, the theory of the progress of knowledge led directly to the theory of social progress, and even more

optimistically, to the dogma of the perfectibility of man.[48]

Friend and correspondent of Jefferson and Franklin, Condorcet provided men of the American Enlightenment with a doctrine of progress which celebrated the American Revolution as the apocalypse in world history revealing the joyous nearness of the heavenly city. Beyond the seas in America, whence came Franklin—Condorcet's and Barbeu Dubourg's "apostle of philosophy and tolerance"—French revolutionaries envisioned a new society in which there would be no limit to the perfectibility of human nature. Had they been more traditionally religious, they might have agreed with Lopez de Gomara, that only the creation and the birth of Jesus outranked in importance the discovery of America.[49] At any rate, their heterodox religious opinions notwithstanding, French revolutionaries like Condorcet possessed a boundless enthusiasm for America.

For Rush, as for Condorcet, Montesquieu, Helvétius, and the other *philosophes,* the theory of progress by government was axiomatic. Like Helvétius, in particular, whose *De l'esprit* (1758) Rush valued in his private library along with the sensationalistic works of Locke and David Hartley, Rush viewed "morals and legislation," in Helvétius's words, "as one and the same science."[50] Unlike them, however, and to his immense profit, Rush early in his life participated in the first great western revolution, in America, which provided him with the real conditions necessary to reform. What was to Barbeu Dubourg and Condorcet mere vicarious

[43] Bury, *The Idea of Progress,* pp. 217–218. For an elaboration of this difference between French and British thought, see Bury, *ibid.,* ch. xii, pp. 217–237. Yet the Englishman, William Godwin, must not be overlooked, believing as he did with his more influential French contemporary, Condorcet, that human life could be indefinitely prolonged. For a comparison of Godwin's and Condorcet's ideas on prolongevity—a possibility in which Rush was greatly interested too—and an excellent discussion of the general conception and its relation to the idea of progress in the Enlightenment, see Gerald J. Gruman, "A History of Ideas About the Prolongation of Life: The Evolution of Prolongevity Hypotheses to 1800," *Trans. Amer. Philos. Soc.* **56,** 9 (December, 1966): pp. 74–90. Macklin Thomas, in a doctoral thesis of 1938, recognized in a comparative essay evidence of the idea of progress in Rush's writings. Unfortunately, however, the study was based on very limited Rush sources, "The Idea of Progress in the Writings of Franklin, Freneau, Barlow, and Rush" (unpublished Ph.D. dissertation, University of Wisconsin, 1938), pp. 228–262.

[44] Robbins, "Algernon Sidney," *Wm. and Mary Quart.,* 3d ser. **4,** 3 (1947): pp. 281–295.

[45] Collingwood, *The Idea of History,* p. 81; Colbourn, *The Lamp of Experience,* pp. 179–180; Ernst Cassirer, *The Philosophy of the Enlightenment,* trans. by Fritz C. A. Koelln and James P. Pettegrove (Boston, 1955), pp. 226–228, and ch. v, pp. 197–233.

[46] Bury, *The Idea of Progress,* p. 109; Kingsley Martin, *The Rise of French Liberal Thought; A Study of Political Ideas from Bayle to Condorcet* (2d ed., New York, J. P. Mayer, 1954), pp. 44–47; John H. Randall, Jr. *The Making of the Modern Mind; A Survey of the Intellectual Background of the Present Age* (rev. ed., Boston, 1940), p. 382.

[47] *Autobiography,* p. 226; Rush, "Catalogue of Books."

[48] Bury, *The Idea of Progress,* pp. 209, 214, 98, 104–105, 111–112; Charles Frankel, "The Philosophy of the Enlightenment," in Vergilius Ferm, ed., *A History of Philosophical Systems* (New York, 1950), p. 273; J. Salwyn Schapiro, *Condorcet and the Rise of Liberalism* (New York, 1963), ch. xiii, pp. 234–270. See Condorcet's *Progrès de l'esprit,* trans. by June Barraclough with an Introduction by Stuart Hampshire (New York, 1955). For a valuable discussion of Cartesian method, see J. Bronowski and Bruce Mazlish, *The Western Intellectual Tradition; from Leonardo to Hegel,* (New York, 1962), ch. xii, pp. 216–229.

[49] "History and Historiography," *Encyclopaedia of the Social Sciences* **7**: pp. 374–375; Thomas Jefferson to Marquis de Condorcet, August 30, 1791, Philip S. Foner, ed., *Basic Writings of Thomas Jefferson* (New York, 1944), pp. 601–602; Dumas Malone, *Jefferson and His Time* **2**: *Jefferson and the Rights of Man* (Boston, 1951), p. 15; Aldridge, *Franklin and His French Contemporaries* (New York, 1957), p. 14; Van Doren, *Benjamin Franklin,* p. 479; Carl L. Becker, *The Heavenly City of the Eighteenth-Century Philosophers* (New Haven, 1963), *passim;* Schapiro, *Condorcet and the Rise of Liberalism,* ch. xii, pp. 215–233. Of general importance for this discussion is R. R. Palmer, *The Age of the Democratic Revolution: A Political History of Europe and America, 1760–1800* (Princeton, 1959–). See John Adams's notes on Condorcet's *Progrès de l'esprit* in Zoltán Haraszti, *John Adams & the Prophets of Progress: A Study in the Intellectual and Political History of the Eighteenth Century* (New York, 1964), ch. xii, pp. 235–258.

[50] Quoted in Sampson, *Progress in the Age of Reason,* p. 56; Rush, "Catalogue of Books."

experience before 1789—the year in which France followed America—was to Rush a personal and dangerous adventure. The republicanism of Sidney and Macaulay among others, at first only a youthful and theoretical enthusiasm for Rush, acquired practical meanings after the thirty-year-old physician and others declared America independent. Then, the Whig philosophy of history and government merged imperceptibly with the French theory of legislative perfection of man and society. Rush's positive conception of government as the molder of men through education and other institutions was—as we shall see—a key principle of his social thought; and fundamentally all of his thought was social, i.e., concerned with the objective relation between man and man, and between man and God.

Recent as well as ancient historical examples were used by Rush to demonstrate the truth of progress and to vindicate this belief against the cynical and pessimistic attacks of the faithless. Had not the timorous once, and not long ago, denied as "visionary" the proposed independence of the colonies? Yet he himself had signed the liberating document. Had not grave realists labeled utopian the abolition of Negro slavery in Pennsylvania? Yet this too had been accomplished by him and others. And what about the United States itself, had not this been called fanciful only to become a living reality within fresh memory? "The seeds of the American Revolution," Rush wrote to his congenial friend, James Madison, another deep student of history,

were sown in the reign of Charles the first. The seeds of the Reformation were sown in England in the reign of Henry IVth. The seeds of the present humane and enlightened policy upon the subject of the slavery of the Negroes were sown in Pennsylvania near 20 years ago. Many other instances of a distant and improbable connection between the first proposition and the accomplishment of events might be mentioned.[51]

---

[51] February 27, 1790, *Rush Letters* 1: p. 541. "Truths resemble trees—some ripen in a short time, while others require half a century or more to bring them to perfection. But the seeds of the latter must be planted, as well as of the former, by *somebody*. To plant a forest tree, says Dr. Johnson, is the most *disinterested* act of benevolence a man can perform, for it is impossible for him to live long enough afterwards to enjoy any benefit from his labor. To sow the seed of a truth or of a revolution in favor of human happiness that requires many years to ripen it, is equally a mark of disinterested benevolence. The seeds of truth differ from the seeds of plants in one particular. None of them are *ever lost*. Like matter, they are indestructible in their very nature. They produce fruit in other ages or countries," *ibid.,* pp. 540–541; Rush, "On the Amusements and Punishments Proper for Schools," *Rush Essays,* p. 72; Rush, "On Imposture in Medicine," Rush MSS, call number Yi2/7400/F5, pp. 41–43. Rush found many of his historical examples and similes from ancient times in Charles Rollin's popular *Roman History* (1738–1748) and Oliver Goldsmith's compilation of the same title (1770), both of which he owned, "Catalogue of Books." His favorite historian, Tacitus, became a perfect Whig apologist in Thomas Gordon's translation (1728), Colbourn, *The Lamp of Experience,* p. 60; *Autobiography,* pp. 333–334; Rush, *An Address to the Inhabitants of the British Settlements in America, upon Slave-Keeping,* pp. 11–12.

These facts, Rush argued, gave the lie to the spiritless majority of men who counselled despair, the futilitarians who saw the future as black as the past. Aware of the Industrial Revolution—heralded by philosophers like Joseph Black and William Cullen—whose outlines he had discerned abroad, Rush sensed a greater revolution in human affairs. With a Baconian determination, he urged his students and himself to exhaustive investigations into nature in order to smooth the progress of moral, political, and scientific truth and happiness. "All the doors and windows of the temple of nature," he said, "have been thrown open, by the convulsions of the late American revolution. This is the time, therefore, to press upon her altars."[52] Thus, in Rush's new revolutionary man, French and English traditions interfused, even to the extent of supplying Deistic metaphor.

Any hint of Deistic rationalism in Rush's doctrine of progress must be simply rhetorical, however, in that he consistently refused to accept the then fashionable view of the omnipotence of reason in all things. Reason, to be sure, was as precious to him as it was to Barbeu Dubourg and other enlightened progressive thinkers of the eighteenth century; but it was not exclusive. Unaided reason was not enough, neither in religion nor in the perfection of man in the earthly city. Rush believed with Pascal, whose *Pensées* he owned and cherished, that "the heart has its reasons, which reason does not know."[53] History, too, was clear on this point.[54] William Godwin, Thomas Paine, and the others notwithstanding, Rush found reason stripped of revelation insufficient for progress and reform. Reason without the motives of religion was "like the clay-formed image of our first parent, before his Creator infused into him the breath of life."[55] Reason and revelation, as David Hartley, the Newton of Christian philosophy had demonstrated, were divine benefactions to man and complemented each other in the progress of human understanding and happiness. To think of one without the other was patently wrong, since the two had been joined by God in the original constitution of

---

[52] Rush, "Observations upon the Duties of a Physician," *Med. Inq. & Obs.* (5th ed.) 1: p. 264; Rush, "On the Application of Metaphysicks to Medicine," Rush MSS, call number Yi2/7400/F2, pp. 11–12. Cf. Rev. Timothy Dwight's remarks on this and the general idea of the rising glory of America in "The Friend. No. **5**," *American Museum* 6 (August, 1789): p. 156. "I have indeed," he wrote, "with no small pleasure, viewed the American revolution, as a new era of improvement in all things natural and moral." Like others, though, Dwight never elaborated this kind of insight into a systematic philosophy of the American Revolution, as did Rush.

[53] Rush, "Catalogue of Books."

[54] Rush, "On the Application of Metaphysicks to Medicine," Rush MSS, call number Yi2/7400/F2, pp. 19–21: Rush, "Three Lectures upon Animal Life," *Med. Inq. & Obs.* (5th ed.) 1: p. 37.

[55] Rush, "On the Causes of Death, In Diseases That Are Not Incurable," *Sixteen Introductory Lectures,* p. 87.

things.[56] "The natural man," Rush read in Sidney's *Discourses Concerning Government,* "is in a perpetual enmity against God, without any possibility of being reconciled to him, unless by the destruction of the old man, and the regenerating or renewing him through the spirit of grace." [57] And all three Protestant thinkers, Rush, Hartley, and Sidney, of course found this "spirit of grace" only in the Gospel.

While philosophic historians of the Age of Reason found revealed religion everywhere opposed to progress in man's decline from the enlightened antiquity of Greece and Rome—and zealously attempted to destroy superstition and the infamies of priestcraft—Rush just as sincerely believed that history demonstrated reason and Christianity to be themselves progressive and that, accordingly, the operations of both were not only complementary but necessary to effect real and lasting progress.

Of the "happy revolution in favour of justice and humanity" which men called the Enlightenment, Rush observed:

It may either be ascribed to the light of the gospel shining in 'darkness, which comprehended it not'—or to the influence of sound and cultivated reason—for reason and religion have the same objects. They are in no one instance opposed to each other. On the contrary, reason is nothing but imperfect religion, and religion is nothing but perfect reason. It becomes christians," [Rush explained his own synthesis of Enlightenment reason and Great Awakening religion,] "to beware how far they condemn the popular virtue of humanity, because it is recommended by deists, or by persons who do not profess to be bound by the strict obligations of christianity.—Voltaire first taught the princes of Europe the duty of religious toleration. The duke of Sully has demonstrated the extreme folly of war, and has proved that when it has been conducted with the most glory, it never added an atom to national happiness. The marquis of Beccaria has established a connexion between the abolition of capital punishments, and the order and happiness of society.

So sure was he of the good done by the humanitarianism of Barbeu Dubourg and the other *philosophes* as agents—if ignorant ones—in God's drama of salvation, that he concluded: "Should any thing be found in the scriptures, contrary to these discoveries, it is easy to foresee that the principles of the deists and the laws of modern legislators will soon have a *just* preference to the principles and precepts of the gospel." [58]

History showed that philosophy and religion had advanced together in the past, edging mankind towards that climax of the ages, that union of the Augustinian Cities, which Rush held to be not distantly removed from his own century. "The light of the Gospel" had "risen gradually on the world." [59] Perfection of all things by the successive disclosures of God's benevolence—this was the ultimate term of progress.[60] Any other position, such as the one taken by the militant Deists, especially Voltaire, was forced to admit the Manichaean dualism of autonomous good and evil, which in Rush's view made real progress impossible. Rush knew that to be valid a theodicy must deny reality to evil, a concession which the Deists were incapable of making because of their conspiratorial enthusiasms.[61]

God acting in history, Rush believed, had wrought the eighteenth century—the age of enlightened inquiry into truth—after centuries of pernicious ignorance. No longer were men to be "deterred in their researches after truth, by the terror of odious or unpopular names." [62] The eighteenth century marked a watershed in the progress of knowledge to perfection, a condition in which truth and common sense, i.e., majority opinion, would be united.[63] Progress was God's design worked out by secondary causes like Newton's law of gravity and, even more directly, Hartley's law of the association of ideas, and made clear by the operations of reason. In Hartley's *Observations on Man* (1749), which Rush hailed as the world's first synthesis of "physiology, metaphysics, and Christianity," the English physicotheologian had shown how the law of the association of ideas led inevitably to perfection and ultimate happiness. The final cause of this natural mechanism of

56 Rush, "Influence of Physical Causes upon the Moral Faculty," *Med. Inq. & Obs.* (5th ed.) 1: pp. 123–124; Rush, "An Enquiry into the Consistency of Oaths with Reason and Christianity," *Rush Essays,* pp. 126–127; Rush, "Outlines of the Phenomena of Fever," *Med. Inq. & Obs.* (3d ed. rev. & enlarged, Philadelphia, 1809) 3: pp. 30–31; Rush, "On the Application of Metaphysicks to Medicine," Rush MSS, call number Yi2/7400/F2, pp. 26–35. Basil Willey's discussion of Hartley's physico-theological progressivism seems to apply equally as well to Rush, his American disciple, and led to many of the same paradoxical complications, complications which the present writer thinks Rush resolved to his own satisfaction in his final years. See Willey, *The Eighteenth Century Background: Studies on the Idea of Nature in the Thought of the Period* (Boston, 1961), ch. viii, pp. 136–154.
57 8: ch. ii, p. 100. *Cf.* David Hartley's *Prayers and Religious Meditations* (2d American ed., Cambridge, Mass., 1829), pp. 53–56, and his *Observations on Man, passim.*
58 Rush, *Considerations on the Injustice and Impolicy of Punishing Murder by Death* (Philadelphia, 1792), pp. 12–13.
59 *Autobiography,* p. 226.
60 Rush, "An Eulogium, Intended to Perpetuate the Memory of David Rittenhouse," *Rush Essays,* p. 351; Rush, "An Eulogium in Honor of Cullen," *ibid.,* pp. 333–334; Rush, "On Imposture in Medicine," Rush MSS, call number Yi2/7400/F5, pp. 24–26.
61 For Rush's theodicy, see especially "On the Origin of Evil of Every Kind," Rush MSS, call number Yi2/7399/F36, "Old & Copied Lectures on Pathology," *ibid.,* call number Yi2/7396/F3, pp. 603–605, and "An Inquiry into the Causes of Premature Deaths," *Rush Essays,* pp. 310–316.
62 Rush, "Influence of Physical Causes upon the Moral Faculty," *Med. Inq. & Obs.* (5th ed.) 1: p. 115.
63 Rush, "Thoughts on Common Sense," *Rush Essays,* pp. 250–253; Rush, "On the Influence of Physical Causes upon the Intellectual Faculties," *Sixteen Introductory Lectures,* pp. 114–119. Here he says that he agrees with Condorcet that someday "all the knowledge we now possess will appear to the generations that are to succeed us, as the knowledge now possessed by children appears to us" (p. 114).

progress to perfection, as of all the mechanisms of nature, Rush agreed, was the will of an all-benevolent God.[64]

Nowhere was divine progress more certain than in the historic materialization of republican government in America. "Republican forms of government are the best repositories of the Gospel," Rush observed to Rev. Elhanan Winchester. "I therefore suppose they are intended as preludes to a glorious manifestation of its power and influence upon the hearts of men."[65] By the Gospel, Rush meant the New Testament promise of divine forgiveness; and it was his belief that republican government had been foreordained by Providence in order to establish not only the worldly happiness of all men in liberty, but the heavenly bliss of all men ultimately through the universal love of Jesus.[66] "I am and have been several years before the memorable 1776 a republican in principle," Rush explained to Jeremy Belknap, another friend and clergyman who shared many of his ideas,

not only because I conceive republican governments are most conformable to reason but to revelation likewise. The pride of monarchy and the servility of that state which it induces in all its subjects are alike contrary to the humility and dignity of the Christian character. It is the Spirit of the Gospel (though unacknowledged) which is now rooting monarchy out of the world. Truth in this case is springing up from that earth which helped the woman. . . . How

truly worthy of a God who styles himself Love is that religion which is opposed to everything which disturbs or violates the order and happiness of society, whether that society consists in the relation of individuals or of nations to each other.

Rush went on to describe his vision of a Christian utopia and his and Belknap's duty as workers in a kind of Great Awakening "Party of Christ" to make ready for the Saviour's millennial rule.

Yes, my friend, I anticipate with a joy which I cannot describe the speedy end of the misery of the Africans, of the tyranny of kings, of the pride of ecclesiastical institutions, whether founded in the absurd ideas of apostolic succession or in the aristocracy of Presbyterianism. Connected with the same events, I anticipate the end of war and such a superlative tenderness for human life as will exterminate capital punishments from all our systems of legislation. In the meanwhile let us not be idle with such prospects before our eyes. Heaven works by instruments, and even supernatural prophecies are fulfilled by natural means. It is possible we may not live to witness the approaching regeneration of our world, but the more active we are in bringing it about, the more fitted we shall be for that world where justice and benevolence eternally prevail.[67]

Republican governments were the natural means now being employed by God in His scheme to redeem fallen man and his world. In the one great Christian Republic of the United States, the "Spirit of the Gospel" was fulfilling prophecies according to the divine plan, and the beginnings of the Millennium could already be seen.

As it were, republicanism was counterpointed to Christianity, and this progressive relationship could be traced down the ages from the beginnings of man recorded in the Old Testament to the near perfection of republicanism and Christianity in Rush's own climactic day. John the Baptist, St. Paul, Hippocrates, Brutus, Locke, Sidney, and Mrs. Macaulay—all were in some way anticipatory of the union of republicanism and Christianity.[68] That consummation of republican government and Christian religion, Rush held, had begun with the American Revolution; and from the new center of world history in America, republicanism and Christianity would radiate someday to the ends of the earth. "At present," he wrote Rev. Elhanan Winchester, "we wish 'liberty to the whole world.' But the next touch of the celestial magnet upon the human heart

[64] Rush to Thomas Jefferson, January 2, 1811, *Rush Letters* 2: p. 1075; Hartley, *Observations on Man, His Frame, His Duty, and His Expectations* (London, 1749) 1, prop. 88: pp. 366–367, *et passim.* "I believe in a general and particular providence," Rush wrote in 1796, "having long been a disciple of Dr. Hartley. *All will end well,*" Rush to James Currie, July 26, 1796, *Rush Letters* 2: p. 780. To John Adams in 1807 Rush described Hartley as "a man whose discoveries in physiological, metaphysical, and theological science mark an era in the achievements of the human mind—I mean the great and good, I had almost said the inspired, Dr. Hartley," *ibid.,* p. 953. On progress as God's design worked out by secondary causes, see Rush, "Lectures on Pathology. On the Influence of Different Religions on the Health of the Body," Rush MSS, call number Yi2/7396/F23, pp. 318–319, Rush, "On Imposture in Medicine," *ibid.,* call number Yi2/7400/F5, p. 2, and the discussion below.

[65] November 12, 1791, *Rush Letters* 1: p. 611; Rush, "Lectures on Pathology. On the Influence of Different Religions on the Health of the Body," Rush MSS, call number Yi2/7396/F23, pp. 317–318; Rush, "An Enquiry into the Consistency of the Punishment of Murder by Death, with Reason and Revelation," *Rush Essays,* pp. 180–181. *Cf.* the sermon, *The Divine Goodness Displayed, in the American Revolution* (New York, 1784), pp. 30, 12–13, *et passim,* by the New Light preacher, Rev. John Rogers. Elhanan Winchester's *Thirteen Hymns, Suited to the Present TIMES: Containing; The Past, Present, and Future State of AMERICA: with Advice to Soldiers and Christians* (2d ed., Baltimore, 1776), pp. 12–13, indicates his own republicanism, as do his letters to Rush, e.g., March 13, 1793, Rush MSS, XXII: pp. 97–98, and July 26, 1793, *ibid.,* p. 98.

[66] Rush, *Considerations upon the Present Test-Law of Pennsylvania* (Philadelphia, 1784), pp. 19–21; Rush, "Lectures on Pathology. Influence of Government upon Health," Rush MSS, call number Yi2/7396/F22, pp. 312–314.

[67] June 21, 1792, *Rush Letters* 1, p. 620.

[68] Rush to Elhanan Winchester, November 12, 1791, *ibid.,* pp. 611–612; Rush to Jeremy Belknap, June 6, 1791, *ibid.,* pp. 583–584; Rush to Thomas Jefferson, August 22, 1800, *ibid.* 2: pp. 820–821; Rush, "A Defence of the Use of the Bible as a School Book," *Rush Essays,* pp. 112–113; Rush, "On the Application of Metaphysicks to Medicine," Rush MSS, call number Yi2/7400/F2, pp. 26–35; Rush, "Of the Mode of Education Proper in a Republic," *Rush Essays,* pp. 8–9. Heimert, *Religion and the American Mind,* p. 545.

will direct it into wishes for the *salvation of all mankind.*" [69]

It was in the "Schools of the Prophets" that Rush had been taught to look for the signs of the world-renewing "Spirit of the Gospel" that he found everywhere in the American Revolution. Gilbert Tennent, Samuel Finley, and Samuel Davies were all premillennialists, i.e., believers in Christ's Advent before the Millennium, and Rush followed them on this point. They saw the Great Awakening of their own day as the coming of the Messianic Kingdom, the most convincing of all signs that the "Spirit of the Gospel" was regenerating the world. In the early '70's, Rush was confident that he was observing the workings of the Gospel in a worldwide movement against slavery and the slave trade. This could be seen particularly in the ministry of saintly Anthony Benezet of Philadelphia through whom God was "bringing about some great revolution in behalf of our oppressed Negro brethren." [70] Rush himself contributed to this revolution against Negro slavery in his *Address to the Inhabitants of the British Settlements in America, upon Slave-Keeping* (1773)—dedicated to Anthony Benezet—and he co-operated with the "Spirit of the Gospel" to redeem the world in other ways, most notably by taking a leading part in the American Revolution which he interpreted not just as a revolution against political slavery but, like the Great Awakening, as a crisis and opportunity, albeit the final one, to reconstruct the world on Christian principles in readiness for the Millennium. America was to be the historic scene of "the triumphs of the Gospel" as well as "the triumphs of liberty." [71] "America has taught the nations of Europe by her example to be free," Rush addressed the clergy of the United States,

and it is to be hoped she will soon teach them to govern themselves. Let her advance one step further—and teach mankind that it is possible for Christians of different denominations to love each other and to unite in the advancement of their common interests. By the gradual operation of such natural means, the kingdoms of this world are probably to become the kingdoms of the Prince of Righteousness and Peace. [72]

Citing Hartley's *Observations on Man* as the source of his ideas, Rush wrote in 1794:

I believe in the rapid approach of a new order of things, from the coincidence of present events with the prophecies of the old and new testaments. These prophecies are now accomplishing by natural means. Events essential to each other, have lately taken place as if by concert in different nations and truths essential to those events, have been discovered, or revived in different parts of the world.

In parentheses he noted that

in former ages the discovery of the art of printing, was connected with the revival of letters, and the change in the moral and religious state of Europe. Thus—too, the application of the loadstone to the purpose of navigation immediately preceded the discovery and settlement of America.

Modern medicine, Rush went on, alluding to his own American system, made possible the conquest of plague by natural, rather than supernatural, means. "Thus" he quoted from Hartley "as the apostles had the power of healing miraculously, future missionaries may in a short time accomplish [natural cures] themselves with the knowledge of all the chief practical rules of medicine." The plague, the scourge of "Asiatic countries" and until now the "one natural obstacle" to the spread of Christianity, was "no longer an incurable disorder." "What Dr. Hartley predicted with respect to diseases in general, has we hope come to pass with respect to the plague." [73]

Reason and Christianity, then, were for Rush progressive in their historical courses and divinely fitted in the eighteenth century to the great end of human happiness. And rational and Christian society, i.e., republican society, was the divine means by which virtuous and enlightened legislators would act as the agents of all-benevolent Providence. The perfection of man and his environment, Rush maintained, would be achieved by republican governments, since they were the chosen of God. [74] The progressively developed truths of

[69] November 12, 1791, *Rush Letters* 1: p. 612. See Elhanan Winchester's *The Three Woe Trumpets; Of Which the First and Second Are Already Past: and the Third Is Now Begun; Under Which the Seven Vials of the Wrath of God Are To Be Poured Out upon the World* (Boston, 1794), pp. 63–64, *et passim,* and his *A Course of Lectures, on the Prophecies That Remain to Be Fulfilled* (2v., 2d ed., Norwich, 1795) 2: pp. 246–258.

[70] Rush to Granville Sharp, October 29, 1773, Woods, ed., "Correspondence of Benjamin Rush and Granville Sharp," *Jour. Amer. Stud.,* 1, 1 (April, 1967): p. 3.

[71] Rush to Charles Nisbet, May 15, 1784, *Rush Letters* 1: p. 335.

[72] Rush "To the Ministers of the Gospel of All Denominations: An Address upon Subjects Interesting to Morals," June 21, 1788, *Rush Letters* 1: pp. 466–467.

[73] Rush, "On the Application of Metaphysicks to Medicine," Rush MSS, call number Yi2/7400/F2, pp. 26–30. See *Observations on Man* (6th ed., corrected and rev., London, 1834), prop. 84, p. 556, for Rush's quotation from Hartley. "It remains for" man, Rush alluded to the millennial ideas of Hartley and Winchester in a letter of 1793, "only to render the air subservient to his will. This I conceive will sooner or later be effected by the improvement and extension of the principles of balloons .... who knows but they may be the vehicles which shall convey the inhabitants of our western world to Jerusalem to pay their annual homage to the Saviour of the World during the period of the millennium?" Rush to Elizabeth Graeme Ferguson, January 18, 1793, *Rush Letters* 2: pp. 627–628; Hartley, *Observations on Man, ibid.,* and props. 82, pp. 83, 551–555, *et passim;* Winchester, *A Course of Lectures on the Prophecies* 2: pp. 217–234.

[74] Rush, "An Eulogium, Intended to Perpetuate the Memory of David Rittenhouse," *Rush Essays,* p. 358; Rush, "Lectures on Pathology. Influence of Government upon Health," Rush MSS, call number Yi2/7396/F22, pp. 313–314; Rush, "Three Lectures upon Animal Life," *Med. Inq. & Obs.* (5th ed.) 1: p. 40. *Cf.* Samuel Cooper, "A Sermon Preached before His Excellency John Hancock . . . October 25, 1780" (Boston,

physical and moral science as they emerged in history would be used to improve society. Newly discovered truths like that of political republicanism, objectified in history at the time of the American Revolution, would be used to reshape the environment and produce new men in accordance with Scriptural prophecy. The natural means for accomplishing this regeneration of man and his society was David Hartley's law of the association of ideas, which God now revealed to man in the eighteenth century. A society constructed on republican and Christian principles—of liberty, equality, and fraternity—would advance God's design by the natural mechanism of the association of ideas in which known true ideas in constant association with one another would dialectically produce true ideas on all subjects. Rush's Hartleyianism, which in its progressivist character was not inconsistent with William Cullen's medical teaching, explains Rush's great interest in devising a system of revolutionary education in which truths like liberty, equality, and fraternity would in association promote other truths.

There is an indissoluble union between moral, political and physical happiness; and if it be true, that elective and representative governments are most favourable to individual, as well as national prosperity, it follows of course, that they are most favourable to animal life [by which Rush means human life in the fullest sense].[75]

Ultimately, Rush believed, in enlightened republican society all truths would stand in their correct relation to one another in correspondence with the divine order which had prevailed before the Fall of Man.[76] In phi-

losophy, religion, government, taste, medicine, technology—in every art and science—each increment of change was in the direction of perfection.

The adoption of the Federal Constitution of the United States which Rush, as a true Commonwealthman and Enlightenment thinker, understood to be the fulfillment of English history in particular and universal history in general was a clear sign to him of the workings of the "Spirit of the Gospel." It was, he boldly declared,

as much the work of a Divine Providence as any of the miracles recorded in the Old and New Testament were the effects of a divine power . . . . Justice has descended from heaven to dwell in our land, and ample restitution has at last been made to human nature by our new Constitution for all the injuries she has sustained in the old world from arbitrary government, false religions, and unlawful commerce.[77]

Rush believed that, more than any other American, his good friend and respected Whig thinker, John Adams, had advanced the science of political happiness in his writings, especially in his *Defence of the Constitutions of Government of the United States* (1787–); and that in this great enterprise, which had already led to the adoption of republican state and federal constitutions, Adams was divinely commissioned to help prepare America as "the theater on which human nature will reach its greatest civil, literary, and religious honors." [78] Because of Adams's success in reducing politics to a science, which was truly providential, the world could now see clearly that the only perfect, "free constitution" was one in which liberty was protected by "representation and checks." [79] The seventeenth-century Whig quest of Locke and Sidney for a perfect science of politics was over. The Glorious Revolution, which had historically inspired Rush as a student and Commonwealthman, was finally being completed in the American Revolution and the triumphant republicanism of the state and federal Constitutions, which Adams so ably defended. Political and social evil, Rush wrote Rev. Elhanan Winchester, was being removed from the world by the "Spirit of the Gospel" which had produced

---

1780), where Cooper asserts that "the form of government originally established in the Hebrew nation by a charter from Heaven, was that of a free republic, over which God himself, in peculiar favour to that people, was pleased to preside" and observes "a striking resemblance between our own circumstances and those of the ancient Israelites; a nation chosen by God a theatre for the display of some of the most astonishing dispensations of his Providence" (pp. 8, 2, *et passim*); John Witherspoon, *The Dominion of Providence over the Passions of Men* (Philadelphia, 1776), pp. 39–41. See Rutherford E. Delmage, "The American Idea of Progress. 1750–1800," *Proc. Amer. Philos. Soc.* **91**, 4 (October, 1947): pp. 307–314; Perry Miller, "From the Covenant to the Revival" in James W. Smith and A. Leland Jamison, eds., *The Shaping of American Religion* (Princeton, 1961) **1**: pp. 322–350; Heimert, *Religion and the American Mind*, ch. x, 510–552; Sidney, *Discourses Concerning Government* **2**: ch. i, pp. 3–5, *et passim*.

[75] Rush, "Three Lectures upon Animal Life," *Med. Inq. & Obs.* (5th ed.) **1**: pp. 40, 17; Rush, "Old and Copied Lectures on Pathology," Rush MSS, Yi2/7396/F3, pp. 59–60.3; Rush, "On the Application of Metaphysicks to Medicine," *ibid.*, Yi2/7400/F2, pp. 24–25; Rush, *Diseases of the Mind*, p. 11; Hartley, *Observations on Man* (6th ed.), conclusion, pp. 602–603. D'Elia, "Benjamin Rush, David Hartley, and the Revolutionary Uses of Psychology," *Proc. Amer. Philos. Soc.* **114**, 2 (1970): pp. 113–115. See below.

[76] Rush, "On the Necessary Connexion Between Observation and Reasoning in Medicine," *Sixteen Introductory Lectures*, where he discusses the "union of prerelated truths" which God "established at the creation of the world" (p. 13). "You see here gent: the simplicity & unity of truth," Rush addressed his

medical students. "Not only moral & political—but physical happiness are all alike promoted by republican governments. Errors are opposed to errors—but truths upon all subjects harmonise with each other," Rush, "Lectures on Pathology. Influence of Government upon Health," Rush MSS, call number Yi2/7396/F22, pp. 313–314.

[77] Rush to Elias Boudinot? "Observations on the Federal Procession in Philadelphia," July 9, 1788, *Rush Letters* **1**: p. 475. Heimert, *Religion and the American Mind*, pp. 545–548, does not mention Rush in his excellent discussion of evangelical republican ministers and their view of the union and the ratification of the Federal Constitution as millennial.

[78] Rush to John Adams, July 2, 1788, *Rush Letters* **1**: pp. 468–469.

[79] Rush to David Ramsay, March or April, 1788, *ibid.*, p. 453. "Liberty consists in being governed by laws made by ourselves, or by rulers chosen by ourselves. This is the true definition of liberty," Rush, *Considerations upon the Present Test-Law of Pennsylvania*, p. 4.

republican governments. "The language of these free and equal governments seems to be like that of John the Baptist of old, 'Prepare ye the way of the Lord—make his paths strait.' " [80] Soon Christ would come again and destroy "evils of *every kind.*"

In Rush's view, post-Revolutionary America was the new Canaan in which there was "room enough for every human talent and virtue to expand and flourish." [81] It was plausible, he said, that Divine Providence had evolved the Christian Republic of the United States through millennia of history as a refuge for the thousands of Europeans who were being displaced by the Industrial Revolution. Also plausible, Rush asserted in keeping with his teleological optimism, was the belief that America by relieving foreign nations of surplus population was advancing the divine plan of benevolence in Europe. "In spite of all the little systems of narrow politicians, it is an eternal truth that universal happiness is universal interest. The divine government of our world would admit of a controversy if men, by acquiring moral or political happiness, in one part, added to the misery of the inhabitants of another part of our globe." [82] Living in new circumstances, free of traditional restraints and authorities, erstwhile Europeans were forced by necessity to adjust to a different environment. The product of this adjustment was the American, who for Rush was in some respects very much like Crevecœur's "new man." Rush's American, too, was almost indistinguishable from Barbeu Dubourg's and the other *philosophes'* "man in general," save for his tenacious Christianity. What made Rush's ideal man of history, the American, really different, was the "Spirit of the Gospel" which was converting him— and ultimately would convert all men—to that state of grace and brotherly love which Christ required on earth for His Second Coming.

On the basis of these remarks on Rush's view of history, it is clear that he was truly a man of his century in regarding history as philosophy teaching by examples. The philosophy he discerned in centuries past, however, was Christian; or more strictly, he found

not rationalistic philosophy but evangelistic Christianity to be the universal truth of human experience. The "Spirit of the Gospel," which could be seen unfolding itself in history in fulfillment of the divine plan of redemption, had wrought in Rush's own time first the climactic event of the Great Awakening and then its counterpart, the American Revolution, converting multitudes to the pure and true evangelical religion of Christ and its political analogue, republicanism. Natural reason was important but secondary to the Gospel in transforming the world into the Kingdom of God. The excesses of the French Revolution, which Rush explained as another crisis in the providential scheme, confirmed him in his belief that natural reason must be complemented by divine revelation. "The present commotions in Europe appear to be the commencement of the third woe mentioned in the book of Revelations," he wrote in 1793, showing the influence of Rev. Elhanan Winchester's eschatological ideas in his *Three Woe Trumpets* (1794). "The conduct of the French Convention seems intended to prove that human reason alone in its most cultivated state will not make men free or happy without the aid of divine revelation and the influences of the Spirit of the Gospel upon the hearts of men." [83]

While Voltaire, Hume, Diderot, Gibbon, and other secular historical thinkers purported to reject the Augustinian conception of divine purpose in history, Rush fully accepted it and made it his most general and ultimate principle for explaining events. While Barbeu Dubourg and other *philosophes* ruled out the Christian historiography of Augustine and the medieval historians as transcendental, placing their faith ironically—as Carl Becker has shown—exclusively in reason; Rush, with a deeper appreciation of mystery, rejected only one of Augustine's Cities, the City of the Damned, and thereby allowed for the plenary operation of divine benevolence in enfranchising all of mankind in an historical City of God. This earthly paradise or perfect society towards which, Rush believed, history was coursing would be analogous to that heavenly paradise, where ultimately all men—not just some—would be made perfect in Christ.[84] Social salvation in a perfect

---

[80] Rush to Elhanan Winchester, November 12, 1791, *Rush Letters* 1: pp. 611–612; Rush, "An Account of the Influence of the Military and Political Events of the American Revolution upon the Human Body," *Med. Inq. & Obs.* (5th ed.) 1: pp. 133–134. In addition to the writings of Winchester already cited, see his *The Universal Restoration, Exhibited in Four Dialogues Between A Minister and His Friend . . .* , a new ed. (Philadelphia, 1792), p. 132, *et passim.* This includes a valuable biographical sketch of the Universalist minister.

[81] Rush, "Information to Europeans Who Are Disposed to Migrate to the United States of America," *Rush Essays,* p. 202; cf. Joel Barlow's *Vision of Columbus* and numerous magazine articles, e.g., "An Oration Delivered at a Public Commencement, in the University of Philadelphia, May 7, 1784," *Columbian Magazine* 1 (October, 1786): pp. 83–86, on "The Former, Present, and Future Prospects of AMERICA."

[82] Rush, "Information to Europeans Who Are Disposed to Migrate to the United States of America," *Rush Essays,* pp. 211, 209–210.

[83] Rush to James Kidd, November 25, 1793, *Rush Letters* 2: p. 746. According to Winchester, Christ would come again at the end of the "third woe" and the Millennium would begin, *Three Woe Trumpets,* pp. 57, 32–34. The success of Islam was the first "woe," the "rise and conquests of the Turkish empire" was the second "woe," and the French Revolution marked the end of the second and the beginning of the third "woes," *ibid.,* pp. 17, 19–25, 32–34.

[84] Rush to Elhanan Winchester, May 11, 1791, *Rush Letters* 1: p. 582; Rush to John Adams, June 10, 1806, *ibid.* 2: p. 919; Rush to Granville Sharp, October 8, 1801, Woods, ed., "The Correspondence of Benjamin Rush and Granville Sharp 1773–1809," *Jour. Amer. Stud.* 1, 1 (April, 1967): pp. 35–36; cf. M. W., "A Breviate of Scriptural Prophecies, Relating to the Revolutions of Nations, and More Particularly of This At Present in America," *United States Magazine* 1 (July, 1779): p. 308, *et passim.* A key study in this context is Ernest L.

republican society of this world, that is, would precede individual salvation in heaven.[85] As Rush's teachers in the "Schools of the Prophets" had said, "The Kingdom of God is come." Perfect, eternal life would now be shadowed forth in the Christian Republic which Rush and others, under the inspiration of the Gospel, were constructing from the ruins of the pre-Revolutionary world.

In short, Revolutionary republican man for Rush was man redeemed progressively by divine goodness operating through history: redeemed from monarchy by political republicanism; from corrupted Christianity by religious republicanism; and from pagan medical systems by medical republicanism, i.e., Rush's American system. The promise of Christ was being fulfilled by the "Spirit of the Gospel" in Rush's America where a new state of personal and social grace was redeeming fallen man in every way.

Rush's millennial enthusiasm did wane, however slightly, near the end of his life, and his unhappy personal experience in the post-Revolutionary years did cast his thought increasingly in other-worldly terms, as we shall see, but his belief in history as the progressive disclosure of God's absolute love for man remained with him to the end.

VI. REPUBLICAN EDUCATION AND SCIENCE: THE REVOLUTIONARY PROGRAM FOR A VIRTUOUS AND FREE CITIZENRY

America seems destined by heaven to exhibit to the world the perfection which the mind of man is capable of receiving from the combined operation of liberty, learning, and the gospel upon it.—to Charles Nisbet, December 5, 1783.[1]

In an enlightened age which produced Locke, Rousseau, and Pestalozzi, it was hardly unusual for other men of talents to favor the public with treatises on education; and given an historical event of the magnitude of the American Revolution, the disposition to express one's own reasonable and correct opinions on education in the new republic became irresistible. Such was the case with Benjamin Rush as with many patriots who, after declaring America independent, filled the newspapers and magazines with essays on edu-

cational reform. Rush's philosophy of national education, however, was comprehensive and scientific, drawing ideas from the Whig and Enlightenment traditions while centered in Great Awakening evangelism. "I consider it is possible," he wrote in a fine Newtonian sentence,

to convert men into republican machines. This must be done, if we expect them to perform their parts properly, in the great machine of the government of the state. That republic is sophisticated with monarchy or aristocracy that does not revolve upon the wills of the people, and these must be fitted to each other by means of education before they can be made to produce regularity and unison in government.[2]

The distinguishing features of Rush's educational thought, applicable to his general thought as well, were evangelical Christianity and republicanism; and it is easy to ascertain the major formative influences in his early and middle years.

Mrs. Rush, his beloved mother, widowed and desperately struggling to raise her children, had early inculcated Benjamin with respect for education, both religious and professional. She managed his education at home in Philadelphia as well as she could, and sent him in 1754 to West Nottingham Academy. There Rev. Samuel Finley ineradicably fixed in young Rush's mind the truths of Christianity, making Rush's belief in revealed religion proof against every doubt.[3] Christianity and philosophy, Finley stressed repeatedly, were in perfect correspondence.[4] Whatever was true was Christian, and whatever was Christian was true. Reason and supernatural faith were not mutually exclusive, as the Deists argued. Education, Finley said, was not divisible into religious and secular parts, but was instead one total experience relating man to God and his finite universe. And the Bible was the paramount and irrefutable source of all truth.[5]

Five years of heavily religious instruction at Nottingham to a precocious, fatherless boy, understandably left a deep mark on the forming man; and this mark was

Tuveson, *Millennium and Utopia; A Study in the Background of the Idea of Progress* (Berkeley, 1949). On America specifically, consult H. Richard Niebuhr, *The Kingdom of God in America* (New York, 1959); Reinhold Niebuhr and Alan Heimert, *A Nation So Conceived; Reflections on the History of America from Its Early Visions to Its Present Power* (London, 1964); and Ernest L. Tuveson, *Redeemer Nation; The Idea of America's Millennial Role* (Chicago, 1968).

[85] *Ibid.*, p. 12, *et passim*. On progressivism and millennialism as intimately associated in the seventeenth century, *ibid.*, p. 39, *et passim*. Although H. Reinhold Niebuhr does not consider Rush in *The Kingdom of God in America*, his discussion of the social gospel movement and millennialism as related phenomena helps illumine the reformer's life and thought, pp. 151–152.

[1] *Rush Letters* 1: p. 316.

[2] Rush, "Of the Mode of Education Proper in a Republic," *Rush Essays,* pp. 14–15. Professor Lawrence A. Cremin's new work, *American Education; The Colonial Experience, 1607–1783* (New York, 1970), provides an excellent background to this chapter, especially his discussion of the impact of the Great Awakening upon education, pp. 310–332, *et passim*. Bernard Bailyn does not discuss Rush in his *Education in the forming of American Society* (Chapel Hill, 1960), an important survey of early American education.

[3] *Autobiography*, p. 31.

[4] Rush, "Influence of Physical Causes upon the Moral Faculty," *Med. Inq. & Obs.* (5th ed.) 1: p. 123.

[5] Rush, "An Enquiry into the Consistency of Oaths with Reason and Christianity," *Rush Essays*, p. 126; A. Alexander, ed., *Biographical Sketches of the Founder, and Principal Alumni of the Log College* (Princeton, 1845), ch. xvi, pp. 302–317. "Our Saviour," Rush wrote of the Bible, "calls it 'Truth' in the abstract," to John Adams, January 23, 1807, *Rush Letters* 2: p. 936; Rush, "Introductory Lecture to a Course of Lectures On the History & Practice of Physic," Rush MSS, call number Yi2/7400/F1, pp. 37–38.

the more profound because of the special, almost filial, relationship between Rush and Finley.[6] The Log College graduate passed on to Rush a total religious vision of life which stayed with the man to his final days.[7]

It was at Finley's boarding school that young Rush was first taught Greek and Latin, subjects which possessed little attraction for him. The Great Awakening schoolmaster did not overemphasize the classical languages in his curriculum, since they were after all essentially pagan languages. The ultimate purpose of education, Finley urged in his "School of the Prophets," was salvation, and Greek and Latin obviously availed little here. Rush's other teachers, Enlightenment and Whig thinkers like Cullen, Black, Sidney, Macaulay, Burgh, and Barbeu Dubourg—in the utilitarian tradition of Bacon and Locke—also found Greek and Latin to be of doubtful use to their purposes.[8] Rush followed his tutors on this point, as can be seen in his polemics against classical language studies.[9]

Unquestionably, Finley's New Side preacher background explained the great value attached to oral instruction at the school. An extraordinary regard for the persuasive force of eloquence, which characterized Rush his life long and almost prompted him to study law, was certainly bred in him by the inspired lectures and excellent conversations of his Nottingham days. In his philosophy of animal life, published in 1799, the philosopher Rush thought so highly of conversation as to denominate it a stimulus to animal life.[10] And in his researches on the American Indian (for which, incidentally, he has not been justly credited), he revealed the savage's famed taciturnity to be not an evidence of wisdom but an effect of dullness.[11] "It is equally true,"

observed Rush, "a silent man seldom possesses a clear and active mind."[12] The thought could have come from the *Spectator* or any number of periodicals with Lockean views of education, with which Rush was familiar. Indeed, Locke, Addison, Burgh, and all Commonwealthmen agreed with Finley and the Great Awakening evangelists on the power of conversation to improve man and society.[13] Certainly, one does not have to search far to find the biographical sources of Rush's views on the educational value of speaking and conversing.

Practical education at Finley's school included farming, which so impressed Rush with its academic merit as both a study and a diversion as to lead him to become one of the republic's earliest proponents of formal agricultural instruction. The extremely rural setting of the school, contrasting vividly with a large city like Philadelphia, made him sharply aware of the advantages—which he perhaps exaggerated—of locating colleges in the provinces. As a promoter of Dickinson College, Rush was able to institutionalize his belief in the excellence of rural colleges.

All in all, Rush's education at West Nottingham Academy was religious, hermetically religious; and although his student days at the College of New Jersey and the University of Edinburgh were freer and more varied, his character and thought remained pervasively religious.

The College of New Jersey, like Nottingham Academy—whence it drew one of its presidents in Samuel Finley—was a New Side Presbyterian institution. Hence, the College was steeped, as was the preparatory school, in that democratic revivalism which typified the Great Awakening in the colonies, and which almost necessarily fostered education. This enthusiasm for knowledge, literary as well as religious, was personified in the College's young president, Rev. Samuel Davies, whose dedicated scholarship fortified Rush's conviction of the worth of education. Davies, known far and wide for his missionary zeal, had earlier founded the Presbyterian Church in Virginia. In 1759 he was called to the presidency of the New Jersey College. The new president quickly saw that Samuel Finley's nephew was excellently prepared in verse, composition, and public speaking. A preacher of international distinction himself—whose influence upon Rush and others through his sermon *Religion and Public Spirit* has already been noted—Davies was gratified with his student's progress in the art of eloquence.

After the rude College of New Jersey, where Rush took his B.A. in 1760, sophisticated Edinburgh, with its new personal freedom and university character, doubtless fascinated and overawed the young Pennsylvanian.

[6] Ramsay, *Eulogium*, pp. 12–13; Binger, *Revolutionary Doctor: Benjamin Rush*, p. 20, *et passim*. For the Quaker influence in pre-Revolutionary Philadelphia, which certainly affected Rush's thought in general—and his educational thought in particular (ideas of universal education and curriculum)—see Frederick B. Tolles, *Meeting House and Counting House: The Quaker Merchants of Colonial Philadelphia 1682–1783* (New York, 1963), pp. 148–149, 207–209; Carl and Jessica Bridenbaugh, *Rebels and Gentlemen: Philadelphia in the Age of Franklin* (New York, 1962), ch. ii, pp. 29–69; and Cremin, *American Education*, pp. 304–310, *et passim*.

[7] E.g. *Med. Inq. & Obs.* (5th ed.) 1: pp. 53–54, 47; Rush, "Lectures on Pathology," Rush MSS, call number Yi2/7396/F17, pp. 24–25.

[8] Cremin, *American Education*, pp. 368, 362, *et passim*.

[9] Rush to Ashbel Green?, May 22, 1807, *Rush Letters* 2: pp. 946–947; Rush, "Observations upon the Study of the Latin and Greek Languages, as a Branch of Liberal Education," *Rush Essays*, pp. 21–56, originally published anonymously in the *American Museum* 5 (June, 1789): pp. 525–535, under a different title. On Rush's own debt to the classics, see Richard M. Gummere, *Seven Wise Men of Colonial America* (Cambridge, Mass., 1967), ch. vi, pp. 64–80.

[10] Rush, "Three Lectures upon Animal Life," *Med. Inq. & Obs.* (5th ed.) 1: p. 38.

[11] Rush, "An Account of the Vices Peculiar to the Indians of North America," *Rush Essays*, p. 259.

[12] Rush, "On the Means of Acquiring Knowledge," *Sixteen Introductory Lectures*, p. 349.

[13] Cremin, *American Education*, pp. 365–368; Robbins, *The Eighteenth Century Commonwealthman*, p. 18.

Certainly helpful in bolstering his confidence for the rigors of overseas medical study, however, were the courses in anatomy and materia medica that he had taken with Drs. Morgan and Shippen, Jr., in Philadelphia. But in "classical and philosophical learning," as Rush put it in his *Autobiography,* the New Side scholar recognized his deficiencies and characteristically removed them by private study. Mathematics, Latin, French, Spanish, and Italian all came in for study or review while he was a medical student at Edinburgh, with German deferred until his return voyage to America.[14] The conspicuous place of modern languages, especially French and German, in Rush's scheme of Revolutionary education for American youth clearly owed something to his personal experience as an American abroad. The utility of these languages and mathematics made an impression on him which he did not forget years later when he joined others in urging educational reform.

The influence of Dr. William Cullen, Rush's principal medical teacher at Edinburgh, helped form Rush's attitudes towards education. The marks of Cullen's genius which deeply impressed Rush were order, regularity, system, ingenuity, punctuality, freedom of inquiry, academic tolerance, speculative intelligence, and, above all, his cautious yet profound belief in progress.[15] Dr. Cullen rebelliously lectured in English to his classes, rather than in Latin, a practice which was surely not uncongenial to the young American who was to become one of his country's most formidable opponents of the "dead languages." Emulating Cullen, Rush later as a teacher habitually inspired his students with an appreciation of free inquiry and universality of outlook.[16]

Rush's studies of chemistry under the celebrated Dr. Joseph Black, besides developing his own inductive powers considerably, made him keenly aware of the broad educational uses of the new science. True, his immediate concern with chemistry was technological, but he also understood the general pedagogic value of chemistry in training men and women to think analytically. Hence, in his proposed system of revolutionary education, he urged and promoted the study of chemistry at all levels of education and among both sexes. Rush's *Syllabus of Lectures, Containing the Application of the Principles of Natural Philosophy, and Chemistry, to Domestic and Culinary Purposes,* which he delivered at Philadelphia's Young Ladies'

Academy in 1787, has been called America's—and perhaps the world's—first textbook on home economics chemistry.[17] And not to be overlooked, Rush the moralist realized, was the happy "sedative" effect that the study of the new science had on the passions.[18] Logically enough, Rush included chemistry in his "Plan of Education for Dickinson College."[19]

Dr. Cullen, Dr. Black, and many other persons warmly, even lovingly, described in his student journal, impressed Rush with their piety, knowledge, benevolence, and humanity. Scotland thus became a kind of educational second country to him, and it remained so until his death. Later, Rush, as the "Father of Dickinson College," almost instinctively appealed to a Scotsman, Dr. Charles Nisbet, to head the institution; and while he was at Edinburgh, he was chiefly responsible for persuading John Witherspoon, another Scotsman, to assume the office of president at the College of New Jersey. From Princeton Witherspoon's influence, as a teacher of the Scottish philosophy of "common sense," was incalculably great in forming the minds of American leaders.[20]

Dr. Cullen's belief in the perfectibility of medicine, which so affected Rush, was akin to another belief widely held in the Age of Reason, i.e., the perfectibility of man by means of education. This Enlightenment doctrine of what the venerable Samuel Miller called, derisively, the *"omnipotence of education"* helped justify the extremest optimism of the period.[21] It was, moreover, a doctrine accepted with great enthusiasm by Rush; and his revolutionary program of education, like

---

[14] *Autobiography,* pp. 39, 42–43, 77.

[15] Rush to John Adams, March 15, 1806, *Rush Letters* **2**: pp. 915–916; Whitfield J. Bell, Jr., "Some American Medical Students of 'That Shining Oracle of Physic,' Dr. William Cullen of Edinburgh, 1755–1766," *Proc. Amer. Philos. Soc.* **94** (June, 1950) : pp. 275–281.

[16] E.g., Rush, "On the Causes Which Have Retarded the Progress of Medicine, and on the Means of Promoting Its Certainty, and Greater Usefulness," *Sixteen Introductory Lectures,* pp. 150, 165; Rush, "Observations upon the Duties of a Physician," *Med. Inq. & Obs.* (5th ed.), **1**: pp. 261–262.

[17] Wyndham D. Miles and Harold J. Abrahams, "America's First Chemistry Syllabus—and Course for Girls," *School Science and Mathematics* (February, 1958), pp. 117, 111; Rush, "Of the Mode of Education Proper in a Republic," *Rush Essays,* pp. 17–18. "Chemistry by unfolding to us the effects of heat and mixture, enlarges our acquaintance with the wonders of nature and the mysteries of art. . ." (*ibid.*). Also see: Rush, "Observations upon the Study of the Latin and Greek Languages," *Rush Essays,* p. 49; Rush, "Thoughts upon Female Education, Accommodated to the Present State of Society, Manners and Government, in the United States of America," *ibid.,* pp. 79–80; Rush "To Friends of the Federal Government: A Plan of a Federal University," October 29, 1788, *Rush Letters* **1**: p. 492.

[18] Rush, *Diseases of the Mind,* p. 337.

[19] Rush MS, p. 5, Dickinson College Library. I am indebted to Dr. Charles Coleman Sellers, Librarian Emeritus of the Dickinson College Library, for the use of this manuscript.

[20] Woodbridge Riley, *American Thought from Puritanism to Pragmatism and Beyond* (New York, 1915), pp. 125–133; Rush, "Scottish Journal"; Rush to Charles Nisbet, April 19?, 1784, *Rush Letters* **1**: pp. 321–325; Gladys Bryson, *Man and Society: The Scottish Inquiry of the Eighteenth Century* (Princeton, 1945), pp. 19–20.

[21] *A Brief Retrospect of the Eighteenth Century. In Two Volumes: Containing A Sketch of the Revolutions and Improvements in Science, Arts, and Literature, During that Period* (2 v., New York, 1803) **2**: p. 296. Cf. Barbeu Dubourg's educational ideas which, again, are very close to those of Rush, Aldridge, "Jacques Barbeu-Dubourg," *Proc. Amer. Philos. Soc.* **95** (1951) : pp. 371, 380.

all of his social thought and action, was an heroic attempt to educate man to a republican perfection.

This perfection of man, Rush believed, could be hastened by applying to man in society the newly discovered scientific principle of the association of ideas, which the English empiricists and David Hartley in particular had elaborated. "It is evident from common observation, and more so from the foregoing theory," Hartley had written of associationism in his *Observations on Man,* "that children may be formed and moulded as we please." [22] In his *Inquiry into the Influence of Physical Causes upon the Moral Faculty,* read before the American Philosophical Society in 1786, Rush, like Hartley before him, synthesized elements of thought from Commonwealth, pietistic, and Enlightenment traditions and proposed a system of "moral education of youth upon new and mechanical principles."

"From this Book," Rush wrote of Hartley's *Observations on Man,*

I derived my system of physiology. . . . It not only imparts new ideas upon all subjects, but it teaches the reader to acquire them in a new manner. It has like Hershel's telescope opened new discoveries to our senses, & greatly extended our knowledge of the moral & theological as well as the mental and physical worlds. . . . It may be compared to a voyage of circumnavigation. It has embraced, & connected the whole globe of the mind. . . . The great object of Dr. Hartley's work is to prove that all the exercises of the mind depend upon certain vibrations communicated to the brain through the medium of the nerves, and that all abstraction of thought is produced by certain associations of these vibrations. The actions of the senses, pleasure & pain, the waking and sleeping states, are all explained by these principles in the most simple and satisfactory manner.[23]

And there is no doubt that he had his beloved Dickinson College in mind as he discussed the physical causes that should act upon the moral faculty of young men to produce Christian republican virtue. From schools and new, revolutionary colleges like Dickinson, Rush believed, the moral regeneration of man would be accomplished by physical causes known to restore the moral faculty to its healthy operation. The restoration of the moral faculty by scientific means, after centuries of diseased operation in the Old World, would mechanically produce in republican America correct associations of ideas and an exact correspondence of ideas and objective reality—a perfected, Godlike understanding denied to man ever since the sin of his first parents, allowing man once again directly to perceive and choose

good over evil, republican virtue over monarchical vice.[24]

Happily for the republic of the United States, Rush argued, its national territory lay in the middle latitudes, where a climate known physically to cause "gentleness and benevolence" operated naturally upon the people. This was nature's education, as it were, but Rush's moral science could improve upon nature by locating schools and colleges in the country, where rural odors calmed the passions and strengthened the moral faculty in its perception of virtue. The Enlightenment scientist could employ many other physical causes to achieve the moral perfection of American youth. He knew that a "temperate and vegetable diet" taken with water— never spirituous liquors—helped promote "the virtues of candour, benevolence, and generosity." These physical causes, these impressions upon the body, when scientifically arranged in a program of moral education with other physical causes like moderate labor, moderate sleep, cleanliness, music, and eloquence, would mechanically produce in the mind correct associations of ideas.[25] Rush as chemist even believed in the moral uses of chemistry, that, for example, "dephlogisticated air, when taken into the lungs, produces cheerfulness, gentleness, and serenity of mind." [26] And as a physician Rush argued for exercise, the cold bath, and "a cold or warm atmosphere" as cures for diseased moral faculties and physical causes of virtue.[27] When he developed his unitary theory of disease—all disease as one, fever— Rush sought to cure diseased moral faculties principally by bloodletting, which in his famous American system of medicine he believed to destroy fever by reducing tension in the arteries and blood vessels of the body.[28]

---

[22] (6th ed., corrected and rev., London, 1834), conclusion, pp. 602–603; George S. Bower, *Hartley and James Mill* (London, 1881), pp. 6–7, 204n.

[23] Rush, "On the Application of Metaphysicks to Medicine," Rush MSS, call number Yi2/7400/F2, pp. 22–25; Rush to John Montgomery, December 28, 1785, *Rush Letters* 1: p. 378.

[24] *Ibid.,* p. 10; Rush, "Lectures on Pathology," Rush MSS, call number Yi2/7396/F16, p. 1; Rush, "Plan of Education for Dickinson College," Rush MS, pp. 1–20. See Richard Price to Benjamin Rush, July 30, 1786, Rush MSS, XLIII: p. 116. In 1774 Rush had written to Granville Sharp in anticipation of this discovery: "If the moral faculty can be injured by physical causes, may it not be improved by the same means? The memory and judgement are strengthened by exercise, and temperance and the imagination is enlivened by a fulness of the blood vessels of the head,—in like manner may not a regimen, or a medicine be discovered which shall improve, or alter the diseased state of the moral faculty? Dr. Stork relieved fatuity by repeated doses of strammonium. An erring judgement (as in maniacal and delirious patients) has been cured by bleeding— and blistering. What the regimen or medicine might be that shall alter false perceptions of moral truths, or correct vicious appetites I shall not pretend to determine. Perhaps hereafter it may be as much the business of a physician as it is now of a divine to reclaim mankind from vice," July 9, 1774, Woods, ed., "The Correspondence of Benjamin Rush and Granville Sharp 1773–1809," *Jour. Amer. Stud.* 1, 1 (April, 1967): p. 8.

[25] Rush, "Influence of Physical Causes upon the Moral Faculty," *Med. Inq. & Obs.,* 5th ed., 1: pp. 107–114.

[26] *Ibid.,* p. 114.

[27] *Ibid.,* pp. 109–110.

[28] Rush, *Diseases of the Mind,* pp. 17–18, 26–27; Shryock, "The Psychiatry of Benjamin Rush," *Amer. Jour. Psychiatry* 101 (January, 1945): p. 430; Eric T. Carlson and Meribeth M.

Rush believed that the American Revolution—which was, like the Great Awakening, an outpouring of the "Spirit of the Gospel"—had given a new, radical direction to human society by greatly increasing the power of reason, religion, and all civilized values. Therefore, it was easy for him to conclude that American medicine must reflect these happy changes in its revolutionary improvements. "In contemplating the prejudices against bloodletting, which formerly prevailed so generally in our country," Rush wrote in the mid-1790's,

I have been led to ascribe them to a cause wholly political. We are descended chiefly from Great-Britain, and have been for many years under the influence of English habits upon all subjects. Some of these habits, as far as they relate to government, have been partly changed; but in dress, arts, manufactures, manners, and science, we are still governed by our early associations. . . . Here then we discover the source of the former prejudices and errors of our countrymen, upon the subject of blood-letting. They are of British origin. They have been inculcated in British universities, and in British books; and they accord as ill with our climate and state of society, as the Dutch foot stoves did with the temperate climate of the Cape of Good Hope.[29]

Indeed, Americans were now living in a revolutionary epoch in medicine as in all departments of human life, a pre-millennial age in which by secondary causes God was redeeming man physically and morally and preparing him for life everlasting. The "physician who is not a Republican," Rush informed his students, "holds principles, that call in question his knowledge of the principles of medicine." [30] The "perfect renovation of the human body," as foretold by St. Paul, had

begun.[31] And the perfect environment of the New Jerusalem, with its pure air and water, in which regenerated man was destined to live, was to be attained here in America by God-given republican science.[32]

Correct physical causes, whether employed by the republican legislator, the republican divine, the republican schoolmaster, or the republican social and medical philosopher, would produce the desired physical environment in America; and it, in turn—by Rush and Hartley's system of physiological psychology—would scientifically restore man to his long-lost direct perception of truth and virtue which God had originally blessed him with before the sin of Adam and Eve.[33] In the Christian Republic of America, where the "Spirit of the Gospel" was realizing itself, men would once again be made whole by a loving God working through secondary causes. And Rush and Hartley's physiological psychology, in the American revolutionary's view, was the physics of moral reform, the ultimate science of the Enlightenment.[34]

Simpson, "Benjamin Rush's Medical Use of the Moral Faculty," *Bull. History of Medicine* 39 (January–February, 1965) : p. 29, *et passim.*

[29] Rush, "A Defence of Blood-letting, as a Remedy for Certain Diseases," *Med. Inq. & Obs.* (5th ed.) 2: p. 223. Rush wrote to his English friend, the eccentric physician Dr. John Coakley Lettsom, who needed no reminding, that he was "still fond of voyages to Otaheite [Tahiti] in medicine," September 28, 1787, *Rush Letters* 1: p. 443.

[30] Rush, "Lectures on Pathology. Influence of Government upon Health," Rush MSS, call number Yi2/7396/F22, pp. 313–314. With Jefferson's election to the presidency in 1800 and the rise of what Alan Heimert has called the "spirit of the Republican revival," Rush's vision of a pre-millennial American society enlightened by true science appeared even closer to fulfillment. He wrote to James Madison, the new secretary of state, on the need to abolish quarantine laws, unnecessary in the light of Rush's discovery of the non-contagiousness of yellow fever, and to replace them with strict laws requiring urban sanitation: "Posterity will be grateful to that government which shall take the lead in this important business. Hitherto science has been scouted from the cabinets of the rulers of the world. It bears the hateful name of philosophy. But we look for more correct associations of things under the present administration," June 23, 1801, *Rush Letters* 2: pp. 835–836; Rush to Thomas Jefferson, November 27, 1801, *ibid.,* p. 840, and June 15, 1805, *ibid.,* p. 896, *et passim;* Heimert, *Religion and the American Mind,* pp. 544–549.

[31] Rush, "Influence of Physical Causes upon the Moral Faculty," *Med. Inq. & Obs.* (5th ed.) 1: pp. 114–115; Rush, "On the Necessary Connexion Between Observation and Reasoning in Medicine," *Sixteen Introductory Lectures,* pp. 13–14. "We live, gentlemen, in a revolutionary age. Our science has caught the spirit of the times, and more improvements have been made in all its branches, within the last twenty years, than had been made in a century before. From these events, so auspicious to medicine, may we not cherish a hope, that our globe is about to undergo those happy changes, which shall render it a more safe and agreeable abode to man, and thereby prepare it to receive the blessing of universal health and longevity; for premature deaths seem to have arisen from the operation of that infinite goodness which delivers from evils to come," *ibid.;* see Winchester, *A Course of Lectures on the Prophecies* 2: pp. 42–44, on this fulfillment of prophecy, which Rush understood according to his friend's exegesis, Rush to Elhanan Winchester, May 11, 1791, *Rush Letters* 1: pp. 581–582; *cf.* Gruman, "A History of Ideas About the Prolongation of Life," *Trans. Amer. Philos. Soc.* 56, 9 (1966).

[32] Rush, *Syllabus of Lectures, Containing the Application of the Principles of Natural Philosophy, and Chemistry, to Domestic and Culinary Purposes,* p. 8; Rush, "Influence of Physical Causes upon the Moral Faculty," *Med. Inq. & Obs.* 1: p. 114; see Winchester, *A Course of Lectures on the Prophecies* 2: p. 47; D. J. D'Elia, "Dr. Benjamin Rush and the American Medical Revolution," *Proc. Amer. Philos. Soc.* 110, 4 (1966) : pp. 227–234.

[33] Rush, "Influence of Physical Causes upon the Moral Faculty," *Med. Inq. & Obs.* (5th ed.) 1: pp. 120–124, esp. p. 122; Rush, "Three Lectures upon Animal Life," *Med. Inq. & Obs.* (5th ed.) 1: p. 17. Professor Joseph Blau's treatment of Rush's social philosophy is very good but necessarily too general in his excellent *Men and Movements in American Philosophy* (Englewood Cliffs, N. J., 1963), pp. 65–72.

[34] See Dugald Stewart's penetrating criticism of Hartley's—and, by extension, Rush's—"grand *arcanum,* the principle of association" and "the unexampled latitude with which the words *association* and *idea* are, both of them, employed, through the whole of his theory." Hartley's "reveries" and "conceits," Stewart asserted, derived from his "error" of trying to "explain the intellectual phenomena by analogies borrowed from the material world . . . ," *Philosophical Essays* (first American ed., Philadelphia, 1811), pp. 167–168, 178–179. What a later critic, George S. Bower, termed Hartley's "physical

Social programs conceived in the light of the principle of the association of ideas could extirpate time-worn and degenerate habits of mind, practices, and manners. In this way, science and religion would raise man to the private and public perfections required of him in the world's first republican society—man would finally be republicanized! When Rush affixed his name to the Declaration of Independence, he quite consistently subscribed to this radically democratic view of the native equality of man. The corpus of his educational writings, collected and dispersed, really amounts to an elaboration of that revolutionary subscription.

In his earliest (1783) tract on the practice of republican education, "Of the Mode of Education Proper in a Republic," Rush explained his purposes as an American educator:

> The business of education has acquired a new complexion by the independence of our country. The form of government we have assumed, has created a new class of duties to every American. It becomes us, therefore, to examine our former habits upon this subject, and in laying the foundations for nurseries of wise and good men, to adapt our modes of teaching to the peculiar form of our government.[35]

Needless to say, the "wise and good" republicans educated in the new schools would be Christians on account of the necessary connection between republicanism and Christianity. In fact, religion was essential to republican education, because education without religion was devoid of virtue, and virtue was indispensable to liberty, which was, "the object and life of all republican govern-

ments."[36] Christianity, as Rush understood it, would make men virtuous and free. This he had learned himself in the "Schools of the Prophets."

Again, as a Commonwealthman and Enlightenment reformer, Rush turned to legislation to effect those changes in education which he deemed necessary to safeguard and perpetuate the American Revolution.[37] It was not enough that republican government, brought about by the late war, had greatly increased what he called the "quantity of mind" as well as the "quantity of animal life" in the United States.[38] Intellect, although twenty times more plentiful in the nation in 1799 than in 1774, and knowledge, although one hundred times more plentiful, still required systematic direction in order to insure a general republican will.[39] Enlightened social legislation was absolutely necessary, particularly in the establishment and subsidization of schools.[40]

---

hypothesis" was charged against Rush, too, as was the more general "error" of arguing too often from analogies rather than from "real causation," Bower, *Hartley and James Mill*, pp. 225, 2, 215, Harriot W. Warner, ed., *Autobiography of Charles Caldwell, M.D.*, With a New Introduction by Lloyd G. Stevenson, M.D. (New York, 1968), p. 316. Dr. Caldwell was a student of Rush, and his criticism of his teacher's mind and method as too analogical and deductive to be original, is important; although it should be noted that Caldwell here was evaluating Rush from what he considered a "modern" (nineteenth-century positivistic) point of view, *ibid.*, pp. 319, 275, 296, 146–147. Of Dugald Stewart's attack on Hartley's *Observations on Man*, Rush wrote Jefferson: "The Scotch philosophers of whom Dugald Stewart has lately become the champion abuse it in intemperate terms, but it is because they are so bewildered in the pagan doctrines of Aristotle and Plato that they do not understand it," January 2, 1811, *Rush Letters* 2: p. 1075; see Professor Butterfield's note on Caldwell, *ibid.*, p. 778.

[35] Rush, "Of the Mode of Education Proper in a Republic," *Rush Essays*, pp. 6–7. *Cf.* Noah Webster, *A Grammatical Institute of the English Language* (Hartford, 1783), preface to Pt. i. There was, of course, even earlier discussion of the need for a distinct program of American education, but it seems to have been more suggestive than systematic. See, e.g., anon., "Thoughts on Quotations from Authors. A Fragment," *United States Magazine* 1 (August, 1779): pp. 352–353, anon., "Remarks on the Magazine for August, in a Conversation of Ladies, &c.," *ibid.* (September, 1779): pp. 404–405, "Senex," to the *Pennsylvania Packet*, September 28, 1782, reprinted from the *Virginia Gazette* for September 7, 1782.

[36] Rush, "Of the Mode of Education Proper in a Republic," *Rush Essays*, pp. 8, 20; Rush "To the Citizens of Philadelphia: A Plan for Free Schools," March 28, 1787, *Rush Letters* 1: p. 414. Rush, as noted above, prized Montesquieu's *De l'esprit des lois* (1748) which held virtue to be the object of republican education, 1: Bk. IV. Unlike Rush's conception of virtue, however, Montesquieu's was neither Christian nor moral, but political.

[37] Rush, "Of the Mode of Education Proper in a Republic," *Rush Essays*, p. 20; Rush, "Influence of Physical Causes upon the Moral Faculty," *Med. Inq. & Obs.* (5th ed.) 1: p. 124; Rush, "A Plan of a Peace-Office for the United States," *Rush Essays*, p. 184; Rush to Richard Price, May 25, 1786, *Rush Letters* 1: pp. 388–389. *Cf.* "The Worcester Speculator," "On Republican Government," *American Museum* 6 (November, 1789): pp. 385–387. See Richard Price's *Observations on the Importance of the American Revolution, and the Means of Making It a Benefit to the World* (Boston, 1784), pp. 43–44.

[38] Rush, "On the Influence of Physical Causes upon the Intellectual Faculties," *Sixteen Introductory Lectures*, pp. 109–110.

[39] *Ibid.*; Rush, "Of the Mode of Education Proper in a Republic," *Rush Essays*, pp. 14–15.

[40] Rush, "Influence of Physical Causes upon the Moral Faculty," *Med. Inq. & Obs.* (5th ed.) 1: p. 124; *Autobiography*, p. 216; Rush, "A Plan of a Peace-Office for the United States," *Rush Essays*, 184; Rush "To the Citizens of Philadelphia: A Plan for Free Schools," March 28, 1787, *Rush Letters* 1: pp. 413–415; Rush, "A Plan for Establishing Public Schools in Pennsylvania, and for Conducting Education Agreeably to a Republican Form of Government," *Rush Essays*, p. 3. Rush's quotation from Beccaria's *Essay on Crimes and Punishments*, a favorite handbook of reform, is on p. 2 of the last entry and exemplifies the *philosophe's*—and Rush's—belief that, "by the radiance of knowledge, power trembles, but the authority of laws remains immoveable." Rush's writings are filled with references to Beccaria, e.g., *Considerations on the Injustice and Impolicy of Punishing Murder by Death,* pp. 10, 13, Rush, "An Enquiry into the Effects of Public Punishments upon Criminals," *Rush Essays,* p. 158. And Rush agreed with Beccaria, Barbeu Dubourg, and other Enlightenment reformers that, to quote from the Italian thinker, "It is better to prevent crimes than to punish them. This is the fundamental principle of good legislation, which is the art of conducting men to the *maximum* of happiness, and to the *minimum* of misery. . . . The most certain method of preventing crimes is, to perfect the system of education," *An Essay on Crimes and Punishments, trans. from the Italian of Caesar Bonesana, Marquis Beccaria. To Which*

The "republican ferment" which Rush said had caused him to reconsider his medical and social opinions, also made him re-examine his opinions on education, and some of these he found to be erroneous. Accordingly, in his educational writings directed to legislatures and the public, he strove to remove what he regarded as pernicious errors in republican education.

Compulsory study of Greek and Latin was high on his list, as was enforced reading of the ancient classics themselves. Personally, he wrote to a skeptical John Adams, early study of the classical languages had forced upon him a "turgid and affected style" of writing which he had broken away from only after applying himself to the model English compositions of Lowth, Swift, and Hume.[41] "Who are guilty of the greatest absurdity," he asked in the same place, "the Chinese who press the feet into deformity by small shoes, or the Europeans and Americans who press the brain into obliquity by Greek and Latin?"[42]

Republicans, obviously, must be free to express their own genius without Old World restraints. A new people required a new idiom, and Rush predicted that, once liberated from servile dependence upon classical and British norms, an American language would flourish.[43] By force of her armies, religion, and lan-

guage, Rome had once unjustly ruled the world; now only her language remained, and Rush proposed to bar it and Greek from the United States along with slavery.[44] In Napoleonic France and corrupt Britain, the study of the "dead languages," Rush maintained, was calculated to distract the people from too close an attention to their tyrannical governments.[45] In the republican United States, any interference with government, however slight, frustrated the design of open and popular rule and was for that reason intolerable.

Greek and Latin were also unrepublican because of their pagan character. Recounting as they did the depraved conduct of the ancients—the murders, rapes, and incests—the classics possessed an "immoral tendency" flatly opposed to Christian republican virtue. Naturally, the virtue of the people must be protected against such licentious influence, in the same way that the virtue of the people had to be protected from the corrupting influence of slavery and militia laws. Declared Rush:

Much more, in my opinion, might be said in favour of teaching our young men to speak the Indian languages of our country, than to speak or write Latin. By their means, they might qualify themselves to become ambassadors to our Indian nations, or introduce among them a knowledge of the blessings of civilization and religion.[46]

Other studies to be avoided because of their immoral nature or uselessness were those of fiction, as in the novel, linguistics, alchemy, occultism, and moral philos-

---

is Added, a Commentary, by M. D. Voltaire. Trans. from the French, by Edward D. Ingraham, (2d American ed., Philadelphia, 1819), pp. 148, 156.

[41] July 21, 1789, Rush Letters 1: p. 524; Rush to James Muir, August 24, 1791, ibid., p. 604; Rush, "Observations upon the Study of the Latin and Greek Languages," Rush Essays, p. 29. A month after Rush's "Observations" appeared, the author sent a copy to Adams. The two friends agreed to disagree and kept up the correspondence on the subject for years; see Rush Letters, passim, and John A. Schutz and Douglass Adair, eds., The Spur of Fame: Dialogues of John Adams and Benjamin Rush, 1805–1813 (San Marino, Calif., 1966), ch. viii, pp. 166–179. Less gentle than Adams was "Glottophilus," who in replying to Rush's anonymous essay in American Museum 5 (June, 1789): pp. 525–535, described the author as "a certain gentleman, of publishing propensity, [who] has learned both Latin and Greek, and is not a whit the wiser." "When a writer requires our assent to certain postulata, which are the very points he ought to prove, his conduct is an indication, either that he has no arguments to support his cause, or that they will not bear the test," ibid. 6 (August–September, 1789): pp. 189, 109.

[42] For Hartley and Saint-Pierre as authorities for his views on classical language study, see Rush's note, Autobiography, p. 346, and Dr. Corner's remarks, n. 45. Rush praised Saint-Pierre's Studies of Nature (1784) which, in the tradition of Rousseau and Barbeu Dubourg, urged the education of the young in love and virtue. Saint-Pierre's vision of a new world order based upon natural reason and the Gospel was one that Rush could share. "He has made our globe to be the echo of the song of the angels at the birth of our Saviour," Rush to Samuel Bayard, September 22, 1796, Rush Letters 2: p. 781. See Jacques Henri Bernardin de Saint-Pierre, Studies of Nature, trans. by Henry Hunter (Philadelphia, 1808) 2: pp. 407–408, et passim, for the "tedious and painful study of dead languages."

[43] Rush "To Friends of the Federal Government: A Plan for a Federal University," October 29, 1788, Rush Letters 1: pp. 492–493; Rush, "Observations upon the Study of Latin and Greek Languages," Rush Essays, pp. 26–28. Cf. John Whittler,

"The Ranger. No. 1," United States Magazine 1 (April, 1794): pp. 17–19, and "P. Q." Columbian Magazine 1 (March, 1787): pp. 313–314. See Myer Reinhold, "Opponents of Classical Learning in America During the Revolutionary Period," Proc. Amer. Philos. Soc. 112 (1968): pp. 221–234.

[44] Rush to John Adams, October 2, 1810, Rush Letters 2: p. 1067; Rush to John Adams, June 15, 1789, and July 2, 1789, ibid. 1: pp. 516, 517–518. Adams's reply was classical in its own right: "I should as soon think of closing all my window shutters, to enable me to see, as of banishing the Classicks, to improve Republican ideas," June 19, 1789, Alexander Biddle (ed.), Old Family Letters: Copied from the Originals for Alexander Biddle, Series A (Philadelphia, 1892), p. 40.

[45] Rush to John Adams, January 10, 1811, Rush Letters 2: p. 1077. "It is one among many other of his [Napoleon's] acts that are calculated and perhaps intended to bring back the darkness and ignorance of the 14th and 15th centuries," ibid.

[46] Rush, "Observations upon the Study of the Latin and Greek Languages," Rush Essays, pp. 55–56. Cf. "Doctor Plainsense," "The Pedantry of Technical Phraseology Condemned." Columbian Magazine 1, 16 (December, 1787): p. 806. Rush, "Observations upon the Study of the Latin and Greek Languages," Rush Essays, pp. 24–25; Autobiography, p. 345; Rush, "On the Means of Acquiring Knowledge," Sixteen Introductory Lectures, p. 359; Rush, An Address to the Inhabitants of the British Settlements in America, upon Slave-Keeping, pp. 2–3; Rush, "Influence of Physical Causes upon the Moral Faculty," Med. Inq. & Obs. (5th ed.) 1: pp. 118–119; Rush, "A Plan of a Peace-Office for the United States," Rush Essays, p. 185; Rush, "An Address to the Ministers of the Gospel of Every Denomination in the United States upon Subjects Interesting to Morals," ibid., p. 116. Rush acknowledged the influence of Hartley in his opinion of Greek and Latin as having an "immoral tendency," Autobiography, p. 345.

ophy.[47] "As yet the intrigues of a British novel," he asserted in his pioneer essay on feminine education, "are as foreign to our manners, as the refinements of Asiatic vice." [48] The republican character was still undefiled by excessive passions. It was true that the novel mirrored life, but not pure and simple republican life as it existed in Revolutionary America.[49]

Unacceptable, too, in Rush's ideal curriculum was moral philosophy, which he regarded as a pagan study wholly out of place in Christian schools. "Infidelity systematized," was what Jonathan Edwards had called it, and Rush fully concurred.[50] Moral philosophy was offensive as a study calculated to misrepresent morals as independent of religion; a proposition clearly untrue and for that reason unrepublican. A people trained in the sophistries of moral philosophy would be a nation bereft of right reason and revealed religion—a veritable nation of Deists. Here, unmistakably, stood forth Rush the Great Awakening evangelist and defender of pious and supernatural truths against the new realism of the Scottish school of thought which tended to abandon revealed religion for moral philosophy.[51]

Corporal punishment in the schools was one of Rush's most disturbing educational aversions. Here, as elsewhere, the influence of Locke's educational ideas is clear. Abusive treatment of American youth, Rush contended in the same Whig tradition, was more becoming a fear-dominated monarchy than a courageous and expansive republic.[52] "The fear of corporal punishments," Rush observed, "by debilitating the body, produces a corresponding debility in the mind, which contracts its capacity of acquiring knowledge." [53] Psychologically, Rush's revolutionary principle of the association of ideas worked here as well as in other connections. Imperious and harshly disciplinary teachers promoted not free inquiry and respect for learning in their classes, as they should in a republican society, but "despotism and violence." [54] And depotism and violence led to monarchism, not republicanism.

Foreign influences in republican education were of course suspect to Rush. Studying abroad was to be discouraged. "An education in our own, is to be preferred to an education in a foreign country," Rush asserted. "The principle of patriotism," he continued,

stands in need of the reinforcement of prejudice, and it is well known that our strongest prejudices in favour of our country are formed in the first one and twenty years of our lives. . . . Passing by, in this place, the advantages to the community from the early attachment of youth to the laws and constitution of their country, I shall only remark, that young men who have trodden the paths of science together, or have joined in the same sports, whether of swimming, scating, fishing, or hunting, generally feel, thro' life, such ties to each other, as add greatly to the obligations of mutual benevolence.[55]

The Old World practice of quartering boys in dormi-

[47] Rush, "On the Means of Acquiring Knowledge," *Sixteen Introductory Lectures,* p. 359; Rush, "On the Influence of Physical Causes upon the Intellectual Faculties," *ibid.,* pp. 112–113; Rush, "On the Education Proper to Qualify a Young Man for the Study of Medicine," *ibid.,* pp. 174–175; untitled lecture by Rush printed in Good, *Benjamin Rush and His Services to American Education,* pp. 240–241; Rush to Ashbel Green?, May 22, 1807, *Rush Letters* 2: pp. 946–947. *Cf.* "Character and Effects of Modern Novels," *Pennsylvania Packet and Daily Advertiser,* August 20, 1785, and "Philalethes" "On the Practice of Reading Novels and Romances," *United States Magazine* 1 (May, 1794) : pp. 81–83.

[48] Rush, "Thoughts upon Female Education," *Rush Essays,* p. 81; Rush, *Syllabus of Lectures, Containing the Application of the Principles of Natural Philosophy, and Chemistry, to Domestic and Culinary Purposes,* pp. 1–2.

[49] Rush, "Thoughts upon Female Education," *Rush Essays,* pp. 81, 89; *cf.* anon., "Original Thoughts on Education," *Columbian Magazine* 1 (September, 1787) : p. 645.

[50] Rush to Ashbel Green?, May 22, 1807, *Rush Letters* 2: p. 947; Rush, "On the Opinions and Modes of Practice of Hippocrates," *Sixteen Introductory Lectures,* p. 292.

[51] Rush, "On the Education Proper to Qualify a Young Man for the Study of Medicine," *ibid.,* p. 174; Rush, "On the Necessary Connexion Between Observation and Reasoning in Medicine," *ibid.,* p. 13; Rush, "Of the Mode of Education Proper in a Republic," *Rush Essays,* pp. 8–9; untitled lecture by Rush printed in Good, *Benjamin Rush and His Services to American Education,* pp. 240–241; Rush, "On the Character of Dr. Sydenham," *Sixteen Introductory Lectures,* p. 53; Rush, "Defence of the Use of the Bible as a School Book," *Rush Essays,* p. 105; Rush, "On the Causes of Death, In Diseases That Are Not Incurable," *Sixteen Introductory Lectures,* pp. 86–87; Rush, "Influence of Physical Causes upon the Moral Faculty," *Med. Inq. & Obs.* (5th ed.) 1: pp. 95–96, 99–100; Rush, "Thoughts on Common Sense," *Rush Essays,* p. 250; Rush to Thomas Jefferson, January 2, 1811, *Rush Letters* 2: p. 1075. Jefferson's philosophical beliefs were consistent with Scottish realism, and, of course, his ideal of education was a secular one, Adrienne Koch, *The Philosophy of Thomas Jefferson* (Chicago, 1964), pp. 45, 48–53, 89; Roy J. Honeywell, *The Educational Work of Thomas Jefferson* (New York, 1964), *passim.* Yet some of

Jefferson's positions on religious instruction in public education are ambiguous, Robert M. Healey, *Jefferson on Religion in Public Education* (New Haven, 1962), ch. x, pp. 202–226.

[52] Rush, "Thoughts upon the Amusements and Punishments, Which Are Proper for Schools," *Rush Essays,* pp. 68–71; Rush, "Observations upon the Study of the Latin and Greek Languages," *ibid.,* p. 56; Cremin, *American Education,* p. 363.

[53] Rush, "Thoughts upon the Amusements and Punishments, Which Are Proper for Schools," *Rush Essays,* p. 67. A letter from Rush's good friend, Rev. Elhanan Winchester, to a "Gentleman in Philadelphia," appeared in *Universal Asylum and Columbian Magazine* 8 (May, 1792) : pp. 318–319, in support of Rush's arguments against corporal punishment in the schools. Rush's essay had been published in *Columbian Magazine* two years earlier, 5 (August, 1790) : pp. 67–74.

[54] Rush, "Thoughts upon the Amusements and Punishments, Which Are Proper for Schools," *Rush Essays,* pp. 70–71, 67; Rush, "Observations upon the Study of the Latin and Greek Languages," *ibid.,* pp. 56. *Cf.* Beccaria, *Essay on Crimes and Punishments,* ch. xxvii, p. 94.

[55] Rush, "Of the Mode of Education Proper in a Republic," *Rush Essays, ibid.,* p. 7. For the popularity of this idea among American writers on education in the post-Revolutionary period, see Allen O. Hansen, *Liberalism and American Education in the Eighteenth Century* (New York, 1926), p. 46, *et passim. Cf.* Thomas Jefferson to John Banister, Jr., October 15, 1785, Julian P. Boyd *et al.,* eds., *The Papers of Thomas Jefferson* (Princeton, 1950–) 8: pp. 635–637.

tories was unrepublican, according to Rush. "The practice," he wrote,

is the gloomy remains of monkish ignorance, and is unfavorable to the improvements of the mind in useful learning, as monasteries are to the spirit of religion. I grant this mode of secluding boys from the intercourse of private families, has a tendency to make them scholars, but our business is to make them men, citizens and christians.[56]

Not surprisingly, Rush recommended that Dickinson College students live with private families.[57]

Probably the most serious error of all in pre-Revolutionary education in America, to be corrected now in the new age of republicanism, was that of not using the Bible in all the schools. Not a few of Rush's compatriots maintained that the schools of the nation should exclude the Bible and religious studies as unrepublican, but for Rush there was no more certain way of nurturing republicanism than by teaching American youth the precepts of Holy Writ. He complained:

We profess to be republicans, and yet we neglect the only means of establishing and perpetuating our republican forms of government, that is, the universal education of our youth in the principles of christianity, by means of the bible; for this divine book, above all others, favours that equality among mankind, that respect for just laws, and all those sober and frugal virtues, which constitute the soul of republicanism.[58]

All that was necessary for America was to form Christians in the tax-supported schools in order to produce republicans for the nation; or, more strictly, Christians and republicans would be joined together in the schools as Christian republicans, since Christianity and republicanism were really inseparable positions. Rush made his point even more strongly:

A Christian cannot fail of being a republican. The history of the creation of man, and of the relation of our species to each other by birth, which is recorded in the Old Testament, is the best refutation that can be given to the divine right of kings, and the strongest argument that can be used in favor of the original and natural equality of all mankind. A Christian, I say again, cannot fail of being a republican, for every precept of the Gospel inculcates those degrees of humility, self-denial, and brotherly kindness, which are directly opposed to the pride of monarchy and the pageantry of a court.[59]

The religious instruction which Rush designed to accomplish this would be, he thought, acceptable to all sects because of its uncontroversial nature. It was to consist of lectures presenting the evidences, the various sectarian doctrines, and the truths of Christianity.[60] And, again, in his "Plan of Education for Dickinson Collge," Rush sought to implement his ideas by having students "taught the catechisms of their respective churches." [61]

A program of this kind was not intended to inculcate a system of religion, in the ordinary sense of the word, but even if it did, Rush asked, why should we not provide our students with a system of religion as we did systems of politics, geography, philosophy, and the other sciences? "I claim no more then for religion, than for the other sciences," Rush continued as a dissenter and Commonwealthman,

and I add further, that if our youth are disposed after they are of age to think for themselves, a knowledge of one system, will be the best means of conducting them in a free enquiry into other systems of religion, just as an acquaintance with one system of philosophy is the best introduction to the study of all the other systems in the world.[62]

Christianity, moreover, promoted knowledge, rather than obstructing it the way other religions did. Isaac Newton, Francis Bacon, David Hartley, and a multitude of other Christian philosophers had been responsible for the greatest scientific discoveries because of the affinity of truths for one another and the wide scope of the Christian understanding itself.[63] Now, in the new Christian Republic of America, which was to be the scene of "triumphs of the Gospel" as well as "triumphs of liberty," there was no predicting how many similarly great Christian philosophers might be

---

[56] Rush, "Of the Mode of Education Proper in a Republic," *Rush Essays*, p. 14.

[57] "Plan of Education for Dickinson College," Rush MS, p. 16.

[58] Rush, "Defence of the Use of the Bible as a School Book," *Rush Essays*, pp. 112–113, 94–95, 98–100; Rush, "Of the Mode of Education Proper in a Republic," *ibid.*, pp. 8–9; Rush, "A Plan of a Peace-Office for the United States," *ibid.*, p. 183. Perhaps the clearest explanation of Noah Webster's position on the use of the Bible in American schools is in his letter to the editor of *Universal Asylum, and Columbian Magazine* 7 (September, 1791): pp. 191–192.

[59] Rush, "Of the Mode of Education Proper in a Republic," *Rush Essays*, pp. 8–9. This is Sidney's thesis in his *Discourses Concerning Government*, 19, ch. i, p. 52, *et passim*.

[60] Rush, "Thoughts upon Female Education," *Rush Essays*, p. 82; Rush, "Observations upon the Study of the Latin and Greek Languages," *ibid.*, p. 49; "Defence of the Use of the Bible as a School Book," *ibid.*, pp. 100–101; Rush to Richard Price, May 25, 1786, *Rush Letters* 1: p. 389; Rush "To the Citizens of Philadelphia: A Plan for Free Schools," March 28, 1787, *ibid.*, pp. 414–415. William Paley's celebrated *A View of the Evidences of Christianity* (London, 1794) was strongly recommended by Rush for this purpose, Rush to Ashbel Green, December 9, 1802, *Rush Letters* 2: p. 854.

[61] MS, p. 1.

[62] Rush, "Of the Mode of Education Proper in a Republic," *Rush Essays*, p. 10; Rush to John Armstrong, March 19, 1783, *Rush Letters* 1: p. 295; Rush, "An Eulogium in Honor of Cullen," *Rush Essays*, p. 333; Robbins, *The Eighteenth Century Commonwealthman*, pp. 12–13, *et passim*. For the importance of this idea of free inquiry in the dissenting tradition, see, e.g. Price, *Observations on the Importance of the American Revolution*, pp. 30–53, and George W. Pilcher, *Samuel Davies, Apostle of Dissent in Colonial Virginia* (Knoxville, Tenn., 1971), ch. vii, pp. 119–134, *et passim*.

[63] Rush, "Influence of Physical Causes upon the Moral Faculty," *Med. Inq. & Obs.* (5th ed.) 1: p. 123; Rush, "Thoughts upon Female Education," *Rush Essays*, pp. 83–84, and n.; Rush, "Defence of the Use of the Bible as a School Book," *ibid.*, p. 101; Rush, "On the Character of Dr. Sydenham," *Sixteen Introductory Lectures*, pp. 60–61.

formed in revolutionary "Schools of the Prophets" like Dickinson College.

On the positive side, education for Rush was the republicanization and Christianization of man in America: the making of the virtuous, well-informed, and patriotic citizen. It was, personally, his dauntlessly optimistic effort—worthy of the age—to accommodate special, evangelistic religious beliefs to a new political order.

Appealing to his own state legislature by title, while in fact petitioning all of the states, Rush outlined a scheme of republican education for Pennsylvania reminiscent of the projects of James Harrington and other writers of the 1650's and '60's in support of governmental responsibility for education. Free schools should be opened in townships and districts with one hundred or more families. Tax-supported, these schools would provide instruction in arithmetic, English, and German; and would send some of their pupils to four colleges, carefully located in the state. Graduates of the colleges, in turn, might study medicine, economics, and natural and international law at a state university in the capital city. All together, the free schools, the colleges, and the university would produce from the diverse populations of the state one great, prosperous, instructed, and enlightened citizenry.[64]

Two of the colleges projected by Rush for the state system were Dickinson and Franklin colleges, located at Carlisle and Lancaster, Pennsylvania, and conceived as places of higher education for the Scotch-Irish and German residents of the state. Rush—for whom higher education was indispensable to freedom—was of course the principal founder of the first institution and a zealous champion and charter trustee of the second.[65]

Nationally, Rush proposed the establishment of a federal university, "where the youth of all the states," he wrote, "may be melted (as it were) together into one mass of citizens after they have acquired the first principles of knowledge in the colleges of their respective states." [66] This nationalization of state college graduates, already instructed in the government and laws of their own states, would be achieved by educating them in "federal principles," that is, the branches of the new federal government, the Constitution, and the laws of the nation. In addition to these subjects, young men at the congressionally financed university should study the practical arts and sciences, including useful rather than ornamental literature, ancient and modern history, agriculture, industry and commerce, applied mathematics, military science—which he said, parenthetically, was regrettable but necessary—natural philosophy and chemistry, natural history, philology, German and French, and physical education.[67]

Rush believed that physical education was necessary in the curriculum not only "to impart health, strength, and elegance to the human body," but to promote "religious, moral and political instruction." [68] Republican students, moreover, should follow a uniform, "temperate diet" mainly of "broths, milk and vegetables. The black broth of Sparta, and the barley broth of Scotland," Rush added, "have been alike celebrated for their beneficial effects upon the minds of young people." [69] The new students of the republic, Rush continued, should refuse "spirituous liquors," since alcohol was damaging to both mind and body, and for that reason the drink of monarchies rather than of republics.[70] Dr. Rush further prescribed moderate

---

64 Rush, "A Plan for Establishing Public Schools in Pennsylvania," *Rush Essays*, pp. 2–4; *Autobiography*, p. 216; Rush to Charles Nisbet, May 15, 1784, *Rush Letters* 1: p. 335; Cremin, *American Education*, p. 423. Rush's copy of Harrington's *The Commonwealth of Oceana* (1656) is in the Library Company of Philadelphia, "Catalogue of Books."

65 Rush, "A Plan for Establishing Public Schools in Pennsylvania," *Rush Essays*, pp. 3–4; Rush to John Montgomery, October 15, 1782, *Rush Letters* 1: p. 290; Rush "To the Citizens of Pennsylvania of German Birth and Extraction: Proposal of a German College," August 31, 1785, *ibid.*, pp. 364–368; Rush to Annis Boudinot Stockton, June 19, 1787, *ibid.*, pp. 420–427; Rush to John King, April 2, 1783, *ibid.*, pp. 298–299; Rush, "Of the Mode of Education Proper in a Republic," *Rush Essays*, p. 20; Lyman H. Butterfield, "Benjamin Rush and the Beginnings of 'John and Mary's College' Over Susquehanna," *Bulwark of Liberty, Early Years at Dickinson College; The Boyd Lee Spahr Lectures in Americana, 1947–1950* (New York, 1950) 1: pp. 30–39; James Henry Morgan, *Dickinson College, The History of One Hundred and Fifty Years* (Carlisle, 1933); James A. Bonar, " 'We Have Aimed Honestly At Doing Good': Trusteeship At Dickinson, 1783–1816," *Boyd Lee Spahr Lectures in Americana, 1962–1969* (Carlisle, Pennsylvania, 1970) 4: pp. 85–137.

66 Rush to Richard Price, May 25, 1786, *Rush Letters* 1: p. 388; Rush "To Friends of the Federal Government: A Plan for a Federal University," October 29, 1788, *ibid.*, pp. 491–495; Rush to John Adams, June 15, 1789, *ibid.*, p. 517; Rush, "An Address to the People of the United States. . . . On the Defects of the Confederation, *American Museum* 1 (January, 1787): pp. 9–10. Both Professor Good, *Benjamin Rush and His Services to American Education*, p. 261, and Professor David Madsen, *The National University; Enduring Dream of the USA* (Detroit, 1966), p. 16, credit Rush's formal proposal of a national university as the earliest. Rush's student and close friend, David Ramsay, had suggested the need for "a great Continental University" in his famous *Oration on the Advantages of American Independence* (Charleston, 1778), printed in *United States Magazine*, 1 (January–March, 1779): p. 105n, but apparently never developed the idea.

67 Rush, "Of the Mode of Education Proper in a Republic," *Rush Essays*, pp. 18–19, 13; Rush "To Friends of the Federal Government: A Plan for a Federal University," October 29, 1788, *Rush Letters* 1: pp. 491–495.

68 Rush, "Of the Mode of Education Proper in a Republic," *Rush Essays*, p. 13; Rush "To Friends of the Federal Government: A Plan for a Federal University," October 29, 1788, *Rush Letters* 1: p. 493. Cf. John Dury's educational program to develop "piety, health, manners, and learning," *The Reformed School* (London, ca. 1649), p. 24, cited by Cremin, *American Education*, p. 422.

69 Rush, "Of the Mode of Education Proper in a Republic," *Rush Essays*, p. 13.

70 *Ibid.*; Rush, "Three Lectures upon Animal Life," *Med. Inq. & Obs.* (5th ed.) 1: pp. 39–40; Rush, "An Inquiry into the effects of Ardent Spirits upon the Human Body and Mind, with

sleep, cleanliness, manual labor, and "occasional solitude" for his revolutionary scholars.[71]

In the early republic, Rush contended, there was little if any place for "ornamental literature":

Such are the histories of the incests and rapes and worship of heathen gods, with which the Greek and Roman classics abound, and which, to the disgrace of reason and religion, form a part of the education of boys in christian countries. Such are most of the fables and traditions of modern and ancient nations. Such are the disputes about words and names which have filled whole volumes, in many of our libraries. Such are all dissertations upon alchemical and mystical subjects; and such are most of the novels in all languages of the world.[72]

Rather than studying the useless "ruins of Palmyra and the antiquities of Herculaneum," American students should apply themselves to ancient and modern history so that they might discover the ways by which the science of government might be perfected.[73] "If the years spent in teaching boys the Greek and Roman mythology were spent in teaching them Jewish antiquities and the connection between the types and prophecies of the Old Testament with the events of the New," he wrote John Adams, "don't you think we should have less infidelity and of course less immorality and bad government in the world?"[74] The true record of God in time must be studied. From Sidney to Macaulay, Burgh, John Dickinson, and John Adams himself, Christian Whigs had demonstrated the power of historical study to vindicate God-given political liberty. And great dissenting English scholars like Joseph Priestley and Richard Price had shown its power to defend religious liberty as well. This is why Rush, true to his Commonwealth and evangelistic heritage, gave the study of history a central place in his republican curriculum.[75]

A practical study of great importance for Rush was that of eloquence, which he held to be vital in American education. "It is well known," he wrote,

how great a part it constituted of the Roman education. It is the first accomplishment in a republic, and often sets the whole machine of government in motion. Let our youth, therefore, be instructed in this art. We do not extol it too highly when we attribute as much to the power of eloquence as to the sword, in bringing about the American revolution.[76]

Thus, eloquence had helped make the Revolution and would now, as part of universal republican education, help preserve it as well.

Federal students must apply themselves to composition, too, in order to learn how to express new republican ideas and feelings. America should be independent in language as well as in politics, and her youth must be taught republican simplicity in writing. In Rush's words: "The turgid style of Johnson, the purple glare of Gibbon, and even the studied and thickset metaphors of Junius are all equally unnatural, and should not be admitted into our country."[77] Americans must write directly and without European affectations. Truths in the new republic were simple and, hence, should be simply expressed. And even those students who might not succeed in mastering republican prose would certainly profit from what Rush the psychologist believed to be the strengthening effect of composing on the operations of the mind.[78]

The study of vocal music ranked high in the new revolutionary curriculum. Music had, what Rush called, "mechanical effects in civilizing the mind, and thereby preparing it for the influence of religion and

---

an Account of the Means of Preventing, and the Remedies for Curing Them," *ibid.*, pp. 169–170.

[71] Rush, "Of the Mode of Education Proper in a Republic," *Rush Essays*, p. 13.

[72] Rush, "On the Means of Acquiring Knowledge," *Sixteen Introductory Lectures*, p. 359; *cf.* "Extract of a Letter to the Hon. William Samuel Johnson, L.L.D. President of Columbia College in New-York, from the Hon. Hugh Williamson, M.D. and L.L.D. Dated 24th Sept. 1789," *American Museum* 7 (February, 1790): pp. 103–105.

[73] Rush, "Of the Mode of Education Proper in a Republic," *Rush Essays*, p. 17; Rush, "Observations upon the Duties of a Physician," *Med. Inq. & Obs.* 1: p. 264; Douglass G. Adair, "Experience Must Be Our Only Guide: History, Democratic Theory, and the United States Constitution," in Ray A. Billington, ed., *The Reinterpretation of Early American History: Essays in Honor of John Erwin Pomfret* (San Marino, Cal., 1966), pp. 129–148, and H. Trevor Colbourn's Boyd Lee Spahr Lecture, "The Historical Perspective of John Dickinson," which formed part of his larger study, *The Lamp of Experience* 6: pp. 107–119.

[74] July 21, 1789, *Rush Letters* 1: p. 525.

[75] See e.g., James Burgh, *The Dignity of Human Nature; Or a Brief Account of the Certain and Established Means for Attaining the True End of Our Existence* (2nd American ed., Hartford, 1802), pp. 137–141; Joseph Priestley, "Lectures on

History and General Policy" in Brown, ed., *Joseph Priestley: Selections*, pp. 101–132, *et passim*; Catharine Macaulay, *Observations on the Reflections of the Right Hon. Edmund Burke, on the Revolution in France, In a Letter to the Right Hon. the Earl of Stanhope* (Boston, 1791), pp. 6, 19, 39, *et passim*; Robbins, *The Eighteenth Century Commonwealthman*, p. 350, *et passim*.

[76] Rush, "Of the Mode of Education Proper in a Republic," *Rush Essays*, p. 16. For the "mechanical action" of eloquence upon the moral faculty, another physical cause which Rush hoped to enlist in his scientific program to educate Christians and republicans for the new nation, see "Influence of Physical Causes upon the Moral Faculty," *Med. Inq. & Obs.* (5th ed.) 1: p. 113. "We find, in every age and country where Christianity has been propagated, the most accomplished orators have generally been the most successful reformers of mankind. There must be a defect of eloquence in a preacher, who, with the resources for oratory which are contained in the Old and New Testaments, does not produce in every man who hears him at least a temporary love of virtue" (p. 13).

[77] Rush "To Friends of the Federal Government: A Plan for a Federal University," October 29, 1788, *Rush Letters* 1: p. 493.

[78] Rush, "On the Influence of Physical Causes upon the Intellectual Faculties," *Sixteen Introductory Lectures*, p. 105; Rush, "Observations upon the Cause and Cure of the Gout," *Med. Inq. & Obs.* (5th ed.) 1: p. 188–189; Rush, "Lectures on Pathology. Influence of Government upon Health," Rush MSS, call number Yi2/7396/F22, pp. 313–314.

government" [79]—of course Christian religion and republican government! Music, too, had great power in controlling the passions which interfered with republican scholarship. And Rush the medical philosopher, once again coming to the aid of Rush the educational thinker, proclaimed music efficacious in curing diseases.[80]

Industry, commerce, and applied mathematics were subjects not to be neglected at the proposed federal university. Indeed, along with agriculture, they were vital studies in the new America, where republican civilization depended upon national prosperity. So much was this the case, Rush believed, that Congress should pay to send agents to Europe for the purpose of acquiring for use at home the latest knowledge in commerce, industry, and agriculture. Concerning the new American businessman, Rush emphasized that he should be as well educated as the American of older professions. "The time is past," he asserted, "when an academical education was thought to be unnecessary to qualify a young man for merchandize. I conceive no profession is capable of receiving more embellishments from it." [81] Business and businessmen were to be raised to a new dignity in republican America!

After the completion of their work at the federal university, Rush pointed out, the university graduates would not only be able to teach republicanism and federalism to their countrymen, but would form a corps of excellently trained civil servants. In fact, after the proposed national university had been in operation for thirty years, Rush urged, with high professionalism,

only its graduates should be allowed to fill civil service positions.[82]

Rush's concern with education was not limited to the men and boys of the Christian Republic. Women, too, had a definite place in Rush's revolutionary program. For too long, he maintained, American women had been oppressed by British-style educations. Now, in an enlightened republic, modish lessons at the harpsichord, novel-reading, and prattle on ladies' fashions and the theater simply would not do. American women must be given the best possible education in knowledge and virtue because of the new and great influence they exerted in republican society.[83] They were, indeed, in a position to form or deform the nation according to how they raised their children and dispensed their affections. Hence, they should be induced to read moral essays, history, theology, poetry, and travels. "It would require," Rush speculated, "a lively imagination to describe, or even to comprehend, the happiness of a country, where knowledge and virtue, were generally diffused among the female sex." [84]

Informing every opinion Rush ever advanced on education was his optimistic Enlightenment belief, which he shared with *philosophes* like Barbeu Dubourg, Beccaria, and Jefferson, in the molding power of education. Reinforced by Rush's new science of the mind, which he based upon the Lockean and Hartleyian principle of the association of ideas, there was no discernible limit to the educability of man.[85] If man could be

---

[79] Rush, "Of the Mode of Education Proper in a Republic," *Rush Essays*, pp. 13–14. "The effects of music, when simply mechanical, upon the passions, are powerful and extensive. But it remains yet to determine the degrees of moral ecstacy that may be produced by an attack upon the ear, the reason, and the moral principle, at the same time, by the combined powers of music and eloquence," Rush, "Influence of Physical Causes upon the Moral Faculty," *Med. Inq. & Obs.* (5th ed.) 1 : pp. 112–113.

[80] Rush, "On the Utility of a Knowledge of the Faculties and Operations of the Human Mind to a Physician," *Sixteen Introductory Lectures*, pp. 265–266.

[81] Rush, "Of the Mode of Education Proper in a Republic," *Rush Essays*, p. 16; Rush "To Friends of the Federal Government: A Plan for a Federal University," October 29, 1788, *Rush Letters* 1 : pp. 492, 495; Rush to Elias Boudinot?, "Observations on the Federal Procession in Philadelphia," July 9, 1788, *ibid.* 1 : p. 472. On the great importance of reading, writing, and arithmetic in the Republic, Rush wrote that "no man should be a voter or a juror without a knowledge of them. They should be a kind of sixth or civil sense," Rush to James Hamilton, June 27, 1810, *ibid.*, 2 : p. 1053. *Cf.* Benjamin Franklin's ideas on civic education, which also derived in large part from Locke, Milton, Harrington, and Sidney, Cremin, *American Education*, p. 377. Commerce, Rush believed, was the "best security against the influence of hereditary monopolies of land, and, therefore, the surest protection against aristocracy. I consider its effects as next to those of religion in humanizing mankind, and lastly, I view it as the means of uniting the different nations of the world together by the ties of mutual wants and obligations," "Of the Mode of Education Proper in a Republic," *Rush Essays*, p. 17.

[82] Rush "To Friends of the Federal Government: A Plan for a Federal University," October 29, 1788, *Rush Letters* 1 : pp. 494–495.

[83] Rush, "Thoughts upon Female Education," *Rush Essays*, pp. 81–89, 91–92; Rush, "Thoughts upon the Amusements and Punishments, Which Are Proper for Schools," *ibid.*, pp. 70–71; *cf.*, e.g., anon., "A Defence of the Female Head-Dress at Present in Fashion," *United States Magazine* 1 (June, 1779) : pp. 268–271, and Timothy Dwight's "The Friend. No. V," *American Museum* 6 (August, 1789) : pp. 154–156. For the little effect of Rush's ideas on girls' schools in Philadelphia, see Thelma M. Smith, "Feminism in Philadelphia, 1790–1850," *Penna. Mag. Hist. Biog.* 68 (July, 1944) : p. 247.

[84] Rush, "Thoughts upon Female Education," *Rush Essays*, pp. 87–88. In his MS copy of the *Syllabus of Lectures, Containing the Application of the Principles of Natural Philosophy, and Chemistry, to Domestic and Culinary Purposes*, Rush suggested to the students at the Young Ladies' Academy that they, as women scientists, could make important discoveries in the new field of home economics. Anthony Benezet's influence in Rush's thinking on the education of women is hard to determine. The Philadelphia Quaker founded schools for the education of girls and Negroes, and, in the latter case, Benezet's example was clearly recognized by Rush as an inspiration for his own efforts to improve the conditions of Blacks, Rush, "Influence of Physical Causes upon the Moral Faculty," *Med. Inq. & Obs.* (5th ed.) 1 : pp. 122–123, and n.

[85] The originality of Rush's conscious and programmatic use of associationism can be seen by comparing plans of education put forward at the time. See, for example, Hansen, *Liberalism and American Education in the Eighteenth Century*, which outlines some of the plans, including Rush's. Professor Hansen and other general students of Rush's educational ideas have failed, understandably, to perceive the radically different nature

shaped by enlightened, indirect legislation in society, as Rush firmly believed, then what could not be done to him by direct, scientifically conducted education? Clearly, every conceivable improvement of man was possible by means of education; but—and this was the crux of Rush's belief—education must be devised in terms of the truths of Christianity and republicanism.

Not unjustly, one might say that Rush's philosophy of revolutionary education for America was a highly idealized and systematized version of his own religious and political education in the Great Awakening "Schools of the Prophets" and the Whig-Enlightenment tradition.

VII. REPUBLICAN THEOLOGY: THE ENFRANCHISEMENT OF MAN IN THIS WORLD AND THE NEXT

A Christian cannot fail of being a republican. The history of the creation of man, and of the relation of our species to each other by birth, which is recorded in the Old Testament, is the best refutation that can be given to the divine right of kings, and the strongest argument that can be used in favor of the original and natural equality of all mankind. A Christian, I say again, cannot fail of being a republican, for every precept of the Gospel inculcates those degrees of humility, self-denial, and brotherly kindness, which are directly opposed to the pride of monarchy and the pageantry of a court.[1]

If Rush was a Christian revolutionary in his visions of history, society, medicine, and education—as we have been arguing—then to propose that he was a revolutionary in theology as well should not appear inconsistent. His *esprit de système* required it. Moreover, his age was one of universality, and for him to analogize boldly from politics to religion, or vice versa, had the clear warrant of the times.[2] The contrary assertion that, say religion and politics should be treated in isolation from each other clashed with Rush's own analogical disposition, for which he was famous in his day.[3] And his broad, mature evangelical principles,

rejecting as they did Calvinistic separation of the elect from the reprobate, lent even more credence to his universality of outlook.

As a boy, Rush observed in his own family that diversity of religious experience which was so true to life in the Middle Colonies. His ancestors had been Quakers and Baptists, his father was Episcopalian, and his mother held fast to evangelical Presbyterianism. His father and mother having different religious persuasions, Rush almost naturally inherited from them a liberal and tolerant—dissenting—attitude towards sectarian differences, an attitude later integral to his mature writings on religion.[4] With so many family circumstances exhorting him to religious freedom—not the least being John Rush's first taking religious sanctuary in America—it is no wonder that he became a revolutionary defender of liberty of conscience.[5]

Although Rush remembered his father as a saintly man, it was to his mother that he owed his evangelical religious character. She introduced him to Gilbert Tennent and Samuel Finley, thereby opening to him the hopeful world of revivalistic Christianity. At Nottingham, secluded from the bustling, everyday world of Philadelphia, Rush was formed by his uncle into a devotee of the evangelical religion of the Great Awakening. In fact, the paternal master of Nottingham did such an exemplary job of impressing his nephew with the benevolence of God that, his early Calvinism in the "Schools of the Prophets" notwithstanding, Rush later embraced the loving heresy of universal salvation. Given these New Side antecedents of family and education, the transition of his religious belief from wide sectarian tolerance to universal salvation was almost inevitable.

Rush's years with Finley succeeded in conforming his every word and thought to some religious purpose, and, consequently, it was never really possible for him in adult life to think secularly. His pietistic mentor, whom he considered one of the saints of the "Apostolic Age of the Presbyterian Church in America," taught him to regard every event, however slight its apparent meaning, as deeply laden with divine import; and thus Rush characteristically sought to fit his thoughts and perceptions into grand religious wholes. There was simply no place for accident in his cosmology. All truth, Rush had learned at Nottingham, was contained in the Bible. "Our Saviour in speaking of it calls it 'Truth' in the abstract," he wrote in 1807 after more than a half-century of experience and reflection.

---

of his philosophy of Revolutionary education, based as it was on his new psychological science which, in Rush's view, constituted a mental physics of social reform—the ultimate science of the Enlightenment.

[1] Rush, "Of the Mode of Education Proper in a Republic," *Rush Essays*, pp. 8–9. Basic studies of religion in the Revolution—a theme largely neglected, as Professor Charles W. Akers and others have shown—are Perry Miller, "From the Covenant to the Revival," in James Ward Smith and A. Leland Jamison, eds., *The Shaping of American Religion* (Princeton, 1961), pp. 322–368, Carl Bridenbaugh, *Mitre and Sceptre, Transatlantic Faiths, Ideas, Personalities, and Politics, 1689–1775* (New York, 1962), and Alan Heimert, *Religion and the American Mind.* See Prof. Akers's review of Heimert's book in the *New York Historical Society Quarterly* **51**, 3 (July, 1967), pp. 283–291.

[2] Willey, *The Eighteenth Century Background*, p. 137, *et passim.*

[3] Caldwell, *Autobiography*, p. 316; Samuel Cooper to William Bache, January 9, 1795, Bache Family Papers, Princeton University Library, cited by Butterfield, *Rush Letters* 1: p. 584n; Mitchell, *The Character of Rush*, p. 7.

[4] *Ibid.*, pp. 18–19; Staughton, *Eulogium*, p. 16; Rush to John Adams, July 13, 1812, *Rush Letters* 2: pp. 1151–1152; *Autobiography*, pp. 24, 27, 162–163.

[5] Rush, "Of the Mode of Education Proper in a Republic," *Rush Essays*, p. 8; Rush, "On the Causes Which Have Retarded the Progress of Medicine," *Sixteen Introductory Lectures*, p. 149; Rush, "An Enquiry into the Effects of Public Punishments upon Criminals," *Rush Essays*, p. 163.

It is the only correct map of the human heart that ever has been published. It contains a faithful representation of all its follies, vices, and crimes. All systems of religion, morals, and government not founded upon it must perish, and how consoling the thought—it will not only survive the wreck of these systems but the world itself. "The Gates of Hell shall not prevail against it." [6]

When Rush risked his life and fortune by signing the Declaration, he took it for granted that he had been chosen to serve a heavenly purpose in freeing America from *"antichristian"* monarchy; and when he later exposed himself—almost fatally—to the yellow fever epidemic of 1793, he just as confidently assumed his divine instrumentality. "Hereafter my name should be Shadrach, Meshach, or Abednego," he wrote his wife during the height of the epidemic, "for I am sure the preservation of those men from death by fire was not a greater miracle than my preservation from the infection of the prevailing disorder." [7] It has been said that Rush was self-righteous. He was, indeed, a great-souled, "messianic" personality, believing himself to be, in some mysterious way, a minister of God's providence and grace. [8] But to say that this made him a self-righteous person, with all the unattractive connotations that this phrase generates in what Rush and other men of his and earlier times considered the narrow, secular mind, is hardly justifiable and betrays a modern coarseness of sensibility.

Princeton was less confining than Nottingham in many ways, but again the heavy religious influence of one man fell upon Rush. Samuel Davies's example was more worldly than Finley's in the sense that the younger man had traveled abroad and had become an intimate of the leading dissenters of the age. Rush's closeness to Davies, so evident in the youth's touching eulogy to the prematurely dead minister, almost swayed his career in favor of law. And this same friendship between teacher and pupil afforded Rush a new scope of religious experience, much more comprehensive than the Nottingham experience, because of Davies's broad

culture and doctrinal learning. [9] Yet the faith of the man was intensely evangelical, like that of the great Jonathan Edwards who had preceded him in the administration of the college.

Back in Philadelphia, this time as Dr. Redman's apprentice, Rush occupied himself with medical duties and grim, pietistic self-examination. His thoughts were filled with death and what he must do to be saved—ultimate concerns Rush shared with his new teacher in the "Schools of the Prophets"—and he longed for that gift of divine grace which was necessary to place him among the elect. [10] A melancholy, brooding young man, almost as grave as Dr. Redman, Rush found the provincial city iniquitous and his fellow youth dissolute. [11] When George Whitefield thundered to a Philadelphia congregation about the redemptive sufferings of the Son of God, Rush became a true convert to Christ. [12]

Religion and public policy were already at this stage of his life inextricably connected in Rush's thought, thanks in large part to the influence of Samuel Davies, whose address to Rush's graduating class at Princeton, *Religion and Public Spirit,* had characteristically linked piety and social action. This his surviving letters amply

---

[6] Rush to John Adams, January 23, 1807, *Rush Letters* 2: p. 936; Rush to Samuel Miller, April 13, 1813, *ibid.,* p. 1193; Rush, "On the Application of Metaphysicks to Medicine," Rush MSS, call number Yi2/7400/F2, pp. 20–21; Rush, "Introductory Lecture to a Course of Lectures on the History and Practice of Physick," *ibid.,* call number Yi2/7400/F1, pp. 8–9; *Autobiography,* pp. 337–338; Rush, "Observations upon Worms, and upon Anthelmintic Medicines," *Med. Inq. & Obs.* (5th ed.) 1: pp. 205–206; Rush, "An Inquiry into the Causes of Premature Deaths," *Rush Essays,* p. 310; Rush, "An Inquiry into the Relation of Tastes and Aliments to Each Other," *Med. Inq. & Obs.* (5th ed.) 1: pp. 142–143.

[7] Rush to Mrs. Rush, September 10, 1793, *Rush Letters* 2: p. 657; Rush to Granville Sharp, March 31, 1801, Woods, "Correspondence of Benjamin Rush and Granville Sharp 1773–1809," *Jour. of Amer. Stud.* 1, 1 (April, 1967): p. 34; Goodman, p. 181.

[8] Rush to Mrs. Rush, August 29, 1798, *Rush Letters* 2: p. 805; Rush to Charles Nisbet, May 15, 1784, *ibid.,* 1: p. 335; *Autobiography,* p. 165.

[9] On Davies's books and reading habits, see Pilcher, *Samuel Davies,* pp. 101–106, 155; for the "relationship between evangelical dissent" and "pre-Romanticism," in Davies's poetry, see Heimert, *Religion and the American Mind,* p. 173. To what extent Berkeleyan immaterialism had infiltrated the College's faculty and students while Rush was there is moot, but it is certain that by 1768, when Rev. John Witherspoon became president at the urging of Rush, the faculty overwhelmingly sided with Berkeley. As to intramural religious strife, Rush's letters to Witherspoon are explicit. (see the untitled lecture by Rush printed in Good, *Benjamin Rush and His Services to American Education,* p. 241; Ashbel Green, "Life of Witherspoon," cited by McCosh, *The Scottish Philosophy,* pp. 187–188; Riley, *American Thought,* pp. 130–131; Rush to John Witherspoon, April 23, 1767, and December 29, 1767, *Rush Letters* 1: pp. 36–38, 48.) In any case, it is not too much to say that Rush at least came to know that belief in Nottingham orthodoxy was not universal; that, to choose a specific issue, there were Christians who preferred, to some degree, reason over revelation and moral philosophy over the plain and simple truths of evangelical Christianity which to him, President Davies, Finley, and Gilbert Tennent were primary.

[10] Rush to Enoch Green, 1761, *Rush Letters* 1: pp. 3–4; Rush to Ebenezer Hazard, September 27, 1762, August 2, 1764, November 7, 1764, March 19, 1765, May 21, 1765, June 27, 1765, November 18, 1765, December 23, 1765, *ibid.,* pp. 5–6, 7, 8–9, 10–11, 13–15, 16, 20, 22; *Autobiography,* pp. 164, 272; Bell, "John Redman," *Penna. Mag. Hist. Biog.* 81, 2 (April, 1957): p. 157; Dr. Redman to Benjamin Rush, April 4, 1767, Rush MSS, XXII: p. 10; Rush to Ebenezer Hazard, July 23, 1765, trans. from the Latin by L. H. Butterfield, ed., "Further Letters of Benjamin Rush," *Penna. Mag. Hist. Biog.* 78 (January, 1954): pp. 5–6.

[11] Rush to Enoch Green, 1761, *Rush Letters* 1: p. 4; Rush to Ebenezer Hazard, August 2, 1764, *ibid.,* p. 7. In 1793, Rush was to view the yellow fever epidemic as a "judgment of God upon our city," Rush to Mrs. Rush, October 30, 1793, *ibid.,* p. 733.

[12] Rush to Ebenezer Hazard, May 21, 1765, *ibid.,* pp. 13–14; *Autobiography,* p. 164.

show.[13] By the very nature of Rush's evangelical temperament, personal and social salvation were becoming gradually interwined for him in a reformed Calvinism which harkened back to the primitive, organic church, while at the same time anticipating his mature, universalistic and chiliastic views.[14] Ultimately, Rush would extend this youthful revivalistic faith—with its philanthropic, integrating, and egalitarian motives—to its logical conclusion in the doctrine of the salvation of all souls. But in the meantime, he needed to know life more directly, to think and feel more profoundly, to become a philosopher as well as a penitent. He had first to go to Edinburgh.

In his *Autobiography* many years after his trip overseas, Rush, in a mood of alienation from the modern world, deplored the effect of travel on his spiritual character and laid it down peremptorily that travel was adverse to religion itself.[15] From what he related about his experiences with Commonwealthmen, dissenters, and *philosophes* in Britain and France, and from the tenor of all the available evidence, a case can be made for the occurrence of a decisive religious change in him while abroad; or better, perhaps, the beginning of what he thought at the time to be a maturation and sophistication of religious belief.

Before and during his voyage, Rush's conception of God was severe, personally exacting, and terrifying—more in the Calvinistic tradition of Jonathan Edwards's *Sinners in the Hands of an Angry God* than in the opposite, liberal tradition of an infinitely satisfying divine love for man.[16] While abroad, however, his

agonizing sense of moral blame and vileness before God was diminished somewhat by the worldly concerns, amenities, and religious latitude of his new friends and associates among the liberals and dissenters.[17] Whether his fervid religious energies were also in part sublimated into directions of study and romantic love is, although a most interesting question, quite beyond the competence of this present writer. It suffices to note in this connection that the effect of his experience in Edinburgh, London, and Paris was religiously moderating, deepening, and universalizing, leading him, as he wrote years later, "to consider all denominations of Christians with a more equal eye than I had done in early life" and causing him to give up "an undue predilection for either of them." [18] Commonwealthmen, dissenters, and *philosophes* in all three capitals of European culture taught this doctrine of religious freedom.

At Edinburgh, a world center of Enlightenment thought, Rush was introduced to skepticism and rationalism, which counseled freedom of conscience without endangering his fundamental evangelical belief. Dr. Cullen's religious skepticism, for instance, disturbed the young American; but Rush explained it as an erroneous attempt to make religion conform to the objective methods of science. "Many of the Truths of Religion are Objects of Faith and not of Reason," he wrote in his student journal, and "we ought to believe them altho' we cannot comprehend them." [19] Indeed, he went on to argue in a manner that Gilbert Tennent, Samuel Finley, and Samuel Davies would approve, science itself was not exempt from reliance upon faith. Everyone agreed, for example, that the sun caused trees and plants to grow despite the fact that this truth had never been fully demonstrated.[20] One suspects from arguments like these that Rush was already a close student of Bishop Joseph Butler's *Analogy of Religion, Natural and Revealed* (1736), a book he admired throughout life.[21]

---

[13] E.g., Rush to Enoch Green, 1761, *Rush Letters* 1: p. 4; Rush to Ebenezer Hazard, September 27, 1762, November 7, 1764, May 21, 1765, November 8, 1765, November 18, 1765, *ibid.*, pp. 5–6, 9, 14–15, 18–19, 20. Prof. Akers has helped open a new vista on the American Revolution by calling for studies of the "effect of the Great Awakening" on Revolutionary leaders, especially in their "personality development," review of Heimert's *Religion and the American Mind* in the *New-York Historical Society Quarterly* 51, 3 (July, 1967): pp. 291, 289.

[14] Prof. Heimert's *Religion and the American Mind* and H. Richard Niebuhr's *The Kingdom of God in America* (New York, 1959) are indispensable general works for this chapter, and for this entire study.

[15] Pp. 164–165. See Dr. Redman's letters to young Rush at Edinburgh, warning him of "the depravity of human nature, the deceitfullness of our hearts, the temptations peculiar to every state," and counselling his ward not to "Trust in man, not even in princes," Rush MSS, April 4, 1767, and May 12, 1768, Rush MSS, XXII: pp. 10–11.

[16] E.g., Rush to Ebenezer Hazard, July 23, 1765, Butterfield, ed., "Further Letters of Benjamin Rush," *Penna. Mag. Hist. Biog.* 78 (January, 1954): pp. 5–6; Rush to Thomas Bradford, October 25, 1766, *ibid.*, p. 8; Rush to Ebenezer Hazard, June 27, 1765, *Rush Letters* 1: p. 16. See Joseph Haroutunian, *Piety Versus Moralism: The Passing of the New England Theology* (Hamden, Conn., 1964), pp. 131–135, *et passim*. Of Edwards's *Freedom of the Will*, Rush was later to write: "This work would have been immortal, had not the author unfortunately misapplied the doctrine of necessity, to support a favourite, but narrow system of religion. Where the doctrine is properly explained," he went on to assert his belief in universal salva-

tion, "it leads to views of the divine government both in time and in eternity, that are benevolent, comfortable and sublime. It does more—it prostrates, or rather annihilates human pride. It places the supreme Being upon his throne of universal power, and however much He may be admired, and adored in the creation or government of the natural world, I cannot help thinking that he appears to be infinitely more a *God* when he comes abroad—not upon the wings of the wind, but upon the wills of all his creatures, thereby demonstrating that there [is] but *one will in the universe*," Rush, "On the Application of Metaphysicks to Medicine," Rush MSS, call number Yi2/7400/F2, pp. 19–21.

[17] *Autobiography*, pp. 164–165, 79; Butterfield, "Love and Valor; or Benjamin Rush and the Leslies of Edinburgh," *Princeton Univ. Lib. Chron.* 9, 1 (November, 1947): p. 12.

[18] *Autobiography*, p. 79.

[19] "Scottish Journal," p. 67.

[20] *Ibid.*, pp. 67–68; *Autobiography*, p. 335.

[21] "I possess Butler's *Sermons*, also his *Analogy*, and have read them over and over and marked and selected passages from each of them. They are monuments of the strength of the human understanding. I feel in reading them as if I were in

With the agnosticism of David Hume, which he apparently mistook for Deism, Rush had far less patience. Yet it was not the infidel, Hume, but the moderate churchman, William Robertson, at whom he lashed out; for, in his Great Awakening view, Robertson and other lukewarm clergy who abandoned the evangelical Christian spirit for rationalism were, in Gilbert Tennent's words, "Scribes and Pharisees" more dangerous to the faith than any number of infidels. Atheists and infidels were at least forthright in their apostasies, not like those unconverted, dissembling ministers, Robertson and John Home, who hypocritically professed belief in Christianity while in fact subscribing to what Rush considered Deism.

Still, if Rush, as a disciple of the American prophets, found excessive rationalism cold and unattractive in religion and its advocates in the Church of Scotland unapproved ministers of God, he did nevertheless begin to admit a greater degree of reliance upon reason in his own defense of evangelical Christianity. Edinburgh University was the home of Enlightenment thinkers like Cullen and Black, and it was only natural that their faithful and very intelligent American pupil should discover in their imaginative use of reason a prop for his convictions. Other graduates of Edinburgh might disavow their orthodox religions altogether after having studied the new scientific curriculum, or perhaps modernize them by adopting intellectually respectable Deism or Scottish realism. But Rush in his absolute, evangelical faith would not compromise; instead he assimilated the new Enlightenment science, improved it by his future work and thought, and employed it— as a greater American thinker, Jonathan Edwards, had done before him—to give his version of Christianity a scientific plausibility. And for his guide in this momentous work of making religion and science once again complementary, he eventually chose David Hartley, pietist and Enlightenment scientist, the master Christian philosopher, who to Rush had "established an indissoluble union between physiology, metaphysics, and Christianity." [22]

Rush followed Hartley—that "saint of the first order" —and not the Scottish philosophers essentially because the English physico-theologian had not abandoned revealed religion for moral philosophy the way Francis Hutcheson and Thomas Reid had done—and Dugald

Stewart would soon do.[23] In a deeply significant passage, Rush mirrored what he called Hartley's "truly evangelical" morality:

If moral precepts alone could have reformed mankind, the mission of the Son of God into our world, would have been unnecessary. He came to promulgate a system of doctrines, as well as a system of morals. The perfect morality of the gospel rests upon a doctrine, which, though often controverted, has never been refuted, I mean the vicarious life and death of the Son of God. This sublime and ineffable doctrine delivers us from the absurd hypotheses of modern philosophers, concerning the foundation of moral obligation, and fixes it upon the eternal and self moving principle of *love*. It concentrates a whole system of ethics in a single text of scripture. "A new commandment I give unto you, that ye love one another, even as I have loved you." [24]

Like Hartley, Rush drew back from the *a priori* moral principles of natural religion, opposing any system which in any way detracted from the Scriptural omnipotence of God.[25] For the same reason, in his phi-

---

company with a visitor from another planet, alike elevated above ours in size and in the intellect of its inhabitants," Rush to John Adams, August 8, 1812, *Rush Letters* 2: p. 1157; Rush, "Observations upon the Duties of a Physician," *Med. Inq. & Obs.* (5th ed.) 1: p. 261.

[22] Rush to Thomas Jefferson, January 2, 1811, *Rush Letters* 2: p. 1075; Rush to John Adams, February 1, 1810, *ibid.*, p. 1035. It is essential to remember that by metaphysics Rush meant the science of the mind rather than the study of ultimate reality; Rush, "On the Application of Metaphysicks to Medicine," Rush MSS, call number Yi2/7400/F2, pp. 17–19.

[23] Rush, "Three Lectures upon Animal Life," *Med. Inq. & Obs.* (5th ed.) 1: pp. 51–54; Rush to Thomas Jefferson, January 2, 1811, *Rush Letters* 2: p. 1075; Rush, "Thoughts on Common Sense," *Rush Essays*, pp. 249–251; Rush, "On the Causes of Death, In Diseases That Are Not Incurable," *Sixteen Introductory Lectures*, pp. 86–87; Rush, "On the Vices and Virtues of Physicians," *ibid.*, p. 129; Rush, "On the Education Proper to Qualify a Young Man for the Study of Medicine," *ibid.*, pp. 174–175; Rush, "Influence of Physical Causes upon the Moral Faculty," *Med. Inq. & Obs.* (5th ed.) 1: pp. 95–97, 99–100, 103–104; McCosh, *The Scottish Philosophy*, p. 22; Grave, *The Scottish Philosophy of Common Sense*, ch. vii, pp. 224–257; *cf.* Witherspoon, *Ecclesiastical Characteristics*, pp. 28–30. "Next to my Bible," Rush confided to John Adams, "I find the most satisfaction in reading the works of Dr. Hartley upon both doctrinal and practical subjects. His morality is truly evangelical. His posthumous letters to his sister show him to have been a saint of the first order," February 1, 1810, *Rush Letters* 2: p. 1035.

[24] Rush, "Defence of the Use of the Bible as a School Book," *Rush Essays*, p. 105; Rush, "Three Lectures upon Animal Life," *Med. Inq. & Obs.* (5th ed.) 1: p. 47. "I fear all our attempts to produce political happiness by the solitary influence of human reason will be as fruitless as the search for the philosopher's stone. It seems to be reserved to Christianity alone to produce universal, moral, political, and physical happiness. Reason produces, it is true, great and popular truths, but it affords *motives* too feeble to induce mankind to act agreeably to them. Christianity unfolds the same truths and accompanies them with *motives*, agreeable, powerful and irresistible. I anticipate nothing but suffering to the human race while the present systems of paganism, deism, and atheism prevail in the world," Rush to Noah Webster, July 20, 1798, *Rush Letters* 2: p. 799.

[25] Hartley, *Observations on Man* (1749), 1: pp. 497–499, 512; Rush, "On the Application of Metaphysicks to Medicine," Rush MSS, call number Yi2/7400/F2, p. 21; Rush, *Diseases of the Mind*, pp. 10–11, 16; Rush, "On the Influence of Physical Causes upon the Intellectual Faculties," *Sixteen Introductory Lectures*, p. 102; Rush, "Three Lectures upon Animal Life," *Med. Inq. & Obs.* (5th ed.) 1: pp. 12, 16–17, 47, 51; Rush, "On the Opinions and Modes of Practice of Hippocrates," *Sixteen Introductory Lectures*, p. 292. Contrast Rush's evangelistic view of moral philosophy with that of more rationalistic dis-

losophy of animal life, he rejected the existence of a principle of life in the body.[26] Man's dependence upon God in ethics, in life itself, and in all things must be total; it was a view perfectly consonant with Rush's evangelical temper.

The "indissoluble union" which, Rush maintained, Hartley had formed between science and religion was cemented in a physiological psychology, which Rush borrowed along with its accompanying Hartleyian doctrines of vibrations and association.[27] Although depend-

ing mechanistically upon material processes, Hartley's psychology—and this was its chief attraction for Rush —began in God, was vitalized by God, and ended in God.[28] Moreover, Hartley's deity was a God of Love and his world was one of "benevolence." [29] There were no *a priori* faculties, like Hutcheson's moral faculty, intervening, however slightly, between God and man; rather, man in every respect was derived *a posteriori* from an omnipotent, infinitely loving God acting through a material world external to man.[30] And most acceptable of all to the American evangelical scientist was the final cause of the divine government, whose laws Hartley had described: the "ultimate happiness of all Mankind." [31]

In his own physiological system, advanced in the famous lectures on animal life, Rush, like Hartley, explained all life as having its only source in external force. "Life is the *effect*," he wrote, "of certain stimuli acting upon the sensibility and excitability which are extended, in different degrees, over every external and internal part of the body. These stimuli are as necessary to its existence, as air is to flame." [32] The opposite doctrine of a vital principle or cause of life in the body, he asserted in tacit agreement with Hartley, gave credence to the "atheism" of Pythagoras and Epicurus. Rush's doctrine of animal life, on the other hand, prevented both atheism and Deism, for "by rendering the continuance of animal life, no less than its commencement, the effect of the constant operation of divine power and goodness, it leads us to believe that the whole creation is supported in the same manner." [33] In accordance with true revelation and his own doctrine of animal life, he continued, the "Being that created our world never takes his hand, nor his eye, for a single moment, from any part of it." [34]

The influence of Edinburgh in Rush's mature thought was of course not exhausted in scientific philosophy. His conversion to republicanism had taken place while

senting thinkers like Joseph Priestley and Richard Price, Cremin, *American Education*, pp. 460–461; Heimert, *Religion and the American Mind*, pp. 282–283, *et passim.*

[26] Rush, "Three Lectures upon Animal Life," *Med. Inq. & Obs.* (5th ed.) **1**: pp. 5, 7, 9–10, 51–52; Rush, "Introductory Lecture to a Course of Lectures on the History & Practice of Physic," Rush MSS, call number Yi2/7400/F1, pp. 4–5; Rush, "Observations upon the Duties of a Physician," *Med. Inq. & Obs.* (5th ed.) **1**: p. 257; *Autobiography*, p. 94. Likewise, Rush objected to the absolute dualism of mind and body which was so precious to the Scottish realists, "Influence of Physical Causes upon the Moral Faculty," *Med. Inq. & Obs.* (5th ed.) **1**: pp. 105, 115; Rush, "Three Lectures upon Animal Life," *ibid.*, pp. 9–10, 46–47, 49–50; Rush, *Diseases of the Mind*, p. 360; Hartley, *Observations on Man* (1749) **1**: p. 512, *et passim;* Grave, *The Scottish Philosophy of Common Sense*, pp. 200–203. In his "On the Application of Metaphysicks to Medicine," Rush MSS, call number Yi2/7400/F2, p. 14, Rush asserted that the mind, whether material or immaterial, is subject to the same laws as animal matter. It was Rush's opposition to strict mind-body dualism which principally led I. Woodbridge Riley to oversimplify Rush's position by classifying him as the "head of the Philadelphia school of materialists," "Benjamin Rush as Materialist and Realist," *Bull. Johns Hopkins Hospital* **18** (1907): p. 101. Riley's perspective on Rush was confined—and understandably so—to that of the historian of philosophy; and as a technical critic of philosophical systems, Riley found Rush's philosophy eclectic, unoriginal, and inconsistent. The intellectual historian's perspective, however, should be wider in range and based not only upon formal consistencies or inconsistencies of ideas but upon larger coherences of ideas and objective historical events. Else, particularly in the case of a thinker like Rush, we risk the danger of failing to appreciate objective events like the Great Awakening and the American Revolution as primary conditions of thought. More careful than Riley, although still missing the profoundly religious character of all of Rush's thought, were Herbert W. Schneider, *A History of American Philosophy* (New York, 1947), pp. 74–76, 228–229, 241, 247, 446, and Joseph L. Blau, *Men and Movements in American Philosophy*, pp. 46, 56, 61, 65–72, 152, 314.

[27] Hartley, *Observations on Man* (1749) **1**: ch. i, pp. 5–114; Rush, "On the Application of Metaphysicks to Medicine," Rush MSS, call number Yi2/7400/F2, pp. 13–14, 22–25; Rush, "Three Lectures upon Animal Life," *Med. Inq. & Obs.* (5th ed.) **1**: p. 5; Rush, "Two Lectures upon the Pleasures of the Senses and of the Mind," *Sixteen Introductory Lectures*, pp. 448–449, 339–340, 427–428. "In short," Rev. Samuel Miller concisely explained Hartley's doctrine of vibrations, "every sensation, idea, muscular motion, affection, and internal feeling whatever, is supposed, by Dr. Hartley, to correspond with some vibratory state of the medullary substance, so that the one may be regarded as the exponent of the other," *A Brief Retrospect of the Eighteenth Century* **1**: pp. 19, 17–20; D'Elia, "Benjamin Rush, David Hartley, and the Revolutionary Uses of Psychology," *Proc. Amer. Philos. Soc.* **114**, 2 (April, 1970): pp. 111–112.

[28] Hartley, *Observations on Man* (1749) **2**: prop. 3, pp. 9–13, 245; **1**: pp. 512, 83.

[29] *Ibid.* **2**: prop. 4, pp. 13–30, 245. "It is the prerogative of man to bring evil out of good, but it is the prerogative of God to bring good out of evil," Rush to John Montgomery, April 9, 1788, *Rush Letters* **1**: p. 456.

[30] Hartley, *Observations on Man* (1749) **1**: pp. 498–499, prop. 4, pp. 11–12.

[31] *Ibid.* **2**: prop. 94, pp. 419–425, esp. 420; Rush to James Currie, July 26, 1796, *Rush Letters* **2**: p. 780.

[32] Rush, "Three Lectures upon Animal Life," *Med. Inq. & Obs.* (5th ed.) **1**: pp. 7, 5–6, 47–51, 43–44, *et passim.* "I have supposed that there is but one self-moving Being in the Universe, that all motion is the effect of his hand imposed upon matter, and all volition the effect of his will imposed upon mind," Rush to John Adams, December 19, 1812, *Rush Letters* **2**: p. 1171.

[33] Rush, "Three Lectures upon Animal Life," *Med. Inq. & Obs.* (5th ed.) **1**: pp. 52–53; Hartley, *Observations on Man* (1749) **1**: p. 512.

[34] Rush, "Three Lectures upon Animal Life," *Med. Inq. & Obs.* (5th ed.) **1**: pp. 53–54, 47; Rush, "Lectures on Pathology," Rush MSS, call number Yi2/7396/F17, pp. 24–25.

he was at the university; and it was, in fact, a political consideration that had given rise to his rational awakening. For Rush, physiology and politics were closely related because of his belief in the unity of truth. Hence, he maintained, truth in physiology should be analogical to truth in politics, just as truth in politics should be analogical to truth in medicine. Writing in his "Three Lectures upon Animal Life," twenty-three years after he had joined with two other Edinburgh graduates in proclaiming America free, Rush put the analogy between politics and physiology this way:

The origin of power which was derived for ages from divine or hereditary right now rests exclusively upon the will of the people, while the origin of animal life which has been, time immemorial, derived from a self moving power . . . now reposes, probably for ever, upon external and internal impressions.[35]

Thus, the inference was clear from this and other statements, animal and political life were both effects of an all-powerful divine cause. Man neither lived because of a principle of life in his body, nor had life, liberty, and property as imprescriptible, *a priori* natural rights. He had life and other rights only because God gave them to him continuously out of his benevolence. "Self-existence," Rush protested over and over again in every imaginable connection, "belongs only to God." [36]

This view of the direct origin of republicanism in an absolute God, without the mediation of Lockean—and Jeffersonian—precepts of nature, was conformable to the language of the Declaration of Independence, especially where it acknowledged the "unalienable rights" bestowed upon man by his "Creator." "I have always considered Christianity as the strong ground of republicanism," Rush asserted to Jefferson.

The spirit is opposed, not only to the splendor, but even to the very forms of monarchy, and many of its precepts have for their objects republican liberty and equality as well as simplicity, integrity, and economy in government. It is only necessary for republicanism to ally itself to the Christian religion to overturn all the corrupted political and religious institutions in the world.[37]

The idea of the Christian republic as the sovereign, immediate work of God was elaborated by Rush in his philosophy of history, as we have already seen.

Rush's doctrine of animal life further reflected his personal synthesis of physiology, evangelical Christianity, and republicanism by arguing that the Christian religion and republicanism were the best stimuli of their

kind to life and health; and that at least in the case of Christianity, the healthful effect of true belief was evidence enough of its divine nature. "For Christianity was intended as much to promote health, as it was the moral happiness of mankind." [38] Christianity, moreover, like republicanism and physiology, had the same life-giving character but in infinitely greater degree. Just as physiologically the forces of life overcame the forces of death in man and the other animals in the natural world, and as liberty surmounted tyranny and revivified man in the political world, so Christianity triumphed over every kind of physical and metaphysical death.

Everywhere in the universe there was evidence of divine benevolence; everywhere there were signs for all to see of the paramountcy of love, of the final victory of everlasting life over death.[39] To Rush, the evangelical Christian physician who battled and lost to death so many times, true religion meant quite simply the conquest of mortality in every extended sense of the word, i.e., the full redemption of man through Christ:

"The Son of Man came not to destroy men's lives, but to save them." Excellent words! I require no others to satisfy me of the truth and divine original of the Christian religion; and while I am able to place a finger, upon this text of scripture, I will not believe an angel from heaven, should he declare that the punishment of death, for any crime, was inculcated, or permitted by the spirit of the gospel.[40]

If the Saviour had come to deliver men from the evil of physical and spiritual death, and if the whole creation bespoke His mercy and love in its economy—propositions which Rush unquestioningly accepted—then true

---

[35] Rush, "Three Lectures upon Animal Life," *Med. Inq. & Obs.* (5th ed.) **1**: p. 47; D. P. Heatley, *Studies in British History and Politics* (London, 1913), p. 46. For another use of this basic republican analogy, see Rush to Granville Sharp, April 22, 1786, Woods, ed., "Correspondence of Benjamin Rush and Granville Sharp 1773–1809," *Jour. Amer. Stud.* **1**, 1 (April, 1967): p. 29.

[36] Rush, "Three Lectures upon Animal Life," *Med. Inq. & Obs.* (5th ed.) **1**: pp. 52, 5, 7, 9–10.

[37] August 22, 1800, *Rush Letters* **2**: pp. 820–821; Rush to John Adams, July 21, 1789, *ibid.* **1**: p. 523.

[38] Rush, "Lectures on Pathology. On the Influence of Different Religions on the Health of the Body," Rush MSS, call number Yi2/7396/F23, p. 318; Rush, "Three Lectures upon Animal Life," *Med. Inq. & Obs.* (5th ed.) **1**: pp. 40, 43, 39, 13; Rush, "On the Causes of Death, In Diseases That Are Not Incurable," *Sixteen Introductory Lectures,* p. 77; Rush, *Diseases of the Mind,* pp. 39, 71; Eva V. Armstrong, "Portrait of Benjamin Rush from A Student's Note-Book," *Univ. of Penna. Library Chronicle* **5**, 2 (June, 1937): p. 45.

[39] E.g., see: Rush, "Three Lectures upon Animal Life," *Med. Inq. & Obs.* (5th ed.) **1**: p. 54; Rush, "Outlines of the Phenomena of Fever," *ibid.* (3d ed., rev. and enlarged) **3**: pp. 31–32; Rush, "On the Necessary Connexion Between Observation and Reasoning in Medicine," *Sixteen Introductory Lectures,* pp. 13–14; Rush, "An Inquiry into the Causes of Premature Deaths," *Rush Essays,* pp. 315–316; Rush, "On the Origin of Evil of Every Kind," Rush MSS, call number Yi2/7399/F36, p. 17 *et passim;* Rush, "An Account of the Bilious Remitting and Intermitting Yellow Fever, as It Appeared in Philadelphia, in 1797," *Med. Inq. & Obs.* (5th ed.) **2**: p. 43; Rush, "A Narrative of the State of the Body and Mind of the Author, During the Prevalence of the Fever," in "An Account of the Bilious Yellow Fever, as It Appeared in Philadelphia in 1793," *ibid.* **2**: p. 181.

[40] Rush, "An Enquiry into the Consistency of the Punishment of Murder by Death, with Reason and Revelation," *Rush Essays,* pp. 176–177; Rush, "Old and Copied Lectures on Pathology," Rush MSS, call number Yi2/7396/F3, pp. 60.2–60.4 (Rush's special pagination); Rush, "A Plan of a Peace-Office for the United States," *Rush Essays,* p. 185.

Christianity and philosophy joined in discrediting any religion which allowed for eternal punishment or spiritual death. Here, again, Rush's science perfectly accorded with and illustrated the great Biblical truth of Christ as the " 'life of the world,' 'the prince of life,' and 'life' itself, in the New Testament."[41] That the power of divine life and love was absolute was a fact certified by the Word and Works of God. In the Christian Republic of America, then in the world, and in the final state of man with God, life would by degrees attain its absolute perfection.

This belief in universal salvation, which came to Rush in various doctrinal forms from Arminian writers like John William Fletcher and Elhanan Winchester—"our Theological Newton"—was the more appealing to him because of its affinities with his characteristic way of integrating and universalizing his experience. "At Dr. Finley's School," Rush summarized his religious development,

I was more fully instructed in these principles [his mother's and Gilbert Tennent's Presbyterian principles] by means of the Westminster Catechism. I retained them but without any affection for them 'till about the year 1780. I then read for the first time Fletcher's [John William Fletcher's] controversy with the Calvinists in favor of the Universality of the atonement. This prepared my mind to admit the doctrine of Universal salvation, which was then preached in our city by the Revd. Mr. Winchester. It embraced and reconciled my ancient calvinistical, and my newly adopted Armenian [Arminian] principles. From that time I have never doubted upon the subject of the salvation of all men. My conviction of the truth of this doctrine was derived from reading the works of Stonehouse [Sir James Stonehouse's *Universal Restitution* (1761)], Seigvolk ["Paul Siegvolk" or George Klein Nicolai, author of *The Everlasting Gospel* (1753)], White [Jeremiah White's *The Restitution of All Things* (1712)], Chauncey [Charles Chauncy's *Salvation for All Men Illustrated and Vindicated as a Scripture Doctrine* (1782)], and Winchester, and afterwards from an attentive perusal of the Scriptures. I always admitted with each of those authors future punishment, and of long, long duration.[42]

---

[41] Rush, "Three Lectures upon Animal Life," *Med. Inq. & Obs.* (5th ed.) 1: pp. 53–54.

[42] *Autobiography*, pp. 163–164, and Dr. Corner's notes; Edwin M. Stone, *Biography of Rev. Elhanan Winchester* (Boston, 1836), pp. 67, 200; Joseph H. Allen and Richard Eddy, *A History of the Unitarians and the Universalists in the United States* (New York, 1894), p. 412; Rush to Elhanan Winchester, May 11, 1791 and November 12, 1791, *Rush Letters* 1: pp. 581–582, 611–612, the latter attributing the phrase *"Theological Newton"* to Dr. John Redman; Elhanan Winchester to Benjamin Rush, July 27, 1792, July 26, 1793, March 13, 1793, March 24, 1794, Rush MSS, XXII: pp. 96–99; Rush to Elizabeth Graeme Ferguson ?, January 18, 1793, *Rush Letters* 2: p. 628. For the background to the eighteenth-century debate on eternal punishment, see D. P. Walker, *The Decline of Hell: Seventeenth-Century Discussions of Eternal Torment* (Chicago, 1964). See William W. Fenn in *DAB*, s.v. "Chauncy, Charles." Very probably, it was Fletcher's *Three Checks to Antinomianism* (1771), so admired by John Wesley, that greatly impressed Rush, see *The Works of John William Fletcher* (first Amer. ed., Philadelphia, 1791); Allen and Eddy, *A History of the Unitarians and the Universalists in the United States*, pp. 376–

Did Rush as a physician ever acquiesce in the death of a patient? Emphatically not! How then could he accede to the orthodox Calvinist doctrine of Limited Atonement? God, the supreme physician, must heal all, must do what His humble assistant, Dr. Rush, tried to do but could not accomplish.[43] Did he love his fellow men to the point of risking his life again and again for their welfare? How infinitely greater, then, must be the love of God for man! Did he find a heavy predominance of good over evil, of pleasure over pain, in this life?[44] How perfectly blissful, then, must be the next. Himself a "minister of hope" in medicine, Rush found the only durable, absolute, most plausibly realizable hope in an all-loving God, whose mercy transcended His justice.[45]

Universalism or the final restoration of all souls, Rush contended, was founded in the human heart itself and easily demonstrable from natural and supernatural revelations. Just as in Rush's physiology the body of man was an entity, responsive to environmental stimuli and living and dying as a unit, so humanity was an entity which must stand or fall as one. Accordingly, the human race as a whole had sinned with Adam; hence it must be redeemed as a whole in Christ. "Truth is a unit. Man is passive in animal life, volition, and salvation by Jesus Christ."[46] Moreover, there were, Rush continued to argue from natural science, "passions" native to man which had for their object the integration of man with man and with God. These

---

377, 382–383. "I have read," Stone quoted Rush, "all Mr. Fletcher's writings, and I thank God that I ever did; for until I read Mr. Fletcher, I never could plead the promises of God with confidence; for being educated a Calvinist, I did not know I was included in the atonement. But Mr. Fletcher convinced me that Jesus Christ died for the whole world, and therefore that he died for Dr. Rush. I could then claim the divine promises addressed to me," *Biography of Rev. Elhanan Winchester*, p. 200.

[43] *Autobiography*, pp. 226, 336–338, 343–344; Rush to Elhanan Winchester, November 12, 1791, *Rush Letters* 1: pp. 611–612; Rush to Jeremy Belknap, June 6, 1791, and October 7, 1788, *ibid.*, pp. 583–584, 490; Rush, "An Inquiry into the Effects of Ardent Spirits upon the Human Body and Mind, with an Account of the Means of Preventing, and the Remedies for Curing Them," *Med. Inq. & Obs.* (5th ed.) 1: pp. 170–171.

[44] Rush, "Two Lectures upon the Pleasures of the Senses and of the Mind," *Sixteen Introductory Lectures*, pp. 454–455, 424–425; Rush to Mrs. Rush, August 29, 1798, *Rush Letters* 2: p. 805.

[45] Rush, "On the Study of Medical Jurisprudence," *Sixteen Introductory Lectures*, p. 377; Rush, "An Enquiry into the Consistency of the Punishment of Murder by Death," *Rush Essays*, pp. 174, 182. Rush read and enjoyed Abbé de Saint-Pierre's *Études de la nature* which, in Rush's words, showed that "everything in nature . . . breathes kindness and good will to man," Rush to Samuel Bayard, September 22, 1796, *Rush Letters* 2: p. 781.

[46] *Autobiography*, p. 229; Rush, "Defence of the Use of the Bible as a School Book," *Rush Essays*, pp. 108–109; Rush to Richard Price, June 2, 1787, *Rush Letters* 1: p. 419. See Haroutunian's discussion of the Universalism of Charles Chauncy, John Murray, and James Relly, *Piety Versus Moralism*, p. 135 ff.

passions for integration showed that man and the natural world were moving inexorably towards the ultimate term of reconciliation with their Creator.[47] And as if this gratuitous endowment of love were not enough to prove His benevolence, the Deity even attached pleasure to the use of the altruistic and religious passions. "It is impossible to advance human happiness," Rush wrote Rev. Jeremy Belknap, "while we believe the Supreme Being to possess the passions of weak or wicked men and govern our conduct by such opinions." [48]

The supernatural revelation granted to man in the Bible likewise demonstrated the truth of the final salvation of all men. But it did so more directly and more credibly than the "hyeroglyphics" of nature.[49] The Bible was the ultimate source of truth, and the one deep, unifying truth of the holy text was final restitution. "The idea of only one Soul being lost either by a defect of mercy to redeem, or of power to save after redemption, is pregnant with despair, and contrary to the universal command and obligation to believe the Gospel." [50] This was why the Bible must be read in the schools of America. "The great enemy of the salvation of man in my opinion never invented a more effectual means of extirpating Christianity from the world than by persuading mankind that it was improper to read the Bible at schools." [51] Progressively, men were discovering hitherto obscured truths in the Scriptures, as they were in the natural world. The "Spirit of the Gospel" was animating philosophers and theologians like Newton, Hartley, Winchester, and Rush himself. And each newly discovered revealed truth, like each discovery in philosophy, confirmed the all-inclusive benevolence of God.[52]

Universalism, which for Rush was synonomous in careful usage with Christianity, was perfectly and historically related to republicanism, in the same way that all truths were related to one another. Universalism and republicanism were both divine correctives, as it were, to man's perverted doctrines of religious and political absolutism, i.e., strict Calvinism and monarchism. "The spring which the human mind acquired by the Revolution has extended itself to religion," Rush happily informed Dr. Richard Price, dissenting minister and author of *Observations on the Importance of the American Revolution, and the Means of Making It a Benefit to the World* (1784).

The Episcopal clergy and laity have held a convention in this city and agreed on such alterations in their discipline, worship, and articles as will render the Episcopal Church the most popular church in America. They have adopted a form of ecclesiastical government purely republican. . . . While these changes are going forward in the Episcopalian Church, the Presbyterians and Baptists are showing an equal spirit of innovation. A considerable body of them who had been educated in the strictest principles of Calvinism, and many of whom are people who have long been eminent for their piety, have separated from their respective churches and are now forming an independent society under the direction of Mr. Winchester, an eloquent and popular Baptist preacher who has openly and avowedly preached the doctrine of final restitution. Tenets of the same kind are now spreading rapidly in New England, &c.[53]

The equality of all men as beneficiaries of divine love and the ultimate restoration and happiness of all men were views which were obviously more congenial to republicanism than to monarchism. Political equality, in fact, drew its very existence from religious equality.[54] God's free and overspreading love for humanity now

---

[47] Rush, "Three Lectures upon Animal Life," *Med. Inq. & Obs.* (5th ed.) 1: p. 28; *Autobiography*, pp. 337–338, 342–343; Rush to Elhanan Winchester, November 12, 1791, *Rush Letters* 1: p. 611.

[48] Rush to Jeremy Belknap, October 7, 1788, *ibid.* 1: p. 490; Rush, "Two Lectures upon the Pleasures of the Senses and of the Mind," *Sixteen Introductory Lectures*, p. 452.

[49] Rush, "Defence of the Use of the Bible as a School Book," *Rush Essays*, pp. 108, 96; Rush, "An Enquiry into the Consistency of the Punishment of Murder by Death," *ibid.*, pp. 166, 169; Rush, *Diseases of the Mind*, p. 116; Rush to Elhanan Winchester, May 11, 1791, *Rush Letters* 1: pp. 581–582.

[50] *Autobiography*, pp. 226, 342–345; Rush, "Defence of the Use of the Bible as a School Book," *Rush Essays*, pp. 96–97; Rush, "An Enquiry into the Consistency of the Punishment of Murder by Death," *ibid.*, pp. 176–177; Rush to Richard Price, June 2, 1787, *Rush Letters* 1: p. 419 and Richard Price to Benjamin Rush, September 24, 1787, Rush MSS, XLIII: p. 118.

[51] Rush to Jeremy Belknap, July 13, 1789, *Rush Letters* 1: p. 521.

[52] Rush, "Three Lectures upon Animal Life," *Med. Inq. & Obs.* (5th ed.) 1: pp. 8–10, 17–18, 24–25; Rush, "On the Origin of Evil of Every Kind," Rush MSS, call number Yi2/7399/F36, pp. 14–15; Rush, "On the Application of Metaphysicks to Medicine," *ibid.*, Yi2/7400/F2, pp. 11–12. "Human reason has at last overturned the errors and abuses of government;—The time I hope is not very distant when it will level all the more pernicious errors and abuses which have crept into religion,"

[53] Rush, "Lectures on Pathology. On the Influence of Different Religions on the Health of the Body," *ibid.*, Yi2/7396/F23, pp. 318–319; Rush, "Introductory Lecture to a Course of Lectures on the History & Practice of Physic," *ibid.*, Yi2/7400/F1, p. 9; Rush to John Dickinson, February 16, 1796, *Rush Letters* 2: p. 770. "To pry into the meaning of the prophecies is certainly a *duty*. Our Saviour condemns his disciples for being slow of heart in believing all that the Scriptures say concerning him, and commends Abraham for beholding his day afar off and rejoicing in the great events which were to follow it," Rush to Elhanan Winchester, May 11, 1791, *ibid.* 1: p. 581. Rush was confirming to Winchester what he had just read in the latter's *A Course of Lectures on the Prophecies* 1: p. 5, *et passim*.

[53] October 15, 1785, *Rush Letters* 1: pp. 371–372; Rush, "Of the Mode of Education Proper in a Republic," *Rush Essays*, pp. 8–9; Rush to Jeremy Belknap, June 6, 1791, *Rush Letters* 1: pp. 583–584; Rush to Thomas Jefferson, August 22, 1800, *ibid.* 2: pp. 820–821; Rush, "On the Application of Metaphysicks to Medicine," Rush MSS, call number Yi2/7400/F2, pp. 26–35.

[54] Rush to Jeremy Belknap, June 6, 1791, *Rush Letters* 1: p. 584; Rush, "Defence of the Use of the Bible as a School Book," *Rush Essays*, pp. 112–113; *cf.* Elhanan Winchester, *A Plain Political Catechism. Intended for the Use of Schools, in the United States of America: Wherein the Great Principles of Liberty and of the Federal Government, Are Laid Down and Explained, By Way of Question and Answer* (Greenfield, Mass., 1796). For a different view, see Rev. Thomas Reese, "Essay on the Influence of Religion in Civil Society. Number 6, *American Museum* 7 (May, 1790): pp. 262–263.

raised men to an equal condition in religion and government.

Whereas before, in the *ancien régime* of religion and government, men had been subjects to arbitrary power; now, in pre-millennial republican society, each man was not only a free and equal citizen but the personally redeemed of God. Just as each man, according to the Declaration of Independence, now held a special place in the new political order; so, according to Rush's doctrine of universal salvation, each man now held a special place in the order to come.[55] Ultimately, all souls would be rendered equal in the enjoyment of universal salvation, in much the same way as the American Revolution had rendered all men equal in the enjoyment of republican government. The perfect republic of men in this life, Rush analogized, would lead directly to the perfect republic of souls in the hereafter. Universalism was a new, revolutionary theology, worthy of the new age signaled by the emergence in history of American republican civilization.

Although Rush himself analogized from his revolutionary political universalism to a revolutionary religious universalism, he did not feel it necessary to convert others to the same experience and faith. Nor did he really desire to institutionalize his belief in a church. "The pride of ecclesiastical institutions, whether founded in the absurd ideas of apostolic succession or in the aristocracy of Presbyterianism" had no place in Rush's utopian Christian commonwealth.[56] He believed that men were by nature religious, possessing what he called variously "the sense of Deity," "the principle of faith," and—after Hartley—"theopathy." [57] Hence, there was no reason to force religion upon men or to importune them to accept sectarian doctrines; the way of the Lord was open to all men who used these divinely given aids to salvation and read the Bible. In religion, as in medicine and government, what mattered were principles not forms.[58] It was a scientific fact, moreover, that "a Religion of some kind . . . is as essential to the mind of man as Air is to Respiration." [59] "The opposite systems of the numerous sects of christians," Rush explained, "arise chiefly from their being more instructed in catechisms, creeds, and confessions of faith, than in the scriptures." [60] There was, however, nothing wrong in having many religious sects, except insofar as they detracted by their special creeds from the Biblical message of universal love. "There is no pagan opinion more contrary to nature and reason, and to the whole tenor, as well as to the most consistent interpretations, of the Scriptures, than the doctrine of men being called into existence on purpose to endure the pains of eternal misery." [61]

Sectarianism was more than a tolerable fact of religious experience in the United States and elsewhere; it was a positive good and evinced the wisdom and benevolence of the Almighty. A diversity of sects, each cherishing a particular religious truth, was God's

[55] Rush to Jeremy Belknap, June 6, 1791, *Rush Letters* 1: p. 584; Rush to Richard Price, June 2, 1787, October 15, 1785, *ibid.*, pp. 419, 371; *Autobiography*, pp. 226, 89.

[56] Rush to Jeremy Belknap, June 21, 1792, *Rush Letters* 1: p. 620; Rush, "Introductory Lecture to a Course of Lectures on the History & Practice of Physic," Rush MSS, call number Yi2/7400/F1, p. 33. Richard Eddy, the Universalist historian too strongly identifies Rush with the Universalist Church, "Dr. Benjamin Rush," *The Christian Leader* 55, 40 (October 1, 1885), and *A History of the Unitarians and the Universalists in the United States, passim.* Staughton's position (*Eulogium*, pp. 29, 16), as eulogist and close friend of Rush, that Rush was an eclectic and belonged to no sect, is more consistent with the available evidence; e.g., Rush to John Adams, April 5, 1808, *Rush Letters* 2: pp. 962–963. Even William Cobbett, the famous satirist and bitter enemy of Rush, recognized Rush's lack of sectarian attachment in his virulent way, Peter Porcupine (William Cobbett), *The Rush Light*, No. 1 (February 15, 1800). Rush wrote John Adams in the above-mentioned letter: "Accustomed to think for myself in my profession, and encouraged to believe that my opinions and modes of practice are just from the success which has attended them even in the hands of their enemies, I have ventured to transfer the same spirit of inquiry to religion, in which, if I have no followers in my opinions (for I hold most of them secretly), I enjoy the satisfaction of living in peace with my own conscience, and, what will surprise you not a little, in peace with all denominations of Christians, for while I refuse to be the slave of any sect, I am the friend of them all. In a future letter I may perhaps give you my creed. It differs materially from Dr. Brown's [Thomas Browne], as expressed in his *Religio Medici*. It is a compound of the orthodoxy and heterodoxy of most of our Christian churches," p. 963. Apparently, Rush never sent his "creed" to Adams.

[57] *Autobiography*, pp. 335, 339; Rush, "Two Lectures upon the Pleasures of the Senses and of the Mind," *Sixteen Introductory Lectures*, pp. 448, 445; Rush, *Diseases of the Mind*, pp. 219–220, 271–275, 358; Rush, "Three Lectures upon Animal Life," *Med. Inq. & Obs.* (5th ed.) 1: p. 43; Rush, "On the Utility of a Knowledge of the Faculties and Operations of the Human Mind to a Physician," *Sixteen Introductory Lectures*, pp. 262–263; Armstrong, "Portrait of Benjamin Rush from a Student's Note-Book," *Univ. of Penna. Lib. Chron.* 5, 2 (June, 1937): p. 45. "There is an irresistible propensity in all men to *believe*, if not in a Saviour, in great men, in certain books, or systems, or in themselves," *Autobiography*, p. 226.

[58] Rush to John Montgomery, February 20, 1786, *Rush Letters* 1: p. 380; John Lathrop to Benjamin Rush, May 5, 1788, Rush MSS, XXIV: pp. 144–145.

[59] Rush, "Lectures on Pathology. On the Influence of Different Religions on the Health of the Body," Rush MSS, call number Yi2/7396/F22, pp. 314–315; *cf.* the Enlightenment religious ideas of Barbeu Dubourg, Rousseau, and Franklin, Aldridge, "Jacques Barbeu Dubourg," *Proc. Amer. Philos. Soc.* 95 (1951): pp. 389, 392, 373–375.

[60] Rush, "Defence of the Use of the Bible as a School Book," *Rush Essays*, pp. 100–101; Rush, "Introductory Lecture to a Course of Lectures on the History & Practice of Physic," Rush MSS, call number Yi2/7400/F1, pp. 32–33. As had Doddridge and other dissenters before him, Rush praised Richard Baxter's comprehensive theology and liberal views of church polity: "He is justly considered as one of the greatest and best men England ever produced. His creed in religion embraced both the Calvanist and Arminian principles," Rush to John Adams, September 4, 1811, *Rush Letters* 2: p. 1101; Robbins, *The Eighteenth Century Commonwealthman*, p. 256.

[61] Rush, *Diseases of the Mind*, pp. 116, 45, 81; Rush to Elhanan Winchester, May 11, 1791, *Rush Letters* 1: p. 581; Rush, "Thoughts on Common Sense." *Rush Essays*, p. 252.

way of making sure that His revelation to man was kept alive.[62] Episcopalians, Roman Catholics, Baptists, Quakers, Presbyterians, Methodists, Unitarians, Lutherans, Moravians, and other denominations, by emphasizing various and different religious truths, safeguarded these precious truths against desuetude and loss. And a synthesis of these truths, Rush argued with his customary ingenuity, produced the grand, supreme truth of universal salvation—"When the different religious sects, like the different strings in a musical instrument, shall compose a harmony delightful in the ears of Heaven itself!"[63] This, of course, was a reason not only for religious freedom and equality, but for active encouragement of all religious sects. "Competition of different religious societies" was the only liberal way of "preserving visible religion in any country."[64] This was another side to Rush's work as a Christian revolutionary: his finding religious, not secular, arguments for the Revolutionary new order. And as if to point up his characteristic use of science to justify his religious beliefs, the Edinburgh-trained evangelist hypothesized sectarian differences to be in some measure physically caused and, therefore, involuntary.[65]

But if all Christian denominations were purposeful and more or less republican in nature, as Rush believed, it was still true that only those which fully subscribed to the doctrine of absolute and universal love in the New Testament were "truly catholic" and merited the title of republican Christianity. "To feel or to exercise the true Spirit of the Gospel nowadays," he wrote disappointedly in 1792, "seems to require a total separation from all sects, for they seem more devoted to their forms or opinions than to the doctrines and precepts of Jesus Christ."[66] Only republicanism and universal salvation together could produce the necessary physical causes required wholly to enfranchise mankind in this world and in the next. Every other combination of politics and religion fell miserably short of the Gospel plan for perfect human equality and happiness in the loving fatherhood of God. "The Son of Man came not to destroy men's lives, but to save them," was Rush's motto. The Son of Man would come again soon. And the revolutionary Christian Republic of the United States, which Rush himself had helped found as a divine agent, heralded the millennial reign of Christ—"the Redeemer's new empire in America"—when sickness, pain, and death of every kind would be conquered by absolute love and all men eventually saved. This was the ultimate American Revolution.[67]

VIII. AMERICA AS A CHRISTIAN REPUBLIC: THE REVOLUTIONARY VISION

Most of the distresses of our country, and of the mistakes which Europeans have formed of us, have arisen from a belief that the American Revolution is over. This is so far from being the case that we have only finished the first act of the great drama. We have changed our forms of government, but it remains yet to effect a revolution in our principles, opinions, and manners so as to accommodate

[62] *Autobiography*, pp. 339, 345, 224; Rush to Granville Sharp, April 27, 1784, *Rush Letters* 1: pp. 330–331; cf. Hartley, *Observations on Man* (1749) 2: prop. 45, 195. At Dickinson College, his "nursery of the Church of Christ," Rush planned to have students taught their respective catechisms, Rush to John Montgomery, June 21, 1799, *Rush Letters* 2: p. 812.

[63] Rush "To the Citizens of Pennsylvania of German Birth and Extraction: Proposal of a German College," August 31, 1785, *ibid.* 1: p. 367; Rush, "Observations upon the Cause and Cure of Dropsies," *Med. Inq. & Obs.* (5th ed.) 1: pp. 120–121; Rush, "Defence of the Use of the Bible as a School Book," *Rush Essays*, pp. 100–101; *Autobiography*, pp. 340, 224. "In the present state of human nature the division of Christians into sects is as necessary to the existence and preservation of Christianity as the divisions of mankind into nations and of nations into separate families are necessary to promote general and private happiness," Rush "To the Ministers of the Gospel of All Denominations: An Address upon Subjects Interesting to Morals," June 21, 1788, *Rush Letters* 1: p. 466.

[64] Rush to Granville Sharp, April 27, 1784, *ibid.*, pp. 330–331. Hence, Rush in public and private life was a member, loyal friend, and backer of many widely different churches, with a special interest in nationalizing and republicanizing their constitutions. E.g., see: Rush to John Adams, April 5, 1808, *ibid.* 2: pp. 962–963; Rush to Richard Price, October 15, 1785 and April 22, 1786; *ibid.* 1: pp. 371–372, 385–387; Rush to Mathew Carey, November 24, 1808, *ibid.*, p. 989; Rush to Granville Sharp, April 27, 1784, *ibid.*, pp. 330–331; Rush to Elias Boudinot? "Observations on the Federal Procession in Philadelphia," July 9, 1788, *ibid.*, p. 474; Rush to Jeremy Belknap, January 5, 1791, *ibid.*, p. 573; *Autobiography*, p. 79. "Religion is best supported under the patronage of particular societies. Instead of encouraging bigotry, I believe it prevents it by removing young men from those opportunities of controversy which a variety of sects mixed together are apt to create and which are the certain fuel of bigotry. . . . Religion could not long be maintained in the world without forms and the distinction of sects. The weaknesses of human nature require them. The distinction of sects is as necessary in the Christian Church towards the perfection and government of the whole as regiments and brigades are in an army," Rush to John Armstrong, March 19, 1783, *Rush Letters* 1: pp. 294–295.

[65] Rush, "Influence of Physical Causes upon the Moral Faculty," *Med. Inq. & Obs.* (5th ed.) 1: p. 120; Rush to Richard Price, June 2, 1787, *Rush Letters* 1: pp. 419–420.

[66] Rush to Jeremy Belknap, June 21, 1792, *ibid.*, pp. 620–621; Rush to Granville Sharp, November 28, 1783, Woods, ed., "Correspondence of Benjamin Rush and Granville Sharp 1773–1809," *Jour. of Amer. Stud.* 1, 1 (April, 1967): p. 21.

[67] Rush to Ashbel Green, August 11, 1787, *Rush Letters* 1: p. 434. "A disposition to search the Scriptures, and a belief in the millenium have lately appeared in different parts of the United States," Rush reported to Granville Sharp "The men who held this belief formerly were called 5th monarchists,—our citizens who hold it call themselves *Christocrats*," April 2, 1799, Woods, ed., "Correspondence of Benjamin Rush and Granville Sharp 1773–1809," *Jour. Amer. Stud.* 1, 1 (April, 1967): p. 33. Ramsay wrote that Rush in 1798 described himself to his former student as "a Christocrat," *Eulogium*, p. 103. For Rush as a latter-day "5th monarchist," preparing for the reign of Christ in the "fifth monarchy," see Rush to Granville Sharp, October 8, 1801 and April 2, 1799, Woods, ed., "Correspondence of Benjamin Rush and Granville Sharp 1773–1809," *Jour. Amer. Stud.* 1, 1 (April, 1967): pp. 32–37.

92   D'ELIA: BENJAMIN RUSH, PHILOSOPHER   [TRANS. AMER. PHIL. SOC.

them to the forms of government we have adopted.—to Richard Price, May 25, 1786.[1]

The social redemption of man, Rush believed, had begun with his own revolutionary generation. As early as 1772, two years after his return to the colonies, the young Christian republican began subjecting his native environment to new and rigorous criteria. Abroad in Britain and France, skepticism, Whig libertarianism, and Enlightenment rationalism had subtly pervaded his thinking, forcing upon him a critical social awareness. Deepened in his political, social, and religious understanding, he was now committed to reform wherever necessary and could no longer uncritically accept established institutions at home. Having gone overseas with the simple intention of becoming a well-trained physician at the University of Edinburgh, the greatest medical school in the world, Rush had returned to Pennsylvania a radical Christian intellectual as well, compelled by his new disposition to test the institutions of his country against the exacting standards of Enlightenment reason and Christian brotherly love.

From 1772, when his *Sermons to Gentlemen upon Temperance and Exercise* appeared, until 1812, the year his classic work on mental disease was published, Rush attempted to reconstruct American society in terms of what he took to be the new order of Christian republicanism. This was his program as a Christian revolutionary.

In his first book, *Sermons to Gentlemen upon Temperance and Exercise,* Rush, while principally arguing for temperance and exercise, struck obliquely at slavery and anticipated his elaborate attack on slave-keeping a year later. Although largely implicit, the new social conscience of the revolutionary—reflecting his anti-slavery correspondence with Barbeu Dubourg at the time—was unmistakably present in this early work; and Rush, as if still a trifle reluctant to offend, had his opinions published anonymously.[2] The ideal of the temperate and well-exercised man, obeying the divine injunction to fruitful activity, was to evolve during and after the Revolution into the new republican man of Rush's conception. "Labor," he emphasized later in another place, "favours and facilitates the practice of virtue."[3] And even though virtuous habits

were simply mechanical, i.e., neither moral nor rational in origin, the happy social effect was no different from what it would be in republican society where virtue was the "soul" of government.[4]

Rush's new republican man must necessarily be temperate. Drunkenness was a Tory vice, he agreed with more than one reformer of the day, but he added that spiritous liquors also produced the seditious and turbulent spirit of "anti-federalism, in every part of the united states. Hence anarchy is the constant companion, and tyranny the certain consequence of the use of these mischievous liquors."[5] Republican man was both enlightened and religious, and reason and religion depended upon sobriety for their unerring operations. Rush in his middle years sought to transform rather than eschew the doctrines and moral values he had inherited from Calvinism. Thus, intemperance was as much a danger to republican society as it was to the soul. For when political sovereignty derived from the people, an intemperate electorate must vitiate government by its choice of legislators. To protect the Christian Republic, laws must be passed regulating the number of drinking places, levying heavy duties on distilled spirits, punishing drunkards, and safeguarding the property rights of the chronic drunkard's family.[6] Here was Rush, the Enlightenment liberal, appealing to government for action in keeping with his new belief in legislative perfection of man and society. Rush the Christian revolutionary likewise asked religious leaders of all denominations to join together with secular governments in opposing the use of ardent spirits. Other Americans, too, were appealing to the new governments to support Christianity, "the professed religion of these states," as both an obligation to God for His assistance in the late war and as the perfect religion "to raise and cherish the seeds of universal love and compassion," as one writer declared in the *American Museum.*[7] But Rush alone had a politico-

---

[1] *Rush Letters* 1: pp. 388–390; cf. J. Franklin Jameson's seminal work, *The American Revolution Considered As A Social Movement* (Princeton, 1926). An excellent general discussion of early American culture is Howard Mumford Jones, *O Strange New World. American Culture: The Formative Years* (New York, 1964). Also important for this chapter are: Henry N. Smith, *Virgin Land: The American West As Symbol and Myth* (Cambridge, Mass., 1950); R. W. B. Lewis, *The American Adam: Innocence, Tragedy and Tradition in the Nineteenth Century* (Chicago, 1955); and Charles L. Sanford, *The Quest for Paradise: Europe and the American Moral Imagination* (Urbana, Ill., 1961).

[2] *Autobiography,* p. 82.

[3] Rush, "Influence of Physical Causes upon the Moral Faculty," *Med. Inq. & Obs.* (5th ed.) 1: pp. 109–110, 123.

[4] Rush, "Defence of the Use of the Bible as a School Book," *Rush Essays,* pp. 112–113; Rush, *Sermons to Gentlemen,* pp. 27–28.

[5] Rush, "An Oration on the Effects of Spiritous Liquors upon the Human Body, and upon Society; Intended to Have Been Spoken at a Late Commencement," *American Museum* 4 (October, 1788): pp. 325–327. See, e.g., "A Citizen," in *Pennsylvania Packet,* February 17, 1781; "Hortensius," "Observations on the Evil Consequences Attending the Excessive Use of Spiritous Liquors," *American Museum* 4 (August, 1788): pp. 123–124.

[6] Rush, "An Inquiry into the Effects of Ardent Spirits upon the Human Body and Mind, with an Account of the Means of Preventing, and the Remedies for Curing Them," *Med. Inq. & Obs.* (5th ed.) 1: pp. 169–170. John A. Krout has described this tract as "the first comprehensive, uncompromising attack upon ardent spirits ever written," *Origins of Prohibition,* p. 296; Asbury, *The Great Illusion,* p. 27.

[7] Rush, "An Inquiry into the Effects of Ardent Spirits," *Med. Inq. & Obs.* (5th ed.) 1: p. 170; Rush, "An Address to the Ministers of the Gospel of Every Denomination in the United States upon Subjects Interesting to Morals," *Rush Essays,* pp. 115, 123–124. See, e.g., Rev. Thomas Reese, "Essay on the

religious program of revolutionary reform to which he even made his science contribute.

Not only as a defender of liberty and prosperity, but as a scientist Rush viewed sloth and the immoderate use of ardent spirits as extremely undesirable. Physiologically, intoxication upset the delicate balance of life by overstimulation, while inactivity had the reverse effect of understimulation. In a Christian republican society, of course, men should be properly and naturally stimulated, without need of such artificial stimulants as distilled liquors and tobacco.[8] And an important natural stimulus to animal life was liberty, which Rush classed in significance with food, clothing, and fuel. This explains, in large part, why he opposed slavery on medical grounds, i.e., depriving men of the natural stimulus of liberty and replacing it with fear, which was destructive of animal life.[9]

Naturally, after revolutionizing America's political habits in 1776, Rush sought to alter her drinking habits as well by promoting wine, beer, ale, and other beverages as substitutes for ardent spirits. Wine, especially, was productive of the cheerful, benign temperament which should belong to the new republican man. Here, again, Rush the Christian republican thinker was synthesizing his political, scientific, and religious ideas in a philosophy of social reconstruction, while other advocates of reform were less ideological and more pragmatic, more concerned with empirical, melioristic reform of social evils than programmatic revolutionary change.[10] The legions of the Roman Republic, Rush noted, had been sustained by an even simpler drink than wine in their mighty exertions, a drink of vinegar and water. The men of the American republic, however, had at their disposal native fruits from which excellent and cheap wines, "truly federal" wines—as

one farmer suggested—could be made.[11] Those who preferred beer to wine could make it by using the syrup of the plentiful American sugar maple tree, which God in His providence had created to benefit humanity in many ways, not the least of which was by removing dependence upon the slave-worked plantations of the West Indies for sugar. The God of history, in Rush's teleological view, had now revealed that the forests of republican America were in the divine scheme of things to provide "innocent" maple sugar as a substitute for slave cane sugar, much the same way as they were to yield other cures for moral and physical diseases. "In contemplating the present opening prospects in human affairs," he wrote Thomas Jefferson, whose interest in sugar maples was more practical and characteristically nonteleological,

I am led to expect that a material part of the general happiness which Heaven seems to have prepared for mankind will be derived from the manufactory and general use of maple sugar, for the benefits which I flatter myself are to result from it will not be confined to our own country. They will I hope extend themselves to the interests of humanity in the West-Indies. With this view of the subject of this letter, I cannot help contemplating a sugar maple tree with a species of affection and even veneration, for I have persuaded myself to behold in it the happy means of rendering the commerce and slavery of our African brethren in the sugar islands as unnecessary as it has always been inhuman and unjust.[12]

To protect the valuable natural resource of the sugar maple tree, Rush called for appropriate laws.[13]

Slavery was for Rush an odious institution, equally condemned by natural and revealed religion; and the synthetic, programmatic nature of his revolutionary social thought, his Christian republicanism, is nowhere better seen, his philosophy of reform nowhere more consistent, than in his treatment of the problem of Negro slavery. In his crusade for the Negro's freedom and prosperity, as in his views on temperance, Rush showed the influence of Anthony Benezet, whom he regarded as God-like in his benevolence; although, unlike both Benezet and another gentle Quaker, John Woolman, Rush had complicated motives for his reform views.[14] All three agreed slavery was incompatible

Influence of Religion in Civil Society," *American Museum* 9 (March, 1791): pp. 153–155, and "E. C.," "The Importance of the Protestant Religion Politically Considered," *ibid.* 6 (July, 1789): pp. 41–42.

8 Rush, "Three Lectures upon Animal Life," *Med. Inq. & Obs.* (5th ed.), pp. 13, 39–40; Rush, "Observations upon the Influence of the Habitual Use of Tobacco upon Health, Morals, and Property," *Rush Essays,* pp. 267–268; Rush, "Lectures on Pathology. Morbid Effects of Cold," Rush MSS, call number Yi2/7396/F18, p. 67; Armstrong, "Portrait of Benjamin Rush from A Student's Note-Book," *Univ. of Penna. Lib. Chron.* 5, 2 (June, 1937): p. 45.

9 Rush, "Three Lectures upon Animal Life," *Med. Inq. & Obs.* (5th ed.) 1: pp. 39–40; Rush, "On the Causes of Death, In Diseases That Are Not Incurable," *Sixteen Introductory Lectures,* p. 77; Rush, *Diseases of the Mind,* p. 39; Rush, "Lectures on Pathology. Influence of Government upon Health," Rush MSS, call number Yi2/7396/F22, pp. 309–310.

10 On temperance, e.g., see anon., "Caution Against Rum!" *American Museum* 4 (August, 1788): p 124; "A Friend to Family Happiness," "Various Uses to Which Might be Applied the Money Saved By Declining the Consumption of Spiritous Liquors," *ibid.,* pp. 124–125; anon., "Plan for Establishing Schools in a New Country, Where the Inhabitants Are Thinly Settled, and Whose Children Are to Be Educated With a Special Reference to a Country life," *Columbian Magazine* 1 (April, 1787): p. 358.

11 *American Museum* 8 (November, 1790): pp. 242–243; Rush, "An Inquiry into the Effects of Ardent Spirits," *Med. Inq. & Obs.* (5th ed.) 1: pp. 161–163.

12 Rush "To Thomas Jefferson: An Account of the Sugar Maple Tree," July 10, 1791, *Rush Letters* 1: pp. 596–597, 595, 587, 592–593.

13 *Ibid.,* p. 595. Plain water, though, was the ideal drink for Americans, Rush, "Lectures on Pathology," Rush MSS, call number Yi2/7396/F21, pp. 207–209. For water as the "common drink" during the coming Millennium, see Winchester, *A Course of Lectures on the Prophecies,* 2: pp. 52, 47.

14 Rush, *Address to the Inhabitants of the British Settlements in America, Upon Slave-Keeping,* p. 9; Rush, "An Enquiry into the Consistency of the Punishment of Murder by Death, with Reason and Revelation," *Rush Essays,* p. 179. See his "Biographical Anecdotes of Anthony Benezet" and "Paradise of Negro-Slaves.—A Dream," *ibid.,* pp. 302–304, 305–310; George

with Christianity, but Rush found it grossly unrepublican as well. Rush believed that republican society and government rested upon virtue, as Montesquieu had pointed out, and further that virtue depended upon liberty. Essential to both virtue and liberty was health, i.e., that fullness of animal life that the Creator had intended for man, but which slavery destroyed in the victim, causing physical and mental disorders like lockjaw, melancholy, and dietary diseases, and in the master, producing mania. Failure to perceive that slavery violated the laws of God and nature was a pathological condition, according to Rush's medical science, and he classified it as "negromania," a collective mental disease prevalent in the slave areas of the world. Fortunately, though, reason and Christianity were becoming ever more powerful in their operations because of the American Revolution, and more and more negromaniacs were being cured of this pre-republican madness.[15]

When Rush signed the Declaration of Independence, he fully and unequivocally subscribed to the self-evident truths of equality and liberty for black and white alike. "Do the rights of nature cease to be such, when a negro is to enjoy them?" asked a freedman in the *American Museum*.[16] Rush answered emphatically not! Hence, consistent with his republican trust in laws, Rush petitioned for legislative action against slavery; and to make his crusade even more effective, he helped found America's first abolitionist society in Philadelphia.

As co-founder, secretary, and president of the Pennsylvania Society for Promoting the Abolition of Slavery, and the Relief of Free Negroes Unlawfully Held in Bondage (1774), Rush had other "romantic schemes" —as he said his critics called them—for the welfare of the Negro. The abolition of slavery in his native state, which was achieved in 1780, was just the beginning. In the Pennsylvania state ratifying convention, Rush worked hard to win acceptance of the proposed federal government. A principal reason he did so was that the Constitution outlawed the slave trade in the United States after 1808—or so in his idealism Rush chose to believe. "To the influence of Pennsylvania chiefly is to be ascribed the prevalence of sentiments favorable to African liberty in every part of the United States," Rush observed with pride to an English abolitionist. "You will see a proof of their operation in the new Constitution of the United States. In the year one thousand seven hundred an eight [*sic*] there will be an end of the African trade in America."[17] Now that revolutionary America was finally about to complete in the late 1780's her moral independence from depraved British civilization, whose legacy of vice to her former colonies and to the world included slavery, Rush believed that programs for the rehabilitation of the freedman must be undertaken. Regenerate white America, having put an end to the monarchical evil of Negro slavery, must now provide for the ex-slaves as citizens of the Christian Republic. As late as 1791, Rush noted that the freedmen of Philadelphia were "still in a state of depression, arising chiefly from their being deprived of the means of regular education and religious instruction."[18] The situation was clear to Rush the Christian social philosopher. With other humanitarians, black and white, he established in Philadelphia America's first Negro church, the African Episcopal Church of St. Thomas (1793). "I conceive it will collect many hundred Blacks together on Sundays who now spend that day in idleness," he wrote in his commonplace book.

It may be followed by churches upon a similar plan in other States, and who knows but it may be the means of sending the gospel to Africa, as the American Revolution sent liberty to Europe? Then perhaps the Africans in America may say to those who brought them here as slaves, what Joseph said to his brethren when they condemned themselves for selling him into Egypt.[19]

It seemed that the freedman might have a divinely appointed place in the Christian Republic, as a missionary of the regenerating American "Spirit of the Gospel" to Africa and—perhaps—as a political missionary there of the American spirit of government, too. It seemed also the case to Rush that the Negro had a

---

S. Brookes, *Friend Anthony Benezet* (Philadelphia, 1937), pp. 93–94, 151; Alice F. Tyler, *Freedom's Ferment; Phases of American Social History from the Colonial Period to the Outbreak of the Civil War* (New York, 1962), p. 465; Rush, "Influence of Physical Causes upon the Moral Faculty," *Med. Inq. & Obs.* (5th ed.) 1: pp. 121–122, and n.

[15] Rush to Granville Sharp, November 28, 1783, Woods, ed., "Correspondence of Benjamin Rush and Granville Sharp 1773–1809," *Jour. Amer. Stud.* 1, 1 (April, 1967): p. 20; Rush to John Coakley Lettsom, April 21, 1788, *Rush Letters* 1: pp. 457–459; Rush, *Diseases of the Mind*, p. 41; Rush, *Address to the Inhabitants of the British Settlements in America, Upon Slave-Keeping*, pp. 12–13, 21–24, *et passim;* D'Elia, "Dr. Benjamin Rush and the Negro," *Journal of the History of Ideas* 30, 3 (July–Sept., 1969): pp. 413–422.

[16] "Letter on Slavery. By a negro," 6 (July, 1789): p. 80. Also, on the Declaration and slavery as incompatible, see the *Pennsylvania Packet,* August 3, 1782, and William Pinckney's speech in the *American Museum* 6 (July, 1789): pp. 74–77. "Slavery," wrote Othello from Baltimore, "should be abolished . . . because it is inconsistent with the declared principles of the American revolution," "Essay on Negro Slavery," *ibid.* 4 (November, 1788): p. 417.

[17] Rush to John Coakley Lettsom, September 28, 1787, *Rush Letters* 1: p. 442; Goodman, p. 298; Rush to Barbeu Dubourg, April 29, 1773, *Rush Letters* 1: pp. 76–77; Rush to Jeremy Belknap, May 6, 1788, *ibid.,* p. 460; Rush to Nathanael Greene, September 16, 1782, *ibid.,* p. 286; Ira V. Brown, *Pennsylvania Reformers: from Penn to Pinchot* (University Park, Pa., 1966), p. 7. See Winthrop D. Jordan, *White Over Black: The Development of American Attitudes Toward the Negro, 1550–1812* (Chapel Hill, 1968).

[18] Rush to Granville Sharp, August, 1791, *Rush Letters* 1: p. 608; Rush, *Address to the Inhabitants of the British Settlements in America, Upon Slave-Keeping*, p. 19.

[19] *Autobiography,* p. 202. "Now therefore be not grieved, nor angry with yourselves, that ye sold me hither: for God did send me before you to preserve life." Genesis XLV, 5.

special relationship to God in which his misery in this world as a slave was substituted for long punishment hereafter as a means to salvation.[20]

Another project for advancing the welfare of the nation's blacks was Rush's planned farm colony of "Benezet," named after the great Quaker reformer. Convinced that the Negro would prosper most and be happiest from farming his own land, Rush in 1794 donated 5,200 acres of his holdings in western Pennsylvania to the Abolition Society for distribution among ex-slaves in fee simple. Later he donated still more land, this time in Cambria County, Pennsylvania, to be used for the same purpose.[21] The Negro, Rush believed, was as well suited to yeoman farming as the white man. The black man had no permanent or special disabilities. Further, Rush hypothesized in a scientific paper read before the American Philosophical Society that a black skin—the principal difference between Negroes and Whites—was only a temporary condition, really a symptom of an inherited leprous disease which republican medical science would someday cure. According to Rush's revolutionary religious, political, and natural science, then, white and black men were equal, save for the Negro's inherited social and physical disadvantages which were temporary and removable by progressive republican social and medical science.[22]

Rush's hostility to slavery was of a piece with his general encouragement of agricultural and commercial values. "Farmers and tradesmen," he declaimed in 1788, "are the pillars of national happiness and prosperity."[23] Republican farmers and tradesmen must, of necessity, be free: labor was not the mean duty of slaves, but a requirement of all men created in the divine image. Agriculture and commerce as modes of labor were conducive to virtue, and virtue was the soul of republican society. Degrade men to slaves, Rush maintained as a true Commonwealthman, and they must adopt the anti-republican vices of theft, idleness, and treachery.[24] Even slaveowners themselves, although free, must become morally corrupted and thereby unfit for republican life by the barbaric sights of slavery. National virtue, it was clear to Rush, depended upon ex-slaves in farm settlements like "Benezet" and other republican farmers tilling the bountiful American soil.[25]

The new republican man must have a heightened sensibility like the pain-conscious Dr. Rush. To this end, vice must be replaced by virtue. As a favorite author, Helvétius, had written, men who lived in "despotic empires" like that of decadent Britain had not respect but "contempt for virtue."[26] The American Revolution was changing this by releasing the forces of virtue which now, after centuries of quiescence, were progressively reforming the world. The assemblies of Pennsylvania and the other states could and must quicken the great moral revolution by wise legislation against all private and public vices. "The preamble of a single law of Congress declaring in strong terms the folly and absurdity as well as inhumanity of war would do more good than a thousand volumes written against it," Rush wrote James Madison.[27] In this crusade against evil, legislators must be joined by philosophers and divines.[28] Together, they must civilize, Christianize, and otherwise ennoble and perfect man by abolishing slavery and regulating the use of ardent spirits.

Rush in his ideal conception of the Christian Republic recommended, on the analogy of the federal Constitution, "a plan of a new species of federal government for the advancement of morals in the United States."[29] A congress of representatives from each Christian sect, he urged, should be established as "an ecclesiastical federal government" to promote national morality. Like the political states in the new federal union, the sects would be protected by a constitution in the enjoyment

---

[20] "And when shall the mystery of providence be explained which has permitted so much misery to be inflicted upon these unfortunate people? Is slavery *here* to be substituted among them for misery *hereafter?* They partake in their vices of the fall of man. They must therefore share in the benefits of the Atonement. Let us continue to love and serve them, for they are our brethren not only by creation but by redemption," Rush to Jeremy Belknap, August 19, 1788, *Rush Letters* 1: pp. 482–483.

[21] Rush to the President of the Pennsylvania Abolition Society, 1794?, *ibid.* 2: pp. 754–755 and n.; Goodman, p. 303.

[22] "I am now preparing a paper for our Society," Rush wrote Jefferson, "in which I have attempted to prove that the black color (as it is called) of the Negroes is the effect of a disease in the skin of the leprous kind. The inferences from it will be in favor of treating them with humanity and justice and of keeping up the existing prejudices against matrimonial connections with them," February 4, 1797, *Rush Letters* 2: p. 786. His paper, "Observations Intended to Favour a Supposition That the Black Color (as It Is Called) of the Negroes Is Derived from the Leprosy," was read before the American Philosophical Society in July 1797 and published in their *Transactions*, old ser., 4 (1799): pp. 289–297. Daniel J. Boorstin compared Rush's and Jefferson's ideas on the Negro in *The Lost World of Thomas Jefferson*, p. 89ff.

[23] Rush to Elias Boudinot? "Observations on the Federal Procession in Philadelphia," July 9, 1788, *Rush Letters* 1: p. 472.

[24] Rush, *Address to the Inhabitants of the British Settlements in America, Upon Slave-Keeping*, pp. 2–3.

[25] Rush, "Influence of Physical Causes upon the Moral Faculty," *Med. Inq. & Obs.* (5th ed.) 1: pp. 118–119.

[26] Rush owned an English translation of *De L'Esprit: or Essays on the Mind, and Its Several Faculties* (London, 1759), p. 153; Rush, "Catalogue of Books."

[27] February 27, 1790, *Rush Letters* 1: p. 540.

[28] Rush, "Influence of Physical Causes upon the Moral Faculty," *Med. Inq. & Obs.* (5th ed.) 1: pp. 120–124; Rush, "An Account of the Vices Peculiar to the Indians of North America," *Rush Essays*, p. 260. Contrast Rev. Timothy Dwight's more general and secular ideas on American culture in "The Friend. No. V," *American Museum* 6 (August, 1789): pp. 154–156; *cf.* Anon., "On Republican Government," *ibid.* (November, 1789), p. 386.

[29] Rush "To the Ministers of the Gospel of All Denominations: An Address upon Subjects Interesting to Morals," June 21, 1788, *Rush Letters* 1: p. 466.

of their sovereign rights. The moral constitution of
the Christian Republic, Rush proposed, should include
an article authorizing the federal congress of clergy to
prevent notorious sinners from communion with the
constituent churches. The purpose of the national
Christian assembly, however, was to be exemplary and
constructive rather than disciplinary. It was to be that
of Christianizing man and society, of achieving in
America that "dominion of grace" which seventeenth-
century Fifth Monarchy Men had failed to achieve in
England. "By the gradual operation of such natural
means," he concluded his "Address" to the clergy of
the United States, "the kingdoms of this world are
probably to become the kingdoms of the Prince of
Righteousness and Peace." [30] And as we have seen,
Rush believed that the natural means of reforming
America and the world, revealed by God in the eighteenth century, was moral science.

The brutalization of man, in Rush's highly subtle
view, was a complicated psychological process, not to
be reversed simply by freeing slaves and encouraging
temperance. Pre-republican evils were many, varied,
and often hidden. They, each of them, had to be
destroyed by right reason and enlightened religion
before man could be perfected in republican society.
Total, scientific control of the environment was necessary to restore man's moral faculty and effect his reconciliation with God. With David Hartley, the great
disciple of John Locke whose system Rush accepted,
the American scientist believed that the association of
ideas was the natural mechanism by which mental
phenomena were combined in the mind after being
derived from physical phenomena. In this system of
physiological psychology, the mind of man was formed
by the physical environment. It was clear to Rush, as
we have already seen, that here was the ultimate social
science of the Enlightenment: a physics of reform by
which republican society and republican man could be
morally perfected by physical means. Change the social
institutions of man by law, education, custom, and other
physical means and man himself would be changed,
willy-nilly, by the mechanical effects of the new social
institutions upon his mind. [31]

An example of an evil with multiple and often
imperceptible effects for Rush was that of disrespect
for the human person. This evil was of course, within
Rush's terms of understanding, diffused throughout
human society by pre-republican, monarchical forms of

government. With the advent of republicanism, produced by the "Spirit of the Gospel" realizing itself in
a new order of love, measures should be taken to
enhance and ennoble the human person. Enlightened,
republican government drew its authority from a united,
confident, and self-respecting people. Intemperance,
slavery, dueling, war, cruel public and capital punishments, selfishness, excessive formalisms of every kind,
narrow loyalties, religious bigotry, political factionalism,
snobbery, and affectation—all of these and more were
for Rush abusive of universal, i.e., republican, man.
These social practices, based upon unnatural associations of ideas, separated men from one another after
the manner of old, decadent aristocratic regimes. "What
have the citizens of the United States to do with the
duels, the elopements, the crim. cons., the kept mis-
tresses, the murders, the suicides, the thefts, the forg-
eries, the boxing matches, the wagers for eating,
drinking, and walking, &c., &c., of the people of Great
Britain?," Rush wrote the editor of the new Federal
Gazette. "Such stuff, when circulated through our
country by means of a newspaper, is calculated to
destroy that delicacy in the mind which is one of the
safeguards of the virtue of a young country." [32] Old
and vicious associations of ideas imposed upon pre-
Revolutionary America by decadent Europeans, associations of ideas like those of dueling and honor, revenge
and public punishment of social offenders, war and
patriotism, must now be replaced with natural, republican associations of ideas, e.g., rational settlement of
differences and honor, brotherly love and reformation,
peace and benevolence to all mankind, so as to form
new, virtuous citizens of the world's first Christian
Republic. Republican society must universalize men,
accommodate them one to another, fit them together in
order "to produce regularity and unison in government." [33] In the Christian Republic, the world's first
community of grace where "no man 'liveth to himself,'"
all men must be brothers. God had ordained it so. [34]

Naturally, then, Revolutionary American society
must venerate man and human life in a new and full
way, unlike societies of the past. To achieve this, Rush
sought to outlaw cruel public and capital punishments,
dueling, war, and to erase sundry other institutions and
practices that detracted from human worth and dignity.
Rush as a physician maintained that fear of any kind
was physically and mentally debilitating; whereas hope,
confidence, and love were tonic. [35] Christianity and

[30] Ibid., pp. 466–467.
[31] D'Elia, "Benjamin Rush, David Hartley, and the Revolutionary Uses of Psychology," Proc. Amer. Philos. Soc. 114, 2
(1970). This was the "secret remaining to be discovered"
which would "cause future generations to grow up virtuous
and happy, and accelerate human improvement to a greater
degree than can at present be imagined," Price, Observations on
the Importance of the American Revolution, p. 43; Richard
Price to Benjamin Rush, July 30, 1786, Rush MSS, XLIII:
p. 116.

[32] Reprinted in American Museum 5 (May, 1789): p. 488.
[33] Rush, "Of the Mode of Education Proper in a Republic,"
Rush Essays, pp. 14–15; cf. Burgh, Political Disquisitions 3:
pp. 119–130.
[34] Ibid. 9: pp. 14–15; Rush, "An Enquiry into the Consistency
of the Punishment of Murder by Death, with Reason and
Revelation," Rush Essays, p. 175.
[35] Rush, "On the Amusements and Punishments Proper for
Schools," ibid., p. 67; Rush, "Three Lectures upon Animal
Life," Med. Inq. & Obs. (5th ed.) 1: p. 13.

republicanism were founded upon hope, confidence, and love. Monarchy and all forms of despotism were bottomed in fear. Corporal punishment was necessarily deleterious, anti-Christian, and unrepublican because it induced fear.[36] The imposition of the death penalty, too, caused fear and morbid weakness not only in the victim, where of course the issue was fatal, but in the spectators as well. War, dueling, and physical violence of all kinds were likewise harmful to animal life. In their opposition to these evils, Rush knew, *philosophes* like Beccaria and Barbeu Dubourg, Commonwealthmen like Burgh, and physico-theological reformers like himself and Hartley, were one.

True religion, i.e., Christianity properly understood as absolute brotherly love in the fatherhood of God, also opposed abuses of the human person; not just because of its necessary agreement with true philosophy on all things, but because of its divinely revealed truth of universal salvation and final restitution. "These principles" of universal salvation and final restitution, Rush wrote Richard Price, a Commonwealthman and dissenter, many of whose social reform ideas Rush shared,

have bound me to the whole human race; these are the principles which animate me in all my labors for the interests of my fellow creatures. No particle of benevolence, no wish for the liberty of a slave or the reformation of a criminal, will be lost. They must all be finally made effectual, for they all flow from the great Author of goodness, who implants no principles of action in man in vain.[37]

Belief in eternal punishment, moreover, was no deterrent to crime, immorality, and social disorder, as religious conservatives alleged[38] "The Son of Man is not come to *destroy* men's *lives* but to save them," emphasized Rush by adding his italics to the Biblical pronouncement. "I wish these words composed the motto of the arms of every nation upon the face of the earth," he continued, "They inculcate every duty that is calculated to preserve, restore, or prolong human life."[39] Himself a leading organizer of America's first Sunday school, opened in Philadelphia in 1791, Rush hoped that every young person in the United States would be taught the revolutionary truth that life and not fear

must be the guiding principle of the Christian Republic, binding citizens one to another in this life and preparing them thereby for the all-loving benevolence of God in the next. In these Sunday schools and in public schools every young person would learn that war, dueling, and violence to man in general were anti-Christian.

War, to Rush's mind, was more than pathogenic: it was a disease itself, "founded in the imperfection of political bodies, just as fevers are founded on the weakness of the animal body."[40] Consequently and by medical analogy, there existed a cure for the disease of war, and that cure was perfected republican government, which by its enlightened legislation—representative of the broad, enlightened electorate—would succeed in converting swords and spears into plowshares and pruning hooks.[41] The perfecting of republican government would be realized, Rush believed, and perfect government here in America and, in time, elsewhere would abolish war; more precisely, war would disappear once it was recognized to be the product of accummulated vices which enlightened laws could prevent. American lawmakers, educated in the basic truths of the new science of physiological psychology (which Rush believed Hartley and he himself had developed from Locke's psychology), could control and improve the environment and the minds of men by passing the right laws and repealing others, knowing as they did that the physical environment shaped men's minds by producing impressions upon the body which in turn caused associations of ideas as predictable as other events in the natural, Newtonian world. Republican legislatures must repeal militia laws, which, Rush was convinced, were productive of the vices which led to war: idleness, intoxication, quarreling, profanity, and violence.[42] The militia was no longer necessary even from a more immediate point of view, as the waging of war had become so simple as to allow fast recruitment of effective troops directly from the people at large. This had been amply demonstrated, he said, by American and French revolutionary experience.[43]

---

[36] Rush, "On the Amusements and Punishments Proper for Schools," *Rush Essays,* pp. 67, 70; Rush, "An Inquiry into the Effects of Public Punishments upon Criminals," *ibid.,* p. 163; Rush, "Lectures on Pathology. Influence of Government upon Health," Rush MSS, call number Yi2/7396/F22, pp. 309–312; Rush, "Defence of the Use of the Bible as a School Book," *Rush Essays,* p. 105; Rush, "On the Utility of a Knowledge of the Faculties and Operations of the Human Mind to a Physician," *Sixteen Introductory Lectures,* p. 270.

[37] June 2, 1787, *Rush Letters* 1: p. 419.

[38] Rush, "An Account of the Manners of the German Inhabitants of Pennsylvania," *Rush Essays,* p. 241.

[39] Rush, "An Enquiry into the Consistency of the Punishment of Murder by Death, with Reason and Revelation," *ibid.,* p. 176. For the Christian basis of American pacifism, see Merle E. Curti, *The Roots of American Loyalty* (New York, 1946), p. 213, *et passim.*

[40] Rush, "An Inquiry into the Natural History of Medicine Among the Indians of North America," *Med. Inq. & Obs.* (5th ed.) 1: p. 66; Rush to Jeremy Belknap, January 5, 1791, *Rush Letters* 1: p. 573, and n. 4 to p. 574.

[41] Rush, "A Plan of a Peace-Office for the United States," *Rush Essays,* p. 186; Rush, "Thoughts on Common Sense," *ibid.,* p. 252; Rush, "An Enquiry into the Consistency of the Punishment of Murder by Death, with Reason and Revelation," *ibid.,* pp. 180–181.

[42] Rush, "A Plan of a Peace-Office for the United States," *ibid.,* p. 185; Rush "To the Ministers of the Gospel of all Denominations: An Address upon Subjects Interesting to Morals," June 21, 1788, *Rush Letters* 1: p. 462. "Pompilius" agreed in his article, "On the Mischievous Effects of Militia Laws," *American Museum* 4 (September, 1788): pp. 224–225.

[43] Rush, "On Imposture in Medicine," Rush MSS, call number Yi2/7400/F5, p. 36. This assertion is a fine example of Rush's belief in didactic use of the past, however close the event. Cf. anon., "Of American Recruits," *American Museum* 4 (August, 1788): p. 128, in which the author wrote that "it

In the Christian Republic, where bellicose influences of every sort must be thwarted, Rush proposed to make elaborate use of the principle of the association of ideas in order to prevent militarism. The "instruments of death"—weapons of every type—should be made unfamiliar to the people and their use discouraged even in hunting. Hunting and gunning were morally dangerous as well as superfluous activities in civilized republican society, where meat was readily available from domestic stock. Nor did Rush, like some other critics of militia laws, favor hunting and gunning as substitutes for military training.[44] And this point helps illustrate how different Rush really was from other reformers of the period in his systematic use of science —his own psychologic science of associationism—in combination with his religious and political ideas. The unnecessary killing of animals served only to vitiate man's moral faculty by diminishing his sensibility to the pain and suffering of other creatures, including men. Witness the Roman emperor Domitian, who "prepared his mind, by the amusement of killing flies, for all those bloody crimes which afterwards disgraced his reign." [45] Witness, too, the savages of North America, whose moral insensibility derived reportedly from their dependence upon hunting wild animals for food.[46] The Indians, like the cruel, benighted ancients, lacked the highly civilized and eminently religious value of sensibility. This was so because of the pejorative associations of savage and ancient life—of wanton hunting in the first instance and gladiatorial contests in the second. All this could and should be changed in the new Christian Republic of America, where different and wholesome associations would produce morally regenerated men. "A receipt to destroy the insects that feed upon turnips, or to prevent the rot in sheep, will be more useful in America, than all the inventions for destroying the human species, which so often fill the columns of European newspapers," Rush asserted.[47] Legislatively, a good beginning would be the passage of laws for the protection of animals against abuse.[48]

The abuse of man, Rush held with Beccaria, John Howard, Barbeu Dubourg, and other Enlightenment reformers, had for too long been practiced by society in its penal and hospital systems, a fact obviously related to the inhumane associations of pre-republican times. The same perverted sensibility which allowed murder and torture as moral in war, allowed public execution and revengeful punishments of criminals as moral in peace. "The operation and progress of truth, though slow, is sure," Rush wrote John Howard in 1789.

Your excellent works I have no doubt will prove a seed of improvements in criminal law for future generations. To me there is no truth in mathematics or even morals more self-evident than that solitude and labor might be so applied for all crimes as to make the punishment of death and public disgrace forever altogether unnecessary.[49]

The callous treatment of patients in the hospitals likewise appalled the Revolutionary physician, who knew first-hand the military as well as civilian hospitals of America.[50] Religion and philosophy were equally outraged by these violations of man. "A belief in God's universal love to all his creatures," Rush argued from his republican theology of universalism,

and that he will finally restore all those of them that are miserable to happiness, is a polar truth. It leads to truths upon all subjects, more especially upon the subject of government. It establishes the equality of mankind—it abolishes the punishment of death for any crime—and converts jails into houses of repentance and reformation.[51]

In a monarchy, where men were mere subjects of a king, to be disposed of in ways he thought fit, cruel and capital punishments had some doubtful plausibility; but in a republic, where men were free, equal, and sovereign, life and personal dignity were inalienable. America was "in a forming state," Rush proudly observed to Howard, whose work he deeply admired.

Shall not the United States be favored with a visit from you? Ignorance and inhumanity prevail everywhere in our jails, though perhaps in a less degree from their size and number than in Europe. While in too many instances you can only deplore without being able to remedy the evils of

must gratify the benevolent mind to observe, that America is altering the method, or rather the want of method, in obtaining military recruits" by insisting upon men of good character.

[44] "Pompilius," On the Mischievous Effects of Militia Laws," *American Museum* 4 (September, 1788): p. 225.

[45] Rush, "Influence of Physical Causes upon the Moral Faculty," *Med. Inq. & Obs.* (5th ed.) 1: p. 118.

[46] *Ibid.*; See Rush's "An Account of the Vices Peculiar to the Indians of North America," *Rush Essays,* pp. 256–260, his corrective to the widely held European myth of the noble savage.

[47] *American Museum* 5 (May 1789): p. 489. *Cf.* Burgh, *Political Disquisitions* 3: pp. 105–106.

[48] Rush, "An Inquiry into the Natural History of Medicine Among the Indians of North America," *Med. Inq. & Obs.* (5th ed.) 1: p. 71; Rush, "Influence of Physical Causes upon the Moral Faculty," *ibid.,* p. 118; Rush, "On the Duty and Advantages of Studying the Diseases of Domestic Animals, and the Remedies Proper to Remove Them," *Sixteen Introductory Lectures,* pp. 295–317; Rush, "Two Lectures upon the Pleasures of the Senses and of the Mind," *ibid.,* pp. 447–448.

[49] October 14, 1789, *Rush Letters* 1: p. 527; Beccaria, *Essay on Crimes and Punishments;* Howard, *State of the Prisons in England and Wales, with Preliminary Observations, and an Account of Some Foreign Prisons* (1777–1780); Aldridge, "Jacques Barbeu Dubourg," *Proc. Amer. Philos. Soc.* 95 (1951): p. 388, *et passim;* Richard Price to Benjamin Rush, September 24, 1787, Rush MSS, XLIII: p. 118.

[50] Rush volunteered his services as a physician to the Continental Army in 1776, caring for the wounded at Trenton and Princeton, and a year later was appointed Physician-General of Military Hospitals, *Autobiography,* pp. 124–138. For his unfortunate tenure in the latter position, see James E. Gibson, *Dr. Bodo Otto and the Medical Background of the American Revolution* (Springfield, Ill., 1937), esp. chs. xv, pp. 185–194, and xvii, pp. 204–237; and Goodman, ch. v, pp. 83–106. Also, see Rush, "Thoughts upon Female Education," *Rush Essays,* p. 87; Rush to Jeremy Belknap, October 13, 1789, *Rush Letters* 1: p. 526.

[51] *Ibid.,* June 6, 1791, *ibid.,* p. 584.

jails in Europe, you may here perhaps forever prevent them by sowing the seeds of justice, policy, economy, and humanity in the minds of the present rulers of our country by your conversation and presence.[52]

Enlightened republican society was cognizant, as other societies were not, of the improvability of man through science, religion, and government. The object of punishment, according to Rush, physician to the Philadelphia Society for Alleviating the Miseries of Public Prisons, should be reformation of the criminal so as to prevent further crime by his example—his living example. Medical science, too, endorsed this humane treatment of offenders by revealing the nature of "vicious actions" to be often involuntary.[53] Men should not be punished simply because they suffered from a disease of the will which compelled them to steal, lie, or even kill. Punishing, instead of curing the morally or mentally ill, was tantamount to punishing the physically ill, and clearly absurd. The new medicine of the eighteenth century held out the promise of cures for all diseases, whether of the body or the will.[54] In America, which was making ready for the Coming of Christ, men should be healed and restored rather than destroyed. Murderers, thieves, drunkards, liars, and other less offensively deranged people should be treated medically in hospitals set aside for their benevolent care.[55] Again, in Rush's mind, enlightened republican science and theology together marked the beginning of a new age in the history of the world, a Millennium of benevolence which even great European reformers like Howard and Beccaria could only dimly perceive. For

America was to be more than the earthly city of the philosophers, more than a paradise of reason for humanity as in Barbeu Dubourg's vision. It was to be the perfect republic of souls. Not a life must be wasted in the Christian Republic, just as not a soul was to be wasted in the final divine government of the universe.

There were other and more subtle pre-republican vices which must be removed before the new American man and his society could be made whole. One of these was selfishness. Enlightened self-interest was good, Rush agreed with Harrington, Milton, Sidney, and other seventeenth-century political writers, because it was consistent with republican duty in promoting private and public happiness; selfishness, however, was bad in that it had a disruptive effect upon society by placing men at war with one another. The one produced universal order, the other particular disorder. The selfish, pre-republican man esteemed family, friends, and property above country; the man of enlightened self-interest put country first. The Republic came rightfully first because it was a whole larger than its parts of family, friends, and property. The republican, discerning this, placed country before all else, realizing that he was "public property."[56] He sought wealth, and was taught to seek it, but only in order to "encrease his power of contributing to the wants and demands of the state."[57] In this manner,

[52] October 14, 1789, *ibid.*, p. 528. For Rush as the earliest Pennsylvanian to condemn the death penalty publicly and wholly, see Albert Post, "Early Efforts to Abolish Capital Punishment in Pennsylvania," *Penna. Mag. His. Biog.* **68**, 1 (January, 1944): p. 41.

[53] Rush, *Diseases of the Mind,* pp. 264, 366; Rush, "On the Study of Medical Jurisprudence," *Sixteen Introductory Lectures,* pp. 389–390; Rush, "Thoughts on Common Sense," *Rush Essays,* p. 253. In an article and later in a book, Negley K. Teeters described Rush's best efforts in prison reform as anticipating many features of modern penology, "Benjamin Rush, Pioneer Prison Reformer," *Prison Journal* **23**, 2 (April, 1943): p. 306; and with John D. Shearer, *The Prison at Philadelphia, Cherry Hill,* p. 225.

[54] Rush, "Influence of Physical Causes upon the Moral Faculty," *Med. Inq. & Obs.* (5th ed.) **1**: pp. 114–115; Rush, "Observations upon the Duties of a Physician," *ibid.,* pp. 263–264; Rush, "On the Study of Medical Jurisprudence," *Sixteen Introductory Lectures,* pp. 384–385, 387–388; Rush, *Diseases of the Mind,* pp. 263–266.

[55] *Ibid.,* pp. 263–270, 243; Rush, "On the Construction and Management of Hospitals," *Sixteen Introductory Lectures,* pp. 208–209; Rush, "On the Study of Medical Jurisprudence," *ibid.,* pp. 389–390; Rush, "On the Causes of Death, In Diseases That Are Not Incurable," *ibid.,* p. 78. For Rush as the "Father of American Psychiatry," see Deutsch, *The Mentally Ill in America,* p. 72, and Shryock, "The Psychiatry of Benjamin Rush," *Amer. Jour. Psychiatry* **101** (January, 1945): pp. 429–432, esp. p. 432. On Rush as the greatest figure in the early history of the Pennsylvania Hospital, see Thomas G. Morton and Frank Woodbury, *The History of the Pennsylvania Hospital, 1751–1895* (rev. ed., Philadelphia, 1897), p. 40.

[56] Rush, "Of the Mode of Education Proper in a Republic," *Rush Essays,* p. 10. On the popularity of this idea, *cf.* "Sidney," "Maxims for Republics," *American Museum* **2** (July, 1787): p. 82, and "The Trifler," in *Columbian Magazine* **1** (December, 1786): pp. 164–165, who wrote that "Society has a right to demand an account of every man's employments. . . . The merit of every method of occupying the mind, must be weighed only by its relation to the benefit of mankind." See Rush's epistolary strictures on the "funding system," which he regarded as a kind of institutionalized selfishness, especially his letters to Thomas Fitzsimons, February 19, 1790, Butterfield, ed., "Further Letters of Benjamin Rush," *Penna. Mag. Hist. Biog.* **78** (January, 1954): pp. 30–31, and John Adams, October 2, 1810, *Rush Letters* **2**, 1067–1068, and August 8, 1812, *ibid.,* pp. 1158–1159, and see below, ch. ix; Rush, "Observations upon the Duties of a Physician," *Med. Inq. & Obs.* (5th ed.) **1**: p. 260; Rush, "Thoughts upon the Cause and Cure of Pulmonary Consumption," *ibid.* **1**: p. 42. "The funding system," he wrote, "and speculations in bank scrip, and new lands, have been fruitful sources of madness in our country," Rush, *Diseases of the Mind,* p. 66; *cf. Pennsylvania Packet,* December 9, 1784. On the identity of self-interest and public interest in Harrington's "equal commonwealth," see George H. Sabine, *A History of Political Theory* (3rd ed., New York, 1961), p. 503; on Harrington, Milton, and Sidney, see *ibid., passim,* Zera S. Fink, *The Classical Republicans; An Essay in the Recovery of a Pattern of Thought in Seventeenth Century England* (Evanston, Ill., 1945), *passim;* Robbins, *The Eighteenth Century Commonwealthman, passim.*

[57] Rush, "Of the Mode of Education in a Republic," *Rush Essays,* pp. 11–12. By this Rush meant that all wealth existed for the doing of good. In fact, God encouraged benevolence by designing it so that we experience pleasure when we do good, "Two Lectures upon the Pleasures of the Senses and of the Mind," *Sixteen Introductory Lectures,* p. 452. "But the unity of disease will derive still more support from comparing [it]

enlightened self-interest operated for the benefit of the nation and the world by drawing men together rather than repelling them from one another. "Freemen love the whole world, and wish to extend the blessings they enjoy to the whole human race. In what part of the globe, was the 'great family of mankind' given as a toast," Rush proudly asked, "before it was given in the republican states of America?" [58] Commerce, as an expression of enlightened self-interest, not only amassed wealth for the republic, but checked the power of hereditary landed aristocracy.

Selfishness was of course bad in religion and politics, where religious intolerance and political factionalism divided men from one another and thereby obstructed republican unity. No wonder tyrannical Great Britain led Europe in the incidence of sedition and rebellion. "Consider that we live three thousand miles from the nations of Europe," Rush instructed the editor of the *Federal Gazette,* "and that we have but little interest in their domestic parties, or national quarrels. The less therefore you publish of them, the better." [59] America must teach her people not suspicion and dislike for one another, but love for one another, thus spreading the healing divine Gospel to the ends of the earth. America must "make up," to use the words of Rush's evangelist teacher, Samuel Finley, "a party for Jesus Christ." [60]

Also unacceptable as coercive and discriminatory in the new republican society of America were oaths and affectations of all kinds. Oaths and test laws had no place in the United States, because it was Rush's belief that whatever was inconsistent with reason and Christianity was unrepublican. Oaths and test laws were unreasonable and pagan, having been first employed in

pre-Christian times to constrain men to act unjustly and unethically. In the Christian Republic, however, men would not have to be forced to obey the laws, since just laws would of themselves enjoin obedience. Oaths would thus become politically unnecessary. Religiously, they were already unnecessary in that every Christian in the very nature of his belief followed "that Being who has inculcated a regard for truth, under the awful consideration of his omniscience, and who has emphatically styled himself the truth." [61] The Christian republican, whose religion and national and state governments aimed for peace, union, justice, and truth did not need the "absurd and improper obligation of oaths." [62] Abolishing oaths and tests laws, moreover, would have the positive effect of discouraging perjury in the courts of the nation and, by association, promoting honesty in all transactions. And if all republicans were honest with one another, Christian with one another, as they should be in the Christian Republic, courts of law themselves would be unnecessary. Brothers in the fatherhood of God would settle their differences, if any, in a spirit of love. This belief of Rush helps explain why he was never really enthusiastic about nationalizing English common law the way, say, John Fenno was.[63]

---

with *moral* evil. I have said there is but one disease. I say—with equal confidence,—There is but one sin—(yes gent: however strange it may sound—I say again.—there is but one sin) —and that is *Self-Love.* When man fell, says a celebrated writer, he fell into *himself,* and into the same abyss he has drawn all his posterity. . . . This primary Sin of self love is the fountain of all his other sins. However different they may appear in their nature or effects they all originate in this inverted principle. We steal and murder only because we love ourselves better than our neighbors. . . . Tyrants and usurpers oppress their subjects and overthrow kingdoms and empires only to feed the principle of self love," Rush, "Old and Copied Lectures on Pathology," Rush MSS, call number Yi2/7396/F3, pp. 59–60.4

[58] Rush, "Lectures on Pathology. Influence of Government upon Health," Rush MSS, call number Yi2/7396/F22, p. 312; Rush, "Of the Mode of Education Proper in a Republic," *Rush Essays,* p. 17.

[59] Reprinted in *American Museum* 5 (May, 1789) : p. 488; Rush to John Adams, July 21, 1789, *Rush Letters* 1 : p. 522; *Autobiography,* pp. 339–340; Rush to Elias Boudinot? "Observations on the Federal Procession in Philadelphia," July 9, 1788, *Rush Letters* 1 : p. 474; *cf.* "Pennsylvanian" in *Pennsylvania Packet,* September 14, 1782.

[60] For the "ecumenical spirit" of the Great Awakeners, from which Rush generalized his ideal of the unity of post-Revolutionary society, see Heimert, *Religion and the American Mind,* pp. 140–141, 78, *et passim.*

[61] Rush, "An Enquiry into the Consistency of Oaths with Reason and Christianity," *Rush Essays,* pp. 131, 134; Rush, "Defence of the Use of the Bible as a School Book," *ibid.,* pp. 112–113, 128, 134, 129, 135. Rush opposed the Pennsylvania Test Law of 1777, and wrote against it in his *Considerations upon the Present Test-Law of Pennsylvania. Cf.* Price, *Observations on the Importance of the American Revolution,* pp. 67–68; Beccaria, *Essay on Crimes and Punishments,* p. 73. For a different point of view concerning oaths in a republic, see Rev. Thomas Reese, "Essay on the Influence of Religion in Civil Society," *American Museum* 7 (March, 1790) : p. 161.

[62] Rush, "An Enquiry into the Consistency of Oaths with Reason and Christianity," *Rush Essays,* p. 135; Rush, "A Plan of a Peace-Office for the United States," *ibid.,* pp. 184–185.

[63] Rush "To the Ministers of the Gospel of all Denominations: An Address upon Subjects Interesting to Morals," June 21, 1788, *Rush Letters* 1 : p. 463. See Fenno's "Essay on National Pride of Character," *American Museum* 6 (November, 1789) : pp. 391–393. *Cf.* Rev. Thomas Reese's "Essay on the Influence of Religion in Civil Society," *ibid.* 9 (January, 1791) : p. 34, where he writes of lawyers: "If the precepts of christianity had that influence upon us, which their excellence naturally leads us to expect, there would be little need of that order of men." However, Rev. Thomas Reese, whose conception of government was orthodox and negative, was much less optimistic than Rush about the successful influence of Christian precepts among men in civil society. For him, religion was a restraining influence on man's corrupted nature, an influence which operated in the conscience of man by keeping before him the awful prospect of final judgment and possible damnation. Rush's conception of man in society was positive and liberal because of his progressivistic religious and scientific ideas. Also, see "Resolutions Entered Into by a Respectable Number of Inhabitants of Germantown," March 1, 1787, *ibid.* 2 (August, 1787) : pp. 166–167, in which they agree to settle disputes among themselves out of court and amicably because of excessive court actions, "the chicane of the law," and "the corruption of our courts of justice."

Rush found affectation of every kind pernicious to republican society. Titles like "my Lord" and "my Lady" were abhorrent to him as harmful features of decadent pre-republican governments.[64] Their use degraded both the titled and the untitled by puffing up the former and debasing the latter, with disastrous consequences for the nation. Again, effete Great Britain exemplified this fact. Titles, moreover, failed the tests of reason and religion, which of course in Rush's view must be the case since titles were unrepublican. A republican way of according recognition to patriots, humanitarian as well as military and political, Rush wrote Jefferson, was by naming places and ships after them. This method of reward was scientifically desirable, too, as it made use of the principle of association. "From the connection between words and ideas," he explained his Hartleyian science to Jefferson, "much good might be done. A map of a state and the history of travels through the United States would fill the mind with respect for departed worth and inspire exertions to imitate it."[65]

Life in the Christian Republic should be simple and unaffected. America was no place for large-wigged dandies. Class-ridden London was the natural habitat for such people—not Philadelphia or Northumberland! Equally incongruous in America were those men who despised the stoutly republican horse, which had so nobly borne the heroes of Seventy-Six, in favor of coaches and liveried servants. It was imperative to Rush that Americans form a new, natural society, where men of simple republican manners would eschew old world affectations—in titles, dress, conduct, food, shelter, writing, medicine, and even thought—in order to achieve useful equality.[66] Americans, especially

legislators, should take their republican example from the Pennsylvania Germans and the Quakers.[67] Let them also look to the great revolutionary Americans in whom republican virtue shone so brightly: to John and Samuel Adams, Jefferson, Franklin, Madison, Hancock, Rittenhouse, Mercer, and legion others. Their very names, to paraphrase a poem of 1789, struck "ev'y title dead."[68] In them America and the world triumphed; they were the first generation of new men.

By these and other programs, Rush sought to construct a Christian republican society in America. "In America," he was convinced, "everything is new & yeilding. Here genius and benevolence may have full Scope. Here the benefactor of mankind may realize all his Schemes."[69] From Edinburgh and London, he had carried to America a new, revolutionary way of thinking about himself, his age, and his country. Evangelistic and scientific, assured both by reason and Christian revelation that man and society were perfectible, Rush tried to build the perfect Christian Republic in America. "Religion and Science," he proudly declared, "will have no prejudices or errors to encounter among us."[70] He began to reform American society even before Lexington, but it was the American Revolution which focused his reform ideas on a grand purpose.[71] "We have changed our forms of government," Rush wrote Richard Price, a staunch friend of America, "but it remains yet to effect a revolution in our principles, opinions, and manners so as to accommodate them to the forms of government we have adopted."[72] In his *Influence of Physical Causes Upon the Moral Faculty* (1786), read to the American Philosophical Society, the leading scientific body of the new nation, Rush provided his countrymen with what he thought to be the natural means for effecting this revolution in morals.

I am not so sanguine as to suppose, that it is possible for man to acquire so much perfection from science, religion, liberty, and good government, as to cease to be mortal; but

---

[64] Rush to John Adams, July 21, 1789 and June 4, 1789, *Rush Letters* 1: pp. 523–524, 514. Adams thought titles necessary in any government. See his letter to Rush of July 24, 1789, Biddle, ed., *Old Family Letters, A*, pp. 45–47. For Rush's rather common opinion, see, e.g., "Mirabeau," "Forerunners of Monarchy and Aristocracy in the United States," *American Museum* 12 (December, 1792): p. 336, and anon., "Rules for Changing a Limited Republican Government Into an Unlimited Hereditary One," *ibid.* (July, 1792): p. 56.

[65] August 22, 1800, *Rush Letters* 2: p. 820. Later, Jeremy Bentham, in the tradition of Hartley, was to classify these words and other words which created proper associations, "eulogistic" as opposed to "dyslogistic," Bower, *Hartley and James Mill*, p. 205. See Rush, "Influence of Physical Causes upon the Moral Faculty," *Med. Inq. & Obs.* (5th ed.) 1: pp. 117–120, *et passim*.

[66] E.g., Rush, "An Inquiry into the Natural History of Medicine Among the Indians of North America," *Med. Inq. & Obs.* (5th ed.) 1: pp. 86–87; Rush, "An Eulogium, Intended to Perpetuate the Memory of David Rittenhouse," *Rush Essays*, p. 361; Rush, "Observations on the Study of the Latin and Greek Languages," *ibid.*, pp. 28, 42; Rush, "Of the Mode of Education Proper in a Republic," *ibid.*, pp. 7, 13; Rush, "Observations upon the Duties of a Physician," 254–255; Rush, *Diseases of the Mind*, pp. 273–274; Rush, "Information to Europeans Who Are Disposed to Migrate to the United States of America," *Rush Essays*, pp. 189–190; Ramsay, *Eulogium*, pp. 102–106; Rush, "On Imposture in Medicine," Rush MSS, call number Yi2/7400/

F5, pp. 40–41. *Cf.* Dr. Hugh Williamson's letter to the *American Museum* 2, 2 (August, 1787): pp. 115–116; anon., "Pernicious Effects of Fashion in Some Cases," *ibid.* 8 (August, 1790): p. 73.

[67] Rush, "An Account of the Manners of the German Inhabitants of Pennsylvania," *Rush Essays*, pp. 233, 247; Rush to John Adams, March 19, 1789, *Rush Letters* 1: p. 507; Rush to James Madison, July 17, 1790, *ibid.*, p. 568.

[68] "Impromptu," "On the Approach of the President of the United States," *American Museum* 6 (November, 1789): p. 412. See *Autobiography*, pp. 115, 139–144, 151-152, 148-149, 217, 156, Rush to Richard Henry Lee, January 15, 1777, Butterfield, ed., "Further Letters of Benjamin Rush," *Penna. Mag. Hist. Biog.* 78 (January, 1954): p. 18.

[69] Rush to William Peterkin, November 27, 1784, *ibid.*, p. 27; Rush, "Defence of the Use of the Bible as a School Book," *Rush Essays*, pp. 112–113.

[70] Rush to William Peterkin, November 27, 1784, Butterfield, ed., "Further Letters of Benjamin Rush," *Penna. Mag. Hist. Biog.* 78 (January, 1954), p. 26.

[71] *Autobiography*, p. 89.

[72] May 25, 1786, *Rush Letters* 1: p. 388.

I am fully persuaded, that from the combined action of causes, which operate at once upon the reason, the moral faculty, the passions, the senses, the brain, the nerves, the blood, and the heart, it is possible to produce such a change in his moral character, as shall raise him to a resemblance of angels; nay, more, to the likeness of God himself.[73]

This other and greater revolution in human affairs—the fulfillment of prophecy by redeeming men in a perfect Christian community of love—was Rush's grand purpose, the real American Revolution for Benjamin Rush.[74]

PART THREE

THE GREAT DRAMA OVER

IX. GRAVE DOUBTS AND OTHERWORLDLY CONSOLATIONS

Since the year 1790 I have taken no part in the disputes or parties of our country. My retirement from political pursuits and labors was founded upon a conviction that all I had done, or could do for my country would be fruitless, and that things would assume the same course in America, that they had done in Europe, and from similar causes, and that disorder would reign every where until the coming of the Messiah. This disorder is perhaps necessary to form a contrast to his divine and peaceful government. "Offences must come." Tyranny, anarchy, war, debt, standing armies &c are the natural consequences of liberty and power uncontrouled by the spirit of christianity. They must therefore exist, perhaps to furnish an opportunity of a display of divine power in destroying them.[1]

In articulating his revolutionary vision of America, Benjamin Rush excitedly described history's transfiguration of "liberty and power" into Christian love. This glorious event, prepared over the centuries by an all-benevolent deity, was the real American Revolution. And the perfect Christian Republic of this world and the next was the final dispensation of God before the Millennium. In his philosophy of the American Revolution, as we have seen, Rush worked out the system of ideas on which the vision of the Christian Republic

must rest. This was, in Rush's phrase, the concluding act of the great drama of the American Revolution; and until his death in 1813 the Pennsylvania idealist allowed no reality, however privately discouraging, to end his dream of the Christian Republic. True, the language of despair and even defeat is plentiful enough in his letters, especially to John Adams, but so is the substance of hope in these same letters and in other writings.[2] Ultimately, Rush never really doubted that the "spirit of christianity" would triumph over all.

In the late 1780's and early 90's, however, this did not seem to be the case. There were signs that, despite fresh republican victories in new state and federal constitutions, pre-revolutionary "principles, morals, and manners" were not only reviving but taking on increasing strength. The spirit of Christianity was not controlling liberty and power to the extent that it must in the perfect Christian Republic. There was cause for alarm.

More vigorously than ever, Rush in 1790 condemned the idolization of Washington and the neglect of other revolutionary heroes as unbefitting a nation of Christian republicans. "What incense is perpetually offered to one of the military characters that acted only an executive part in the Revolution," he wrote Vice-President John Adams in obvious allusion to Washington,

and that too after the foundation of it was laid in principles and opinions disseminated by [James] Otis, [Josiah] Quincy, yourself, Saml. Adams, [John] Dickinson, and a few others. Had I leisure, I would endeavor to rescue these characters from oblivion and give them the first place in the temple of liberty.[3]

A "bitter and unchristian spirit" was abroad in the land, a counter-Revolutionary spirit which, Rush believed to his final day, was destroying hard-won republican equality by the "idolatrous worship" of one man. Indeed, he explained to John Adams as late as 1812, the deification of Washington was one of our

---

[73] Rush, "Influence of Physical Causes upon the Moral Faculty," *Med. Inq. & Obs.* (5th ed.) 1: p. 122.

[74] There is a further observation that should be made on the historical background of Rush's Christian Republic. As Butterfield has noted, Rush was fond—very fond, we might add—of the *Mémoires* of Maximilien de Béthune, Duc de Sully (1559–1641), which he possessed in the English translation. Although the present writer has never found in Rush's writings a specific reference to Sully's famous project for a Christian republic of Europe with an international amphicytonic assembly, the similarity of Rush's Christian Republic with its "ecclesiastical federal government" is too evident to be dismissed as coincidental. See Rush to John Adams, April 3, 1807, *Rush Letters* 2: p. 938–939n; Rush to John Adams, September 4, 1811, *ibid.*, p. 1103; Rush to John Adams, October 17, 1809, *ibid.*, p. 1021; Rush, "Catalogue of Books"; *Memoirs of the Duke of Sully, Prime Minister to Henry the Great. Trans. from the French, a new ed., rev. and corrected; with Additional Notes, and An Historical Introduction, Attributed to Sir Walter Scott* (4 v., London, 1856) 4: pp. 217–259.

[1] Rush to Granville Sharp, April 2, 1799, Woods, ed., "Correspondence of Benjamin Rush and Granville Sharp 1773–1809," *Jour. Amer. Stud.*, 1, 1 (April, 1967): p. 33.

[2] *Rush Letters, passim;* Schutz and Adair, ed., *The Spur of Fame, passim.*

[3] Rush to John Adams, February 24, 1790, *Rush Letters* 1: p. 534. See Rush's "Characters of the Revolutionary Patriots" in *Autobiography*, pp. 138–158.

"national sins," for which a wrathful Heaven called down the punishment of a new war.[4]

Another threat to the Christian Republic in Rush's view, another and even greater national sin which derived from the apparent failure of Christian spirit to control "liberty and power" in the years after the Revolution, was Alexander Hamilton's funding plan. In his Report on Public Credit of January, 1790, the secretary of the treasury had urged that foreign and domestic debts be funded at par and that the depreciated paper which Congress had issued be redeemed at par. Opposition was fast in coming from debtor and agrarian interests, and James Madison rose in the House to defend the original holders of certificates from exploitation by the increasing number of speculators. His motion to distinguish between the former and the latter in payment was rejected in February, but not before Rush had written to Madison in praise of the action. When Rush learned of the fate of the Virginian's proposal, he was shocked "that a man of any character should have opposed it." [5] And yet the truth was that Madison's just and patriotic motion had been defeated almost three to one and in the House of Representatives of the United States! "In reviewing the decision upon your motion," Rush wrote more sorrowfully than angrily to Madison, "I feel disposed to wish that my name was blotted out from having contributed a single mite towards the American Revolution. We have effected a deliverance from the national injustice of Great Britain, to be subjugated by a mighty act of national injustice by the United States." [6] The patriots living and dead, the widows and orphans of the fallen heroes, those impoverished by devotion to their country, and the lovers of republican virtue all cried out for justice.

But there was no justice forthcoming. Instead, as it became clear with every depressing year, Hamilton's corrupt funding scheme was the "pomum Adami" of all national evil, the black act by which a nation had fallen from the grace of God.[7] "The funding system, founded in rapine and fraud, begat universal speculation," Rush told a less pessimistic John Adams over and over again, "speculation begat banks, and banks have ruined our country. A city in flames kindled by the hand of war is not so melancholy a sight as a whole nation absorbed in the love of money." [8]

As the seventeen-nineties wore on, every new year seemed to bring more distressing evidence of national apostasy. Political enmities, which had no place in the

ideal Christian Republic, were dividing Americans into Federalists and Democratic-Republicans, turning brother against brother in the manner of pre-revolutionary governments.[9] Although it was clear that the arts of peace must be taught and practiced in the new nation, as Rush himself had shown in his "Plan of a Peace-Office for the United States (1793)," new armies were being raised and used against other Americans, as in the case of the Whiskey Insurrection.[10] Social injustices of the *ancien régime* persisted. Even the revolutionary example of America's struggle for liberty was being perverted in France by Deists and atheists who failed to learn from the New World that liberty was impossible without true Christianity.[11] While at home plague after plague of yellow fever as if by divine visitation killed countless numbers of America's people. Now was the time for the jeremiad, now the time to lament the "melancholy spectacle of human misery." [12]

Rush's pessimism, though, was still not complete. It could never be as long as his final prophet was the author of Revelation rather than Jeremiah. "The Bible assures us that the time will come when the kingdoms of this world shall become the kingdoms of our Lord, and that the knowledge and love of his name shall cover the land as the waters cover the sea," he wrote Granville Sharp in 1799.

Under the influence of these, and other prophecies, I have abstracted my attention from the operations of human governments, and directed it wholly to that kingdom in which there shall be absolute monarchy with perfect freedom, un [con] trouled power, with universal justice, perpetual safety without fleets and armies, unparalleld splendor supported without taxes or a national debt, and general equality of rights without disrespect for superiors. This kingdom I believe will be administred in person by our Saviour upon our globe.[13]

Like a latter-day Fifth Monarchy Man disappointed in his sanguine hope for total revolution by a kind of Washington-Hamilton protectorate, and unwilling to use force in his attempt to establish the true Kingdom of God—as had his seventeenth-century counterparts—Rush was now moderating his revolutionary idealism. His revolutionary America had failed to realize the

---

[4] Rush to John Adams, July 8, 1812, and to William Marshall, September 15, 1798, *Rush Letters* 2: pp. 1146, 807.

[5] Rush to James Madison, February 27, 1790, *ibid.* 1: p. 538.

[6] *Ibid.*, p. 539. *Cf.* Rush to Thomas Fitzsimons, February 19, 1790, Butterfield, ed., "Further Letters of Benjamin Rush," *Penna. Mag. Hist. Biog.* **78** (January, 1954): pp. 30–31.

[7] Rush to John Adams, December 21, 1810, *Rush Letters* 2: p. 1073.

[8] August 8, 1812, *ibid.*, pp. 1158–1159.

[9] Rush to William Marshall, September 15, 1798, *ibid.*, p. 807. Himself the object of personal attacks by the Federalist writers, John Ward Fenno and William Cobbett (alias "Peter Porcupine"), Rush began libel suits against both of them in 1797. Such action was, philosophically, neither Christian nor republican, but Rush felt compelled to take it nevertheless. See Butterfield's discussion of "The Cobbett-Rush Feud" in *Rush Letters*, append. iii, pp. 1213–1218.

[10] Rush to James Madison, February 27, 1790, *ibid.* 1: p. 540.

[11] Rush to John Adams, November 25, 1806, *ibid.* 2: p. 935; Rush to Granville Sharp, April 2, 1799, Woods, ed., "Correspondence of Benjamin Rush and Granville Sharp 1773–1809," *Jour. Amer. Stud.* 1, 1 (April, 1967): p. 32.

[12] Rush to William Marshall, September 15, 1798, *Rush Letters* 2: pp. 806–807.

[13] April 2, 1799, Woods, ed., "Correspondence of Benjamin Rush and Granville Sharp 1773–1809," *Jour. Amer. Stud.* 1, 1 (April, 1967): pp. 32–33.

Kingdom of God, as had John Cotton's and Jonathan Edwards's Puritan America. The New World Israel had come ever so close to divine perfection in Rush's day, when all seemed in readiness for the Christian Republic, only to demonstrate again by its worldliness that the time was not right. What good men must do, then, was to prepare the way for Christ by works of love, never doubting that "he that cometh—will come." [14] This, Rush resolved, would be his course in his remaining years; and in Rush's pre-millennial works of love, he adhered to this course with few deviations.

As the seventeen-nineties came to an end in uncertainty and disillusionment, Rush, as if to ring down the curtain on the Great Drama and on his life, began his autobiography. While the "Travels through Life," in its very title, revealed his increasing otherworldliness, the text nevertheless reaffirmed his evangelical republican principles. And, as Rush in 1800 was writing his final testament in a mood of resignation, there suddenly appeared new hope for America in the election of his trusted revolutionary friend, Thomas Jefferson, to the presidency.

For a very brief moment at least it seemed to Rush that the republican unity of '76 could be restored after all and, fittingly enough, by "the penman of the Declaration of Independence" himself. "You have opened a new era by your speech on the 4th of March in the history of the United States," a jubilant Rush hailed the new president's inaugural.

Never have I seen the public mind more generally or more agreeably affected by any publication. Old friends who had been separated by party names and a *supposed* difference of *principle* in politics for many years shook hands with each other immediately after reading it, and discovered, for the first time, that they had differed in *opinion* only, about the best means of promoting the interests of their common country.[15]

Jefferson, in a masterpiece of old-fashioned republican simplicity, had "concentrated whole chapters into a few aphorisms in defense of the principles and form of our government." [16] Let the youth of America and their apostate fathers read the pure republican sentiments of this truly great American and learn or remember the forgotten truths of Seventy-Six.

"In contemplating the change you have produced in the public mind," Rush went on in his joyous letter of March 12, 1801,

I have been carried back to an interesting conversation with you about two years ago in which you predicted it. I did not concur with you, for our country was then so much under the influence of the name of——, the plans of——

[here Jefferson correctly wrote the names of Washington and Hamilton], and the press of Peter Porcupine, that I despaired of a resuscitation of its republican spirit. You said the death of two men (whom you named) would render your prediction speedy as well as certain. They both died in 1799. In the third month of the year 1801 we have become "all Republicans, all Federalists." [17]

It was, Rush told his English friend, Granville Sharp, later that month, "a great revolution . . . in the power of the government of the United States." [18] And to make Rush's joy in the seeming deliverance of his country even greater, President Jefferson had in his inaugural invoked the blessings of God upon their troubled country, thus giving the lie to rumors of his infidelity.[19]

But, alas, Rush's joy was short-lived, for the ghosts of Washington and Hamilton were not to be so easily exorcized.

Jefferson's noble and patriotic sentiments were to be of no avail against hard realities. True, Jeffersonian America in the ensuing years was to prove closer to Rush's ideal than federalist America, but liberty and power were to remain "uncontrouled by the spirit of christianity." For all Jefferson's good intentions, Americans were not to become "all Republicans, all Federalists," even though Rush himself was in the spirit of Jefferson's first inaugural to effect the reconciliation of Federalist John Adams and Republican Thomas Jefferson before he died.[20] The national sins of Washington's administration, of which party spirit was just one, were too deeply marked on the American nature to be removed by human power, Rush became more convinced over the years. The failure of Jefferson's presidency and then Madison's to save republican America confirmed him in his millennial belief. Only the Messiah could redeem America. Only God by supernatural means could right what was wrong with Rush's America and produce the Christian Republic of his dream.

The sermon for the times, Rush wrote John Adams in 1812, was one that he had heard Samuel Finley preach during the Great Awakening on "The Madness of Mankind." "And Madness is in their Heart while they live, and after that they go to the Dead," the evangelist had thundered out of Ecclesiastes. "Whoever seriously views and wisely considers the Manners of Mankind, and brings them to the Test of right Reason, will be forced to receive the same melancholy

---

[14] *Ibid.*, p. 33.

[15] March 12, 1801, *Rush Letters* **2**: p. 831. For the "revolution" of 1800–1801 as reviving "the evangelical hope of the great community," see Heimert, *Religion and the American Mind*, pp. 544–550.

[16] *Rush Letters* **2**: p. 831.

[17] *Ibid.*, p. 832.

[18] March 31, 1801, Woods, ed., "Correspondence of Benjamin Rush and Granville Sharp 1773–1809," *Jour. Amer. Stud.* **1**, 1 (April, 1967) : p. 34.

[19] *Ibid.*

[20] "We are not 'all Federalists and all Republicans,' but we are (with the exception of a few retired and growling neutrals) all Frenchmen or all Englishmen," Rush to John Adams, March 13, 1809, *Rush Letters* **2**: p. 998. See Butterfield's "The Dream of Benjamin Rush: The Reconciliation of John Adams and Thomas Jefferson," *Yale Review* **40** (1950–1951) : pp. 297–319.

Idea of them, represented in this Text." [21] Truly, mankind was mad, Rush the author of *Diseases of the Mind* and social pathologist of America and the world, agreed. "The Scriptures speak of nations being drunk and of all the individuals of the human race being mad," Rush kept on telling Adams in the closing years of his life. "What sober man or what man in his senses would think of walking in company or reasoning with either of them?" [22] As the new nation's first psychologist, Rush pronounced the United States as mad as the Old World. The only hope for man lay not in history and Enlightenment liberalism but in Christ, who had conquered death and disease on the Cross and would come again soon to destroy forever the Evil One and all his works. [23]

So Rush in his final years tried to redeem his own increasingly grave doubts about the American Revolution and his part in it with millennial and otherworldly consolations, while keeping up his pre-millennial works of love in social reform. When, in Rush's phrase from his last letter to John Adams, his "night . . . of death" began on April 19, 1813, Rush died with the Christian conviction that his night of death would be followed by a morning of eternal life. [24] Still another precious and unchanging conviction of the dying idealist on the thirty-eighth anniversary of Lexington and Concord was that the American Revolution was "big with important consequences to the world, and that the labor of no individual, however feeble his contributions to it were, could have been spared." [25]

EPILOGUE

The cause of freedom, and the universal happiness of man, were dear to his inmost heart. He exulted for joy as he beheld their approach. . . . America shared his best affections, but he felt himself like Cato born for the human race.—William Staughton[1]

Thus wrote Staughton of his intimate friend after Rush's death in 1813; and the characterization, although biased with love for a departed comrade, rings no less true in the lengthened perspective of our century and a half.

The eulogist, a classical scholar of broad outlook, discerned that philanthropic nature of Rush's genius which others failed to see or, like William Cobbett, saw only as messianic self-absorption. His comparison of Rush to the Stoical philosopher, Cato, in respect of great humanity, was more felicitous than the ordinary reader of eulogies might at first suspect. For both men were the consciences of their republics and historical personalities of the first order; and, more important, both worked for the organization of mankind into a community of brotherly love, excluding neither the poor nor the enslaved.

But while Rush labored to produce a revolution in human affairs, by constructing a new society on the lines of evangelical Christianity, he could not strike from his mind the painful consciousness of the necessity of reform in a divinely created world. If an all-benevolent God had made the world, as he steadfastly believed, then why was it not perfect? Why were there slaves in Virginia and Santo Domingo, why soldiers and undertakers, why pain, sickness, and death? The problem of evil, however one states it, is familiar enough to all men of good will, whatever their century. Simply because of his deeply religious nature, the problem was extraordinarily troubling to Rush; but as an enemy of the *status quo*, as a Christian revolutionary, the problem of reconciling the world-as-it-was with the world-as-it-ought-to-be was not just greatly troubling, it was seemingly without solution.

Had Rush been a less practical man, more concerned with thought than action, he might have been able, like certain of the Stoics, to dismiss slavery and other kinds of injustice as merely external discrimination. But Rush, at least in this sense, was too practical a man to gloss over wrongs. He was impatient of tedious, metaphysical theodicies; and, perhaps in typical American fashion, he demanded full resolution of the problem of evil in simple terms. Political republicanism, as we have seen, was for him the simple and providentially designed system by which political evil was to be destroyed. Medical republicanism, similarly, was to put an end to physical and moral evil. But these evils were merely temporal. The restoration of all men to God, or the destruction of spiritual evil, was to be accomplished by Christian republicanism.

The tension between the world as Rush found it and the world as he knew it ought to be was, apart from its long history in human thought, peculiarly relevant to Rush as a person whose life spanned two centuries as widely different as the eighteenth and the nineteenth. The pietistic tradition of the eighteenth and earlier centuries, with its otherworldly anxieties about death and salvation, clashed in Rush with the forming secular and humanitarian tradition of modern times. From the first tradition, Rush derived his compulsion to view the world and its institutions as secondary to ultimate religious concerns. This essentially anti-reform com-

---

[21] Samuel Finley, *The Madness of Mankind, Represented in a Sermon Preached in the New Presbyterian Church in Philadelphia* . . . (Philadelphia, 1754), pp. 3–4. See Rush's letter to Adams, August 8, 1812, *Rush Letters* 2: p. 1159.

[22] September 22, 1808, *ibid.* 2: pp. 984–985.

[23] Rush to Granville Sharp, June 20, 1809, Woods, ed., "Correspondence of Benjamin Rush and Granville Sharp 1773–1809," *Jour. Amer. Stud.* 1, 1 (April, 1967): pp. 36–37.

[24] April 10, 1813, *Rush Letters* 2: p. 1192.

[25] *Autobiography*, pp. 161–162.

[1] *Eulogium*, p. 19.

pulsion enhanced his underlying and more general religious acquiescence in things as they were. The other *Zeitgeist,* which the years at the turn of the century prefigured, moved Rush to attach importance to the earthly condition of man and to seek ways of remedying outstanding temporal wrongs. This was the Enlightenment source of his character as a reformer.

In a more intellectually conventional man, Rush's two disparate and paradoxical actions of overturning the established political and social order as a revolutionary, while extolling the rightness of things in general as a Christian, would never have intersected. But in Rush they did, precisely because Rush believed in the relatedness and wholeness of truth. This conviction, as we have seen, led him unsuspectingly to reason from analogy on all subjects however unrelated, never questioning the paradoxes that constituted his life and thought. The supreme paradox of Rush's life as a Christian and as a revolutionary, the strange opposition of conservative thesis and radical antithesis, was partly resolved and synthesized in his eschatological doctrine.

Universal salvation perfected the earthly world-as-it-was by referring it to the heavenly world-as-it-ought-to-be of full restoration. All would come out well in the end; not a soul or a thing would be lost. History would terminate in perfection, so why profoundly—existentially—worry about apparent, short-term discord. Worry a little, even translate worry into action, but never substantially doubt that the seeming conflict of the two worlds, regardless of the effect of one's own efforts, will find resolution. This was Rush's controlling assumption, which he shared with David Hartley and the other great optimists of his age. Alexander Pope, whose *Essay on Man* he naturally read and quoted, voiced the sentiment in an immortal couplet:

All discord, harmony not understood;
All partial evil, universal good.

It was a happy creed for the reformer, assuring him of ultimate success whatever his temporary reverses.

This synthesis of two apparently contradictory traditions of Great Awakening pietism and Enlightenment humanitarianism produced a new momentum for Rush's reform impulse, in much the same way that his organic union of evangelism and rationalistic science gave a new force and confidence to his philosophical world-view. Rush combined opposites and made them subserve his ultimate purpose of discovering a grand design of love in the universe. Had he not like Gilbert Tennent, Samuel Finley, and Samuel Davies found it there in unmistakable detail, he would have found it within himself and superimposed it upon the universe. "If God did not exist," said Voltaire in a famous epigram, "it would be necessary to invent Him." If love were not at the center of things, Rush might very well have observed, it would be necessary to put it there.

Another and somewhat different judgment from that of Staughton is appropriate here. As intimate with Rush as Staughton, if not more so, was John Adams; and the New England realist would have agreed with the characterization of his friend as an American Cato. But Adams, for all his love of Rush, was not blind to his friend's weaknesses of thought and character. He saw that Rush was a "prophet of progress" like Richard Price, Joseph Priestley, Condorcet, and other visionaries of the Enlightenment who "in a fit of enthusiasm" about the perfectibility of man had been "carried away by the popular contagion of the times." [2] "For these moral and political Histericks," he continued in this letter to Dr. Rush, "are at least as infectious as the small Pox or yellow fever." Adams saw, too, that his benevolent but dreamy friend—like Rev. Dr. Richard Price, about whom he made the observation—had "forgot his Bible which pronounces an irrevocable Decree of Death on every human Being, almost in every page of it." [3] And, more directly, he cautioned Rush, while pointing the remark ostensibly to Dr. Priestley, not to indulge in wild millennial speculations about the meaning of prophecy. "I must confess to you," Adams the statesman and historian wrote in 1806,

that the Data, upon which we reason from the Prophecies concerning the future amelioration of the condition of Mankind, are too obscure and uncertain, to authorize us to build any systems upon them for the conduct of Nations. It is well to understand as much of them as we can: but the Rulers of Men would presume too much, if they neglected History, Experience and Philosophy and depended upon Theological Interpretations of mysterious Predictions, which were not intended to be perfectly understood untill the time of their accomplishment. Our Friend Priestley believed, that France would establish a free Government because the King of France was the first of the ten Horns, which were to fall off. [4]

Rush, always deferential to his friend and senior, offered nothing in reply.

The point, though, is that Rush ultimately cared little about the realities of "History, Experience and Philosophy" nor about Old Testament pronouncements of death and disease that regulated the thinking of Calvinist-bred John Adams. Rush's thinking about all things was Christological, New rather than Old Testament, idealistic and transcendental rather than realistic. Deep down, one suspects, John Adams knew this and loved his comrade of '76 more for it. But Adams' judgment of his "enthusiastic" friend stands as the best from Rush's contemporaries.

The present writer has now, he hopes, shown at least that the tenacious image of Benjamin Rush as a figure of secondary importance in American history, memorable only because of isolated accomplishments in

---

[2] John Adams to Benjamin Rush, November 11, 1806, Biddle, ed., *Old Family Letters, A,* p. 116. See Haraszti, *John Adams & the Prophets of Progress, passim.*

[3] *Ibid.,* p. 116.

[4] John Adams to Benjamin Rush, June 22, 1806, Biddle, ed., *Old Family Letters, A,* pp. 99–100.

politics, reform, and—negatively—medicine, is not consistent with the historical evidence. The persistence of such an image is, moreover, hardly excusable now that primary materials of historical discovery have been made available in print through the superlative editorship of Drs. Corner and Butterfield. There is no disagreement among Rush scholars on this point. The same consensus, however, is not apparently true of the historical profession, not to speak of the public at large. Generally, this present work should help revise our historiographical attitude towards Rush, if not our understanding of his place in our national history.

Beyond this, the present study argues that Rush was an original American thinker who devised a *Weltanschauung* to fit the special revolutionary circumstances of his day. Christianity and republicanism were integral to this world view at a time when revolutionaries in America and Europe were denouncing any truck of one with the other. Rush made Christianity acceptable to republicanism by revolutionizing its tenets to provide full religious equality in this world and in the next, much the same way as republicanism provided full political equality. And he appealed to Scripture as well as to reason for his authorizations, finding in both places great cause for joy in divine benevolence.

The Revolutionary republic of Rush's vision was to be founded upon Christianity, not in a superficial way—as a merely external system of human relationships—but in a deeply spiritual community of souls in love. It was to harken back to the primitive, organic church, while preparing for the climax of salvation history in the Millennium. It was to be truly a Christian Republic, and Rush as its herald was a Christian revolutionary whose program of social and religious construction, which we have treated above, was unique in America. It is not too much to claim that Rush was second to none of the American revolutionary leaders in the originality of his thought. If the present study fails to show this, it must be charged to the inadequacies of this writer, not to any paucity of original ideas in Rush himself.

It has been argued with little serious opposition that the American character is pragmatic and not ideological. Whatever the character of the American, this new man, the fact is that Benjamin Rush, one of his early national leaders, possessed, cherished, and taught a revolutionary ideology worthy of the moral and intellectual productions of any age.

If Rush's life has any special relevance to our times, it is as a revolutionary counsel to love God and one another, to think and live boldly and manfully. Let us remember, he would say, that we Americans were the world's first true revolutionaries and that "The Revolution is not over!"

MEMOIRS

OF THE

AMERICAN PHILOSOPHICAL SOCIETY

TRANSACTIONS

OF THE

AMERICAN PHILOSOPHICAL SOCIETY

TRANSACTIONS

OF THE

AMERICAN PHILOSOPHICAL SOCIETY

HELD AT PHILADELPHIA
FOR PROMOTING USEFUL KNOWLEDGE

———

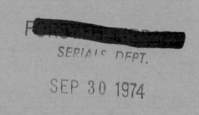
NEW SERIES—VOLUME 64, PART 5
1974

———

BENJAMIN RUSH: PHILOSOPHER OF THE AMERICAN REVOLUTION

DONALD J. D'ELIA

Professor of History, State University of New York, New Paltz

———

THE AMERICAN PHILOSOPHICAL SOCIETY
INDEPENDENCE SQUARE
PHILADELPHIA

September, 1974

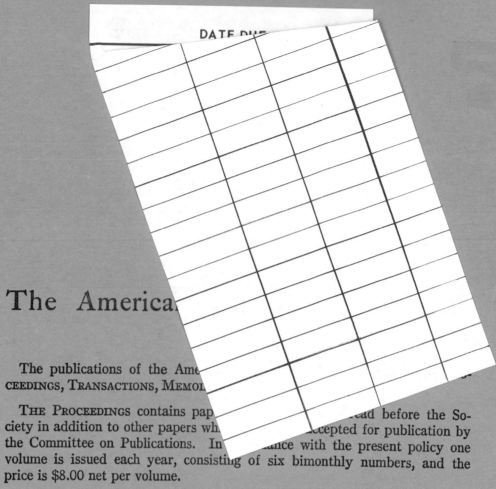

The America[...]

The publications of the Ame[...]
CEEDINGS, TRANSACTIONS, MEMO[...]

THE PROCEEDINGS contains pap[...] [r]ead before the Society in addition to other papers wh[...] [a]ccepted for publication by the Committee on Publications. In [...]ance with the present policy one volume is issued each year, consisting of six bimonthly numbers, and the price is $8.00 net per volume.

THE TRANSACTIONS, the oldest scholarly journal in America, was started in 1769 and is quarto size. In accordance with the present policy each annual volume is a collection of monographs, each issued as a part. The current annual subscription price is $20.00 net per volume. Individual copies of the TRANSACTIONS are offered for sale. This issue is priced at $5.00.

Each volume of the MEMOIRS is published as a book. The titles cover the various fields of learning; most of the recent volumes have been historical. The price of each volume is determined by its size and character.

The YEAR BOOK is of considerable interest to scholars because of the reports on grants for research and to libraries for this reason and because of the section dealing with the acquisitions of the Library. In addition it contains the Charter and Laws, and lists of present and former members, and reports of committees and meetings. The YEAR BOOK is published about April 1 for the preceding calendar year. The current price is $5.00.

An author desiring to submit a manuscript for publication should send it to the Editor, George W. Corner, American Philosophical Society, 104 South Fifth Street, Philadelphia, Pa. 19106.